America's Women in Uniform
1898-1973
(VOLUME 2)

by
Jill Halcomb Smith

1st Printing 2004

Copyright 2004 Jill Halcomb Smith

Published by R. James Bender Publishing,
P.O. Box 23456, San Jose, CA 95153 USA
Ph: (408) 225-5777, Fax: (408) 225-0407
Web: www.bender-publishing.com
E-mail: order@bender-publishing.com

Printed in China

All rights reserved. This book or parts thereof, may not be reproduced in any form without the permission of the author.

ISBN No.: 0-912138-85-8

In memory of
Chaney Carolyn King
March 25, 1982—January 18, 2003
c/Captain, Colorado Wing, CAP
Cadet 3rd Class, United States Air Force Academy

Contents

Office of Civilian Defense (OCD)	10
Policewomen of New York City, Wartime	19
Relief Wings, Inc.	19
The Salvation Army in America	23
Serbian Relief Committee of America	37
United Service Organizations (USO), Stage Door Canteen, American Theatre Wing War Services	39
State of Texas Auxiliary Reserve	52
Texas Guardettes	54
United States Army Telephone Operators of the Signal Corps ("Hello Girls")	56
United States Coast Guard Women's Reserve (SPARS)	65
United States Food Administration	78
United States Public Health Service Reserve Corps	81
United States Shipping Board—Emergency Fleet Corporation	87
United War Work Campaign	89
Victory Girls	91
Volunteer Army Canteen Service (VACS)	92
War Camp Community Service	95
Women Veteran's Organizations (The American Legion, American Legion Auxiliary, Veterans of Foreign Wars and Auxiliary, Survivors of Corregidor and Bataan, AMVETS and other organizations)	98
Women Accepted for Volunteer Emergency Service (WAVES), or US Navy Women's Reserve	107
Women Employed at Army Air Forces Posts	144
Women Flyers of America	150
Women in Aviation (Women's Auxiliary Ferrying Service (WAFS) and Women Airforce Service Pilots (WASP)	151
Women in the United States Air Force (WAF), Air Force Nurse Corps and Air Force Women's Medical Specialist Corps	224
Women Ordnance Workers (WOWs)	262
Women's Overseas Hospital of the U.S.A.	271
Women War Correspondents	272
Women War Department Civilian Employees	286
Women War Workers	288
Women's Air Reserve	293
Women's Ambulance and Defense Corps of America (WADCA)	296

Women's Ambulance Safety Patrol.	304
Women's Army Auxiliary Corps (WAAC) and Women's Army Corps (WAC)	305
Women's Land Army of America (WLAA), Women's Land Army of the U.S. Crop Corps	413
Yeomen (F): United States Naval Reserve (F)	416
Young Men's Christian Association (YMCA)	424
Young Women's Christian Association (YWCA)	446
Other Organizations.	450
Appendix 1: Honor Roll.	495
Appendix 2: "Hello Girls".	523
Index.	529
Bibliography.	538

ERRATUM

In Volume 1 of this series, photographs of items from the collection of The National Society of The Colonial Dames of America were incorrectly identified only as, "Colonial Dames of America–NMAH/Smithsonian." In Volume 2, those items from The National Society of The Colonial Dames of America Collection are identified as, "NSCDA Collection–NMAH/Smithsonian." The author apologizes for any inconvenience.

Acknowledgements

This book is the result of a vast amount of time and co-operation of many individuals and institutions. First, I'd like to thank the late Brad Mann for pointing me in the direction of the US Army Medical Department Museum at Fort Sam Houston and the museum at Brooks Air Force Base, "Hanger 9," the Edward H. White, II Memorial, USAF Museum of Aerospace Medicine, which helped get the research for this book started. P-38 "Lightning" ace, Major Jack Ilfrey, helped me locate several former Wasps who in turn graciously allowed me to study and photograph their uniforms, wings and look through their photo albums. Especially helpful were former Wasps Mary Lou Colbert Neale, 43-W-1, Dorothy Ann Smith Lucas, 44-W-7, Madge Leon Moore, 44-W-4, and Betty Williamson Shipley, 44-W-4.

I am greatly indebted to the curator and staff of the US Army Medical Department Museum at Ft. Sam Houston, Texas. Thomas O. McMasters, Johanna Koehn and Lieutenant Colonel Ron Burkett were indispensable. Johanna spent hours with me, going through uniforms and insignia, and pulling the items I needed to photograph for my research. Likewise, Paula Ussery, of the Admiral Nimitz Museum in Fredericksburg, Texas, went through box after box of Navy Nurse Corps and Women Marine Corps uniforms, and helped me photograph some of them. Paula also let me go through the museum's collection of photographs, reproductions of which are found in this book. Thanks must also go to William C. Moore, Director of the Greensboro Historical Museum and Susan Webster, Curator of Collections, and to Patt Anthony, who photographed items from the museum's collection for use in this book. Patt Anthony was also of invaluable assistance, sending many items from his inventory and personal collection for me to photograph.

George A. Petersen, one of the busiest people I've ever known, heard about my research and graciously sent for my use box after box of uniforms and valuable documentation which he has amassed over the years. A large part of the information in this book came from documentation or uniforms provided by him. I am also very grateful to David I. George, who shipped to me a wonderful and rare example of the World War I Navy Nurse Corps outdoor uniform so that it could be photographed for this book.

I am greatly indebted to several women who made it possible for many of the World War I uniforms from The National Society of The Colonial Dames of America Collection in the Smithsonian Institution to be photographed. First is Josephine Clapp Osbun, National Committee Chairman of The Colonial Dames, whom I met through a happy accident, when she allowed me to use a copy of a photograph of her wearing her World War II United States Public Health Service uniform. Jo was the driving force behind The Dames' collection of World War I uniforms being donated to the Smithsonian. She and Margaret Vining, Armed Forces Collections, Division of the History of Technology of the National Museum of American History, made it possible for me to photograph these extremely rare uniforms. I am also grateful to Colonel Pat Jernigan, USA (Ret.) and intern Cindy Sherman for their help in pulling these uniforms and helping me set up the shots.

Jo also met with me about my research and provided a large amount of documentation about Colonial Dames who served in the World Wars.

Thanks must also go to the Jewish Welfare Board Jewish Chaplains Council, JCCA/NA for the archival material provided about the women in the Jewish Welfare Board During World War I.

I am also grateful to Brigadier General Wilma Vaught, USAF (Ret.), WIMSA (Women in Military Service for America) Foundation President and the WIMSA staff. Britta Granrud, WIMSA Collection Manager, was of much assistance. Even though being extremely busy with the opening of the WIMSA memorial, she somehow found time to provide my research with World War I photographs from the WIMSA collection, and to point me in the direction of collections where pertinent photographs could possibly be found. Britta also pulled several rare uniforms from the WIMSA collection and helped me photograph them. Thanks must also go to Judith Bellafaire, Ph.D., the WIMSA curator.

I would also like to thank the staffs of the National Archives, Still Pictures Branch, the Library of Congress, and the US Navy Historical Section. E.C. Finney, Jr., Curator Branch, Photographic Section, Naval Historical Center and his staff did an outstanding job in locating photographs and regulations for this research. Likewise did the staffs of the National Archives, Still Pictures Branch and the Library of Congress. The results of their assistance are illustrated on many pages in this book.

I am also deeply indebted to the American Red Cross National Headquarters and their personnel, such as Mary D. Doering, Elizabeth Hooks and ARC Volunteer Historian Shirley Powers. Their assistance in this project was vital. Shirley Powers provided a great deal of information about Red Cross uniforms, even though she is conducting her own research of ARC uniforms.

Historian Lettie Gavin, author of *"American Women in World War I. They Also Served,"* was very gracious to loan me photographs from her files and to allow me to use the information about women who were decorated for service during World War I. I am also grateful to George W. Connell, who sent me his files concerning the Cadet Nurse Corps, the Office of Civilian Defense and the WASP.

Women veterans also contributed to this project. First was Barbara Kishpaugh, Colonel, ANC (Ret.). Colonel Kishpaugh really got this project off the ground by giving me a wonderful grouping of photographs from her service in World War II, the Korean War and the Vietnam War. Lucy Wilson Jopling, Captain, ANC, allowed me to photograph her A-2 jacket and copy many of her photographs. "Air Wac" Sergeant Frances Dupree Harris loaned me her uniforms and insignia to photograph, and even gave me one of her uniforms for my collection. Alice Strong Barber, Captain, WMSC, allowed me to photograph her beautifully preserved taupe uniform and some of her photographs, as did Maryann Haucke Munroe, Lieutenant, ANC. The late Maria Lourdes Torres Maes, Coporal, USM-CWR, had photographs made of her World War II items of uniform and period photos for use in this book. The cooperation and generosity of these women is to be commended.

Collectors, of course, also helped with this book. Foremost is Sylvia Leasure, who generously allowed me to photograph uniforms and insignia from her extensive collection. Likewise, Phil and Linda Darling provided a large group of images and uniforms to be photographed from their extensive "Home Front" collection. John Coy was kind enough to send several very rare uniforms to me for use in this book.

Most importantly, I would like to thank my husband for his patience, tolerance and very much needed assistance, which made this project run much more smoothly and pleasantly. It's a pleasure to have such a handsome helper!

Many others were of much valued assistance. They are listed in alphabetical order:

Jason Akai
Michael Albanese
John Angolia
Brett Bailey
Roger Bender
John Bond
Bryan Bowerman
Renée Boyd
Ursel D. Boyd
Thomas W. Braniger
Susan H. Brosnan
Karen E. Buchannan
General Edward R. Burka, USAR (Ret.)
Adin B. Capron, Jr.
David Carmichael
Judy N. Chelnick
Sander Cohen
George W. Connell
Patrick E. Consadine, Sr.
Stewart S. Corning, Jr.
Garry Corson
Fernando Cortez
Mary Lou Cummings
Mark Day
Frances Q. Deel
Frances Dingman

Barbara S. Dlugokinski
Fred W. Elwell
William K. Emerson
William "Billy Bob" and Mary Edith Engle, WASP, 43-W-4
Alan S. Fine
Thomas Fleming
Charles Bracelen Flood
Kathy Burnam Flood
Stefan Frank
Richard L. Gilbert
Randy L. Goss
Connie Hagood
Yashka K. Hallein, Ph. D.
Andrea Hinding
Henry E. Hodge, Colonel, USA
Ann Russ Holaday, WASP, 43-W-7
Barry Hooper
Jim Hammack
Marsha Hunt
Jennifer Jukes
Diane Kiser, First Lieutenant, ANC, Vietnam War

Lorna Knight
Jim LaChute
Rabbi Nathan Landman, JCCA
Kenny Lane
Niles Laughner
Marguerite Lavier
Clive M. Law
Ken Lazier
Elden Leasure
Jeannine Mayes
Dennis H.J. Medina
Jon A. Maguire
Tucker Malishenko
Anna McDonald
Ron Manion
Elias San Miguel
John Mull
Keith Ness
Duane Netzley
Helen Novodvotsky
Charles B. Oellig
Kenya Ostermeier
Mrs. Donna Owens
John Parascandola, Ph.D.
D.B. Patterson
George A. Petersen
Frèdèric Pineau
Gloria Rand
Mark and Raylene Riese
Steve & Mary Anne Rohde
Neva I. Rohr, Major, ANC (deceased)
James H. Rufener
Bee Savage, 2nd Lieutenant, ANC
Ronda Sheel
William John Shepherd, Sr.
Melvin Schroeder
Ryan Schroeder
Jim Speraw
Frank Storer
Richard Strauss
LTC (ret.) Mary L. Stremlow, USMC
Kathleen A. Struss
Ken Tassie
Cora P. Teel
Charles R. Waude
Mike Weidner
Barbara Williams
John Wilson, Jr.
Yvonne Wood, WASP, 43-W-7
Noelle Young

Institutions

Admiral Nimitz Museum
Allegheny University of the Health Sciences Conference Center
American Red Cross National Headquarters
American Legion Auxiliary National Headquarters
Archdiocese of Denver
Aurora Public Library and Staff
The Catholic University of America
Cornell University
Delaware State Archives
Denver Public Library and Staff
Department of the Army
Department of Defense
Department of Health and Human Services
Dwight D. Eisenhower Library
Fort George G. Meade Museum
Greensboro Historical Museum, Greensboro, North Carolina
Jewish Welfare Board Jewish Chaplains Council, JCC Association/NA
Kautz Family YMCA Archives, University of Minnesota Library
Knights of Columbus Supreme Office
Library of Congress
Marshall University
Museum of the City of New York
USAF Museum of Aerospace Medicine, Brooks Air Force Base ("Hanger 9")

US Army Medical Department Museum, Fort Sam Houston
US Army Museum, Fort Sam Houston
Montana Historical Society
National Air and Space Museum
National Archives, Still Pictures Branch
National Museum of American History—The Smithsonian Institution
National Museum of American Jewish Military History
Naval Historical Center
National Society of The Colonial Dames of America
Peterson Air Force Base Clothing Sales
Peterson Air Force Base Museum
Pikes Peak Library and Staff
The Salvation Army National Headquarters
The Salvation Army Territorial Headquarters Museum
The State Museum of Pennsylvania
The USAF Museum of Aerospace Medicine
University Press of Colorado
University of Texas, Institute of Texan Cultures
Wings Over the Rockies Air and Space Museum
Women in Military Service for America (WIMSA) Memorial
Wright-Patterson Air Force Base Museum
YMCA of the USA Archives, University of Minnesota Libraries

Special thanks are extended to Ruth D. Bender and Paul Oostmeyer for their editing skills and dedication to accuracy.

Ed Anderson Jr. must be given special recognition for his enthusiastic assistance and knowledge of numerous women's organizations, most especially noted in the WAFS and WASP chapter.

In addition to those contributors listed in Volume 1 of this series, the following individuals and institutions provided additional assistance to the compilation of Volume 2:

American Friends Service Committee
Bill Block
Greg Ciesielski
Patrick E. Consadine, Sr.
Michael von Deckbar
Stephen Durant
PT Gavin
Tom Golden
David O. Hall
Jeanne M. Holm, Brig. Gen., USAF (Ret.)
David Johnson
Steve Johnson
Peter Knepton
Shirley Kramer
E. Mejia
Daniel J. Miller
Mike Minnich
Stephen R. Nelson, Fort MacArthur Museum
Ted Paulson
Thomas C. Schultz
Janet Sims
Mike Staccy
Mary Stremlow, Col., USMC (Ret.)
Ken Tassie
"The Last Post"
Mac West
Richard Williams
Brian K. Williamson

Office of Civilian Defense
(OCD—World War II)

Volunteers working for Civil Defense wore uniforms particular to their job. To become volunteers, women had to be between the ages of eighteen and fifty, attend a twenty-hour first aid course, have the equivalent of a high school education, and serve without pay. Civilian Defense volunteers worked in hospital wards and clinics, helping nurses make beds and attend to patients, as air raid wardens, canteen workers and the like. OCD uniforms were introduced just a week after the bombing of Pearl Harbor. Nine regional offices were established in New York City, Boston, Atlanta, Baltimore, Cleveland, Omaha, Chicago, San Antonio (later, Dallas) and San Francisco. The well-known insignia of the OCD was designed by Col. Walter P. Burns, who held patents on them, in cooperation with Charles T. Coiner.[660] There were sixteen patches which identified the wearer's area of work:

Air Raid Warden;
Auxiliary Police;
Civil Defense;
Bomb Squad;
Auxiliary Firemen;
Fire Watcher;
Road Repair Crew;
Decontamination Corps;
State Staff Corps;
Rescue Party; Need
Medical Corps;
Nurses' Aides Corps;
Messenger;
Drivers Corps;
Emergency Food and Housing;
Demolition and Clearance Crew.[661]

Air Raid Warden patch.

Air Raid Warden lapel pin. (Courtesy: Sylvia Leasure)

"Air Warden" patch. This piece may date from after WWII. (Courtesy: Sylvia Leasure)

Auxiliary Police patch, possibly worn after WWII. (Courtesy: Sylvia Leasure)

Kansas Civil Defense brassard. (Courtesy: Sylvia Leasure)

Auxiliary Police lapel pin. (Courtesy: Sylvia Leasure)

---

[660] Published by the Defense Civil Preparedness Agency Information Services, *Significant Events in the United States Civil Defense History,* 1975, p. 3.

[661] *Significant Events in United States Civil Defense History,* p. 3.

In early 1942, the nation was critically short of trained nurses. The Army and Navy Nurse Corps had enlisted 15,000, the U.S. Public Health Service needed 10,000 more and civilian hospitals were understaffed by 10%. The problem was solved with 100,000 women volunteers. As nurses' aides, they released nurses by taking over routine duties. At this time some 2,000 women had enrolled in the OCD-Red Cross training courses or worked in hospitals. While three years were required for the title of Registered Nurse, the OCD-Red Cross program called for only 80 hours of classroom study and ward practice. The unpaid volunteer pledged to give 150 hours of hospital service every year, preferably in a three-month period, and to be available for permanent duty if war demands required it. These nurses' aides worked under direct supervision of a nurse and her concern was the comfort of patients. In addition to mastering the art of hospital bed making and bathing and feeding her patients, she had to take pulse and temperature and to discern changes in their condition.

Female office workers wore a blue rayon shirt-dress which had a collar that could be worn open or closed. The dress had a four button closure and the was belted at the waist. Buttons were gold and were embossed with the OCD triangle insigne. The color of the belt buckle was gold. Detachable shoulder straps, much like those worn by members of the American

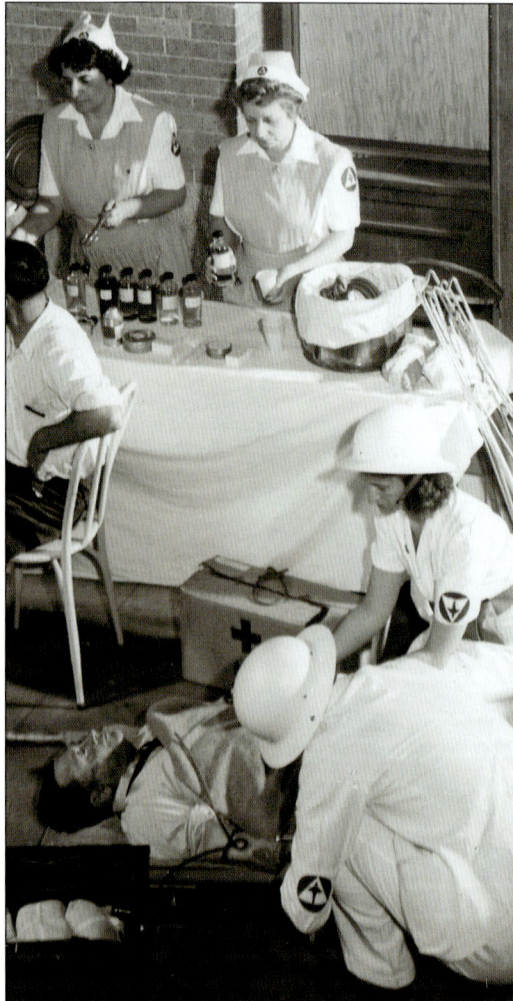

Uniform worn by female OCD workers. This woman wears the "CD" headquarters or unassigned sleeve patch. (Courtesy: George Petersen)

These Civilian Defense workers are going through a casualty drill. The man and woman in the foreground wear the Medical Corps brassard, albeit the woman is wearing hers upside down. The women behind the table are wearing the OCD nurse's aide uniform. (Courtesy: Museum of the City of New York)

Fire Watchers lapel pin. (Courtesy: Sylvia Leasure)

Medical Corps lapel pin. (Courtesy: Sylvia Leasure)

Red Cross, were worn at the shoulders and had a section of colored grosgrain ribbon on them,[662] the color indicated the wearer's area of service.

The round, blue OCD patch with a white triangle and red "CD" letters in the center was sewn to the upper left sleeve. A small white unit number embroidered upon a black rectangular piece of cloth was sewn about two inches below this.

The Driver's Corps Patch in wear. (Courtesy: Marshall University)

Nurse's Aide Corps patch. (Courtesy: Sylvia Leasure)

Mrs. Verne W. McKinney wears the shirtdress with detachable shoulder straps. (Courtesy: George Petersen)

The "defense blue" garrison cap was patterned after that worn by men, and appeared to at some time been piped in white. The round metal badge of the OCD was worn on the left curtain.[663]

---

[662] Document titled, "Women into Uniform." Wartime, but no date.
[663] Period photograph of Mrs. Verne W. McKinney, chairman of the volunteer Office of Civilian Defense, shows her wearing this dress and garrison cap, January 29, 1943.

WWII period OCD uniforms, (L to R): winter outdoor uniform; nurse's aide; shirtdress; summer outdoor uniform; overcoat and canteen worker uniform. (Courtesy: Library of Congress)

The winter outdoor uniform was made of "defense blue" Shetland wool and consisted of a blouse, skirt, white crêpe shirtwaist and headdress. A brown leather belt[664] and blue gloves were optional for wear.

The blouse had breast patch pockets with flaps and buttons and bellows pockets with flaps and buttons on the skirt of the blouse, at the hips. The front of the blouse was secured with gold buttons. The skirt was of the same color and material and had one inverted pleat in the front center.

Period photographs show this uniform being worn with a billed hat that had a bow in front and a round Civilian Defense badge above it, a blue garrison cap with a small Civilian Defense badge affixed to the left curtain, and a hat that resembles that worn by today's women in the military. Another period photograph shows what appears to be a pair of round, metal CD insignia being worn alternately on the collar and on the lapels of the winter outdoor uniform.

The summer outdoor uniform was made of light blue cotton denim called "defense blue." The blouse had no collar and was secured at the front by three gold buttons. Two bellows pockets with flaps and buttons were at

---

[664] Virginia Pope, "Civilian Defense Uniforms," *The New York Times,* December 14, 1941, sec. Fashion: D3.

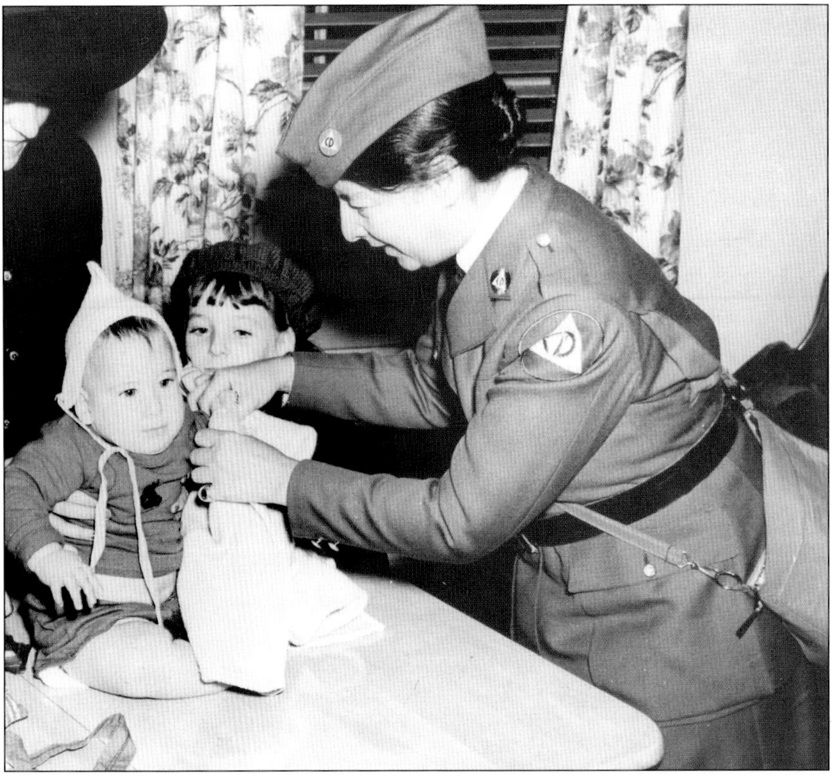

OCD uniform worn by a woman from the Emergency Welfare Division. (Courtesy: Museum of the City of New York)

the skirt of the blouse, and two pleated patch pockets with flaps and buttons were at the bodice. The blouse had a cloth belt, held by belt loops, and a gold, embossed metal buckle. A white shirtwaist was worn with the collar extended over the blouse. The matching skirt had an inverted pleat in the front.[665]

Two hats of the same material were authorized for wear with the summer uniform. One was a garrison cap, the other a visored hat with a bloused top. The round CD badge with the red and white striped triangle in the center was worn in the front center of this hat.

WWII period photograph showing an unusual hat being worn with the OCD uniform. (Courtesy: George Petersen)

---

[665] Ibid.

Canteen workers wore a shirt-dress of light blue denim which closed with four white buttons. The bodice had two styled pockets with buttons. The dress was belted with a cloth and leather belt. The dress had a four button closure on the left side. The skirt was slightly flared and was made of eight gores. The short sleeves had cuffs.[666]

Canteen workers could wear the circular CD blue denim hat with the CD badge on front with a red coffee cup in the center of the badge. (See also, "American Red Cross" Vol. 1.)

Volunteer nurses' aides wore a light blue blue jumper with a white short-sleeved shirtwaist underneath. A matching light blue cap with a white upturn was worn also. The OCD/ARC combination patch was worn on the right sleeve of the shirtwaist and a smaller version of the patch was worn in the center of the cap. This uniform was authorized by the American Red Cross and the Office of Civilian Defense.[667]

A photograph in an unidentified newspaper clipping dated June of, possibly, 1942, shows uniforms whose style was a bit exaggerated, and designated for "U.S. Women [sic] in defense jobs." New insignia were introduced as well, and shown on these uniforms and was designated for wear by "civilians enrolled in defense work." It is doubted that any of these uniforms or insignia were ever used.

WWII CD volunteer nurse's aide jumper.

"Vicky Victory," your Hair Aid warden. A hair pin kit with a OCD theme. (Courtesy: Ed Anderson, Jr.)

Shown in this photograph is a uniform like the previously described nurses' aid, except the apron was called a "utility apron." The new insignia was worn on the apron bib and CD nurse's cap. A white dress with a white headdress like that worn by nuns, except falling just above the line of the shoulder was prescribed for a "working nurse." The new insignia were

---

666 Document, "Women into Uniform."
667 Document, "Volunteer Nurse's Aides Needed in Civilian Defense, October 1941.

Volunteer nurse's aid cap. (Courtesy: Phil & Linda Darling)

worn on the headdress and on the left sleeve. The third uniform looked like the summer outdoor uniform, but the hat, while of similar style, has a higher band, making the top look bigger. This uniform was described as being for an air raid warden. The winter version, like the winter outdoor uniform, was called the "dress uniform for air raid warden." The new insignia were worn on both uniforms on the headdress and on the left sleeve. The canteen dress was similar to the one described earlier, but opened down the front and had a twelve-button closure. The bodice pockets were slanted, but had flaps with buttons, and there were pockets with flaps and buttons on the sides of the skirt. The dress had no sleeves, but a white, long sleeve shirt was worn under it. The new insignia were worn in the center of the hat band and on the left sleeve. The final uniform is called the "working nurse" uniform. It appears to be a white, double-breasted dress with long sleeves that puff at the shoulder seams. There are four pair of buttons down the front. The nurse's cap is a large, boxy affair, with the new badge affixed to the front[668] and a new insigne worn on the left sleeve.

Air Raid Wardens had no official uniforms, although helmets and arm bands were official.

---

[668] Wartime newspaper clipping, no date.

Tom Golden

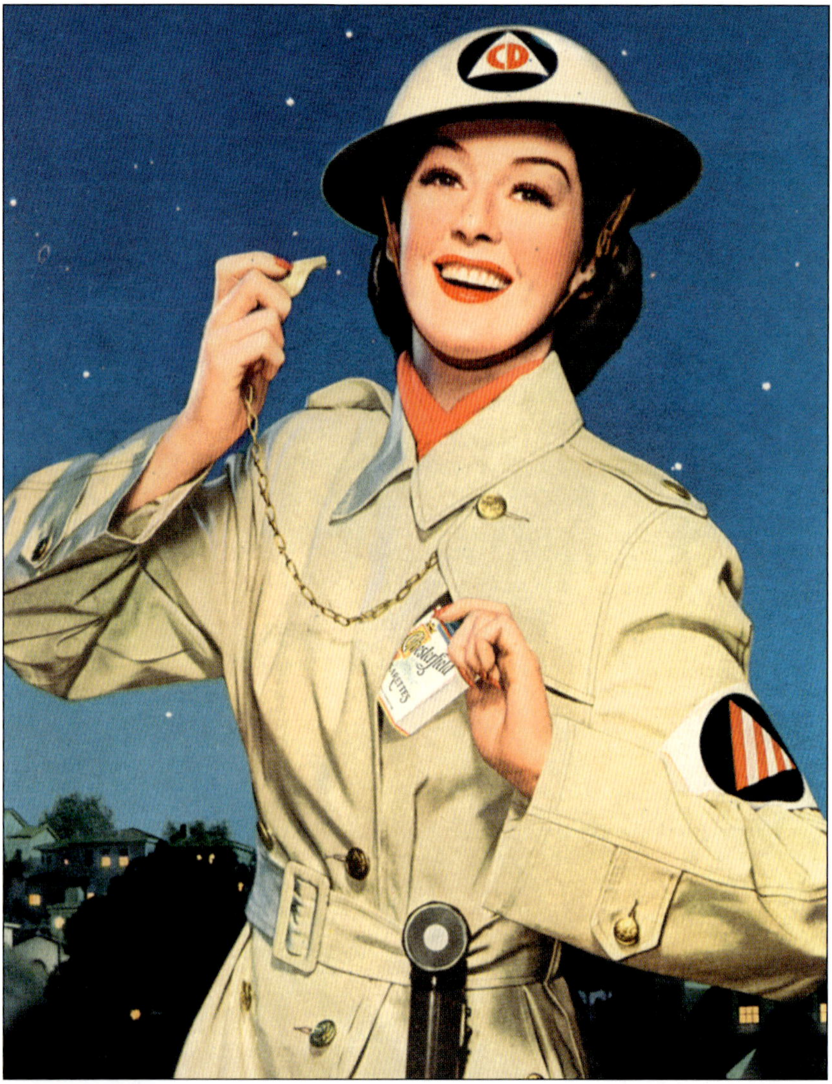

Rosalind Russell wears the official CD helmet and arm band in this 1942 Chesterfield cigarette ad. (Courtesy: Tom Golden)

To achieve high morale, the OCD authorized six ribbon bars to recognize the long hours its volunteers contributed. They were officially known as "Office of Civil Defense Service Ribbon Awards" and had the following color schemes:

500 hours

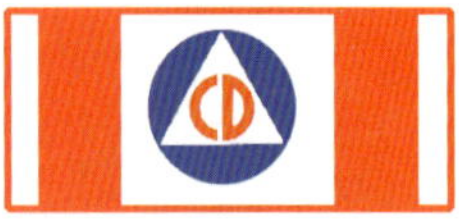

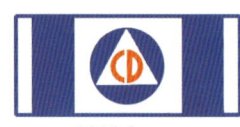

1000 hours

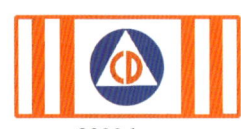

2000 hours

3000 hours

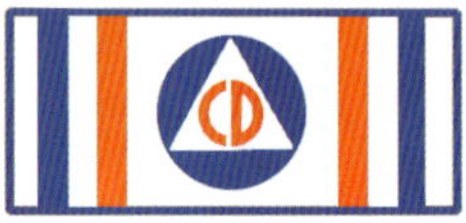

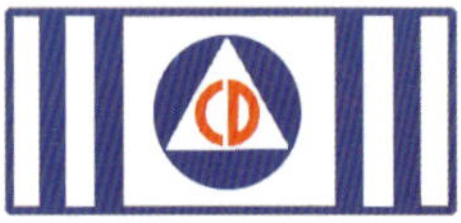

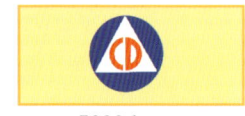

4000 hours

5000 hours

Policewomen of New York City, Wartime
(WORLD WAR I & WORLD WAR II)

Women replacing policemen who were in the service during World War I were organized into the Women's Police Reserves, Women's Police Training Corps, and the Women's Mounted Police Reserve Corps.[669] During World War II, women replacing policemen who went into the service wore blue police uniforms. A few of them carried black leather shoulder bags which had sections to hold the policewomen's .32 caliber revolver and a make-up kit, consisting of lipstick, a compact for face powder and dry rouge. These shoulder bags were gifts of Grover A. Whalen, Director of the Civil Defense Volunteer Office, and chairman of the board of Coty, Inc. They were presented to 103 of New York City's policewomen by mayor Fiorello LaGuardia at ceremonies held at City Hall on September 25, 1943. LaGuardia said,

"Use your gun as you would your lipstick—only when you need it. And use it intelligently."[670]

Relief Wings, Inc.
(World War II)

Created along the same lines as the Aerial Nurse Corps of America, Relief Wings, Inc., came into being in May 1940, as an organization prepared to provide emergency medical aid through air ambulances. It's motto was, "Humanitarian Service by Air." It was sponsored by leaders of civic, aviation, church, medical and business. More than two hundred flight nurses and flight surgeons were enrolled in the organization in eleven sectional units throughout the United States. It offered its services to the Office of Civilian Defense, the American Red Cross and the Civil Air Patrol.

Members worn a single-breasted, horizon blue belted blouse and matching skirt, which covered culottes and trousers, needed for climbing in and out of airplanes. Members also wore a matching garrison cap.

---

[669] "Times Photo Section," *The New York Times,* May 19, 1918, Sunday ed.
[670] *The New York Times,* September 25, 1943: p. 12.

All members wore a pair of stylized 2-1/2 inch wings on the upper left breast of the blouse, and a smaller pair on the left forward section of the garrison cap curtain.

The large wings were all silver with an unmarked reverse and pin with a roll catch. The small wings were blue and silver.

The large wings had a globe in the center. An arc above the globe spanned with wings and bore the raised designation, "Relief Wings." Wings worn by all national chairmen had a gold globe.

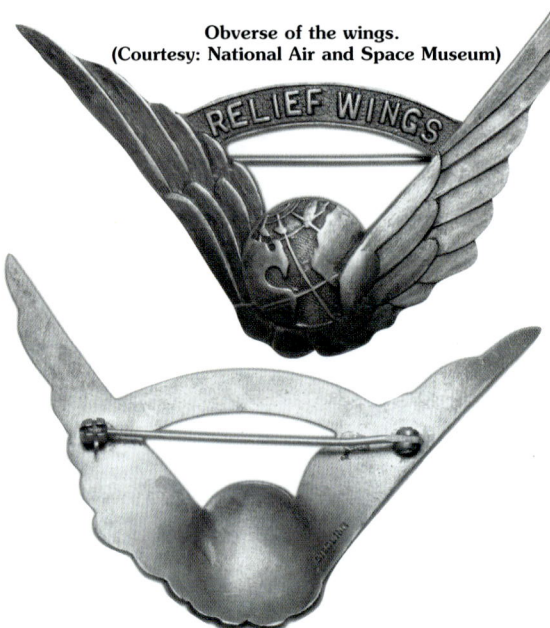

Obverse of the wings.
(Courtesy: National Air and Space Museum)

Reverse of the wings.
(Courtesy: National Air and Space Museum)

Relief Wings uniform.
(Courtesy: George Petersen)

The wings worn by the national coordination chairman, section and state directors had wings with an additional arc above the first one, with the person's job title on it. The wings worn by volunteer flight surgeons had a caduceus on the right wing. Flight nurse's wings had the caduceus, plus an "N" above it on the right wing. Pilots, airplane owners and coordinators and leader's wings had a vertical propeller, while personnel having to do with communications had a lightning bolt on the right wing. (The departments of aircraft owners, pilots and amateur radio operators were suspended during the war, therefore, these wings were not worn.)

Ranks or titles were shown, probably engraved, on the upper section of the left wing.

The following wings were worn:
National Officials
National Coordination Chairman—Additional arc with "CO-ORD. CMR;"
National Chairman, Flight Surgeons— Caduceus on right wing, "NAT. CHAIRMAN" on the left;
National Chairman, Flight Nurses—Caduceus and "N" on right wing, "NAT. CHAIRMAN" on left;
National Chairman, Airplanes and Pilots—Vertical propeller on right wing and "NAT. CHAIRMAN" on the left; (Suspended during the war.)

DEPARTMENTS

CONTRIBUTORS PIN
2 SIZES: LARGE 2¼ INCH IS ALL SILVER. SMALL BLUE & SILVER

These two departments temporarily suspended for the duration of the war

LEADERS	FLIGHT SURGEONS	FLIGHT NURSES	AIRCRAFT OWNERS AND PILOTS	AMATEUR RADIO OPERATORS
NATIONAL Coordination Chairman	National Chairman Flight Surgeons	National Chairman Flight Nurses	National Chairman Airplanes and Pilots	National Chairman Am. Rad. Oper's.

INSIGNIAS OF ALL NATIONAL CHAIRMAN BEAR A GOLD WORLD

SECTION Sectional Director	Sectional Coordinator of Vol. Flight Surgeons	Sectional Coordinator of Vol. Flight Nurses	Sectional Coordinator of Vol. Airplanes and Pilots	Sectional Coordinator of Am. Rad. Oper's.
STATE State Director	State Leader of Vol. Flight Surgeons	State Leader of Vol. Flight Nurses	State Leader of Vol. Airplanes and Pilots	State Leader of Am. Radio Oper's.
CORPS (No General Corps Director)	Corps Leader of Vol. Flight Surgeons	Corps Leader of Vol. Flight Nurses	Flight Leader of Aircraft	(No Corps Leaders of Am. Radio Oper's.)
VOLUNTEER	Flight Surgeon Volunteers	Flight Nurse Volunteers	Aircraft Owner or Pilot Volunteer	Am. Radio Oper. Volunteers

National Chairman, Amateur Radio Operators (Suspended for the duration of the war.) —Lightning bolt on the right wing, "NAT. CHAR-MAN" on the left;

Section Officials

Sectional Director—Additional arc with "SEC. DIR;"

Section Coordinator of Volunteer Flight Surgeons—Caduceus on right wing and "SEC. CO-ORD." on left wing;

Sectional Coordinator of Volunteer Flight Nurses—Caduceus and an "N" on right wing, "SEC. CO-ORD," on left wing;

Sectional Coordinator of Volunteer Airplanes and Pilots (suspended for the duration of the war)—Vertical propeller on the right wing, "SEC. CO-ORD." on left wing;

Sectional Coordinator of Amateur Radio Operators (suspended for the duration of the war)—lightning bolt on the right wing, "SEC. CO-ORD" on left wing;

State Officials

State Director—Additional arc with "STATE DIR;"

State Leader of Volunteer Flight Surgeons—Caduceus on right wing, "Captain" on left wing;

State Leader of Volunteer Flight Nurses—Caduceus and "N" on right wing, "Captain" on left wing;

State Leaders of Volunteer Airplanes and Pilots—Vertical propeller on right wing, "Captain" on left wing;

State Leader of Amateur Radio Operators—Lightning bolt on right wing, "Captain" on left wing;

Corps Leaders

No General Corps Director

Corps Leaders of Volunteer Flight Surgeons—As before, but with "FL. Leader" on left wing;

Corps Leader of Volunteer Flight Nurses—As before, but with "FL. Leader" on left wing;

Flight Leader of Aircraft—As before, but with "FL. Leader" on left wing;

No Corps Leader of Amateur Radio Operators.

Volunteers

Flight Surgeon Volunteer—As before, but no designation on the left wing;

Flight Nurse Volunteer—As before, but no designation on the left wing;

Aircraft Owner of Pilot Volunteer—As before, but no designation on the left wing;

Amateur Radio Operator Volunteer—As before, but no designation on the left wing.[671]

---

[671] Mary Steele Ross, *American Women in Uniform* (Garden City, NY: Garden City Publishing Co., Inc., 1943) pp. 49-51.

The Salvation Army in America

The Salvation Army was created by William Booth in England in 1865. It was founded on Booth's belief of two basic principles: First, "The absolute and inescapable necessity of conversion—of accepting in faith that man is born under the power of original sin and can escape from its consequences only by accepting that the grace of Christ on the Cross alone is the sovereign cure—and second, that after conversion sinful tendencies remain, but that God offers His children a kind of perfection in grace whereby His love, and theirs for Him and for each other, purges the last traces of selfishness, self-will and pride."[672] Booth began to see America as a great mission field, and organized a small group of six women and their leader, George Scott Railton for that. They sailed from England on February 14, 1880 aboard the *Australia*.[673] They were referred to as the "American Detachment" and the "Hallelujah Seven." Their comrades in England presented them with two Salvation Army flags to take with them to the states. One was to be given to an American missionary couple, the Shirleys, who lived in Philadelphia and the other one was for the future first Salvation Army district, "Blood and Fire New York No. 1."[674] Both flags had an American flag sewn to the ensign. With their military tradition, the Salvation Army called areas "corps" and named posts, "New York No. 1," the "7th Pennsylvania," etc Around 1885, this changed to refer to a city, rather than a state, e.g. "Chicago No. 13," and "Brooklyn No 1.," etc. "Divisions" had been established in 1884. The New York Times wrote of their arrival:

> "They...created quite a sensation in the [Castle] Garden [the station for immigrants at the Battery in New York City] and...in the streets as they proceeded to the lodging house .... They were all attired in a uniform of dark blue cloth, edged with bright yellow binding and around their hats were broad bands of scarlet ribbon inscribed with the words: 'The Salvation Army' in gold letters."[675]

The motto of the Salvation Army, "Blood and Fire" is found on many Salvation Army insignia and uniforms. "Blood" referencing the Blood of Christ and "Fire" referring to the Holy Spirit From the onset of

---

[672] Edward H. McKinley, *Marching to Glory* (New York: Harper & Row, Publishers, 1980) pp.2-3.

[673] Sallie Chesham, *Born to Battle. The Salvation Army in America*. (New York: Rand McNally & Company, 1965) p. 57.

[674] McKinley, p. 11.

[675] Chesham, *Born to Battle,* pp. 58-59.

the Salvation Army, women held positions as officers, just like the men. Evangeline Booth was the first female commander of the Salvation Army (1904). She was awarded the Distinguished Service Medal for her service during World War I in 1919.[676]

Prior to the American expedition, William Booth's organization had grown so rapidly that the rigors of a military organization were needed. That explains why the Salvation Army came to wear uniforms, use ranks and military nomenclature.

The Salvation Army also made a conscious decision to wear uniforms in order to make themselves stand out from the crowds and to make everyone in its membership equal, regardless of rank. Railton was the first officer to appear in uniform, at the farewell given him and the "Sacred Seven" before they left England for America.

The uniform colors were red, for the Blood of Christ; yellow for the fire of the Holy Spirit and blue for purity. The first bonnet worn by Salvation Army women was simple white Quaker-style, and had two long white ribbons which tied in a bow under the chin. The black straw bonnet appeared in 1887, and was first worn by Catherine Booth. The idea of the bonnet, and the uniform as well, was to "combine simplicity with the testimony of separation from the world. In public it was meant to be a perpetual reminder to the careless and ungodly, forcing them to think of the 'eternity to which they are hurrying"[677] Said Catherine Booth: "It was cheap, durable, protective and solidly unwordly, the bonnet with its red band and huge bow and ribbons became a symbol of the Great Salvation War."[678] It was called the "Hallelujah bonnet" or the "helmet of salvation."[679] It had a rather large brim, and two dark blue or black ribbons which tied to the left of the chin.

Mrs. Captain McIndoe wrote in an 1893 edition of *"War Cry,"* Salvationists on the West Coast "....didn't just go out and buy a bonnet. You would take the old bonnet to have it blocked (there were only two or three hat blockers on the West Coast.) I wore the first blue bonnet in the West." [680]

Sometimes salvationists were pelted with tomatoes and the like. Due to the possibility of such behavior from those to whom the Salvation Army was trying to minister, the "coal scuttle" bonnet was adapted in the latter 1890's. It had a deeper brim and offered more protection. The bonnet was modified in the early 1900's to have the more familiar short brim, covered with shirred dark blue material. The red ribbon with "Salvation Army" was worn across the top of the brim, with three sections of this ribbon directly behind. This bonnet had two long navy-blue ribbons, which tied under the

---

[676] Phyllis J. Read and Bernard L. Witlieb., *The Book of Women's First*. (New York: Random House, 1992) pp. 61-62.
[677] Untitled article by Frances Dingman of the Salvation Army. Section titled, "The Bonnet and the Modern World," p. 1.
[678] McKinley, p. 40.
[679] Frances Dingman, p. 1.
[680] Ibid, p. 1.

chin with the bow high on the left side. The ribbon on the right side was longer than the ribbon on the left side. This form of bonnet was modified so that the ribbon was permanently attached to the hat on the left side. The bonnet also had a chin strap. Wearing of the Salvation Army bonnet was discontinued in 1978.[681]

Salvation Army dark blue straw bonnet. The right ribbon was longer than the left, so that the bow could be tied high on the left side.

English bonnet actually worn by Mrs. Commissioner Adam Gifford, Western Territorial Commander 1920-31. White on ribbon denotes rank. Ribbon tied in large bow with ends hanging in front. (Courtesy: The Salvation Army Western Territorial Headquarters Museum)

"Summer hat" introduced in 1904 and seen as late as 1930 on older women. (Courtesy: The Salvation Army Western Territorial Headquarters Museum)

In the 1880's, women of the Salvation Army wore a long, dark blue dress with a standing collar and the ever-present bonnet. Some wore a silver shield-shaped brooch with the words "Salvation Army" cut-out on it. A period photograph of Maud Booth, wife of Commissioner Balllington Booth, shows her wearing a dress with a turn-down collar and false collar underneath, with large Salvation Army crests on each side of the collar.[682] Another photograph shows Maud Booth wearing an officer-type blouse, close-fitting with three wide pleats down the front. On the turn down collar are large Salvation Army crests and she wears passants on the shoulders of the blouse with at least three stars on them.[683] Consul Emma Booth-Tucker is shown wearing a dark blue dress with high, stiff collar, which is piped, button-on passants with stars, and piped sleeve cuffs. A photograph, ca. 1907, shows National Commander Evangeline Booth wearing a single-breasted jacket of heavy material with at least seven cloth covered buttons down the front. The collar is the stand and fall type, and appears to be stiffened. It is piped and has the Salvation Army crests and the "S" on both sides. The insignia are embroidered upon separate pieces of matching cloth and sewn to the collar. There are a pair of button-on passants on the shoulders of the jacket, with at least three stars. She appears to be wearing a high-collared shirtwaist under this, with the Salvation Army crest on it. The uniform has a matching skirt and the ever-present bonnet.[684] By 1915 Miss Booth is shown wearing a long, single-breasted blouse with a dark stand and fall collar, shoulder straps, two lower pleated patch pockets with flaps and buttons. The cuffs of the blouse had a narrow soutache of piping which came to a point and descended around the cuff on each side.[685]

In 1889, Captain Emma J. Brown created the "Slum Sisters," to minister to the nation's poorest. They traveled in pairs and went door to door, ready to handle a drunken husband, feed hungry boys and girls, bathe a dead baby, scrub floors, and share the Gospel of Jesus Christ.

They wore plain garb, so as not to alienate the very people they wanted to minister to. It consisted of a plain dark colored dress, usually dark navy or brown in color. Over this was a large white apron, sometimes having blue or brown pinstripes. Rank was displayed at the hem of the apron: A yellow stripe denoted a lieutenant, red tape, a captain and a white tape indicated an adjutant. Instead of the bonnet, Slum Sisters wore a sailor hat, i.e., a blue straw or felt hat with a brim and a large band and bow.[686]

---

[681] Dingman, photo caption.

[682] McKinley.

[683] Herbert A. Wisbey, Jr., *Soldiers without Swords*. (New York: The MacMillan Company, 1955.) photographic section.

[684] Wisbey, photographic section.

[685] Sallie Chesham, *Born to Battle. The Salvation Army in America*. (New York: Rand McNally & Company, 1965), photo section.

[686] Chesham, p. 138.

Major and Mrs. Jesse Roe, Life Saving Scout and Guard Leaders, the Salvation Army. (Courtesy: The Salvation Army Western Territorial Headquarters Museum)

Major Connie Sly, Territorial Guard and Sunbeam Director, the Salvation Army. (Courtesy: The Salvation Army Western Territorial Headquarters Museum)

The Life Saving Girl Guard was established in 1915.[687]

The first eleven members of the Salvation Army (the group consisting of seven men and four women) arrived at Bordeaux on August 21, 1917. In all, 109 Salvation Army women served overseas.[688] Since General John J. Pershing had awarded them the rank of privates first class, the group went to a Paris tailor and were fitted for regulation olive drab uniforms. The women ordered khaki skirts in lieu of trousers. The men and women wore typical red Salvation Army shoulder straps edged in black on their army blouses and the red cloth Salvation Army badge on their garrison caps.[689]

Female members of the Salvation Army also wore a military style blouse which had four bellows pockets. The front was secured by six embossed metal buttons. The stand and fall collar was fastened at the throat by two sets of metal hooks and eyes. The blouse was belted. Red shoulder

---

[687] Chesham, p. 148.
[688] WIMSA Calendar, 1996, see, "September."
[689] Breech, p. 126, and *The War Romance of the Salvation Army*. (Philadelphia: J.B. Lippencott Company, 1919) by Evangeline Booth and Grace Livingston Hill, p. 55.

straps with black edging were worn at the shoulders. The words, "Salvation Army" were machine embroidered on the shoulder straps near the shoulder seam of the blouse. Women and men often wore the patch of an army or division to which they were attached. Gold bullion or tape overseas service chevrons were sewn to the lower left sleeve. A matching olive-drab, divided skirt was worn under the tunic. The brimmed hat with a Montana peak[690] with a gold or silver metal, screw-back S.A. device, maroon band with "Salvation Army," was worn by enlisted women, while officers wore a padded bullion patch in the front of the hat and cords with acorns or a garrison cap, sometimes with the blackened-bronze "S.A." pin attached to the left side. Normally, though, the shield-shaped Salvation Army patch was sewn to the left curtain flap. It had the words, "The Salvation Army" embroidered in white on a red backing and had an inner or outer white border as well. Female salvationists also wore a round "Salvation Army War Service USA" patch on their garrison caps.

Stella Young, whose parents also served in the Salvation Army, is shown wearing the WWI woman's uniform. Of interest is the British style garrison cap. The faint outline of the 26th Infantry Division (the "Yankee Division") patch sewn to the upper left sleeve of her blouse can just be seen. She wears three overseas service chevrons on the lower section of the sleeve. Her blouse is unusual in that it has cuffs. (Courtesy: Lettie Gavin)

---

[690] *Our Women at the Front. A Little Story, as Told by One of the New York Tribune's Special Writers, and a Few Other Incidents.* World War I period, p. 13.

World War I Salvation Army woman's uniform. (Courtesy: NSCDA Coll.–NMAH/Smithsonian)

Detail of the left epaulet and the patch of the 41st Division of the US Army. (Courtesy: NSCDA Coll.–NMAH/Smithsonian)

Tailor's label inside a blouse. (Courtesy: NSCDA Coll.–NMAH/Smithsonian)

Woman's blouse with a 2nd Army patch sewn to the upper left sleeve. (Courtesy: The Salvation Army Western Territorial Headquarters Museum)

Major and Mrs. Charles (Sarah L. Wheeler) Van Leusen and their daughters, Edna and Grace. Major Van Leusen and daughter Grace are wearing the 3rd Army patch on their upper left sleeves. (Courtesy: The Salvation Army National Headquarters)

National Commander Evangeline Booth wearing a unique version of the overseas uniform, complete with cuff and collar braid. The padded bullion hat badge and cap cords were worn by officers. Although she was the National Commander, Booth did not serve overseas. (Courtesy: The Salvation Army Western Territorial Headquarters Museum)

Silver metal screwback hat device worn on the brimmed hat. Officers wore the device in gold.

Salvationist Della Rapson Ringle wears the brimmed hat with the metal hat device and "Salvation Army" band. (Courtesy: Lettie Gavin)

This Salvation Army officer wears the brimmed hat with bullion, padded badge and cords. Note the cape with frogging on the front. (Courtesy: National Archives)

This Salvationist wears a non-regulation blouse with a turn-down collar. Note the "S.A." pin on her garrison cap. (Courtesy: The Salvation Army National Headquarters)

WWI female Salvationist's garrison cap with the patch sewn on the front of the curtain. (Courtesy: NSCDA Coll.–NMAH/Smithsonian)

Commander Evangeline Booth's garrison cap. The insigne is gold bullion on a red cloth backing. (Courtesy: NSCDA Coll.–NMAH/Smithsonian)

Below: A female Salvationist takes a letter for a doughboy. She wears the round "Salvation Army War Service" patch on the left forward curtain of her garrison cap. (Courtesy: The Salvation Army National Headquarters)

Signa Saunders (right) preparing doughnuts at a Salvation Army canteen. (Courtesy: National Archives)

Salvation Army "lassies," as they came to be known, fried innumerable doughnuts for American soliders during World War I. Photos show these women wearing a simple dress with open, wide collar, sleeves which could be pushed up, and a self belt. A red "The Salvation Army" shield-shaped patch was worn on the left bodice. When necessary, a gas mask kit and steel helmet completed this uniform.

Stella Young (in background) and Gladys McIntyre wear steel helmets and gas mask kits while making pies. (Courtesy: The Salvation Army National Headquarters)

At least two medals were issued to Salvationists who served in the World War. They are illustrated here.

This Salvation Army medal (type 39) is for service in World War I. The planchet is bronze and the ribbon is red. This example has a slot broach and was made by Whitehead and Hoag. The obverse shows a Salvation Army man and woman wearing overseas uniforms standing in front of an SA hut. The Salvation Army shield is to the right. (Courtesy: Stuart S. Corning, Jr. via Lettie Gavin)

Reverse of the medal showing the slot broach and planchet, which reads, "World War, for heroic and faithful service to" with a rectangular space for the recipient's name to be engraved. Below this is the Salvation Army shield, flanked on the left by "1914" and "1919" on flowing ribbons. This medal also incorporates a laurel leaf branch motif.

World War service medal. (Courtesy: The Salvation Army Western Territorial Headquarters Museum)

Below: A group of Salvationists in France, 1926. Note the unique dresses and garrison caps worn by the women. Many are wearing some sort of medal. (Courtesy: Wide World Photos)

The Salvation Army was also active during World War II. While the dark blue dress and bonnet remained basically the same style, the service uniform was greatly modified. It consisted of a gray blouse, skirt and garrison cap made of light weight serge. The blouse had two patch bodice pockets and a self belt and closed with three buttons. A shoulder strap with dark blue trim was sewn on each shoulder. A soft gray silk shirtwaist was worn with a navy-blue tie. The garrison cap was piped in red cord. The wearer's rank insigne was worn on the left forward portion of the cap. A so-called "Stetson" felt hat was worn on dress occasions.

Two SA officers photographed in front of a Service Men's Club, probably during WWII. They wear the silver, false embroidered "S" and star on red collar tabs. Note the shoulder straps and cuff ornamentation. (Courtesy: The Salvation Army National Headquarters)

Silver metal false embroidery style "S" for wear on the red collar tabs.

Blue enamel "S" with silver lettering and accents for wear on the collar. Period unknown.

Commander Evangeline Booth talking with General Wainright. Booth always wore unique uniforms. Several ribbons are sewn to the bodice of her blouse, one of which is for the Distinguished Service Medal. (Courtesy: The Salvation Army National Headquarters)

The service uniform worn by female Salvationists during WWII. (Courtesy: The Salvation Army National Headquarters)

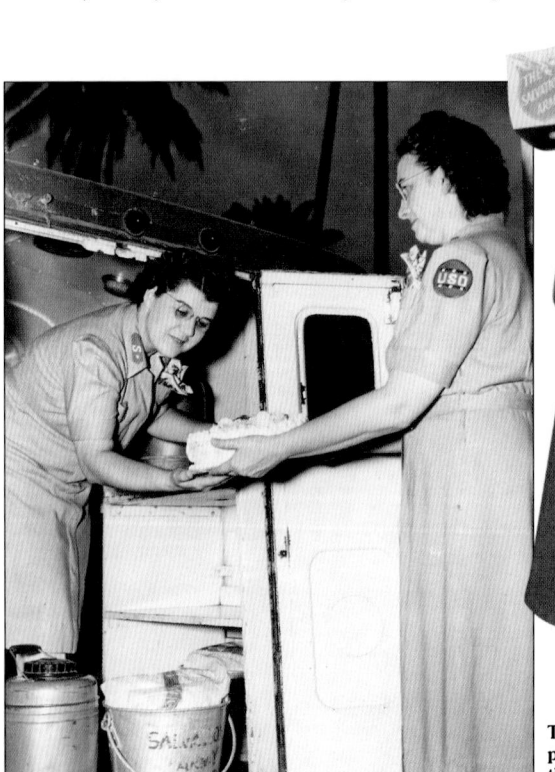

These Salvationists wear a simple dress with collar tabs. Note that the woman on the right also wears a USO patch. (Courtesy: The Salvation Army National Headquarters)

Blue felt patches, each with a metal "S" in the center and a rank insigne, were worn on the collar. Black shoes, blue or black gloves and gunmetal hose completed the uniform. A coat made of oxford gray material was worn during cold weather.

Members of the Salvation Army also served during the Korean War and Vietnam War.

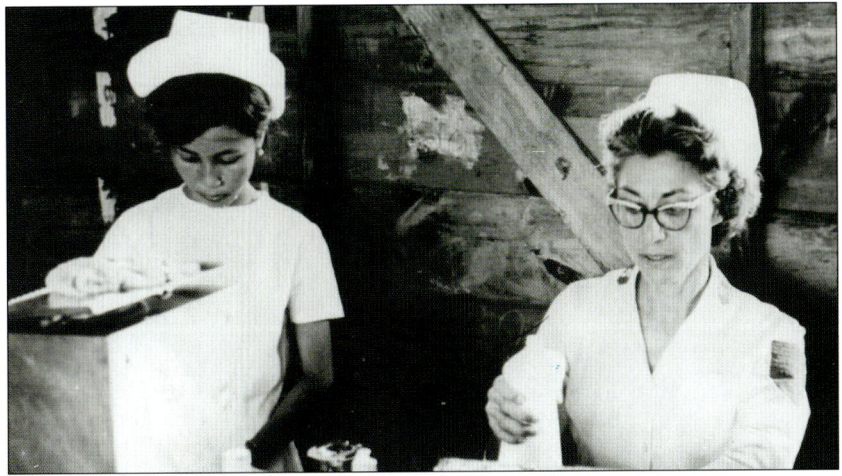

A Salvationist in Vietnam. (Courtesy: The Salvation Army National Headquarters)

Serbian Relief Committee of America
(World War I, 1919-1920)

This organization was created by the daughter of the noted Serbian Professor and Mme. Sima Losanitch, Helen Losanitch (she later married American John Whipple Frothingham, Major, ARC, in Brooklyn Heights, New York, in 1921). Her relief work began in 1915, when she was named the Serbian Red Cross delegate to America. In 1919, she established "Serbia House" in New York City. It was a relief organization, concerned mainly with the welfare of starving and orphaned Serbian children. For her outstanding work, Helen Losanitch Frothingham was awarded her native country's "Order of the White Eagle" and the "Order of St. Sava." During World War II, she was instrumental in the establishment of the American Friends of Yugoslavia.

An American, Ruth S. Farnam was well-acquainted with Serbia, being friends with the American wife of Prince Alexis of Serbia and having visited there several times. However, when she volunteered to serve there, she was rejected for lack of training. She went anyway and then returned

Helen Losanitch Frothingham.

Woman wearing the uniform of the Serbian Relief Committee of America. Note the cloth shield insignia with the initials "SRCA" on her hat and collar.

to the United States to raise money to aid the devastated Serbs. When she returned to Serbia, Farnam was received by the Serbian Army commander-in-chief, who told her,

"Madame, I have the honor to inform you that you are the first woman of any nationality to enter reconquered Serbian territory." For a moment, they watched a bloody battle raging below them. The colonel asked her, "Would you like to give the signal for our guns to recommence firing?" She nodded.

"So in the name of American Womanhood, I gave the signal which sent shells roaring...to fall in the Bulgarian trenches.... I was shaking with excitement."

She was told to calm down, that she would be removed if the battle became a danger to her. "Do you think I'm afraid?" She asked. "I've never lived before. " On the spot, in October 1916, Ruth Farnam was made a member of the First Cavalry Regiment of the Royal Serbian Army.[691]

One photo has been found which shows Helen Losanitch wearing a garrison cap with an upturn behind the front of the curtain and a shield-shaped insigne sewn in the center with the embroidered initials, "SRCA." In the photo she is also wearing a coat with a large fur collar, a white waist and dark tie.[692]

---

[691] Breach, pp. 48-49.
[692] Helen Losanitch Frothingham and Matilda Spence Rowland, ed., *Mission for Serbia. Letters from America and Canada.* (New York: Walker and Company, 1970) pp. 234, 297, 298, 301, 305 and 224.

United Service Organizations

(USO—World War II-The Vietnam War)

USO FLYING SQUADRON, STAGE DOOR CANTEEN, HOLLYWOOD CANTEEN,

AMERICAN THEATRE WING WAR SERVICES, INC.

The United Service Organizations, or USO, was made up of six service organizations: The YMCA, YWCA, the National Jewish Welfare Board, National Travelers Aid Association, the National Catholic Community Service and the Salvation Army.[693] The United States government signed a contract with this organization in March of 1941. The USO sponsored several forms of entertainment for servicemen and women during World War II. The most well-known were provided by Camp Shows, Inc., which had more than seven thousand entertainers. They became known as "soldiers in greasepaint," and included such stars as Bob Hope, Hedy LaMarr, Danny Kaye, Mickey Rooney, Dinah Shore, Joe E. Brown (who lost a son during the war), Martha Raye, the Andrews Sisters, and Nancy Walker, to name only a few.[694]

Perhaps one of the most well-known of the USO performers was Marlene Dietrich. Born in Germany, she came to America and became a citizen. Hitler had put a bounty on her head. Serving with the USO in Europe during the war, she often found herself in situations that were dangerous to anyone, but especially dangerous to her. Oftentimes, she found herself with a unit that was surrounded. While driving from place to place, singing for troops with French actor Jean-Pierre Aumont, they lost their way. Aumont recalled this incident:

> "To be taken prisoner wasn't a particularly agreeable prospect for me, but to be responsible for Marlene's capture.... Without doubt she would have been shot."[695]

---

[693] Maxine Andrews and Bill Gilbert, *Over Here, Over There: USO Stars in World War II.* (New York: Zebra Books, Kensington Publishing Corporation, 1993) p. 30.

[694] Julia M.H. Carson, *Home Away from Home.* (New York: Harper & Brothers, 1946), p.55.

[695] Patrick O'Connor. *Dietrich: Style and Substance.* (New York: The Penguin Group, 1991), p. 79.

Marlene Dietrich was decorated by the French and United States governments not only for service, but for bravery as well.[696]

USO "Camp Shows" patch, worn on the left forward curtain of the garrison cap and on the upper left sleeve of uniforms.

Patch with gold "USO" on eagle and "Camp Shows" embroidered in white. (Courtesy: The Johnson Bros.)

Flocked "Camp Shows" patch. Courtesy: The Johnson Bros.)

At the El Alamein Reunion in London during the 1960's, Dietrich probably reflected the feeling in the hearts of the audience when was asked about what she found important about the war. She responded, "The sharing. Share my food, my water, my danger." [697]

The Army authorized female USO members to wear the uniform of the Army Hostess and Librarian Service without insignia while en route to various stations and in all of the theaters of operation.[698] (For the description of this uniform, see "Army Hostess and Librarian Service," Vol. 1, pp. 160-169.) Some of these entertainers wore WAC officer uniforms with the "USO Camp Shows" patch sewn on the upper left sleeve of the uniform blouse. The patch had a red concave background with a white spread-wing eagle with blue details and "USO" in blue thread on its breast. The words, "Camp" and "Shows," embroidered in blue thread, were below the eagle's wings. Officer's "U.S." insignia were pinned near the edge of each end of the collar and clutch back "USO Camp Shows Volunteer" insignia were pinned near the end of each lapel. These insignia consisted of a horizontal metal badge, surcharged with a white enamel eagle with silver details and "USO" on its breast. The lower section was red, with "Camp Shows" in silver. Below this was a smaller horizontal silver bar with "Volunteer" in red letters. The reverse of some of the insignia viewed during this research were profusely hallmarked.[699] These insignia had tines and clutches on their reverse.

---

[696] Ibid.

[697] Ibid, p. 80.

[698] George Petersen, ed, *World War II US Army Regulations for the Service and Field Uniforms: Clothing, Headgear, Insignia, Medals, and Equipment Enlisted and Officer, Male and Female Personnel.* (Fredericksburg, VA: Reprinted by George A. Petersen, NCHS, Inc.), p. 69. AR 600-36, 1-2, 1 c, Washington, DC: February 25, 1944.

[699] "USO Camp Shows" lapel insignia in the collection of the Admiral Chester Nimitz Museum.

USO Camp Shows lapel insigne, worn by actress Lynn Mayberry. Mayberry toured with Marlene Dietrich throughout WWII.

"Camp Shows Volunteer" lapel insigne. (Courtesy: Sylvia Leasure)

USO Camp Shows lapel insigne with the designation "staff" on the bottom bar. Note that the bar, wording, frame and detail of the eagle are done in silver instead of gold. This example has a screw back and was made by Bastian Brothers.

Reverse of a "Camp Shows Volunteer" lapel insigne, showing four hallmarks. This example was made by Bastian Bros. Company of Rochester, NY. (Courtesy: Nimitz Museum)

This USO member wears a cut-out "US" on her right lapel and the "USO Camp Shows" insigne on her left lapel. (Courtesy: Ed Anderson, Jr.)

Lynn Mayberry (left) and Marlene Dietrich (right) with some GI's from the 101st Airborne Division. They wear the blouse with no pockets or regular lapels, but have placed the "Camp Shows" insignia on their blouses in the approximate location of where they would be if the blouses had regular lapels. Note that their shoulder bags are like those carried by Army nurses.

These twin entertainers pose proudly in their USO uniforms. The woman on the left wears what appears to be a khaki uniform, consisting of a short jacket and trousers. She wears a pair of "U.S." insignia on the collar and five overseas service bars on the lower left sleeve. The woman on the right wears the typical USO overseas uniform with a turban in lieu of the garrison cap.

"Dress" made from a shirtwaist and what appears to be khaki army officer's material. (Photo by Ronda Sheel)

    Because of their civilian status, USO volunteers wore plastic olive-drab four-hole buttons on their uniforms or US Army buttons covered with olive-drab material. There were several variations on the basic uniform, some of which are shown here.

    A dark olive-drab elastique garrison cap, designed like that worn by WAC officers or Army nurses, was also worn. The "USO Camp Shows" patch sewn to the left forward curtain. The curtain was piped in an emerald green piping.

    Other forms of USO sponsored entertainment was the Hospital Circuit, which provided entertainment at military hospitals, and the Blue

Lynn Mayberry and Marlene Dietrich with other USO entertainers, pose with members of a flight crew. Note Lynn Mayberry's visored hat with the USO "Camp Shows" patch on the front. (US Army Signal Corps photo)

USO Camp Shows woman's garrison cap. This example has a rust colored lining and the Knox Hats trademark.

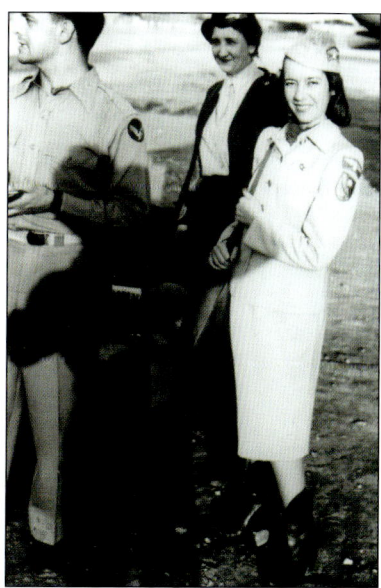

Coloratura soprano Lily Pons wears a very unusual uniform with cowboy boots! Note the USO "Camp Shows" patches on her garrison cap and upper sleeve. She wears the U.S. Army Persian Gulf Service Command patch below the sleeve patch. (Courtesy: Joe Stone)

Larry Adler, Wini Shaw, Anna Lee and Jack Benny plan their upcoming USO itinerary.

Circuit, which provided small troupes of Vaudevillians to entertain at smaller facilities.[700]

USO Hostesses wore civilian clothing with only a possibly paper or cloth brassard on just above their left elbow. Brassards were held in place by a narrow elastic band or cloth ties. The field was white with the letters, "USO" printed in blue. Two red horizontal stripes had three white stars in them. A pin, with the initials, "USO" entwined, was also worn by volun-

---

[700] Frank Coffey, *Fifty Years of the USO. Always Home.* (Washington, DC: Brassey's (US), Inc., 1991) p. 26.

USO volunteer wearing a civilian dress with a USO brassard. (Courtesy: George Petersen)

USO printed brassard. (Phil & Linda Darling)

teers who had accumulated enough work hours. There were other assorted USO pins, some of which are illustrated here.

USO volunteer's pin.

Miniature USO pins, purpose unknown. Examples exist with stars on the top and bottom, probably indicating time of service. (Courtesy: Ed Anderson, Jr.)

Probably one of the early USO volunteer pins. (Courtesy: Patt Anthony)

USO volunteer pin variation. (Courtesy: Patt Anthony)

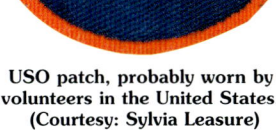

USO patch, probably worn by volunteers in the United States. (Courtesy: Sylvia Leasure)

Young professional women from Honolulu, Hawaii formed a group which went to military posts to provide dance partners for the enlisted men. For undetermined reasons, they were dubbed the "USO Flying Squadron." Its director was Peggy Johnson; the assistant director was Fern Parks.[701] One of its members, Frances Hurd Buxton* wrote, "...I don't remember why we were called the Flying Squadron—none of us flew." They wore a USO pin, bracelet and wings.[702]

Known members of the USO Flying Squadron were:

Eleanor Anderson	Grace Fern	Carol Guthrie
Pearl Anderson	Kathaleen Finnigan	Frances Hurd*
Margaret Archer	Sophie M. Frandsen	Dorothy Johnson
Doreen Barker	Maxine L. Freedman	Alberta Kemple
Betty Charlock	Angeline Gomes	Athalie Keough
Isabella De La Fuente	Ella Marie Grau	Mary Martin
Vivi Evars	Barbara Greer	Sylvia McLean

---

[701] Souvenir Program, USO Flying Squadron Anniversary Dance, Barber's Point Naval Air Station, Oahu, Hawaii, April 11, 1943.
[702] *Fifty Years of the USO*, p. 6.

Eleanor O'Conner
Watty Owens
Fern Parks
Myrtle Paul
Pat Prindiville

Kirsten Rasmussen
Theresa Slavazza
Lucinda Smith
Barbara Wall
Florence Walsh[703]

Chaperones were:
Miss Abertine Sinclair
Mrs. Esther Freedman
Mrs. Walter Wall[704]

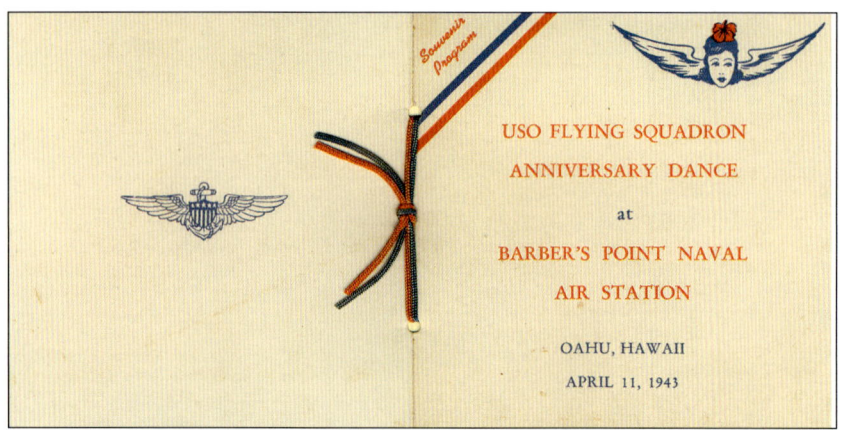

USO Flying Squadron Anniversary Dance souvenir program, April 11, 1943.

Apparently, the Flying Squadron was disbanded in October 1943. Commander Stockard R. Hickey, US Navy, Office of the Commandant of Fleet Recreation wrote on October 16, 1943:

"To the Ladies of the U.S.O. Flying Squadron: As the Recreation and Morale Officer of the Pacific Fleet for the past thirty months it has been my pleasure to see the U.S.O. Flying Squadron come into being as a vital factor in maintaining the morale and fighting spirit of the men of our armed forces here in Hawaii."

Commander Hickey closed by saying:

"When the war is over and old [sic] Glory is flying triumphantly from the highest towers in Berlin and Tokyo, none of your names will appear in the list of those receiving medals, [sic] your reward will be the knowledge that "The Flying Squadron also Served."[705]

The "Stage Door Canteen" was organized by Brock Pemberton, the most famous of the canteens was the one in San Francisco, California, on the block of 30 Mason Street. During its lifespan, the Stage Door Canteen served 4,000,000 sandwiches and provided 108,000 hours of manpower. Nothing by way of documentation could be found about the aprons worn by volunteers, but according to the movie, "Stage Door Canteen," they wore a bibbed apron with wide red, white and blue verticle stripes. Though

---

[703] Program from "The Breakers." Aloha to the USO Flying Squadron Twilight Supper-Dance. Saturday, October 16, 1943.
[704] Ibid.
[705] Ibid.

not shown in the movie, at least one example of a pair of "American Theatre Wing, Stage Door Canteen San Fransisco" wings exist. Five thousand soldiers and canteen workers danced the last dance there until 2:00 am on December 25, 1945, when the Canteen closed its doors for good.[706]

USO "Flying Squadron" identification bracelet.

Reverse of the "Flying Squadron" bracelet which reads, "Official Penalty for Misuse." The woman's name, "Delia Samons" and "Hawaii" appear to be hand engraved. The bracelet is marked "sterling" on the bottom.

Certificate of Appreciation. (Courtesy: Helen Novodvotsky via Sylvia Leasure)

American Theatre Wing: Stage Door Canteen, San Francisco. (Courtesy: Ed Anderson, Jr.)

---

[706] Marie Hicks Davidson, "5,000 Boys, Girls Sing Swan Song," Article from untitled newspaper, December 1945.

The "Hollywood Canteen" was founded by Bette Davis and actor John Garfield. Davis wrote, "The whole idea of the canteen was to give the men fun, relaxation and the chance to meet personally and be served by the stars of Hollywood and not be charged one cent. Some [stars], like Dietrich, not only contributed glamour out front but backbreaking labour in the kitchen."[707]

Hollywood Canteen worker's pin.

The various canteens were under the control of the American Theatre Wing War Service, Inc., of New York. Female members of the American Theatre Wing War Players serving overseas wore an olive-drab military style blouse, sometimes worn buttoned at the collar, with bodice pockets that had no flaps, an olive-drab skirt or trousers, khaki or olive-drab waist, khaki or olive-drab tie and an olive-drab visored hat with a self bow above the visor. A machine-embroidered "USO Camp Shows" patch was sewn to the left sleeve of the blouse, but somewhat lower on the sleeve. Volunteers wore wings which had a blue theatrical mask the center, and were apparently identical to the wings shown at the top of the Certificate of Appreciation (shown at left). Above this was a ribbon with the words, "American Theatre Wing." Oddly, sometimes the wings were pinned to the sleeve of the olive-drab blouse, just below the "USO Camp Shows" patch.[708] They were also pinned just above the breast pockets of khaki shirts and uniform blouses. (Male members of the American Theatre Wing wore the same wings.) Members also wore a pin on the left forward curtain of their garrison cap. The American Theatre Wing War Services, Inc., had originated from the World War I organization, "Stage Women's War Relief."[709]

Actress Katherine Cornell wears the usual uniform described in the text. Note the position of the USO "Camp Shows" patch and the wings pinned below it.

---

[707] "Dietrich," p. 75.

[708] Period photograph of Katherine Cornell in the book, The B.O.W.S. (New York: Harcourt, Brace and Company, 1945), p. 177.

[709] Charlotte Palmer Seeley, ed., *American Women and the US Armed Forces*. (Washington, DC: The National Archives Trust Fund Board, 1992) p. 245, No. 389.6.

Screw-back badge worn on the forward left curtain of the garrison cap. Actual size is 2.5cm wide. Note the initials, "A.T.W." on the white part of the ribbon.

Pair of American Theatre Wing War Service wings. (Courtesy: Ed Anderson, Jr.)

A male member wears a khaki uniform with a tooled leather belt. The wings over his left breast pocket and his cap insigne identify him as being a member of the American Theatre Wing of the USO. Both male and female members wore these wings. Actress Madeline Carroll stands at his right. (Courtesy: Joe Stone)

Unit 319, the troupe of actors who toured overseas with the "The Barretts of Wimpole Street" (who came to be known as the "B.O.W.S."), were given a citation from the Fifth Army, awarded to them on-stage in Italy personally by General Mark Clark. Earlier, Clark had passed out Fifth Army patches to them backstage. The citation read:

"The Barretts of Wimpole Street is awarded the Fifth Army plaque for exceptionally meritorious service, during the period of 14th October to 10th November, 1944. During this period the distinguished cast of this history-making production, in a manner befitting the artistry of its members, presented performances which were attended by thousands of Fifth Army troops. The memorable entertainment provided by the members contributed materially to the enhancement of the morale of the Fifth Army troops."[710]

---

[710] Margalo Gillmore and Patricia Collinge, *The B.O.W.S.* (New York: Harcourt, Brace and Company, 1945) 113.

Some members of the Fifth Army had also given their artillery red or infantry blue ascots to the B.O.W.S., who wore them proudly.[711]

Certificate for "Meritorious Service in USO War Work," dated November 28, 1944. (Courtesy: Joe Stone)

The USO provided entertainment for servicemen and women during the Korean and Vietnam Wars.

USO entertainers in Korea during the war. Note the new patch style. (Courtesy: National Archives)

---

[711] Ibid, p. 99.

USO Victory Belles

The "Victory Belles" originated in Dallas, Texas. Some 1,500 Dallas girls volunteered to serve the USO and American servicemen as secretaries, hostesses, and bridge and dance partners. The June 29, 1942 issue of *Life* Magazine shows Margaret Mary "Bunny" Bekins wearing the USO "Vicory Belle" medal.

Marines jitterbug at the Dallas USO.

State of Texas Auxiliary Reserve

(STARS)
(Post-World War II)

In December 1952, a proposal for the creation of a women's auxiliary section of the Texas State Guard was put to the Executive Committee of the Texas State Guard in Austin. It was brought forward by Lieutenant Colonel Earl C. Dunn, Commanding Officer, 2nd Battalion, 9th Infantry, TSGRC, Corpus Christi. A resolution was presented by Colonel Huson, Commander, 9th Regimental area. It was Captain Samuel D. Beard, Adjutant, 2nd Battalion, who created the name of "STARS," the acronym for "State of Texas Auxiliary Reserve." Committeewomen were selected from each battalion: Ellen L. Humes, wife of Captain Harold K. Humes, assistant adjutant, 9th Regiment; Wilma J. Allen, wife of 1st Lieutenant Orval E. Allen and Lieutenant Ester Spencer, Texas Wing, Civil Air Patrol, wife of 1st Lieutenant Sherman L. Spencer, Commanding officer, 3rd Battalion.

By April 1952, it was suggested that STARS wear khaki uniforms, similiar to the WAC shirtwaist, skirt and garrison cap. A blue star patch was to be worn on the left side. The TSGRC patch was worn on the upper left sleeve, with the small, gold "TEX" insignia pinned to each side of the shirtwaist collar. However, in the March 1952 issue of *"The Guardsman,"* three women officer's are shown wearing men's khaki shirtwaists, and gar-

Wilma J. Allen

Ellen L. Humes

Ester Spencer

rison caps with officer's piping. The waists have rank pinned to the right side of the collar and infantry officer crossed rifle insignia pinned to the left. Rank is also sknown on the left forward curtain of the garrison cap. Distinctive insignia are worn on the shoulder straps if the waist had them, or pinned at the shoulders in the appropriate position.

By June 1952, STARS are shown wearing a belted shirt dress and unpiped garrison cap. A blue star patch is worn on the left side of the cap by some of the women. (*"The Texas Guardian,"* March, April, June and November 1952 issues.)

Six of the nine Corpus Christi STARS. Standing, left to right: Ira Beard, Florence Dupont, Mrs. Mitchell, Mrs. Leggett. Seated: Captain Wilma J. Allen, 1st Lt. Dottie Beard.

Texas Guardettes
(WWII)

This organization was created on October 21, 1942. Comprised of a hundred women, the 5th Battalion of the Texas Guardettes was located in Ft. Worth, and was an auxiliary of the Texas State Guard. It was created by Major Marshall H. Kenady and Captain Jack Massengale, TSG. Captain Lester Painter, Sergeant Leon Harris and Corporal L. Wallace gave the unit instruction in military procedures and infantry drill.

The goals of the Guardettes were to become accomplished in military courtesy and drill, to be prepared to assist groups such as the Red Cross and Civilian Defense in the event of an emergency, to participate in the selling of war bonds, enlisting recruits for the Armed Services, and other wartime activities.

Members wore a blue four-pocket blouse, skirt and piped garrison cap. Presumably, the color of the shirtwaist was white and the tie was black. Some members wore a Sam Browne belt, with or without cross strap. The red, white and blue "Texas Guardette" patch was worn on the upper left sleeve of the blouse. Some wore the "Ft. Worth" tab below this. The smaller red, white and blue star patch was worn on the left forward

Cap star
(Courtesy: Bill Block)

Above: Texas Guardettes membership card.
Right: Shoulder patch. (Courtesy: Bill Block)

section of the flap of the garrision cap. Officers wore rank insignia on their shoulder straps, while enlisted women wore chevrons on their sleeves. This organization was still viable as of 1952. (*The Texas Guardsman,* "Texas Guardettes Doing Fine Job," January 1944, courtesy of Bill Block.)

Texas State Guard Women's Motor Corps Auxiliary patch, 36th battalion. (Courtesy: Johnson Bros.)

United States Army Telephone Operators of the Signal Corps
("HELLO GIRLS")

In 1917, General Pershing notified his superiors in the War Department that he needed American and Canadian women who were fluent in French to serve as telephone operators and translators. Some 7,000 women volunteered as telephone operators, but only 233 were accepted to serve with the AEF in France. The War Department turned to the American Telephone and Telegraph Company to train the women in the operation of switchboards and how to code and decode messages. Some were trained at Grand Central Station in New York City.[712] Organized into six units, these 'soldiers of the switchboard' sailed for France in the spring and summer of 1918.[713] The sound of an American female's voice over the line brought joy to the hearts of many homesick soldiers:

> "Oftentimes...after saying 'number please,' there would be a silence, broken by an awed, 'Oh!' Sometimes it would be, 'Thank heaven, you're here at last!'"[714]

They were under strict Army discipline and "...were subject to court martial same as any other soldier."[715] Set up in seventy-five AEF exchanges throughout France, these women had to work with antiquated French telephone equipment and contend with frequent breakdowns and long hours. Some units worked more than forty hours without relief, because there weren't enough telephone operators initially.[716] Girls working at the Toll Emergency Exchange at Le Bell Epegine (built to replace the one in Paris, should the city fall to the Germans) had to wear surgical masks during an outbreak of influenza.[717]

---

[712] Helen Rogan, *Mixed Company. Women in the Modern Army.* (New York: G.P. Putnam's Sons, 1981) p.125.

[713] "A Stroll Down Memory Lane. "Hello Girls" of WWI." Government Issue. *AT&T's Newsletter for its Government Customers,* Volume 4, No. 4 (July/August 1995): pp. 41-43.

[714] Dorothy and Carl J. Schneider, *Into the Breach. American Women Overseas in World War I.* (New York: Viking Penguin, 1991) p. 268.

[715] Breach, pp. 178-179.

[716] "A Stroll Down Memory Lane. "Hello Girls" of WWI," Government Issue. *AT&T's Newsletter for its Government Customers,* Volume 4, No. 4 (July/August 1995): p. 43.

[717] Caption from a period photo of Hello Girls in France, Fort George G. Meade Museum.

Some "Hello Girls" were assigned to the First Army during the Argonne Offensive in October 1918. Adele Hoppock Mills recounted:

> "Our work during the offensive was tense and confusing as the rapidly advancing army made constant changes in headquarters.
>
> We were expected to use the utmost caution in our conversations over the wires, due to wire tapping by the enemy."[718]

"Hello Girls" at Tours, October 3, 1918.

After the Armistice of November 11, 1918, some "Hello Girls" were seconded to the American delegation for the Paris Peace Conference. Merle Anderson, chief operator at the Crillon Exchange, handled the calls between President Wilson, and Prime Ministers Clemceau of France, Orlando of Italy and Lloyd George of Great Britain.[719] An exchange was set up in Coblenz, Germany in 1919, at Third Army Headquarters. Its code name was 'Doodle Bug.'[720]

Lauded for their performance of duty during the war by General Pershing, the "Hello Girls" returned to the United States only to find that they had been reduced in status to that of civilian employees of the army, which made them ineligible for veterans' benefits. A bitter Merle Anderson wrote,

> "Those blue uniforms...that we so proudly wore were a delusion. We had signed no contracts. We were sworn into service and were constantly reminded by our officers of our responsibilities as 'Army Women.' It was a rude awakening."[721]

Anderson fought long and hard, and without success, for the U.S. Government to recognize these women as legitimate veterans.

---

[718] "A Stroll Down Memory Lane. "Hello Girls" of WWI." Government Issue. *AT&T's Newsletter for Government Customers,* Volume 4, No. 4. (July/August 1995): p. 43.
[719] Ibid, p. 44.
[720] Gavin, p. 100.
[721] AT&T, p. 45.

"Those brave operators of the Meuse Argonne battle—whose Chief Operator, Grace Banker, [who received] the Distinguished Service Medal[722] from 'A Grateful Congress'—have been forgotten."[723]

When Merle Egan Anderson's husband wrote to the government for her Victory Medal, they were told, "that [she] was not eligible for an honorable discharge or a medal for service, since [she] had not been a member of the armed forces. They said the "Hello Girls" were considered 'civilians,' or 'contract employees' of the Signal Corps, not military. ....We had signed no contracts. We had proudly worn the Signal Corps uniform, black bloomers and all. We had served in a war zone under military orders and military discipline, and we had been constantly reminded of our duties and responsibilities as 'Army women.' Now that the war was won, they wanted to forget us."[724]

She also said: " If I do get a Victory Medal, it should be for fighting the Army all these years."[725]

The "Hello Girls" were finally accorded veteran status by the government in 1971, but by that time, most of them had died,[726] and it wasn't until 1979 that Army officers were sent out to give the surviving women their honorable discharges and Victory Medals.[727]

The Hello Girls had to come up with the money for their own uniforms—they were not supplied by the Army. They wore a dark blue Norfolk uniform, consisting of a blue serge blouse with two side patch pockets with flaps and a self belt, which passed through loops on the blouse. It had a stand-and-fall collar. Some women wore a white false collar under this. Period photos also show "Hello Girls" wearing the blouse open at the top with a large white sailor-type collar over it. A blackened-bronze, officer-style "U.S." insigne was pinned to the right collar, about an inch from the forward edge. A blackened-bronze, officer-style Signal Corps device was pinned to the left collar. The blouse fastened by five blacken bronze Army buttons, with four smaller buttons at each sleeve cuff.

A matching blue serge skirt was worn with black shoes or boots with black stockings. Some of these young telephone operators wore 'extra-high tan walking shoes' while they worked the telephones during the battle of Saint-Mihiel.[728] "Hello Girls" also wore black sateen bloomers, in case the wind blew their skirts up.[729]

---

[722] Charlotte Palmer Seeley, ed., *American Women and the U.S. Armed Forces*. (Washington, DC: The National Archives Trust Fund Board, 1992) p. 137, Item # 120.29.
[723] AT&T, p. 45.
[724] Gavin, p. 92.
[725] Breach, p. 278.
[726] AT&T, p. 45.
[727] Gavin, p. 93.
[728] Helen Rogan, *Mixed Company. Women in the Modern Army*. (New York: G.P. Putnam's Sons, 1981) p. 126.
[729] Gavin, p. 79.

General John J. Pershing inspects a group of "Hello Girls" at Third Army Headquarters in Coblenz, Germany, March 15, 1919. They are wearing the white sailor-type collar. (Courtesy: National Archives)

Unpiped garrison cap.
(Courtesy: NSCDA Coll.–NMAH/Smithsonian)

A rare example of the uniform worn by "Hello Girls." Normally, the rank insigne would be worn on the left sleeve, instead of the right, as shown here. (Courtesy: NSCDA Coll.–NMAH/ Smithsonian)

Hello Girls wore a blue serge garrison cap in the Belgian or French styles. Some girls wore orange and white cord piping around the cap curtain upturn, while others wore no piping. The officer style US Army Signal Corps insigne was pinned to the left forward section of the cap curtain. They also wore a dark blue fedora, of velour, felt or rough straw, with the "...orange and white cord ribbon of the corps...on the hat."[730]

Signal Corps girl's orange and white piped garrison cap. (Courtesy: NSCDA Coll.–NMAH/Smithsonian)

Signal Corps girls being awarded citations for meritorious services at Tours, France, on June 25, 1919. Some of the women are wearing the patch of the Second Army. The woman on the right wears a piped garrison cap. (Courtesy: National Archives)

Initially, these telephone operators wore a white brassard with the wearer's rank embroidered on it in black thread. Supervisor's wore embroidered brassards with the outline of a telephone mouthpiece with two laurel leaves below it. A chief operator wore the same insigne, with the addition of two yellow lightning bolts above the mouthpiece. Other operators wore the brassard with the outline of the mouthpiece only.[731] The brassard was replaced by a rank patch was worn on the left shoulder of the blouse. Period photographs show that some of these consisted of a half-wreath of laurel leaves embroidered at the bottom of the patch with a telephone

A young Signal Corps girl prior to her departure for France. Note the heavy velour or, possibly beaver brimmed hat. The acorns on the hat cords are just visible. She wears the brassard, which proceeded the "rank" insigne. (Courtesy: Lettie Gavin)

mouthpiece embroidered above this, facing left. One photograph shows a woman wearing the aforementioned patch with the addition of lightning bolts above the mouthpiece, while another is shown wearing the mouthpiece with a downward pointing chevron. The embroidery was gold bullion. Hello Girls could wear the patch of the army or unit to which they were attached on the upper left sleeve of the uniform blouse. Overseas service chevrons, sometimes in miniature, were sewn on the lower left sleeve.

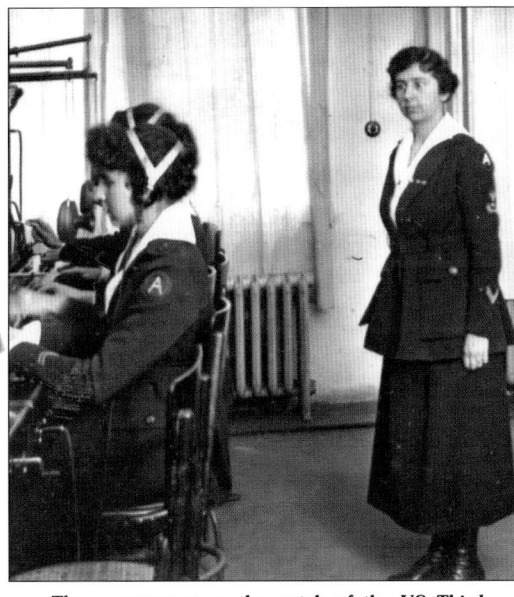

These women wear the patch of the US Third Army on their upper left sleeve as well as overseas service chevrons. (Courtesy: National Archives)

730 The National Society of The Colonial Dames of America, Report of the Committee on Relics (Washington, DC: Colonial Dames of America, 1922) p. 15.

731 Alan Archambault and Ed Milligan. "Lady Telephone Operators of the American Expeditionary Force, 1917-1918," fairly recent publication, the title of which is unknown.

This "Hello Girl" wears an unidentified patch on her left sleeve. (Courtesy: Daniel J. Miller)

Top: Patches with the "Hello Girl" telephone mouthpiece insigne in olive-drab. They appear to be original, however, no indication was found during this research that suggested this color of uniform was worn by the girls. Bottom left: Bullion sleeve rank. Bottom right: Felt sleeve rank.

The uniform illustrated here is unusual in that the "rank" patch is sewn to the upper right, instead of left sleeve. It belonged to chief operator Miss Helen Cook, who served at Pershing's General Headquarters in France,[732] hence the red, white and blue patch on the upper left sleeve.

Uniform worn by Chief Operator Miss Helen Cook. Note that the "rank" insigne is wrongly sewn to the right sleeve. The red, white and blue patch is for General John J. Parshing's Headquarters in France, where Miss Cook served. (Courtesy: NSCDA Coll.–NMAH/Smithsonian)

Rank insigne for a chief operator. (Courtesy: NSCDA Coll.–NMAH/Smithsonian)

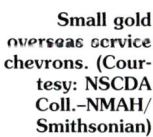

Small gold overseas service chevrons. (Courtesy: NSCDA Coll.–NMAH/Smithsonian)

[732] Report of the Committee on Relics, p. 26.

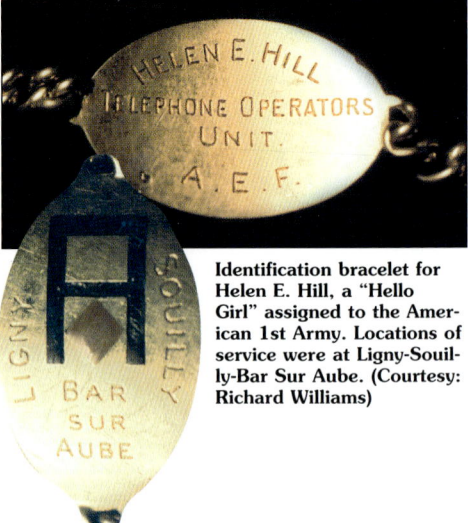

Identification bracelet for Helen E. Hill, a "Hello Girl" assigned to the American 1st Army. Locations of service were at Ligny-Souilly-Bar Sur Aube. (Courtesy: Richard Williams)

M. Olive Shaw, US Army Signals Corps telephone operator during WWI, March 1918-June 1919. Ms. Shaw was one of 18 surviving operators present when they received veteran status in the 1970s. Shaw entered the Signal Corps during the war while already in France, where she was studying music at the Sorbonne. She remained at the Sorbonne following the war and later served as private secretary for Congresswoman Edith Nourse Rogers in Washington, DC. Note that Shaw's insigne of rank consists of a telephone mouth piece over a chevron. She is wearing a British-style garrison cap with the two button front closure. (Courtesy: Mary Birse, Women's Memorial Archive)

Note:
See Appendix 2 for additional information and photos.

United States Coast Guard Women's Reserve

(SPARS)/(World War II)

On December 29, 1942, it was stated, "Tradition took a trimming today...as thirteen women sailed into the portals of the United States Coast Guard Academy." Twelve of the women were Waves who resigned their commissions to serve in the Coast Guard. Enlisted Spars underwent training at Palm Beach, Florida. In all, 13,000 women served as Spars during World War II. The SPARS was disbanded on July 1, 1946[733] and then was reactivated in 1948 and continued to exist through the Korean War.[734] In November 1950, former SPARS officers and enlisted women were recalled to enlist in the newly formed Volunteer Women's Reserve of the United States Coast Guard.[735]

Already in November 1942 SPARS director Captain Dorothy C. Stratton* suggested to Vice Admiral Russel R. Waische, Commandant of the Coast Guard, that the group of women reservists of the United States Coast Guard should be called SPARS, combining its motto, Semper Paratus ("Always Ready").

She stated:

> "...The press would emphasize and publicize the motto of the Coast Guard. Moreover, there is no problem of inventing titles to fill out the word. As I understand it, a spar is often a supporting beam and that is what we hope each member of the Women's Reserve will be.
>
> "...If we do not create a name, we shall be called WARCOGS or something worse. I like SPARS because it has meaning."[736]

Enlistees trained at Iowa State Teacher's College, Oklahoma A&M University, Manhattan Beach, New York, Hunter College, New York and at

---

*After World War II, Dr. Stratton was chosen to lead the Girl Scouts of America.[737]

---

[733] "What the Others are Doing," *WAC News Letter,* Vol. 3, No. 9 (September 1946): p. 2.
[734] Willing, p. 32.
[735] Dorothy Tuttle, "Call to the Colors," *Woman Veteran,* Vol. IV, No. 6 (June 1950): p. 8.
[736] Judy Barrett Litoff and David C. Smith, *We're in this War, Too.* (New York: Oxford University Press, 1994) pp. 38-39.
[737] Dorothy Tuttle, "Wartime SPAR Director Heads Girl Scouts," *Woman Veteran,* Vol. IV, No. 7 (July 1950): p. 8.

the Palm Beach Biltmore Hotel in Florida. Officer candidates were trained at the US Coast Guard Academy or at the Naval Reserve Midshipman School at Northampton, Massachusetts.[738]

The uniforms worn by SPARS officers and enlisted women were identical to the WAVES uniform, differing only in the insignia and clothing labels. SPARS officers wore the standard gold and silver Coast Guard officer's device on their combination hats and a smaller version on the left forward curtain of the garrison cap. Enlisted women wore the "U.S. Coast Guard" tally on their brimmed hats. Both officers and enlisted women wore the Coast Guard insignia in gold metal on their collars. It was a screw-back insigne, having a circle with a federal shield in the center with "SEMPER" at the top and "PARATUS" at the bottom. This was encircled by a band with "United States Coast Guard 1790."

WWII SPARS officer's combination hat.

Sterling United States Coast Guard officer's hat insigne, worn by male and female officers.

---

[738] WIMSA Calender, 1997, see "May.'

SPARS screw-back collar insignia worn by all ranks. Enlisted woman also wore it on the left forward curtain of the garrison cap.

Ensign Mina Brown wears the SPARS officer's combination hat with USCG officer's insigne and the blue top. (Courtesy: Delaware State Archives)

The round badge was superimposed over two crossed anchors. The SPARS uniforms studied during this research had finished holes on the collars to accommodate the screw-back insignia. However, one pair of pin-back insignia were found affixed to the collar of a SPAR uniform. The collar insignia measured approximately one inch square. This insigne was also worn by enlisted women on the left forward curtain of the garrison cap.

SPARS enlisted woman's brimmed hat with the removable white crown.

SPARS officers wore a silver bullion Coast Guard shield above their reserve-blue cuff braid. Enlisted women wore their Coast Guard rates on

Three Spars wearing the gold, screw-back United States Coast Guard insigne on their uniform collars and garrison caps. (Courtesy: Ken Tassie)

SPARS officer garrison cap. (Photo by Ronda Sheel)

USCG small insigne for wear on the left forward curtain of the garrison cap by both male and female officers.

the left or right sleeves of their uniforms and the Coast Guard shield, machine-embroidered in white thread, on the lower right sleeve of the blouse. Officers wore four gold Coast Guard buttons on their uniforms, while enlisted women wore four blue plastic Coast Guard buttons. These buttons had a horizontal striped field, embossed with a spread-winged eagle, facing right, clutching a vertical fouled anchor. A laurel leaf wreath extended under this and to just under the wings of the eagle.

A SPARS Lieutenant (j.g.) wearing the blue uniform with garrison cap in Alaska. (Courtesy: Nimitz Museum)

SPARS officer's blue uniform with cuff stripe rank for a lieutenant (j.g.). (The collar brass is missing.) (Photo by Mark Riese)

Enlisted women were required to have the following items of uniform:

2 Navy-blue wool uniforms;
2 Navy-blue cotton uniforms;
1 lined overcoat/raincoat;
2 reserve-blue cotton shirtwaists;
3 Navy-blue rayon shirtwaists;
4 white short-sleeved shirtwaists;
2 reserve-blue rayon ties;
2 black rayon ties;

Enlisted USCG sleeve shield. (Photo by: Ronda Sheel)

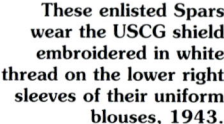

These enlisted Spars wear the USCG shield embroidered in white thread on the lower right sleeves of their uniform blouses, 1943.

1 blue garrison cap;
2 blue and white brimmed hats;
1 havelock (enlisted);
4 pairs of regulation beige lisle hose;
2 pairs of black shoes (laced oxfords of plain leather, plain or moccasin toe. Heel height not to exceed 1-1/2 inches);
1 pair of black galoshes or rubbers;
1 regulation black leather shoulder bag;
White handkerchiefs (no others could be used);
An adequate supply of easily laundered underwear.
Optional items of uniform:
Dress overcoat;
Dress shoes, plain black calf pumps or buckles shoes, heel height not to exceed two inches, closed toe.
Plain white pumps of similar construction could be worn with the white uniform;
White wool or silk muffler;
White Palm Beach summer uniform.[739]

The winter working uniform consisted of the navy-blue shirtwaist worn with the reserve-blue tie and were worn under the navy-blue uniform blouse with the navy-blue skirt. The enlisted woman's hat was worn with either the navy-blue or white cover.

---

[739] "Memorandum for Enlisted Personnel, USCG (WR)," United States Coast Guard, Washington, DC, April 20, 1943, p. 1.

Spars having a night on the town. The Spar on the right wears the "X" in a diamond on her sleeve indicating that she is unassigned. (Courtesy: Larry Pistole)

Regulation SPARS black leather shoulder bag. (Photo by Ronda Sheel)

Enlisted SPARS blue winter uniform. Both SPARS and WAVES wore the "Ruptured Duck," honorable discharge patch on the right pocket flap of the uniform blouse. (Photo by Ronda Sheel)

The blue summer uniform was similar, except that the white short-sleeve shirtwaist was worn with the black tie and the white hat cover. No rate was worn on the white shirtwaist. The Coast Guard shield, embroidered in navy-blue thread, was sewn to the right sleeve. These uniforms could be worn for dress occasions.

The winter uniform for Spars working in Washington, DC and environs was the navy-blue blouse and skirt with the white shirtwaist and black tie, white hat cover, black shoes and white gloves. Their summer uniform was classified as "Service Dress, White," and was made up of the white Palm Beach blouse and skirt with a white shirtwaist, black tie, white hat cover, white shoes and gloves. This uniform was worn only for dress occasions. The wearing of the navy-blue or reserve-blue waists was not permitted. Enlisted women wore the short-sleeved white waist. Officers wore long sleeve waists with their rank pinned to the collar.[740]

---

[740] "Clarification of the Uniform of the Day." United States Coast Guard, Washington, DC, July 6, 1943.

The gray and white seersucker uniform worn by SPARS was like that worn by Waves (only the tags inside differed).

WWII SPARS recruiting poster (Courtesy: K. Lazier)

USCG Women's Reserve Identification Tags
(Courtesy: Steve Rohde)

M-1943 style: Silver, Type 1. This tag was privately purchased and then machine-stamped on base. Note "USCGR-W" designation on this officer's tag—United States Coast Guard Reserve—Women's. Below: An additional tag made into a bracelet.

M-1943: Type 2. An officer's tag with blood type and religion.

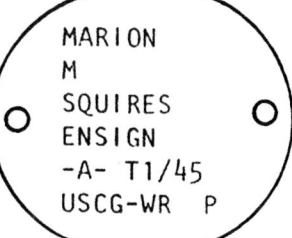

M-1943: Type 1. Enlisted with full "T" date.

M-1943: Type 2. Enlisted. The wearer served from Jan. 1945 to May 1946 at the USCG station at Manhattan Beach, N.Y.

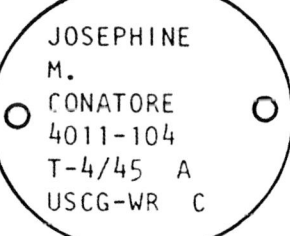

WWII award tag without "T" date or serial number, probably for a port security force volunteer. She would work part-time, 12 hours per week, with no pay. The "T" on this USCG Reserve tag indicates "temporary."

SPARS pharmacist's mate sleeve rate. (Photos by Ronda Sheel)

SPARS winter working uniform.

Summer working uniform.

Ensign Annabel Murray wears the "Service Dress, White." (Courtesy: Institute of Texan Cultures, San Antionia Light Coll.)

The SPARS enlisted version of the "Service Dress, White." Betty Caughill, 1943. (Courtesy: Institute of Texan Cultures, San Antionia Light Coll.)

Spars were to affix name tapes to their uniforms in specific places:
Hats and caps—Inside the sweatband;
Gloves—Initials to be printed on gloves inside the wrists;
Shirtwaists—Below the collar, inside;
Handkerchiefs—On the hem;
Overcoat—Below the collar, inside;
Skirt—On the waistband, center, back;
Blouse—Below the collar on the inside;
Slips—On the inside at back;
Girdles—On the inside at back;
Hose—At the top of the seam.[741]
Black and reserve-blue ties—center underside hem.

Blue and white machine-woven SPARS uniform label.

Two special labels identified official SPARS clothing: The first was a dark blue Coast Guard eagle with the words, "U.S. Coast Guard Clothing Division" woven on a light blue rectangle. The second label was a white rectangular label of coarse material. Two anchors and the words, "U.S. Coast Guard, Name........., Rate........" were printed on it in black. These labels were affixed to the uniform in the following locations:

	Light blue tag	**White tag**
Blouse:	Outside of right interior bodice pocket	Inside this pocket:
Skirt:	None	None;
Garrison Cap:	Left rear, behind size tag	Right rear of cap;
Navy-blue shirtwaist:	Lower left front interior	None;
White shirtwaist:	Lower left front interior	None;
Reserve blue shirtwaist:	None	None.
Black leather purse:	Right interior.[742]	

SPARS enlisted women going to the beach for some exercise.

---

[741] "Memorandum for Enlisted Personnel, USCG (WR), Washington, DC, April 20, 1943, p. 4.
[742] Pharmacist's Mate Erma S. Smith uniform.

SPARS Lieutenant (j.g.) wearing a very none-regulation jacket in Alaska. (Courtesy: Nimitz Museum)

SPAR recruit brassard. (Courtesy: Women in Military Service for America Memorial Archive)

SPARS identification card.

ARC card issued to Spar Erma Smith, January 12, 1944.

Spar Shirley Kephart sits in a Link trainer at the Bond Center in Wilmington, Delaware. (Courtesy: Delaware State Archives)

Spar's Pledge to Her Uniform

This is my uniform
It is the symbol of my membership in our country's service
It is the emblem of my voluntary departure from civilian life
To aid in our mighty war effort
To this uniform I pledge myself
Until the world is at peace again.
I promise to wear it faithfully
I promise to keep it clean
And to wear it properly along with its accessories.
I will not change its appearance in any way
To please my stylish whims
No matter what rating or rank insignia it may carry
It will be worn with pride.
Wearing this uniform,
I shall live up to the ideals and virtues of my service.
Obedience—which is cheerful, willing and intelligent
Loyalty—to my country, service, and fellow members
Self-control
Courage—both physical and moral
Truthfulness—the most important virtue of all
Faith—in myself, my job, and my country
Honor—my conduct shall be above reproach
And last—cheerfulness,
I shall smile and not complain
When things go wrong.
My uniform is my courage,
It is the blue of loyalty
It is my expression of the fighting spirit of America
This is my pledge to the uniform I wear as a Spar
In the United States Coast Guard Women's Reserve.[743]

(For more information about SPARS uniforms, see the chapter on "WAVES," p. 107)

---

[743] Pharmacist's Mate Erma S. Smith papers.

United States Food Administration

(World War I)

Members of this volunteer organization worked to stop the waste of food and help save food for the army. Its director was Dr. Kay Lyman Wilbur. The women each signed a pledge card, and were given a sign to hang in their window, which showed the national shield, surrounded by heads of wheat. The women in the photograph are prominent ladies of the Washington, DC area. Their uniform consisted of a blue dress and white cap. A round embroidered emblem was sewn to the front of the cap and on the left sleeve, midway between the shoulder and the elbow.[744]

US Food Administration emblem.

Group of Washington, DC women who served in the US Food Administration. (Courtesy: Keystone)

---

[744] Keystone stereo view card no. 19062. "Prominent Washington Women that Will Help Feed the Armies of the Nation by Organizing Kitchen Economy Under Dr. Kay Lyman Wilbur." World War I period.

Blue and white uniform of the Food Administration.

Achievement Award issued by the War Food Administration.

Food Administration cap and bonnet.

United States Public Health Service Reserve Corps

The Public Health Service was established in 1798 as the Marine Hospital Service with the mission of caring for sailors.[745] It was not established as a national hospital system until the 1870's and it was headquartered in Washington, DC. Its head, the Supervising Surgeon, was the forerunner of the Surgeon General. In 1902 the name of this organization was changed to the Public Health and Marine Hospital Service and then finally to the United States Public Health Service in 1912. At first, the PHS consisted only of physicians, but from necessity expanded to include many different types of health professionals, from dentists to nurses, scientists, sanitary engineers and pharmacists. With the influx of immigrants into the United States in the late eighteenth century, PHS nurses worked at Ellis Island where medical examinations were conducted. By 1914, to deal with the delicate matter of examining women immigrants, two female physicians were hired by the PHS, but they did not hold commissions. When America enter World War I in 1917 women were hired by the PHS as dietitians or laboratory researchers. In the meantime, Director of the Hygienic Laboratory of the PHS (forerunner of the National Institutes of Health), George McCory, strongly supported women in this field, and saw to it that many women were hired. The first women McCory hired in 1916 was bacteriologist, Ida Bengston. She went on to isolate a new strain of botulism bacillus. Another woman hired by McCory was Alice Evans, who became well-known for her discovery that Bang's disease in cattle was caused by the same organism which caused brucellosis in humans.

By 1943, women were gaining leadership roles within the PHS. The first such woman was Lucile Petry, who was appointed to lead the PHS Cadet Nurse Corps (see Vol. 1, pp. 283-293).

Former commander of the Women's Army Corps (WAC), Oveta Culp Hobby, was the first of four women to head of the Department of Health, Education and Welfare in 1953.

Women with little or no medical training had served as practical nurses from the earliest days in the Marine Hospital. By 1912, those women who had attended and graduated from some formal medical training were

---

[745] Unless otherwise noted, all information about the US Public Health Service was found in the article by John Parascandola, PhD., Public Health Historian, "Women in the Public Health Service," Leadership in Public Health Volume 3, Number 2. (Summer, 1994).

employed. In 1932, the first woman was admitted to the PHS Regular Corps (also called the "Commissioned Corps"). She was Dr. Estella Ford Warner.[746] By 1942, Dr. Warner had risen to the rank of Senior Surgeon.[747] She was the exception: Women did not receive commissions until 1944. As the number of women serving in the PHS grew, quarters for them became a problem. "There was never any idea in the minds of those in authority that women nurses would be placed in these hospitals and, therefore, no quarters were built for them."

During World War II, the US Public Health Service and its Reserve Corps were given full military status and became the fifth branch of the armed forces. To this day, it is the source of medical care for the United States Coast Guard.

By spring break of 1944, Josephine Mobley Clapp (Osbun),[748] a senior pre-med student at Smith College, joined the United States Public Health Service Reserve Corps while home on vacation in Savannah, Georgia. She was commissioned as a Second Lieutenant (the PHS rank was "Junior Assistant Sanitarian Reserve.") and stationed at the Carter Memorial Laboratory where research was being done on the new insecticide, DDT (dichloro-diphenyl-trichloroethane). This insecticide was desperately needed in the tropical theaters of war to protect soldiers from mosquitoes carrying malaria, typhus and dengue fever. In two months Lieutenant Clapp was promoted to Junior Biologist. She and her comrades were successful in their work with DDT. It was one of the major medical breakthroughs of World War II.

Army Nurse Lieutenant Barbara Kishpaugh (L) and an unidentified officer in the US Public Health Service Reserve (note insignia on the lapels of her uniform jacket). Frankfurt, Germany, 1945, 97th General Hospital. (Courtesy: Col. Barbara Kishpaugh, ANC, (Ret.))

---

[746] Ralph Chester Williams, MD, Assistant Surgeon General, USPHS, *The United States Public Health Service, 1798-1950*. (Washington, DC: Commissioned Officers' Association of the United States Public Health Service, 1951) p. 493.

[747] Bibliographical information provided by the Department of Health and Human Services.

[748] Unless otherwise noted, all information from this point is from the transcript of an interview conducted by Barbara Board and Dorothy Grotz, "Colonial Dames Oral History Interview," Subject: Josephine Clapp Osbun, Wilmington, DE (April 23, 1988).

Some female members of the USPHSR wore the standard uniform of the Army Nurse Corps, but with the gold cap insigne of the USPHS, gold officer's "U.S." collar insignia and gold USPHS lapel insignia. Rank insignia were worn on the shoulder straps of the blouse. The USPHSR insignia sometimes caused confusion. Jo Osbun related that she got so tired of being asked to which branch of service she belonged, her pat answer became, "I am a Second Lieutenant in the Submarine Air Corps."

Actual cap device, shown in the photo of Josephine Clapp Osbun. (Courtesy: Jo Osbun)

Actual lapel insigne shown in the photograph of Josephine Clapp Osbun. (Courtesy: Jo Osbun)

Josephine Clapp Osbun, US Public Health Service. (Courtesy: Josephine Clapp Osbun)

Doing their bit to hold down expenses during wartime, Lieutenant Osbun and comrades chipped-in to buy a drum of dry-cleaning fluid. She put her uniform on a stick, dipped it into the barrel and hung it out to dry. It worked, and saved money, too.

Other women served with the United States Navy and Coast Guard and wore the appropriate uniforms, but with gold USPHS buttons and USPHS insignia above the rank stripes on the sleeve.

The Public Health Service uniform could be navy-blue or olive-drab, according to assignment. The Corps insignia, however, was the same for both styles of uniform. Illustrated is an officially converted WAVES uniform with USPHS insignia.

A converted WAVES cap for USPHS use.

85

WAVES style uniform with gold sleeve braid and bullion USPHS insigne. The blouse has gold USPHS buttons and is named and dated April 1945. (Photo by Ronda Sheel)

Ranks

US Public Health Service	Navy	Army
Surgeon General*	Rear Admiral	Major General;
Medical Director	Captain	Colonel;
Senior Surgeon	Commander	Lieutenant Colonel;
Surgeon	Lieutenant Commander	Major;
Senior Assistant Surgeon	Lieutenant	Captain;
Assistant Surgeon	Lieutenant (jg.)	1st Lieutenant;
Junior Assistant Health Service Officer (Student)	Ensign	2nd Lieutenant.

*This insigne is also worn by the ranks of Deputy Surgeon General, Associate Surgeon General and Assistant Surgeon General. In regard to pay grade, these ranks are equivalent to either a Brigadier or Major General.[749]

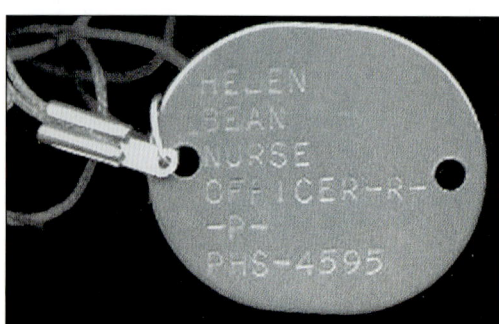

Public Health Service identification tag for a female nurse. (Courtesy: O. Spronk Photo Coll.)

---

[749] *The Commissioned Officer in the US Public Health Service*, (1960's) p. 6.

United States Shipping Board-Emergency Fleet Corp.

(World War I)

When the United States declared war against Germany the purpose and policy of the Shipping Board and Fleet Corporation changed from a body to restore the American Merchant Marine to its old glory, to a military agency to bridge the ocean with ships and to maintain the line of communication between America and Europe. Originally, it was supposed that the function of the Fleet Corporation would be that of developing designs and placing contracts for ships. But all the yards were busy completing 431 hulls for the Corporation or were clogged with orders for the Navy. The shipyard owners could not control the supply of either material or labor, hence the Fleet Corporation stepped in to manage the yards. Entirely new yards had to be built at an expense so huge it could not be defrayed by private companies. In the end the Fleet Corporation had to build the yards with government money. The Plant Protection Section of the Fleet Corporation was organized and charged with the duties of guarding yards against fires and possible attempts by the enemy to destroy buildings, machinery, and material; and of supervising the issuance of passes for admission to the yards and mills in which work was being done.

US Shipping Board Emergency Fleet Corporation uniform. (Courtesy: NSCDA Coll.–NMAH/Smithsonian)

Detail of a button. (Courtesy: NSCDA Coll.–NMAH/Smithsonian)

Sleeve patch. (Courtesy: NSCDA Coll.–NMAH/Smithsonian)

Tricorn hat. (Courtesy: NSCDA Coll.–NMAH/Smithsonian)

    Its female members wore a blue-gray four-pocket blouse and skirt with a navy-blue felt tricorn hat. The blouse closed with three gray metal shankless buttons, each embossed with a foul anchor with nine stars above. These buttons were also worn on the pockets, shoulder straps and on the sleeve cuff "belts." The blouse had a long box pleat in back which ran from the edge of the collar seam to the waist. A self belt was worn with this uniform. The skirt had two slash pockets on the front.

    A round patch with a red, white and blue federal shield, superimposed over a silver bullion anchor, was worn on the upper section of the left sleeve. The federal shield has three white embroidered stars and was bordered with silver bullion. The field of the patch is white with blue border, encircled by a silver bullion edging.

    The tricorn hat was made of navy-blue felt. The upturn of the brim was edged in gold grosgrain. A bullion badge, similar to the one worn on the sleeve of the blouse, was sewn to the left side of the upturn. It has the red, white and blue federal shield, but the anchor is worked in gold bullion, with bullion oakleaves on a white field with a blue border, edged with gold grosgrain.

"War Work" pin issued by the Emergency Fleet Corporation.

United War Work Campaign
(World War I)

The United War Work Campaign was made up of eight independent benevolent organizations: The American Library Association, the National Catholic War Council, Knights of Columbus, the Jewish Welfare Board, the YMCA, the YWCA, the Salvation Army and the War Camp Community Service. Women from all of these societies, except the War Camp Community Service, served overseas during World War I. For information about the uniforms worn by these women, see their respective chapters.

Small United War Work Campaign Poster. (Courtesy: Sylvia Leasure)

Poster announcing donations received by the various components of the United War Work Campaign.

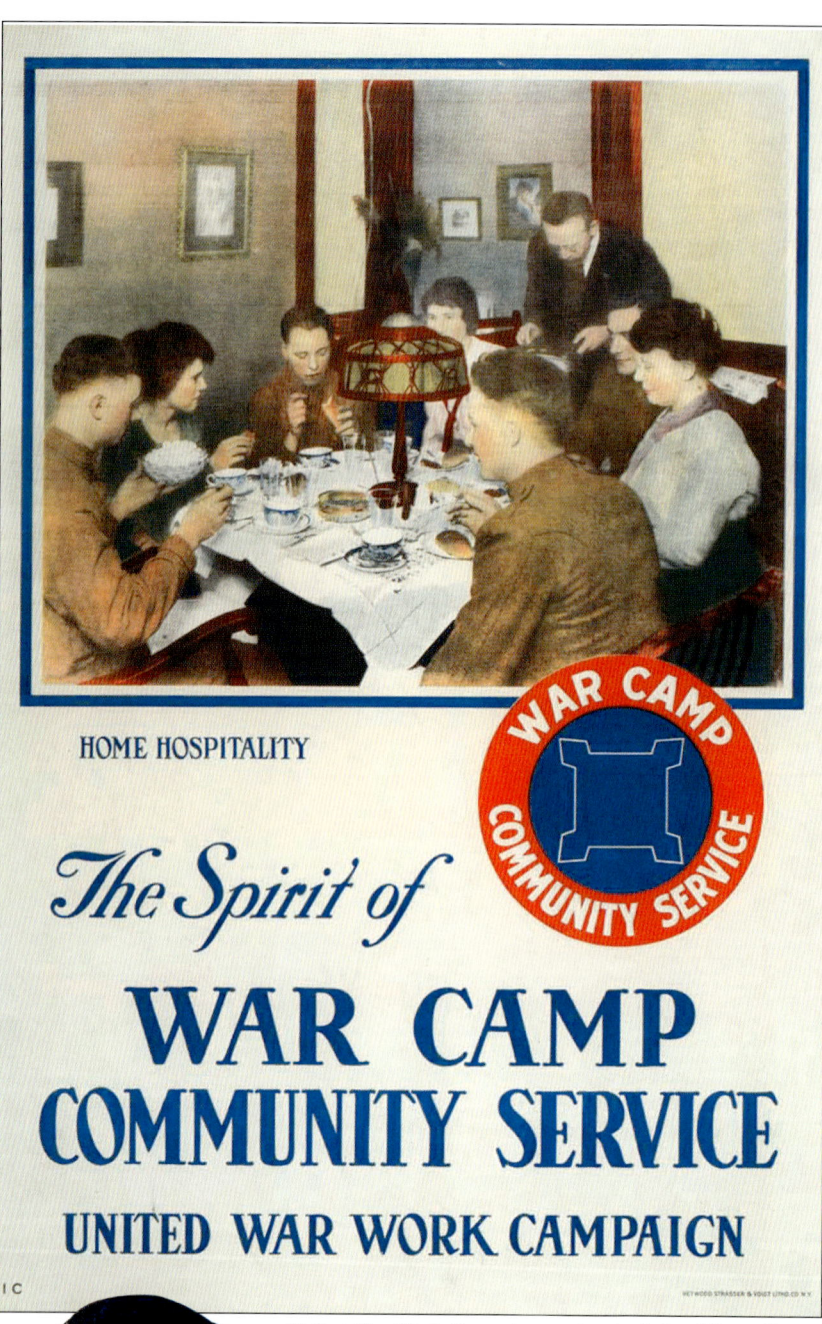

United War Work Campaign poster depicting "Home Hospitality," the Spirit of War Camp Community Service.

United War Work Campaign button.

Victory Girls
(World War II)

According to the book, *United States Army in World War II, Special Studies: The Women's Army Corps*, the term, "Victory Girls" referred to women who were actually members of the world's oldest profession. Some of these women, especially in Baltimore, Maryland and Newport News, Virginia, had even taken to wearing uniforms very similar in style to the WAAC uniform. A few of these ladies were so bold as to meet servicemen at the Hampton Roads Port of Embarkation, while claiming to be Waacs who were there to pick up G.I.'s. Director of the WAAC, Colonel Hobby complained to the Army Quartermaster Corps about the availability of surplus uniforms and material, but nothing was done, since "...the WAAC is a comparatively new corps, [and] the casual and uninformed observer is apt to believe that every woman in o.d. uniform is a Waac. It is believed that this situation will be overcome in due course." To make matters worse, the Quartermaster General, as part of a lend-lease deal, provided some 5,000 uniforms to the French "WAAC" in North Africa. It was comprised of mostly native women, there was no military organization, and they '"obeyed no military commands."[750]

Evidently, though, there was a legitimate organization know as "Victory Girls" during World War I and they were associated with the United War Work Campaign (See poster below.)

Victory Girls button. (Courtesy: Sylvia Leasure)

---

[750] Mattie E. Treadwell, *United States Army in World War II. Special Studies: The Women's Army Corps.* (Washington, DC: Office of the Chief of Military History. Department of the Army, 1954) pp.199-201.

Volunteer Army Canteen Service
(VACS—World War II)

The Volunteer Army Canteen Service was created in February 1942, and was unique to Ft. MacArthur, California. The canteen was the creation of a group of Hollywood women and was so often frequented by movie stars that it was often referred to as "Ft. Hollywood." (Letter of September 19, 2001, from Stephen R. Nelson, Director/Curator of the Fort MacArthur Museum.) The first canteen was opened in the old Battery D mess hall and was open from 11:00 a.m. until midnight. The old mess hall soon proved to be too small, so another canteen was opened at the Service Club. This was located on the Middle Reservation and served the Reception Center and Middleside soldiers. In addition to serving innumerable doughnuts, the canteens had pinball machines and a circulating library. (*The Alert,* "VACS Honored with Parade," May 14, 1942, No. 22.)

Actresses and notables such as Mary Pickford, Mrs. Charles Boyer, Mrs. Clive Brook, Clare Trevor and Mrs. Douglas Fairbanks, Sr. were among the "staff."

Actress Barbara Stanwyck in her VACS uniform.

VACS EXECUTIVE OFFICERS

Mrs. Louis B. Mayer, *Honorary Chairman*
Mrs. Edwin H. Knopf, *President*
Mrs. William Goetz, *Chairman of Executive Committee*
Mrs. Jock Lawrence, *Executive Vice-President*
Mrs. Jack Benny, *Vice-President*
Mrs. Charles Boyer, *Chairman of Ways and Means*
Mrs. Adolphe Menjou, *Secretary-Treasurer*

BOARD OF DIRECTORS

Mrs. Robert Arthur
Mrs. Walter J. Brunmark
Mrs. William M. Clyde
Miss Claudette Colbert
Mrs. Gary Cooper
Mrs. Alexander Hall
Mrs. Ida R. Koverman
Miss Dema Harshbarger
Miss Anita Louise
Miss Anna Q. Nilssen
Mrs. Arthur Rubinstein
Miss Barbara Stanwyck

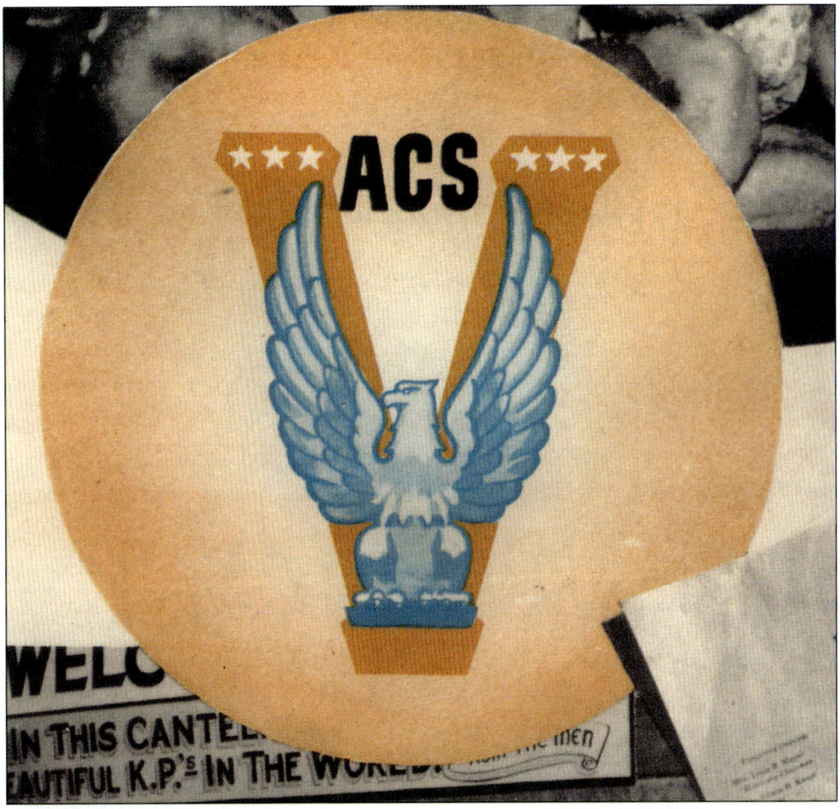

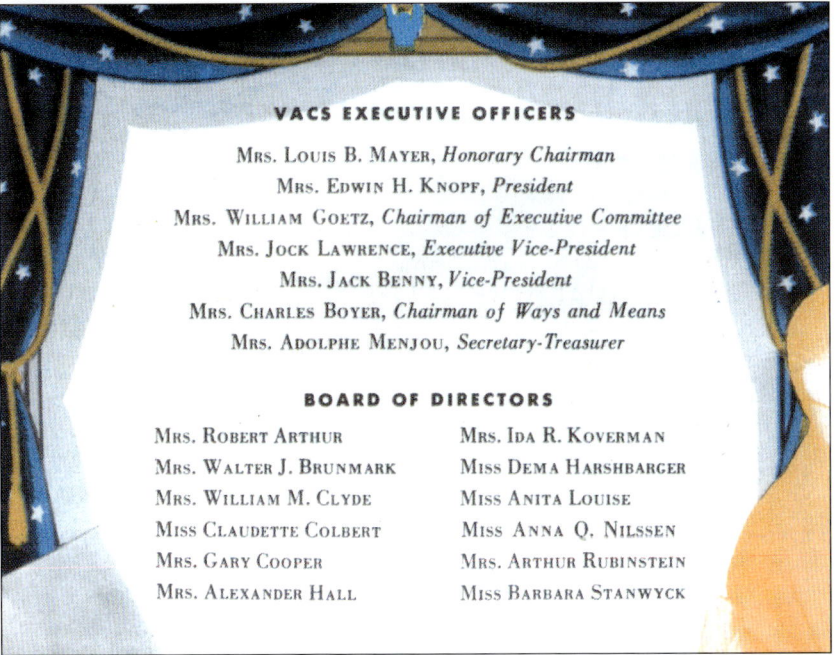

VACS senior member roster showing some of the Hollywood connections of the organization. (Courtesy: Ft. MacArthur Museum)

Volunteer Army Canteen workers could have been local girls or movie stars. Their "uniform" consisted of a cap, similar to that worn by nurses, but with pointed edges and a blue, red and white border. They wore a white bibbed apron over a white dress. A metal "V.A.C.S." pin was attached to the right side of the apron bib, while a white patch with a red "V," embossed with a white eagle with raised wings, with the letters "ACS" in blue between the arms of the "V was sewn to the left side of the bib.751/752

Left: Volunteer Army Canteen Service (VACS) patch. Above: Claudette Colbert as a VACS worker in a 1942 Chesterfield cigarette ad.

Civilian staff at Fort MacArtur also wore a uniform, consisting of a blue blouse, skirt, tie, and a garrison cap with red piping, and a white waist. A matching cloth purse was provided.

---

751 Period soda advertisement showing Barbara Stanwyck wearing the VACS uniform.
752 Ibid.

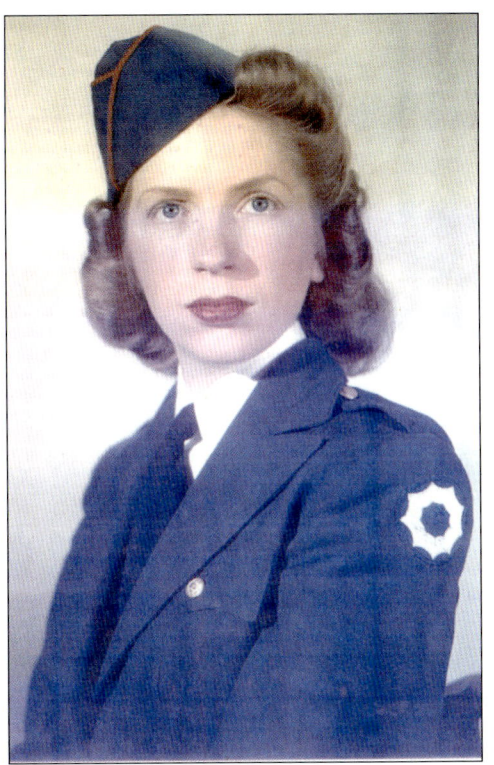

Bobbye MacIntyre in the blue uniform designated for civilian staff at Fort MacArthur Headquarters. Miss MacIntyre was the personal secretary for the Commanding Officer, Col. William W. Hicks. On her left shoulder she wears the 9th Service Command patch as she worked for the Special Services branch at the Fort. The red piping on the cap may not have had any significance except that the majority of men were attached to the Coast Artillery and wore red piping. The uniform was special ordered and had to be purchased by the civilian employee. It came with one tunic, two skirts, a cap and a handbag, shoes were not included. Col. Hicks wanted all civilian employees at the Fort to be dressed in a uniform and ordered its wear shortly after Pearl Harbor. At some point in 1942, Col. Hicks was informed (we think by Gen. Wilson, C.O. of Southern California Sector) that civilian workers could not be ordered to wear uniforms and the practice died out. Ft. MacArtur was the only facility where this uniform was worn. (Courtesy: Ft. MacArtur Museum)

War Camp Community Service

(World War I)

The War Camp Community Service was one of the organizations overseen by the Commission on Training Camp Activities (the others were the YMCA, American Library Association, YWCA, Jewish Welfare Board, Knights of Columbus, American Red Cross and the Salvation Army). Unlike its fellow organizations, this organization did not send any members overseas,[753] Like its compatriot organizations, the WCCS provided clubs for servicemen and also introduced them to the locals.[754]

---

[753] Raymond B. Fosdick, Report to the Secretary of War on the Activities of Welfare Organizations serving with the A.E.F. (Washington, DC: War Department, 1919) p. 3.

[754] Edward M. Coffman, *The War to end all Wars. The American Military Experience in World War I.* (Madison, Wisconsin: The University of Wisconsin Press, 1986) pp. 77-78.

Women in this organization wore one of the more unusual uniforms of the period. It consisted of a dark blue blouse and skirt. The blouse had a stand-and-fall collar, which closed with three blue buttons, whose design resembled train wheels, and three corrsponding loops. Additionally, the collar ends fastened to the blouse with snaps. The front closed with six blue "train wheel" buttons. The blouse was a semi-Norfolk style, having the pleats running over the shoulders and down the front, but on this blouse, the pleats crossed each other at the waist and buttoned on each side to the incorporated belt. On each side of the blouse was a slash pocket with flaps which opened at the top, and closed with three buttons. The matching skirt had two similar pockets on the front. At the back of the sleeve cuffs was decorative braid (see photographs). The WCCS red, white and blue patch was sewn to the upper left sleeve. The matching blue furfelt or velour brimmed hat had a grosgrain band with the War Camp Community Service patch sewn to the front. The uniform illustrated was worn by Colonial Dame Mrs. Charles H. Farnsworth, who was the National Director of Work for Women and Girls.[755]

Unusual closure of the blouse.

War Camp Community Service uniform. (Courtesy: NSCDA Coll.–NMAH/Smithsonian)

---

[755] Report of the Committee on Relics, p. 27.

Unusual hip pocket with "train wheel" buttons.

War Camp Community Service sleeve patch.

Detail of the left sleeve cuff decoration.

Blue fur felt or velour brimmed hat.
(Courtesy: NSCDA Coll.–NMAH/Smithsonian)

War Camp Community Service pin.

Women Veterans' Organizations

(The American Legion, American Legion Auxiliary, Veterans of Foreign Wars and Auxiliary, Survivors of Corregidor and Bataan and other organizations)

The American Legion is often thought of as a "men's only" organization, but women have been members for quite some time. Former World War I Marine Minnie Arthur joined the American Legion in 1919, and she is presumed to be the first woman to do so. "A man I knew told me it was something being organized by one of Theodore Roosevelt's sons, and I said if he was [in] back of it, I'd join up."[756] The Maryland Nurses Post No. 44 was Chartered on September 19, 1919 and held the distinction of being the only post made up completely of women who served during World War I. Its chief work was rehabilitation of veterans. As of 1934, the post commander was Mary E. Carver, and the Post Adjutant was Ruth C. Bennett. Past Commanders were Florence Hunt, Katherine Ellicott, Estelle Wheeler, Margaret, I. Collison, Katherine Webster and Emily Williams.[757] Post No. 185 was named after Jane A. Delano. There were posts for WAVES, Marines and SPARS as well.[758]

An example of an American Legion WWI helmet. Note the Legion decal and "Post 190" on the top, and the owner's name, "June Van Meter" and "American Legion" on the rim. (Courtesy: Patrick E. Consadine, Sr.)

---

[756] Gavin, p. 36.
[757] Walter F. Richardson, Department Historian, *History, Department of Maryland, The American Legion, 1919-1934.* (Baltimore, MD: The American Legion, Department of Maryland, 1934) pp.104-107.
[758] Program, *Wac Post Installation,* Illinois, April 28, 1946.

While only white males who were members of the American Legion were eligible to be members of the *La Societe des 40 Hommes et 8 Chevaux,* more commonly known as the "40-8,"[759] at least one photograph has surfaced, showing Mrs. Mabel T. Dement, president of the American Legion Auxiliary, filling the office for the deceased Mrs. Frances Howard Birely, and then elected president in August 1927, wearing a garrison cap with a round patch with an "8" over "40," and a cape.[760]

Mrs. Mabel T. Dement, President of the American Legion Auxiliary in 1927, wearing a garrison cap with a patch on the left curtain that reads, "8/40." (Courtesy: Patrick E. Consadine, Sr.)

A modern "40 and 8 Nurses Training" patch. (Courtesy: Sylvia Leasure)

The purpose of the American Legion Auxiliary was the, "...perpetuation of the Legion, and ... [to] hand down to coming generations a complete and as nearly as possible...an authentic record of all activities."[761] The auxiliary was active in a great deal of charity and fund raising work.

Listed in the Maryland American Legion Auxiliary section was the all female US Marines Unit No. 1 of Baltimore. Presumably these were former "Marinettes," but they also could have been wives of former Marines. It was organized by the US Marines Post and was the first to be established in the Department of Maryland. It received its charter on May 6, 1926. Its charter members were Mrs. Florence Blake, Mrs. John Briscoe, Mrs. Mary Byers, Mrs. Marie Collins, Mrs. Theodore Lednum, Mrs. Emma Giles Parker, Mrs. Lillian Wroten, Mrs. Elizabeth Wroten, Mrs. Daisy Wroten and Mrs. Ethel Wroten.[762]

Corregidor Post 570 of the American Legion, was comprised exclusively of female World War II veterans. It was headquartered in Cleveland, Ohio.[763]

---

[759] Walter F. Richardson, Department Historian, *History, Department of Maryland, The American Legion, 1919-1934.* (Baltimore, MD: The American Legion, Department of Maryland, 1934) pp. 130-131

[760] Ibid, p. 144.

[761] Ibid, p. 135.

[762] Ibid, p. 158.

[763] Dorothy Tuttle, "Bulletin Board," *Woman Veteran,* Vol. II, No. X (October 1948): p. 5.

Female members wore the standard blue four-pocket blouse with yellow trimming and American Legion buttons. The unit patch was worn on the upper left sleeve. A matching blue skirt was also worn, along with a men's- or women's style garrison cap. In the January 31, 1949 issue of *Woman Veteran* it was announced that, "Women members of the American Legion now have their choice of three uniforms—the old skirt and jacket; the gored skirt and Eisenhower jacket; and this 'New Look' which was designed by the women veterans who are members of the Greater Cincinnati Women's Post No. 664." The new uniform was navy-blue, one-piece gabardine belted dress which buttoned down the front with American Legion buttons. The top of the sleeve cuffs had a band of yellow. The cuffs were fastened with metal cuff links. The post patch was sewn to the upper left sleeve. The legion number insignia were pinned to the collar of the dress and the American Legion lapel insignia were sewn to the lapels of the dress. The navy-blue American Legion garrison cap was worn with the dress.[764]

Adjutant Maxine L. Sweet, seated left, who served in the WAC during WWII, is shown wearing the American Legion uniform for women. She is with other officers of WAC Post No. 919, the first all-WAC post in the American Legion. It was chartered on November 10, 1945. The uniforms for WAC Post No. 919 were made by Garfield Custom Tailoring Company. The garrison caps were made by Camel Cap and Cloth Belt Co.

American Legion woman's blouse. Although this blouse buttons like a man's jacket, it is fitted for a woman's figure. It is also name inside to a woman and dated July 26, 1934. The sleeve patch reads, "Engstrom Duncan Post No. 22." The blouse was made by Craddock Uniforms of Kansas City, Missouri. (Photo by Mark Riese)

---

[764] Ibid.

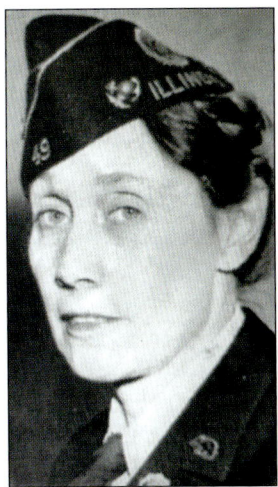

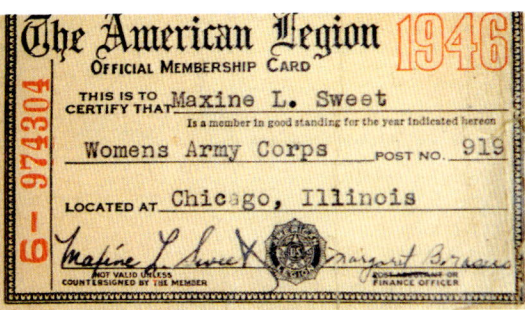

The godmother of WAC Post No. 919 was WWI Marine Blanche Slater Osborne, Roseland, Illinois Post 49. Note the Marine Corps insigne on her garrison cap.

The American Legion 1946
Official Membership Card
6-974304
This is to certify that Maxine L. Sweet
Is a member in good standing for the year indicated hereon
Womens Army Corps Post No. 919
Located at Chicago, Illinois
Not valid unless countersigned by the member
Finance Officer

American Legion membership card and former WAC, Maxine L. Sweet.

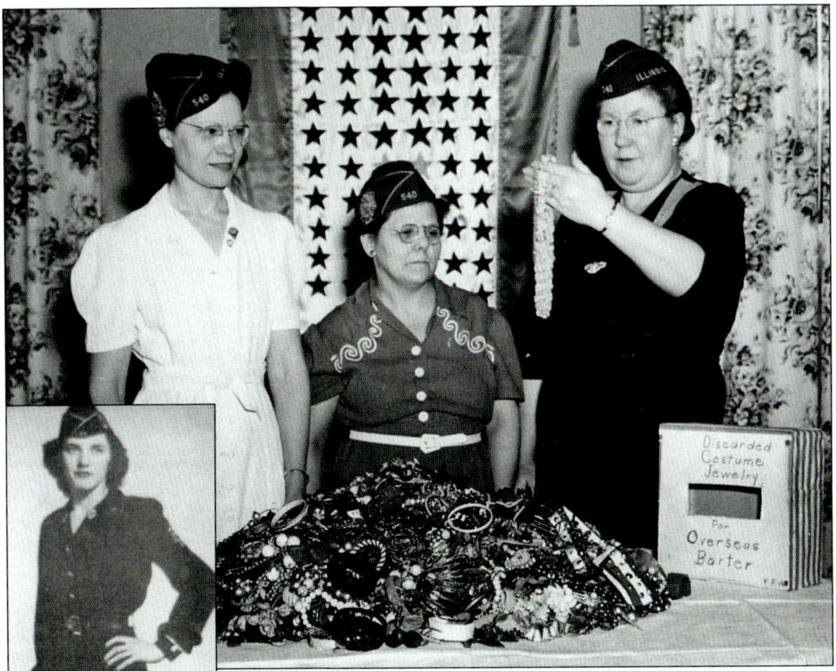

These women appear to be wearing American Legion garrison caps. (Courtesy: John Coy)

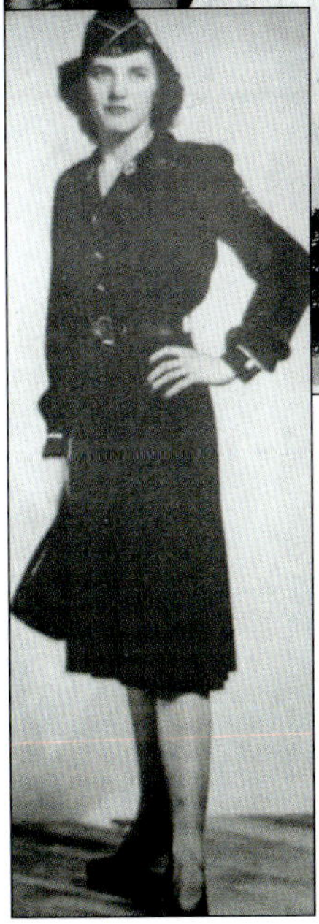

The new one-piece gabardine belted dress. (Courtesy: *Women Veteran*)

This American Legion flag indicates that there were enough women veterans in the Inglewood, California area to have their own post. (Courtesy: Ken Lazier)

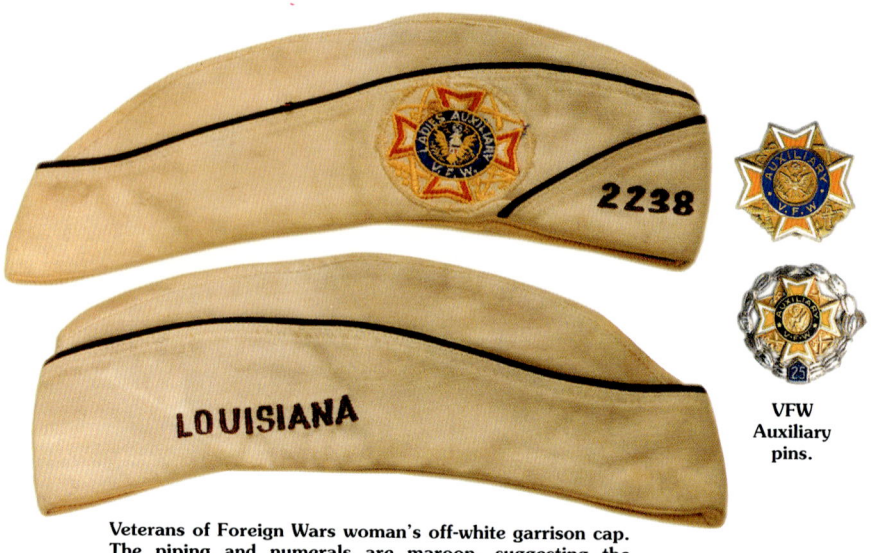

Veterans of Foreign Wars woman's off-white garrison cap. The piping and numerals are maroon, suggesting the owner was an Army nurse. The cap was made by "Salyna by St. George." "Louisiana" is in maroon thread. (Photos by Ronda Sheel)

VFW Auxiliary pins.

Presumably, there were women members of the Veterans of Foreign Wars and there were auxiliaries.

Although chartered by Congress after World War II, little is known about the "American Veterans of World War II (AMVETS)." But by 1948 this organization had celebrated its 4th National Convention in Chicago. The outgoing National Vice-Commander-at-Large in 1948 was former Army nurse Florence Redelsheimer.

Unknown garrison cap with "American G.I. Forum Aux." patch.

In the only photograph found showing the uniforms of this organization, Mrs. Redelsheimer seems to be wearing a light-colored "Ike" jacket with ANC caducei on the lapels of the blouse, a shirtwaist and tie, piped matching garrison cap with, "Tennessee" embroidered on the left curtain, along with the AMVETS patch, the design of which is unknown. She is also wearing an aguillette under the left epaulet of her jacket, and a lieutenant's bar on the left collar of the waist. There also appear to be convention badges being worn on the jacket. A WAVES veteran, also in the photograph with Mrs. Redelsheimer is wearing a civilian suit with a possibly khaki garrison cap with the AMVETS patch and "Illinois" embroidered on the left curtain. Both garrison caps are cut like those worn by men.[765]

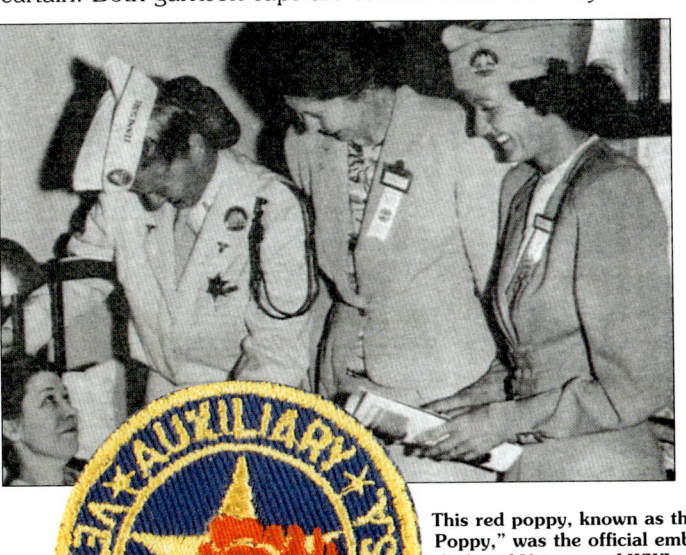

Mrs. Florence Redelsheimer, Vice Commander-at-Large of the American Veterans of WWII (AMVETS) is shown on the left in her special uniform. Former Wave Joy Murray, right, wears an AMVETS garrison cap, September 1948. (Courtesy: Woman Veteran)

This red poppy, known as the "Buddy Poppy," was the official emblem of the Order of Veterans of WWI of the U.S.A., Inc. The red poppy of Flander's Fields denoted the blood shed by American soldiers during WWI.

---

[765] Dorothy Tuttle, "AMVETS Visit Hospitalized Wave Veteran," *Woman Veteran*, Vol. II, No. IX (September 1948): p 7.

Unusual woman's American Legion Auxiliary cap.

Right side view of the cap, showing the unusual skull piece.

Another group was called, FEMVETS, and was part of Omaha, Nebraska American Legion Post No. 1. It was created in 1946 by former Wac, Erma Quinn.[766]

The Women's Relief Corps was founded in 1883 and was an auxiliary of the Grand Army of the Republic (Federal Civil War Veterans' Association). Membership requirements probably were that the ladies be somehow related to a veteran. The Corps had 138,444 members in 1896 and is still active today with descendants of Civil War veterans participating.

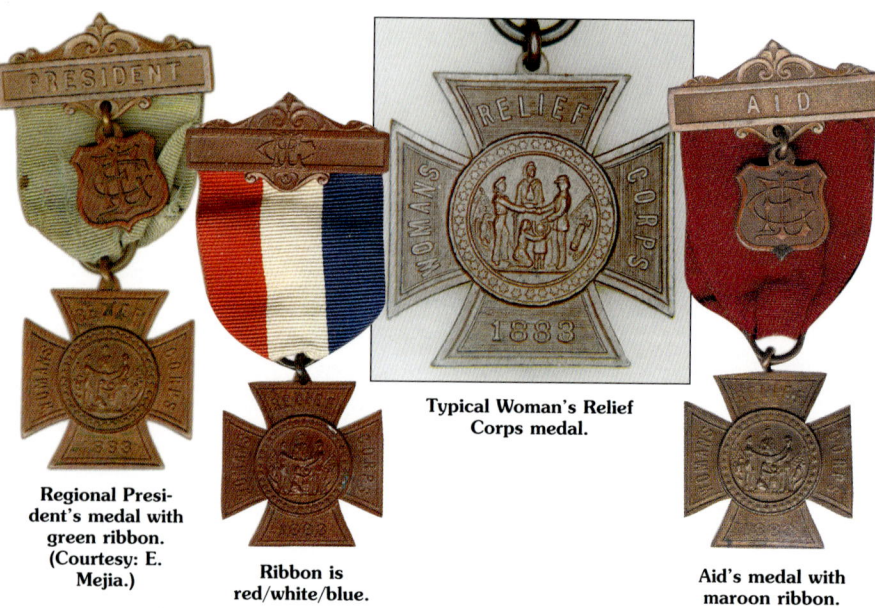

Regional President's medal with green ribbon. (Courtesy: E. Mejia.)

Ribbon is red/white/blue.

Typical Woman's Relief Corps medal.

Aid's medal with maroon ribbon.

---

[766] Dorothy Tuttle, "Bulletin Board," *Woman Veteran,* Vol. II, No. XI (November 30, 1948): p. 6.

Note the patriotic garb worn by WRC members at a meeting on September 8, 1917. (Courtesy: *"The Last Post"*)

Booklet detailing events at a WRC national convention. (Courtesy: E. Mejia)

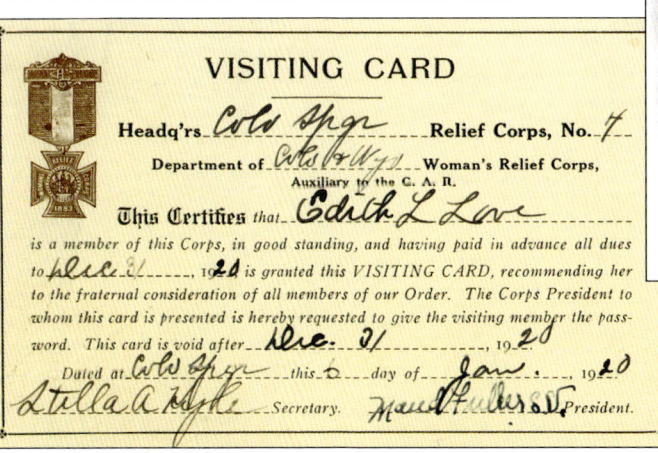

Woman's Relief Corps Visiting Card dated December 31, 1920.

Woman's Relief Corps broach with bars indicating years of service.

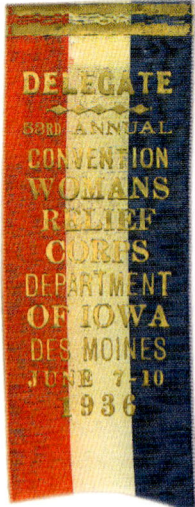
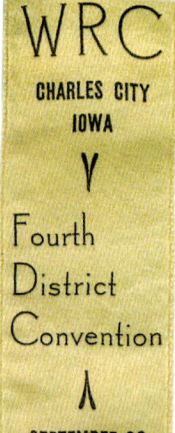

Gold medals presented to the Regional President. Top: 1939. Bottom: 1891.

Delegate ribbons for various Woman's Relief Corps conventions. (Courtesy: E. Mejia)

This medal was issued by the Ladies of the Grand Army of the Republic. The society was the ladies auxiliary to the GAR and membership required marriage or blood relationship to a Union veteran of the Civil War. There was a loose affiliation with the Women's Relief Corps. (Courtesy: *"The Last Post"*)

Women Accepted for Volunteer Emergency Service
(WAVES)
or
U.S. NAVY WOMEN'S RESERVE

Perhaps better known by the acronym, "WAVES' (Women Accepted for Volunteer Emergency Service), the United States Navy accepted women into its ranks during World War II on July 30, 1942, the WAVES having been established by an act of Congress.[767] This was not that unusual, since the Navy had accepted women for service during the First World War (see "Yeomanettes"). The director was Lieutenant Commander Mildred H. McAfee,[768] the first woman to be commissioned in the United States Naval Reserve. She was awarded the Distin-

Mildred H. McAfee, WAVES director, shown here as a Captain.

---

[767] Department of the Navy, *The Story of You in Navy-Blue,* 1943, p. 10.
[768] "First Lady Sees the WAVES March," *The New York Times,* August 3, 1943: p. 21.

guished Service Medal in 1945.[769] The first Wave to be decorated was Lieutenant Elizabeth Reynard, USNR. She was given the Naval Commendation Ribbon for her service at the US Naval Training School (WR) in The Bronx, New York, where 50,000 enlisted Waves received their training during World War II.[770]

Mounted set of medals awarded to a Wave.

Reverse of two US Navy Good Conduct medals awarded to Waves. Both are dated 1946.

Terms of enlistment were that the applicant must be at least twenty years old and no older that thirty-six. Unmarried Waves could not marry until their training was finished, and then they were not allowed to marry a man who was in the Navy. Doing so resulted in resignation or discharge. Women with children were not accepted and pregnancy was cause for resignation or discharge. The applicant had to be of good moral character and be in good physical condition. She had to have at least two years of high school or business school, and was to submit a resume of their work experience since high school. Waves were to weigh no less than ninety pounds and their weight had to be distributed proportionally.

Officers were held to the same requirements, but with a few additions: They could range in age from twenty to fifty years old and had to have a college degree or have passed two years of college.

Upon being accepted for officer training, enlisted Waves were designated reserve midshipmen. A few enlisted women who had attained the grade of Midshipmen, wore the officer style hat with the Midshipmen's fouled anchor insigne on the front of the cap (1942). Officer candidates began training as apprentice seamen for their first month, and then became reserve midshipmen during their second month. They wore the

---

[769] Obituary of Mildred McAfee Horton, September 2, 1994.
[770] Bureau of Naval Personnel Information Bulletin August 1944: p. 59.

WAVES blouse with gold officer eagle buttons when they reported to training.[771] After completion of their training at Smith College at Northhampton, Massachusetts, they were commissioned as officers.[772] The first woman to join the WAVES and, subsequently, become an officer, was Ann Stahlman Hill.[773] While at the Naval Reserve Midshipman's School (WR) Waves purchased items of uniform and insignia. The hat insigne worn by Midshipmen was a vertical anchor. It was issued to them by the Uniform Officer. Upon graduation the insigne had to be returned, since it was property of the United States Government.[774]

During training, designated Waves wore a dark colored brassard with the initials, "MAA" on it, which stood for "Master-at-Arms."[775]

"Dear Mother and Dot,
Well, I am here and passed my physical, evidently, because I have been fitted for uniforms—a navy-blue wool, 2 grey seersucker, and a raincoat. I have a big pile of blouses, a seaman's cap, and lisle hose, and 2 pairs of big ugly black oxfords, which I wear with my civilian clothes."[776]

U.S. Naval Reserve Midshipmen's School
Smith College, Northhampton, Massachusetts
Acceptance and Oath of Office

I, [Name], having been appointed a Midshipman, Volunteer Reserve, U.S. Naval Reserve, do hereby accept such appointment, and do solemnly swear (or affirm) that I will support and defend the Constitution of the United States against all enemies, foreign and domestic; that I will bear true faith and allegiance to the same; that I take this obligation freely, without any mental reservation or purpose of evasion; and that I will well and faithfully discharge the duties of the office on which I am about to enter: So help me God.[777]

Initially, Waves were supposed to serve only within the continental United States, but later several were stationed in Hawaii and Alaska.[778]

Contrary to other women's reserves, WAVES enlisted rates and officers' ranks were equivalent to those held by men.[779] Waves gave salutes to

---

[771] Edwards, p. IX-A-20.
[772] *Navy Blue*, p. 41.
[773] Document from Jo Osbun.
[774] Receipt for "one Midshipman hat insignia [sic],...for which I hold myself accountable." from the Naval Reserve Midshipmen's School (WR), Northampton Massachusetts, June 26, 1944.
[775] Josette Dermody Wingo, *Mother was a Gunner's Mate*. (Annapolis, Maryland: Naval Institute Press, 1994) p. 13.
[776] Letter from M.M. Koumrian from Midshipman's School, June 3, 1944.
[777] Acceptance and Oath of Office taken by Mary Margaret Koumrian, June 27, 1944.
[778] Admiral Chester M. Nimitz Museum Memo, item no. 2, p. 1, January 26, 1993.
[779] *Navy-Blue*, p. 13.

A beautiful portrait of members of the WAVES and SPARS.

Insignia for new recruits.
Oct. 21, 1948–Aug. 10, 1951:
4" x 3-1/2"–orange. Aug. 10, 1951–Oct.
17, 1969: 3-1/2" x 2-3/4"–orange. Oct. 17,
1969–1975: 3-1/2" x 2-3/4"–yellow.

Left and facing page: Examples of
WAVES recruiting posters.

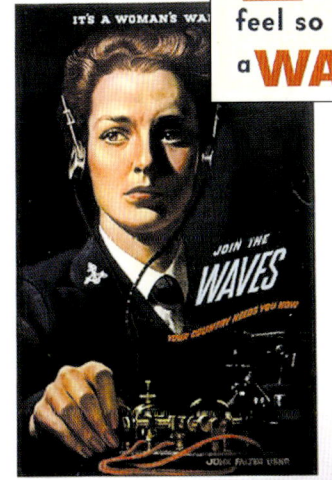

and received salutes from Navy officers. They were assigned to various jobs, such as parachute riggers, secretaries, pharmacists mates, photograph analysts, gunnery and pilot instructors, radio and telephone operators, mechanics, flight orderlies,[780] and even to the position of Admiral's Yeoman, which was basically an admiral's personal secretary and receptionist. After initial training a Wave may have been sent directly to a naval station or back to school for more specialized training.[781]

Waves continued to serve during the Korean and Vietnam wars. The first Wave assigned to duty in Vietnam was Lieutenant Elizabeth G. Wylie. She was ordered to duty on the staff of the Commander Naval Forces Vietnam in Saigon, February 10, 1967.[782]

On March 7, 1967, the Navy approved a 20 per cent increase in the number of Waves in service, (the first increase in the number of Waves since the Korean War) bringing their total strength to 600 officers and 6,000 enlisted women. This increase was made to ease the rotation of male personnel, especially those on duty in naval aviation.[783]

Secretary of the Navy John H. Chaffee announced that the Navy Recruit Training Command (Women) was to be moved from Bainbridge, Maryland to the Naval Training Center at Orlando, Florida, effective July 3, 1972.[784]

In 1942 Mrs. James V. Forrestal asked the designer, Main Rousseau Bocher, known professionally as "Mainbocher", to design a uniform for the WAVES. He did so and charged the Navy only $1.00 for his services. Mainbocher was able to combine style with efficiency and military tradition when he designed the simple, but smart WAVES uniform. Lieutenant Commander McAfee noted this about the wardrobe:

> "One thing we have kept in mind is that there should be no effort to dress the women up to look like men. Their uniforms will be becoming and functional—we are not concentrating on making them look impressive."[785]

But the public was impressed by the WAVES uniform, and it was an incentive for some girls to join up:

> "I made up my mind to join when I saw that dress uniform. A good two-piece suit is one of the most valuable things a girl can own. I can detach the insignia after the war, and get at least three or four years good wear out of it."[786]

---

[780] Bureau of Naval Personnel, "First Waves Assigned to Training as Flight Orderlies," Information Bulletin January 1945: p. 48.
[781] *Navy-Blue*, p. 17.
[782] Chronicle. p. 95.
[783] Chronicle, p. 97.
[784] Chronicle, p. 269
[785] Susan M. Samek, "Uniformly Feminine: The "Working Chic" of Mainbocher," *Dress*, 1993: pp. 34-35.
[786] Ibid, p. 36.

Lucille Halcomb wearing her sister's modified WAVES uniform. (Courtesy: Lucille Mason Halcomb)

Waves board a streetcar with "Join the WAVES" on the front.

Mainbocher called his design, "working chic." He stated: *"Clothes should be practical and wearable. A well-dressed woman always appears to have forgotten what she is wearing."*[787]

The dress blue (i.e. "service") uniform for enlisted women and officers consisted of tailored navy-blue wool blouse which had slightly padded shoulders. It had a distinctive collar that was rounded at each end, and overlapped the blouse lapels. All members wore the WAVES insignia at each collar end, consisting of a "reserve-blue" ship's screw superimposed by a white fouled anchor embroidered on a navy-blue cloth circle. Four navy-blue plastic buttons, embossed with the Navy emblem, secured the front of the enlisted woman's blouse. (At least one period photograph shows an enlisted Waves wearing plain blue buttons on her blouse.) Officer's blouses had four gold metal like-embossed buttons. Officers wore light blue ("reserve-blue") cuff stripes in lieu of the gold stripes worn by male Navy officers. On the prototype uniform, which was never mass produced or issued, the rank stripes were made of red, white and blue braid, which Director McAffee found distasteful. She agreed that WAVES officers should wear the reserve-blue cuff stripes, but later regretted this decision, after realizing that

---

[787] Ibid, p. 33.

Washington D.C. Waves in the blue uniform. (Courtesy: Nimitz Museum, Ray Coll.)

Enlisted Wave's blue uniform. (Photo by Mark Riese)

Small WAVES pin.

WAVES collar insigne worn by all ranks.

the WAVES had been slighted by the Navy when it prohibited its female officers from wearing gold cuff braid, showing them to be equal to their male counterparts. McAfee called this "a terrible slap in the face." (WAVES would not achieve equal status until they became a permanent part of the Navy).[788]

---

[788] Maj. Gen. Jeanne Holm, USAF (Ret.), *Women in the Military: An Unfinished Revolution,* Revised Edition (Novato, CA: The Presidio Press, 1992) p. 41.

WAVES officer's uniform blouse.

WAVES wearing the blue shirtwaist with the reserve-blue seaman's tie. (Courtesy: Delaware State Archives)

In 1942, it was ordered that enlisted Waves were to wear the reserve-blue shirtwaist, instead of the white one, with the dress uniform. But by 1943, enlisted Waves and officers were permitted to wear the white short sleeve shirtwaist with the blue uniform.[789] A white cotton or rayon shirtwaist was worn under the blouse, along with a black seaman's tie.[790] (In 1942, Waves on duty in Washington, DC, were also permitted to wear either the reserve-blue or navy-blue shirtwaist with Service Dress, Blue A.) Black seaman's ties were to be worn with both shirts, until the reserve-blue ties were procured. Likewise, they were ordered to not wear the white shirtwaist at the office.[791]

The navy-blue blouse was lined in dark blue satin. A hidden breast pocket was installed in the lining on each side. The left pocket had no labels, but the right pocket had two labels. The outer label was a medium blue rectangle, machine-woven in dark blue, "Made and Sold Under Authority of the U.S. Navy," over "W.A.V.E.S." The WAVES insigne of a blue anchor upon a white ship's screw was woven in the center of the label. Later, possibly immediately after World War II this label was changed to read, "Made & Sold Under Authority of U.S. Navy, U.S. Women's Naval Reserve." The

---

[789] Edwards, p. IX-A-21.

[790] Price List, Women's Naval Reserve, Officer Personnel, Enlisted Personnel, Uniforms and Accessories. Items no. 602, 603 and 702. Sold under supervision of the U.S. Navy, Official Distributor, March 15, 1944.

[791] Edwards, p. IX-86, IX-87.

inner label was also rectangular in shape, but made of white (or off-white) coarse material. It was printed, "W.A.V.E.S., Name, Rate, Contract No." The wording was later changed to, "Women's Naval Reserve, Name, Rate, Cont. No." The owner could stitch a small label printed with her name under the loop in the back of the neck of the blouse.[792]

WAVES label found on the outer side of the hidden breast pocket in the lining of the blouse.

Second style label.

Interior pocket label.

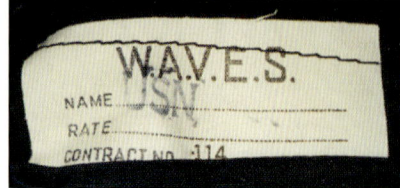

WAVES Mascot Erin Hennessey wears a tiny version of the WAVES uniform on the occasion of the WAVES second birthday party.

The WAVES uniform worn with hat with white top.

---

[792] Sally Berk uniform.

The navy-blue skirt had six gores and was slightly flared, and fastened on the left side by a zipper, topped by a plain navy-blue button.

The white summer uniform consisted of the same items, but was made of light-weight material. Both uniforms were worn with beige lisle or rayon[793] hose and black oxfords or pumps, with heels no higher than 1-1/2" and 2" respectively.[794] White shoes were optional with the summer uniform. Blue plastic buttons were worn by enlisted personnel, while officers wore gold embossed buttons. Enlisted women's grades were indicated by the standard Navy rate patch sewn on the left sleeve of the uniforms.

Enlisted WAVES on parade in the white summer uniform.

---

[793] Ibid.
[794] *Navy-Blue*, p. 18.

Removable WAVES collar insignia for wear on the white uniform.

Detail of a WAVES officer's white blouse. (Courtesy: Greensboro Historical Museum, photo by Patt Anthony)

Enlisted Wave wearing the white uniform with the white garrison cap. (Courtesy: Nimitz Museum)

Enlisted women wore a soft-brimmed hat, which had interchangeable tops of navy-blue to white to grey and white striped seersucker. A navy-blue tally with "U.S. Navy" in gold letters was worn across the front. Officers wore a hat with upturned sides, which Mainbocher patterned after an 1813 seaman's hat.[795] This form of headdress was often referred to as a "combination hat." It, too, had interchangeable navy-blue, white tops and gray and white seersucker tops. Chief Petty officer's wore the combination hat with their fouled anchor insigne. Though against Navy regulations, enlisted Waves below the rank of Chief Petty Officer were permitted to wear the soft-brimmed hat with the navy-blue or white crown until March 1945.[796]

Excellent study of the hat worn by enlisted Waves. (Courtesy: Joe Stone)

Brimmed hat with gray and white striped seersucker top. (Photo by Ronda Sheel)

WAVES enlisted woman's brimmed hat with white top.

---

[795] Susan M. Samek, "Uniformly Feminine: The "Working Chic" of Mainbocher," *Dress*, 1993: p. 33.
[796] Edwards, p. IX-A-24.

WAVES tag in the brimmed hat.

WAVES officer's combination hat.
(Photo by Ronda Sheel)

WAVES officer Elinor F. McCormick wearing the combination hat. (Courtesy: Delaware State Archives)

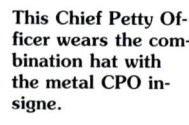

This Chief Petty Officer wears the combination hat with the metal CPO insigne.

Miniature Navy officer's insigne for wear on the garrison cap.

WAVES officer's garrison cap.

Enlisted Wave wearing the garrison cap without insignia, as first ordered.

WAVES officers and chief petty officers were permitted in 1944 to wear men's white and slate-gray garrison caps with the white service uniform or the grey work uniform. Rank insigne was worn on the right curtain of the cap, and the miniature US Navy commissioned officer's insigne was worn on the left curtain. Enlisted women and officers could also wear a women's style navy-blue garrison cap, which was authorized for wear on January 15, 1945.[797] Prior to this, Waves serving in Alaska in November 1942 were permitted to wear the men's navy-blue garrison cap, since the hood of their coats did not fit over their combination hat or enlisted hat. The wear of the men's garrison cap did not officially extend outside of Alaska,[798] but it is possible that other Waves wore the men's garrison cap as well. Men's garrison caps were not popular, since they didn't fit well over women's hairstyles. When first authorized on January 15,[799] 1945 the

---

[797] Bureau of Naval Personnel, "New Waves Garrison Cap May Be Worn 15 January," Information Bulletin January 1945: p. 75.

[798] Edwards, p. IX-115.

[799] "New WAVES Garrison Cap May be Worn 15 January," Bureau of Naval Personnel Information Bulletin January 1945, p. 75.

navy-blue garrison cap was worn without insignia. By order of the Chief of Naval Personnel, dated March 15, 1945, enlisted women were authorized to wear a sterling silver and gold-plated WAVES insigne pinned to the left side of the cap curtain.[800] The rank of Chief Petty Officer wore the standard metal CPO cap insigne in miniature on the garrison caps.[801] A white garrison cap was made for wear with the white uniform. Enlisted women wore a white cloth circular patch with the WAVES emblem sewn to the left forward curtain of the cap. The ship's screw was embroidered in blue and the anchor in light blue. The wear of the white garrison cap was abolished for all Navy personnel on June 1, 1947.[802]

WAVES enlisted garrison cap. (Photo by Ronda Sheel)

WAVES enlisted woman's garrison cap insigne.

Garrison cap labels.

Black or white fabric or leather gloves could be worn with the winter uniform; white gloves could be worn with the summer uniform.

A black leather shoulder bag could be carried with either uniform, but at least one period photograph shows a Wave carrying a white bag.[803] A white cover could be worn over the black bag

WAVES shoulder bag. (Courtesy: Greensboro Historical Museum, photo by Patt Anthony)

---

[800] Bureau of Naval Personnel, "Pin-on Insignia Approved for Wave Garrison Cap," Information Bulletin April 1945: p. 77.

[801] Edwards, p. IX-A-34.

[802] Ibid, p. IX-148.

[803] *Dress*, "Uniformly Feminine: The "Working Chic" of Mainbocher," p. 35.

WAVES tag in a black shoulder bag. (Courtesy: John Mull)

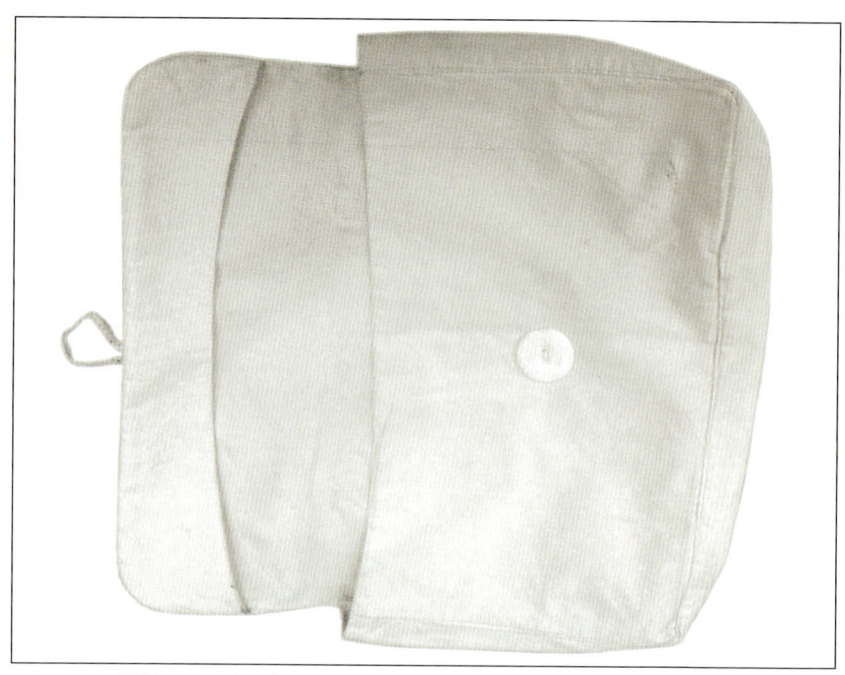

White cover for the WAVES black should bag. (Courtesy: John Mull)

WAVES tag in a white shoulder bag without strap. (Courtesy: John Mull)

for use with the white summer uniform, and it was permissible to remove the strap.[804]

The WAVES overcoat was dark navy-blue and double-breasted, with three pairs of gold Navy buttons on the front. A simple "belt" was sewn on the reverse. Officers wore reserve-blue ranks stripes and corps emblems on the lower sleeves. Two vertical welted pockets were on the front of the coat.

The overcoat was modified to have a two piece belt, two inches in width, on the reverse which had two gold Navy buttons, 40 linge in size, sewn horizontally on it.

**WAVES officer overcoat.
(Courtesy: Mark Riese)**

The WAVES belted raincoat.

Waves could wear a navy-blue, double-breasted and belted raincoat. A navy-blue havelock, in winter or summer weight, was worn as well, when needed. It had plain dark blue plastic buttons.

Introduced in 1943,[805] the uniform dress was made of grey and white pinstripe seersucker, had an open rounded collar, short sleeves, and a zipper on the left side, which extended about five inches below the waist and under the sleeve. The fitted waist had a sewn-in band which secured over the zipper by a white button. A very small hidden pocket was incorporated into the upper left bodice. The front of the skirt had one large pleat. The black seaman's tie was worn by both officers

---

[804] Edwards, p. IX-A-24.
[805] Dress, p. 35.

and enlisted women when the collar of the dress was worn closed. Officers wore their rank insignia pinned on each collar. Enlisted women wore their rate, embroidered on matching grey and white striped seersucker material, sewn the the left sleeve of the dress.

A group of WAVES wearing the gray and white seersucker dress. (Courtesy: National Archives)

A smaller, rectangular light blue label was sewn in the neck of the dress. Its design was as previously described. Another label was sewn inside the dress, on the opposing side of the fitted waist band. It was of white material and read, "W.A.V.E.S., Name, Rate, and Contract No."

Officers and enlisted women could wear a grey and white pinstripe seersucker single-breasted jacket over the dress. The jacket had no collar, since the collar of the dress was worn over the jacket. The WAVES ship's screw and anchor was worn by all Waves on the rounded lapels of the jacket. The screw was embroidered in navy-blue while the anchor and rope were embroidered in reserve-blue. The cloth background for these insignia was white. The jacket had two scalloped flaps on the bodice and two scalloped flaps on the lower section. Only the flap on the lower right side had a pocket.

Lapel insigne on the jacket.

The enlisted dress and jacket. (Courtesy: Naval Historical Center)

The officer's dress and jacket. (Courtesy: Naval Historical Center)

Detail of officer's cuff stripe and supply corps insigne.

Officers wore navy-blue sleeve stripes according to their rank and the appropriate emblem above, indicative of their service specialty. Enlisted Waves wore the same sleeve insigne as on the seersucker dress on the upper left sleeve of the jacket.

An official WAVES machine-woven tag was sewn at the back of the jacket at the neck. A WAVES white specification tag or name tag, with black lettering, was sewn onto the back of the pocket on the lower section, on the interior of the jacket. All ranks wore four navy-blue embossed plastic buttons down the front of the jacket.

The metal anchor and ship's screw emblem was worn by enlisted women on the grey and white pin stripe seersucker garrison cap. WAVES officers wore the standard Navy officer's sterling crossed anchors and eagle pin instead. The combination hat with a grey and white striped seersucker cover was also worn. Enlisted Waves wore a seersucker top on their brimmed hat.

WAVES seersucker garrison cap with officer's insigne.

WAVES physical education instructor wearing a unique jacket.

Some Waves were issued a "tennis dress," for wear during physical training and sports. It was made of light-colored material, had an open collar and buttoned down the front. The waist was belted. The dress was hemmed about two inches above the knee.[806]

Uniforms were not issued by the Navy, rather they were purchased from companies who had contracts with the government. Marshall Fields set up a store in a gymnasium at the University of Wisconsin where Waves could buy items of uniform with their allowance. Alterations were sent to Chicago and returned within a week.[807] Department stores like Gimbels and Macy's sent tailors to Hunter College to measure new Waves for their uniforms. (New Waves were called, "Ripples," i.e., "Little

---

[806] United States Naval Training School Storekeeper (W), Picture Parade. WAVES, MARINES (Milledgeville, GA: Georgia State College for Women, No date.).
[807] Weatherford, American Women and World War II, p. 49.

WAVES blue athletic jacket with white piping. (Courtesy: Wings Over the Rockies Air & Space Museum)

Label inside the jacket. (Courtesy: Wings Over the Rockies Air & Space Museum)

Waves.")[808] Waves were given a $200.00 allowance, $150.00 of which went towards the various uniforms required. The remaining $50.00 was used to purchase items not furnished by the contractors, such as gloves, shoes and underclothing.[809]

The WAVES wardrobe consisted of the following:
1) The multi-stitched, soft brimmed hat. Officers wore a more formal combination hat with upturned sides;
2) Garrison caps, dark blue, white, and grey and white pinstripe;
3) Navy-blue wool blouse and skirt;
4) White summer blouse and skirt;
5) Dark blue and white shirts;
6) Seaman's ties, black and reserve-blue (i.e. light blue; worn with the dark blue shirt);
7) Black leather shoulder bag;
8) Grey and white pinstripe seersucker work dress with matching jacket;
9) Beige hosiery;
10) Black oxfords or pumps (optional);
11) Waterproof havelock and raincoat;
12) Overcoat (optional);
13) Blue denim coveralls, slacks or working blue smock (optional item. Worn only as protective cover during appropriate working conditions);[810]

This Wave wears blue slacks, a white shirtwaist, seaman's tie and garrison cap while serving in the Naval Air Transport Service (NATS).

14) Blue wool slacks.[811]
15) Dungarees;
16) Blue chambray workshirts[812]
17) Cotton anklets in the appropriate color, with slacks only.
18) White muffler.

"Mainbocher, bless him, ... neglected to design us Waves an elegant designer sweater."[813] (Some Waves were eventually provided with a blue cardigan and its wear was limited by station limits and by the commanding officer.) Waves who immediately received a duty assignment after recruit school were designated as Seamen, Second Class.[814] They could hold the following jobs: Airplane cammoufleur, messenger, escort, file clerk, truck and tractor driver, line assistant, poster artist, assistant printer, bookkeeper, librarian, map and chart proofreader, multilith operator, photostat operator, teletype operator, mechanical draftsman, statistical clerk, lithographer and research assistant.[815]

Enlisted Waves who joined the Navy Hospital Corps began their training as technicians with the rank of Apprentice Seamen. After their training, they were rated as Hospital Apprentices, Second Class. After an orientation period, they were assigned to duty and given new ratings of Hospital Apprentices, First Class, Pharmacist's Mate, Third Class or Pharmacist's Mate, Second Class. The Hospital Corps Had 13,000 members during World War II.[816]

Waves classified as Regular Service were given special instruction in anatomy and physiology, minor surgery, first aid, hygiene, sanitation and nursing.

Badge worn by Waves who served at the Naval Hospital in Washington.

---

[808] Josette Dermody Wingo, *Mother was a Gunner's Mate.* (Annapolis, Maryland: Naval Institute Press, 1994) pp. 21 and 35.
[809] *Navy-Blue*, p. 18.
[810] Ibid, p. 18.
[811] Josette Dermody Wingo, *Mother was a Gunner's Mate.* (Annapolis, Maryland. Naval Institute Press, 1994) p. 95.
[812] Ibid.
[813] Ibid, p. 97.
[814] Edwards, p. IX-116.
[815] US Navy Publication, *The Story of You in Navy-Blue*, p. 35.
[816] Willenz, p. 23.

Advanced courses were given to Hospital Corps Waves who wished to specialize in a certain area: Clerical Procedures, Dental Technology (General), Dental Technology (Prosthetic), Electrocardiography and Basal Metabolism, Clinical Laboratory Technician, Operating Room Technician, Fever Therapy, Physical Therapy, X-Ray Technician, Property and Accounting,[817] Occupational Therapy and Physiotherapy.[818]

Hospital Corps Waves could advance to Pharmacist's Mate, First Class, to Chief Pharmacist's Mate.

In 1944, Vice Admiral Ross T. McIntire (MC), Surgeon General of the Navy, expressed the wish to retain WAVES hospital corpsmen in the Navy after the war.

WAVES officers who served in the Hospital Corps wore the corps emblem, which consisted of a caduceus and an oakleaf. (The corps emblems were not worn by a majority of officers until September 1944.)[819] On the blue uniform, the caduceus, serpent and oakleaves were embroidered in reserve-blue. The staff of the caduceus and acorns were embroidered in white. This insigne was worn above the rank stripe(s) on the sleeve cuffs. The colors were changed for wear on the grey and white seersucker jacket: The serpent and oakleaves were embroidered in navy-blue, while the acorns and staff of the caduceus were embroidered in reserve-blue.[820]

Enlisted Waves wore standard Navy rating insignia on the left sleeves of their uniforms. Enlisted Waves who had completed service school training wore only the specialty mark on the left sleeves of their uniforms, positioned midway between the elbow and wrist. As of September 30, 1944, the diagonal stripes worn by enlisted Waves were moved to the same position as rating patches. Navy-blue stripes were worn on the grey seersucker uniform, the smock and the white summer uniform. White stripes were worn on the blue uniform. Previously, enlisted women who had completed training school were allowed to wear that school's specialty mark. Later, women who had also completed a training school and were in line for promotion to Petty Officer were allowed to wear the specialty mark above the Seaman mark until their promotion came through.[821] The ranks of Petty Officer, Third Class, Petty Officer, Second Class, Petty Officer, First Class, and Chief Petty Officer wore red chevrons, white eagle and job designation on navy-blue for wear on the blue uniform (or navy-blue rayon for wear on the navy-blue rayon shirt); The eagle and job designation were blue on the white insigne, worn on the summer uniform; the eagle and job designation were blue on the light blue insigne, for wear on the "reserve-blue" shirtwaist and smock. The chevrons, job emblem and eagle were in navy-blue on the grey and white seersucker backing.

---

[817] US Navy Publication, *Enlist in the WAVES. Serve in the Hospital Corps,* pp. 8-9.
[818] "On 2nd Anniversary...Waves Pass 70,000 Mark," Bureau of Naval Personnel Information Bulletin August 1944: p. 9.
[819] Edwards, p. IX-105.
[820] Ibid, p. IX-105.
[821] Ibid, p. IX-A-35.

Rate for wear on the blue blouse and shirtwaist. CPO recruiter (Emergency Service rating).

Rate for wear on white blouse and shirtwaist. Mail Clerk 3rd Class.

Rate for wear on the "reserve-blue" shirtwaist and smock which was in use from May 2, 1947 to September 1955. Photographic Specialist 2nd Class (or Photogammetry Assistant, 1948-1960).

Yeoman 2nd Class rate for wear on the light blue service dress, which first appears in the March 20, 1959 Navy Uniform Regulations, and was no longer in use by July 1985.

The Waves on the left and right wear "non-rated marks of a pay grade" on their upper left sleeves.

U.S. Navy Enlisted WAVE Ratings for the Gray Seersucker Dress
(Courtesy: Steve Rohde)

Seaman Apprentice, Non-Rated.

Airman (AM), Non-Rated. Note the manufacturer's error—the background stripes are horizontal instead of vertical. The green stripes are post-1948, as are red (fireman) and light blue (construction).

Aerographer's Mate (AG), Third Class.

Aviation Photographer's Mate (AF), First Class. Authorized on April 21, 1948.

Printer (PI), Second Class. (Merged into Lithographer rate in 1955).

Radioman (RM), Second Class.

Yeoman (YN), Third Class.

Teleman (TE), Third Class. Authorized on April 21, 1948. (Merged into Yeoman and Radioman rates in 1956.)

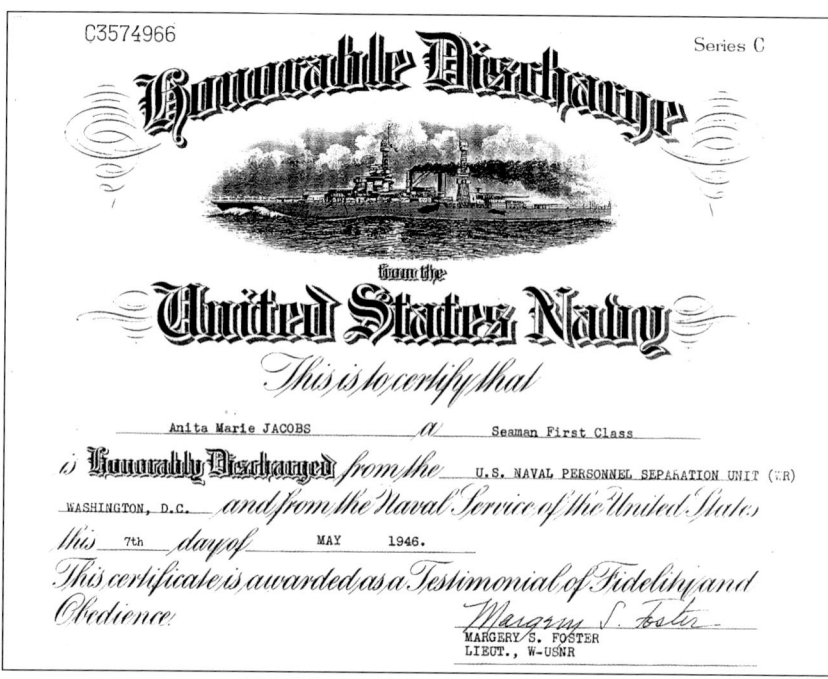
WAVES honorable discharge document.

In June 1948,[822] Airmen and Airmen Apprentices were to wear three and two emerald green diagonal stripes on the left sleeves of all uniforms, sewn midway between the elbow and shoulder. Also in 1948, the term, "specialty marks" was changed to "striker marks."[823]

Enlisted Waves could hold numerous jobs, which had their own symbol and was shown on the sleeve insigne, below the eagle.

Aerographer's Mate—Duties were to direct installation of Naval meteorological observatory ashore, make weather observations, draw weather charts, read weather codes, compute pilot balloon soundings, and make upper air soundings;

Aviation Machinist's Mate I*—Aviation instrument mechanic. Other duties were to assemble and service airplanes and their engines, manufacture small aircraft parts, do seamanship work necessary to airplane ground work, know the principles and theory of flying, and splice aircraft wiring.

Aviation Metalsmith—Duties were to repair airplane metalwork and be able to forge, braze, weld, electroplate and bend pipe, and to use welding outfits and use hand and power tools for woodworking.

Aviation Ordnanceman*—

Aviation Radio Technician*—

Baker—Duties were to do any kind of baking, know how to set up field ovens.

---

[822] Ibid, p. IX-A-48.
[823] Ibid, p. IX-A-48.

Cook—Duties were to supervise and prepare food for cooking and operate all cooking apparatus. Must be able to plan menus, estimate provisions, take charge of galley, inspect provisions and be responsible for food storage.
Hospital Apprentice—
Electrician's Mate*—
Parachute Rigger—(also known as "silkworms.") Duties were to pack and repair parachutes and know how to operate a sewing machine and have knowledge of fabrics. Riggers must also know about rigging and the use of cargo parachutes and aviation life-saving equipment.
Pharmacist's Mate—Duties were to be able to do minor surgery and give first aid, to prepare and administer simple medications, give anesthesia, account for medical and hospital supplies, and have a basic knowledge of anatomy, medications, hygiene, and nursing.
Printer*—
Printer L*—Lithographer
Printer M*—(Offset Duplicating Process)
Radioman—Duties were to send and receive radio messages on all frequencies used by the Navy, to decipher and encipher Navy code messages, and adjust and repair radio direction finders and sound equipment.
Radio Technician—
Ship's Cook*—
Ship's Serviceman—
Storekeeper*—
Specialist (C)*—Classification Interviewer,
Specialist (G)—Aviation free gunnery instructor,
Specialist (I)—Duty was to operate punch card tabulating machine.
Specialist (M)—Mail clerks in Navy post offices. The job emblem was changed from an "M" in a diamond to an "M" in a circle followed by waves (like those found on a canceled stamp) on September 15, 1944.[824]
Specialist (P)—These were photographers who had to be able to mix and handle chemicals used to develop film, check and repair cameras, operate motion picture cameras, cut and edit motion pictures, and do photomicrography.
Specialist (Q)*—Communication specialist,
Specialist (R)—WAVES recruiters.
Specialist (S)—Served as Master-of-Arms at Navy stations (a.k.a. "personnel supervisor"), assist officers in discipline, promulgation of orders, cleanliness of barracks, recreation and physical education and enforcement of fire precautions.
Specialist (T)—Link trainer instructors (who taught instrument flying to naval aviators). They must also have been able to operate control towers and photoelectric devices for training free gunnery to aerial gunners.

---

[824] BuPers. Circ. Ltr. 263-44 (NDB, 15. Sept. 1944, 44-1069, "Bureau of Naval Personnel Information Bulletin," January 1945, p. 77.

Specialist (T)**—Celestial navigation.[825]
Specialist (U)—Supervised the service of food and housekeeping functions in WAVES quarters and messes. They were responsible for the proper storage, care and maintenance of equipment and materiel. Changed to "teacher" in 1944.
Specialist (W)—Naval welfare. Changed to chaplain's assistant in 1944.
Specialist (X)*—Specialist not assigned.
Specialist (Y)*—Control Tower Operator.[826]
Storekeeper—Duties were to keep inventory of stock and issue, store, report, invoice and requisition stocks. They also issued and accounted for clothing and small purchases and had to know pay and allowances and general accounting forms and procedures.
Telegrapher—Operated teletype in a communications office, know Morse, telegraph and cable codes, and know the Navy regulations on communications and security.
Yeoman—Must have been able to take dictation, prepare reports, operated duplicating machines, know the Navy filing system, keep personnel records, handle routine details of enlistments, discharges, transfers and promotions.[827]
Gunner's Mate—Must be able to fire Swiss-made 20mm Oerlikons and Swedish Bofors 40, and instruct others to do the same.[828]

In 1946, enlisted Waves were permitted to wear one service stripe, in red for wear on the blue uniform and navy-blue on the seersucker jacket., to represent four years of active duty in the United States Navy Reserve.[829] The stripes were sewn diagonally on the lower left sleeve.

Officers wore the appropriate corps emblem above their reserve-blue sleeve stripes, the emblem being in the appropriate reserve-blue and white backgrounds to match the uniform. Regular Navy officers resented WAVES officers wearing the line star above their cuff stripes, but WAVES officers were authorized to wear the line star on September 15, 1944. It was worn on the uniform blouses and overcoat.[830] When the blouse was not worn, a metal version of the corps device was worn on the left collar of the shirtwaist with the metal rank insigne worn on the right collar. Officers who were medical specialists wore a caduceus in lieu of the Medical Corps device. Some WAVES officers served as Naval Aviation Observers, but they were not allowed to wear the the insigne until November 29, 1945. The metal or embroidered insigne was worn centered above the left pocket flap

---

[825] **Our Navy, "Congratulations to the WAVES," September 1, 1944, p. 21.
[826] *"WAVE Enlisted Rates," Bureau of Naval Personnel Information Bulletin May 1944: p. 27.
[827] US Navy Publication, *The Story of You in Navy-Blue*, pp. 32-35.
[828] Josette Dermody Wingo, *Mother was a Gunner's Mate*. (Annapolis, Maryland: Naval Institute Press, 1994), p. 54.
[829] Edwards, P. IX-A-47.
[830] Ibid, p. IX-126.

on the blouses and shirtwaists. It was worn 1/4" above any service ribbons.[831]

Waves who had served with honor during World War II were given several honorable discharge insignia (the so-called "Ruptured Duck" emblem) on navy-blue or white backgrounds. It was sewn on the right breast pocket flap of the uniform blouse.[832]

Uniforms were classified into four categories:
1. Service Dress, blue, A—consisted of blue blouse, blue skirt, blue hat cover, black gloves and black shoes;
2. Service Dress, blue, B—As above, but with a white hat cover and white gloves;
3. Service Dress, white—consisted of a white blouse and skirt, white shirt, white hat cover, white shoes and gloves;
4. Working Uniform—consisted of a reserve-blue blouse and skirt, white hat cover, black shoes, white gloves.[833]

By 1944, Waves wore a dungaree uniform for physical work. It consisted of dungaree trousers and a blue chambray shirtwaist. This uniform also doubled as a sports outfit. Enlisted Waves wore this uniform more often than officers.

Women who worked on aircraft wore cotton medium blue aviation coveralls and a turban. The coveralls had long sleeves and opened down the front and had five plain medium blue buttons. A single pocket was on each side of the bodice, and two vertical pockets were below the waistline. The collar was small and had rounded ends. The drop seat closed with five plain medium blue buttons. The legs were full cut, the width of the trousers at the ankles being adjusted by a cloth tab. The "cap" worn with the coveralls was actually a navy-blue, woolen turban. It was a piece of material about 35 inches in length and 18 inches in width. It was wrapped about the head, covering most of the wearer's hair, and shirred at the front.[834]

Sometime during 1943, WAVES officers became the first bona fide naval aviation crewmembers, serving as aerial navigation instructors. They received training, along with male students, at the Naval Air Navigation School (NANS) at Hollywood, Florida. The training lasted seventeen weeks, beginning in the classroom, studying aerology, weather forcasting, and navigation techniques. Flight training began during the middle of the second month, with students navigating Beech SNB's from Florida and its vicinity to the Bahamas or Cuba. A total of fifty flight hours were required. WAVES training on the West Coast navigated Martin PBM-3's. After graduation, however, most WAVES were given training jobs. Only about fifty WAVES

---

[831] Edwards, pp. IX-141, 142.
[832] "Bureau of Naval Personnel Information Bulletin," Honorable Discharge Emblems to be Given to Naval Personnel, January 1945, p. 78.
[833] Arthur A. Ageton, *The Naval Officer's Guide*. (New York: McGraw-Hill Book Company) p. 205.
[834] Edwards, pp. IX-97, 98.

NAS San Diego, California, 1945. WAVES officers wearing USN Air Navigator Wings (L to R): Lieutenant (j.g.) Cecilia Heimlich, Ensign Helen Mayer and Lieutenant Elizabeth Allan. (Courtesy: Mike Minnich)

completed this training and were awarded the US Navy's gold Aerial Navigator's wings. These WAVES navigators were disbanded in 1945.[835]

By 1947, WAVES officers who qualified as Naval Aviation Observers (radar), Naval Aviation Observers, Naval Aviation Observers (navigation), or Naval Aviation Observers (aerology) were permitted to wear a pair of gold Navy wings with an "O" in the center in silver. In this was a vertical, plain silver anchor. The wings measured 2 3/4 inches in width. They could be made of bullion wire, embroidered upon the correct backing to match the uniform.[836]

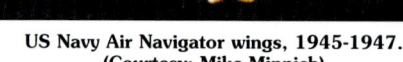

US Navy Air Navigator wings, 1945-1947. (Courtesy: Mike Minnich)

WAVES officer Lieutenant Elizabeth Allan wears the Air Navigator wings in this photo, from her WWII identification card.

Commander Betty Turbiville wears her USN Air Navigator wings on her uniform during the 1950's. (Courtesy: Mike Minnich)

With the passage of the Women's Armed Services Integration Act of 1948, all Navy women's branches were incorporated into the regular Navy and Coast Guard. Consequently, all uniforms worn by female personnel, whether they were worn by a Navy Nurse, Wave or Spar, were changed to the popular style of the WAVES uniform. (The World War II SPARS uniform was already of this style.) Navy nurses no longer wore the double-breasted blouse, but the Mainbocher-style uniform, with its rounded edge collar. For further information about uniforms worn by Waves and Navy nurses, see the chapter "Navy Nurse Corps," Vol. 1, p. 447.

Prayer of a Wave
Dear Lord, as I kneel down to pray I have so much to ask;
my prayers are for the strength to serve a nation's might task.
I need the grace with which to wear in dignity and pride
my uniform and take with its meaning in my stride.
Teach me O Lord obedience—that I may do my best
until our country once again is peaceful and at rest.
And having these to guide me while our Navy's in the war,
I have but then to thank You—I cannot ask for more.
Thank You for our country, for our people free and brave,
and make me ever worthy, Lord, to be a Navy Wave.[837]

---

[835] Mike Minnich, "WAVES Air Navigators: Charting a New Course," *Aviation History*, January 1999, pp. 34-38.
[836] United States Navy Uniform Regulations (Navy Department, 1947) p. 3-18.
[837] Author and date unknown.

WAVES Identification Tags
(Courtesy: Steve Rohde)

M-1943: Type 2. WAVES officers' tags, as indicated by the six-digit number. Note the two different neck cords. On the Bercaw tag the listing of the religion was optional.

M-1943: Type 1. This enlisted WAVES tag carries the blood type but no religion.

M-1943: Type 2. As above, but with both the religion designation and blood type.

M-1943. Type 3. This post WWII tag has no date but has the blood type (B) and religion designaton (C).

M-1943: Type 1. This tag was issued to an enlisted female. "WR"=Women's Reserve.

```
JOSEPHINE
ANNE
KAPUSCIK
733-37-83
T-8/43
USNR-WR A
```

M-1940 Army style tag: Type 2. The "W" suffix denotes USN female personnel in the post WWII period. The religion is Catholic and the blood type is "O."

M-1960: Type 1B. With this style, the Navy adopted a non-notch tag. Note the six-digit number and "W" suffix denoting a female officer, and the full designation for religion and blood type.

```
RUNNING,
JAMIE R.
564602W
USN    AB NEG
PROTESTANT
```

M-1960: Type 3. This tag was issued to an enlisted female in 1981. Note no branch of service is designated, and that the information is stamped on the reverse of the tag.

```
LAHAM LYNNE B
539    1641  A
CHR SCI
```

M-1960: Type 3B. This tag is also from the 1980s and is for an enlisted female. Note the smaller stamped lettering.

143

Women Employed at Army Air Forces Posts
(World War II)

Large numbers of women were employed to serve as civilians at Army Air Forces installations. Some of them were permitted by the local commanders to wear uniforms.

Women serving with the Army Air Forces Technical Training Command in the Los Angeles area wore a blue

Civilian employee Bettey Eager worked at Duncan Field, Texas, 1942. Note the photo ID badge over the left breast pocket, together with a name tag. (Courtesy: Institute of Texas Cultures, the San Antonio Light Coll.)

Army Air Forces Technical Training Command distinctive insigne.

single-breasted blouse with two pocket flaps and buttons on the bodice and two patch pockets with straight flaps and buttons on the side. The blouse closed with three gold buttons, and there was a button at the end of each shoulder strap. All these buttons were possibly regular US Army issue. The skirt was of the same color material as the blouse. A white shirtwaist, with or without a dark tie, was worn under the blouse.

Some women wore the standard Army Air Forces winged star patch, apparently in bullion embroidery, sewn to the upper left sleeve of the blouse. Army Air Forces officer's wing and propeller insignia were worn on the lapels of the blouse.

The visored hat was of self material, having a cloth-covered visor, band, and an oversized top, which bloused over the band. A distinctive insigne was pinned to the center of the hat top.

These *"Chauffeurettes"* served at the AAF Technical Training Command in California. (L to R): Ida Lee Carrillo, Jane Ford and Jean Kelly.

Female civilian employees working at Lowry Field wore the "Lowry uniform." It was made up of a single-breasted blue gabardine blouse and skirt. There were two straight pocket flaps at the bodice, and two interior pockets with straight outside flaps on the sides. The blouse closed with four gold buttons and there were smaller gold buttons on the shoulder straps. Army Air Forces officer's wing and propeller insignia were worn on the lapels.

Chauffeurette Pamela Harris backs up a truck. Note the AAF patch on the sleeve of her blouse.

Polly Vandenburgh awaits order from Captain R.H. Underhill. The women were taught to change tires, make repairs and recognize engine trouble.

Civilian employees worked at Lowry Field, Colorado. They wore a blue gabardine uniform, with wing and propeller insignia on their lapels and on the right side of the garrison cap. Note the sleeve patch with the winged "LF" designation. (Courtesy: Wings over the Rockies Air & Space Museum)

Sleeve patch worn by Lowry Field civilian employee Nettie M. Sherwood. Note the different positioning of the "LF" than shown in the period photo above.

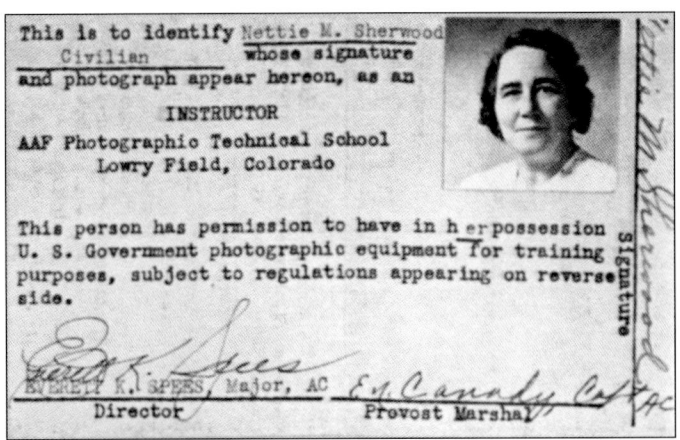

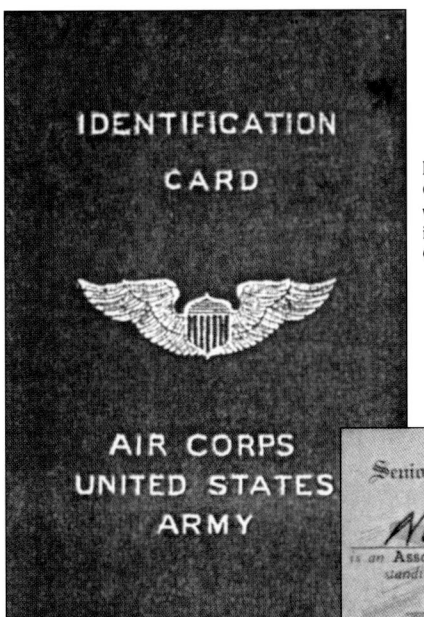

Identification card, pass to the Senior NCO Club and leather wallet of Nettie M. Sherwood, who served as an Army Air Forces photographic nechnical school instructor at Lowry Field, Colorado.

A white shirtwaist was worn open, its collar being worn over the blouse collar.

A matching blue gabardine garrison cap was worn with the uniform. The wing and propeller insigne was attached to the right forward curtain of the cap.

These women wore a round blue patch with a pair of embroidered, upswept wings over the embroidered letters, "LF", on the upper left sleeve of the blouse.

This uniform was approved by Brigadier General Harvey S. Burwell in 1942 but was later prohibited by the War Department.

U.S. Army Air Forces civilian employee's uniform blouse. The Oklahoma City Air Depot patch is sewn to the upper left sleeve. (Courtesy: Jon A. Maguire)

Civilian flight instructor's uniform.

Uniformed civilian emploee of the U.S. Army Air Forces Oklahoma City Air Depot. (Courtesy: Jon A. Maguire)

Detail of the Shoulder bag.

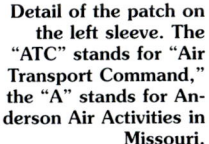

Detail of the patch on the left sleeve. The "ATC" stands for "Air Transport Command," the "A" stands for Anderson Air Activities in Missouri.

Detail of the "Instructor" patch on the right sleeve. Note the "A" designation, which matches the patch on the left sleeve.

Women Flyers of America

The Women Flyers of America was a non-profit, civilian organization, actually a club, which offered lessons to women who wanted to learn to fly. They attended ground school classes and were instructed by certified pilots. Students were then taken to an airfield where arrangements had been made for them to be taught to fly. As of 1942, there were six hundred members.[838] It is not known if these women were uniformed.

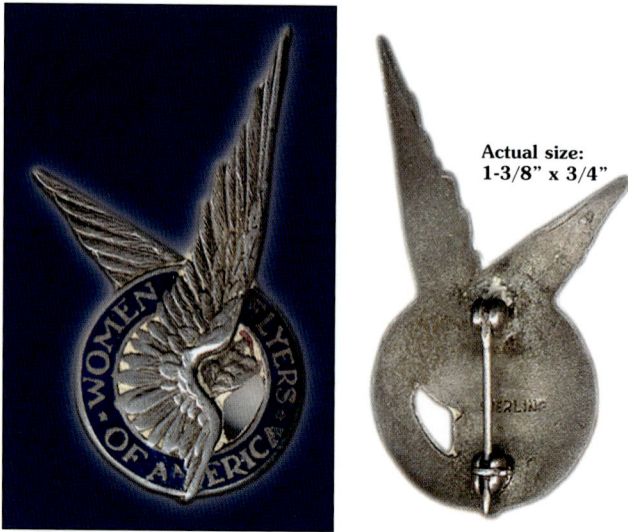

Actual size:
1-3/8" x 3/4"

Blue enamel on silver Women Flyers of America membership pin.
This pin also exists in gold with blue enamel.

---

[838] Charles E. Planck, *Women With Wings*, (New York: Harper & Brothers Publishers, 1942) p. 301.

Women in Aviation

The first American woman to slip the surly bounds of earth was Mrs. D. Klumpke-Roberts, an astronomer from San Francisco who went up in a balloon to better study the heavens in 1898. America's first documented female pilot was Blanche Scott, who began flying in 1910.[839] She was shortly followed by Harriet Quimby, who qualified for her license in 1911. Quimby was notorious for her trademark violet flight suit. An editor, feature writer and drama critic for *Leslie's Weekly,* Quimby was killed on July 1, 1912 while flying with a friend at a Boston, Massachusetts air show. She and her companion, the show director, were killed when her plane flipped over in rough winds, dumping both out and into Dorchester Bay. The plane landed in the water, albeit upside down.[840/841] Incidentally, women who were flying before 1914 were allowed to become members of the "Early Birds," of which there were only six females.

Sisters Marjory and Katherine Stinson started their own flight training school at San Antonio, Texas in 1917 and began training military pilots there. The school was sometimes refered to as the "Texas Escadrille." That same year, Ruth Law went to Europe to study military aviation. When she returned to the United States, she joined the "US Aviation Corps" and helped recruit men for the Army Air Service.[842]

Women like Louise Thadden, Ruth Nichols, Ruth Haviland, Amelia Earhart, Jacqueline Cochran and Nancy Harkness Love became prominent fliers, and their pioneering experience paved the way for the creation of the Women's Auxiliary Ferrying Service and the Women Airforce Service Pilots. Less well-known is Bessie Coleman of Atlanta, Texas. She became the world's first black aviator. Facing discrimination because of her race, Coleman saved her money, learned to speak French and went to France to learn to fly at the prestigious *Fèdèration Aeronautique Internationale,* re-

---

[839] Phyllis J. Read and Bernard L. Willieb., *The Woman's Book of Firsts,* (New York: Orion Books, 1992) p. 396.

[840] Ibid, pp. 353-354.

[841] Walter J. Boyne, *The Smithsonian Book of Flight,* (New York: Orion Books, 1987) p. 68.

[842] Planck, *Women with Wings,* pp. 304-305 and 33.

Harriet Quimby

Katherine Stinson

Ruth Nichols

Trophy won by Genevieve M. Savage for the "Spot Landing Contest" in 1934 at the Washington Women's Air Meet. (Courtesy: Ed Anderson, Jr.)

Early "Powder Puff Derby" pin. (Courtesy: Ed Anderson, Jr.)

Note: The first Women's Transcontinental Air Derby took place in August 1929. Humorist Will Rogers coined it "Powder Puff Derby."

ceiving her pilot's license in 1921, a year before Amelia Earhart.[843] She was killed in a plane crash at a Florida air show on April 30,1926.[844] To this day, pilots fly over her grave in Lincoln Cemetery at Alsip, Illinois, and drop flowers.[845]

After the deaths of Harriett Quimby and Bessie Coleman, a new generation of female aviators emerged from the rebellious times of the Great Depression and the Roaring 'Twenties. Again, women were taking to the skies, and in larger numbers. In general, the women pilots who had not been socially acceptable in the 1920's were viewed as pioneers of aviation and treated like celebrities in the 1930's. As more women took up flying, aero clubs like the Ninety-Nines (so-called for its original ninety-nine members. Established in 1929.) and the Betsy Ross Corps (established in 1931) became more prominent. During the Depression these clubs kept at least one plane to be used by its members so that they could keep their piloting skills current. In 1941, their services as auxiliary pilots were offered to the military after the attack on Pearl Harbor, but were turned down.[846]

Many men, especially those in the military, refused the notion that women could be competent enough to handle such a masculine thing as an airplane. However, as early as 1930 some army officers suggested there be an inquiry into the use of women pilots. The reply was that the idea of female pilots was "...utterly unfeasible..., since women [are] too high strung

Lapel pin with propeller superimposed. (Courtesy: Ed Anderson, Jr.)

A membership card and pin for the "Ninety-Nines" organization. (Courtesy: Ed Anderson, Jr.)

---

[843] Dennis Maurizi, "Breaking Barriers—The Bessie Coleman Story," *Flight Journal*, August 1998: pp. 48-49.

[844] Kirstin Olsen, *Remember the Ladies: A Woman's Book of Days*, (New Jersey: Pittstown: The Main Street Press, 1988) p. 26.

[845] Maurizi, "The Bessie Coleman Story," p. 52.

[846] Adela Riek Scharr, *Sisters in the Sky, Vol. I: The WAFS*, (St. Louis, MO: The Patrice Press, 1986) p. 6.

Poster and emblem of the Betsy Ross Corps. "The Betsy Ross Corps, First Women's Air Corps in the World of licensed women pilots and student flyers, a non-profit patriotic organization, chartered in 1931 under the laws of the State of New York, with members coast to coast...Open to all American citizens over eighteen years of age...For every woman trained to do non-military, civilian air work a man is released for military service." (Courtesy: Ed Anderson, Jr.)

for ...flying."[847] However, some women pilots did achieve professional status: Phoebie Fairgrave Omlie was the first woman to receive a federal pilots license in the 1920's. During Franklin Delano Roosevelt's 1932 campaign for the presidency, Omlie flew speakers around the country. In 1942 she was appointed as the head of a Works Progress Administration (WPA) program that trained civilians as ground personnel at airports.[848]

Women's Auxiliary Ferrying Service (WAFS)
Women Airforce Service Pilots (WASP)

Two women emerged during World War II with plans for women pilots to be used by the military within the United States: They were Jacque-

---

[847] Craven, W.F. and J.L. Cate, *The Army Air Forces in World War II: Services Around the World*, (Chicago, IL: The University of Chicago Press, 1958) p. 528.

[848] Read and Witlieb, *The Book of Women's Firsts*, (New York: Random House, 1992) p. 325.

line Cochran and Nancy Harkness Love. Their philosophies of the role of women in military aviation differed dramatically, and only one of their organizations would survive.

Jacqueline ("Jackie") Cochran had been raised in terrible poverty by a family which was not her own. She was working as a hairdresser when she met and married the wealthy financier, Floyd Odlum. Cochran went on to create a very successful cosmetic business. In the meantime, she discovered airplanes. After competing in and winning many competitions, including the Bendix Race, Jacqueline Cochran became well-known and respected in the field of aviation.

She and her husband were friends of President and Mrs. Roosevelt, since Floyd Odlum saw to much of FDR's financial affairs. Therefore, Cochran had the president's ear, not to mention that of his wife, Eleanor. It is thought that the mention of a trained group of women ferrying pilots was first presented to the President and First Lady at a luncheon with Cochran and her husband in 1941. The President and his wife acknowledged the merit of using female ferrying pilots to allow the United States to have a greater pool of combat male pilots. Roosevelt sent Jacqueline Cochran first to the office of Robert A. Lovette, the Assistant Secretary of War for Air, to discuss the formation of a group of women to be used as auxiliary pilots by the military. Apparently, Cochran wasn't taken seriously and was politely given the run-around. There would be no action taken on behalf of female auxiliary pilots at this time.[849]

In 1940, the Battle of Britain was raging and exacting a terrible toll on the Royal Air Force pilots. More were urgently needed. At a ceremony for the presentation of the Collier Trophy in Washington D.C. (Cochran was a committee member), she and others went to lunch with General H.H. "Hap" Arnold, Chief of the Army Air Forces. He suggested that if she wanted to ferry planes Cochran should get on as a pilot with the British Air Transport Auxiliary (ATA), which used female pilots to ferry airplanes in England. A friend of Cochran's, Lord Beaverbrook, arranged for her to apply for service in the ATA in Canada. She was put through rigorous tests, which she passed. However, a greater amount of effort was required of her since, seemingly, the main obstacle to her flying was her gender. There were frequent attempts to sabotage Cochran's goal of serving in the ATA. Someone even contacted the State Department to prevent her from procuring a special visa for operating in a war zone. Equipment on her plane was damaged, parts and tools mysteriously vanished. Someone even broke the windshield of a plane she was to fly. Men did not like the idea of a woman piloting airplanes, and the ever-determined Cochran was stepping on their turf.

Despite these hindrances, Cochran got the job as the director of women pilots with the British Air Transport Auxiliary and was given the honorary rank of Flight Captain. She proved a skilled and determined or-

---

[849] Scharr, Adele Riek, *Sisters in the Sky,* Vol. I, (St. Louis, MO: The Patrice Press, 1986) p. 7.

ganizer; the Royal Air Force soon asked her to recruit twenty-five American women to come to England and serve with her. While she did serve in the British ATA, Cochran did not actually ferry a plane while she was in England. The British wouldn't risk losing a single precious plane—not even to her. When she traveled, Cochran was flown by her pilot, Mary Nicholson.[850]

At this time, Cochran advocated to General Arnold the use of a thousand member women's flying group to be used as ground and flight instructors, ferrying pilots, glider pilots, and for towing targets—most every task except combat. General Arnold said no to her plans. He believed there were enough male pilots to fill all billets.

Another accomplished aviatrix was Nancy Harkness Love, the wife of the president of Boston's Intercity Airlines, Robert M. Love. In 1940, she became the first American woman to ferry an aircraft to the United States/Canada border. The Canadians pushed her plane across the border and Love boarded another plane and flew back to the states.[851]

Nancy Love wrote to Lieutenant Colonel (and later, general) Robert Olds in May 1940, saying that she knew of at least forty-nine qualified women pilots who could quickly be put to use ferrying military aircraft from the factories to the airfields. She suggested that these pilots be given commissions as second lieutenants in the Army Air Corps Reserve.[852] Olds presented the plan to General Arnold that month but Arnold promptly dismissed it. He was a very outspoken opponent of using women as pilots or copilots. He preferred using male pilots, including those who flew for commercial aviation, as well as Air Corps cadets. The latter, he felt, would gain valuable flying experience while ferrying planes, accomplishing two things at once.

About this same time the US Navy was trying to push a bill through Congress which would allow women to serve within its ranks, and those of the Marine Corps, as ferrying pilots. Not surprisingly, the bill was defeated. There remained a great deal of animosity in the military towards women serving in their ranks in capacities other than nursing or secretaries.

While on business in England, General Arnold assured Cochran that if women were permitted to fly in the military, she would be appointed the director of the organization. Whether Arnold was serious or just trying to pacify Cochran isn't known, but she took him quite seriously and eventually achieved that goal.

In 1941, Cochran and her plans for a women's air force were shuffled back and forth to Secretary of War, Henry L. Stinson, and from Stinson to General Arnold, who was now chief of the Army Air Corps. General Arnold sent the paperwork to the desk of the hardly enthusiastic

---

[850] Granger, Byrd Howell., *On Final Approach. The Women Airforce Service Pilots of World War II*, (Scottsdale, AZ: Falconer Publishing, 1991) p. 17.

[851] Scharr, Adela Riek, *Sisters in the Sky, Vol. I: The WAFS*, (St. Louis, MO: The Patrice Press, 1986) p. 3.

[852] Ibid, p. 5.

Colonel Olds, who was now the commander of the Air Corps Ferrying Command (ACFC). Olds turned down a similar plan that had been submitted by Nancy Love a year prior. Cochran's plan was also rejected.[853]

Undaunted, Cochran presented another plan to General Arnold in August 1941. Briefly, female pilots would be involved in a ninety-day test period, serving in organizations such as the Ferrying Division (now called FERD). At the end of this probationary period, those who had successfully completed the training would be commissioned second lieutenants, first lieutenants, or captains in the Army Air Corps Reserve. Cochran would then become "Chief of Women Pilots." She was again turned down by General Arnold.[854]

Despite these numerous rejections, Colonel Olds began keeping a list of the qualified women pilots in the United States who could be quickly mobilized. This list was passed on to Fiorello LaGuardia, who was head of the Office of Civilian Defense.[855]

In January 1942 Colonel Olds submitted his own plan for the use of women pilots to General Arnold. Olds suggested that the government hire female certified civilian pilots. They would have no military status and be paid a monthly salary. Upon hearing of Old's plan, Cochran hurriedly sent a letter from England to General Arnold, giving reasons why Old's plan was not a good one. First, as mentioned earlier, Cochran had been asked by the British government to recruit American women to serve in the ATA. Colonel Olds' plan would be in direct conflict with her responsibilities in England. Her attempt to recruit American women for service in the ATA would cease, since pay and living conditions were better in the United States. It would have washed Cochran out of the supervision of women fliers in England. Cochran also feared that an organization of women as free-lance pilots would be an unregulated mess. She wrote to Arnold that it would be essential that a woman be placed in charge of the women pilots. Lastly, she stated that Colonel Olds' plan should be delayed to such a time as she had completed her service overseas.

Cochran's time in England was up on July 2, 1942. She was no doubt enraged when she learned that General Harold George, head of the Air Transport Command (ATC), had written headquarters staff on June 11th about the possibility of using commissioned women officers from the Women's Auxiliary Army Corps (WAAC) to ferry airplanes for the ATC. Upon her return to the United States, Cochran was summoned to the Washington, DC office of Colonel Oveta Culp Hobby, director of the WAAC (which became the Women's Army Corps [WAC] in 1943), who suggested to Cochran that women pilots should become a branch of the WAAC. Hobby's plan was, after passing a flight check, the names of the pilot candidates would be reported to Colonel Hobby, who would then

---

[853] Ibid, p. 7.
[854] Ibid, p. 8.
[855] Ibid, p. 9.

commission them. These women would be assigned as second lieutenants at the Second Ferrying Group, Newcastle Army Base at Wilmington, Delaware. Hobby assured Cochran that she would be allowed to be this organization's director.[856]

To quote Jacqueline Cochran:

"I told [Colonel Hobby] that there was just about as much sense putting the women pilots under the WAC as putting the Air Force pilots back in the Army Signal Corps; that I was unalterably opposed to it, and if the scheme were to mature, she would have to find another leader.... I think Colonel Hobby never liked me after that...."[857]

Now a brigadier general, Olds approved a plan for using female pilots as auxiliaries, which surprisingly passed through the offices of Generals Arnold and George before coming upon an unforeseen obstacle: There was no legal precedent or authority which would allow these women to receive the same flight pay as their male counterparts. The way for using women as ferry pilots was finally cleared when it was realized that they could be hired by the government as civil servants. Nancy Love had access to Colonel William Tunner, who knew that she commuted daily by air from Baltimore to Washington, DC. Love was chosen to be the director of these civilian pilots. (Love's husband, Robert, was commissioned a major and was assigned as Colonel Tunner's assistant in FERD.) Tunner wanted to employ twenty-five women pilots, who would be commissioned as second lieutenants in the WAAC.[858]

Jacqueline Cochran in the cockpit of a P-40 "Warhawk" fighter plane.

---

[856] Ibid, p. 13.

[857] Cochran, Jacqueline, with Floyd Odlum as Wingman. *The Stars at Noon*, (Boston & Toronto: Little, Brown and Company, 1954), p. 121.

[858] Granger, *On Final Approach*, p. 23.

Nancy Love by a PT-19 trainer on the day she tested the first applicants to the WAFS.

The result of Brigadier General Olds and Nancy Love's plans for a women's auxiliary ferrying service was formed under the title of "Women's Auxiliary Ferrying Service, or WAFS, being officially established on September 5, 1942 at Newcastle Air Base, Delaware. Twenty-eight women were accepted into the program. The Wafs had the specific goal of releasing men from aircraft ferrying duties to more pressing assignments. Qualification for service were: The applicant must have proof of American citizenship, have fifty hours of recent flying time with a total of five hundred hours of previous time, possess a commercial pilot's certificate, have at least a high school diploma, be between the ages of twenty-one and thirty-five, have a 200 horsepower rating, and be able to submit two letters of recommendation.[859] WAFS members served in the Air Transportation Command of the Army Air Forces. They would be civil servants, albeit ones in uniform.

Upon his own initiative, Secretary of War Stinson appealed for eighty-six experienced women pilots who would require very little additional training to volunteer for service. These women would also be paid civil servants and not members of the armed forces. Each applicant was required to have five hundred flight hours. This group of fliers was call the WFTD, or Women's Flying Training Detachment (emphasis on the word training) and was to be under the direction of Jacqueline Cochran. Members were nicknamed "Woofteddies."[860] They began training at Howard

---

[859] Petersen, George, ed. *American Women at War in World War II, Vol. 1: Clothing, Insignia and Equipment of the US Army, WACs and Nurses, American Red Cross, USO, AWVS, Civil Defense and related Wartime Woman's Organizations*, 1943, p. 68.

[860] Granger. *On Final Approach*, p. 76.

Hughes Airport in Houston Texas on October 1, 1942.[861] The facilities there proved to be too limited, so another site had to be found.

On September 3, 1942 General George sent out the message that recruiting for WFTD fliers was to begin in twenty-four hours.[862] George's idea was that Nancy Love would be in charge of the women pilots who would actually be ferrying planes, whereas Jacqueline Cochran would train less experienced women pilots at an airfield in Houston, Texas. In effect, Cochran would be training pilots in the WFTD for later service in the WAFS.

That same day General Olds warned General Arnold that if Congress delayed the approval of the Women's Auxiliary Ferrying Troops (WAFT, as he called them),[863] the plan might never come to fruition. Women who applied but did not qualify to serve as Wafs were sent by Nancy Love to Houston where they could apply for service in the WFTD, Cochran was to send her graduates to serve with the WAFS in the 6th Ferrying Squadron at Long Beach, California.[864]

General Arnold reiterated that he wanted to use only male pilots and co-pilots, especially cadets, who would benefit from the flight experience. He instructed General Olds to contact the Civil Aeronautics Authority (CAA) and the Civil Air Patrol (CAP) to get from them as many qualified male pilots as possible. General Arnold would only consider using women pilots after the nation's supply of male pilots had been exhausted. General Arnold did not approve of using women auxiliary pilots (Specifically, the WAFS) until September 1942.

Nancy Love and Jacqueline Cochran had two very different goals for the use of these women pilot auxiliaries: Love saw the need for a temporary, yet exemplary group of women pilots to fly for the duration of the war. Cochran envisioned the eventual creation of a military organization of women pilots. She and General Arnold shared the dream of an air force that would be a branch of the military in its own right. Cochran realized that further along, women would have duties other than ferrying aircraft. That is why she disliked the term WAFS—Women's Auxiliary Ferrying Service. The title was too limited. Cochran submitted the following alternate names for the forthcoming organization: Women's Auxiliary Pilots, Women's Supplementary Pilots and Women's Army Support System.[865] All of these titles were rejected by General Arnold. It was he who came up with the catchy acronym, "W.A.S.P.," which stood for "Women Airforce Service Pilots." It was made the official name of all women's auxiliary flight organizations in 1943. General Arnold realized that the WAFS and the WFTD

---

[861] Thomas A. Manning, Command Historian, *History of Air Training Command, 1943-1993*, (San Antonio, TX: United States Air Force, 1993), p. 212.
[862] Scharr, *Sisters in the Sky*, Vol. I, p. 423.
[863] Ibid, p. 14.
[864] Granger, *On Final Approach*, p. 99.
[865] Williams, Vera S. *WASPs: Women Airforce Service Pilots of World War II*, (Osceola, Wisconsin: Motorbooks, International, 1994), p. 23.

were similar organization with overlapping duties. He notified the ATC and Jacqueline Cochran that he, "...would not have two women's pilot organizations in the AAF—that they would have to get together." Thus, on August 5, 1943 those WAFS pilots who so desired to continue ferrying planes were merged into the WASP. Both organizations would soon be absorbed by the WASP. As promised, Jacqueline Cochran was appointed the Director of Women Pilots, while Nancy Love was named to a rather vague position known as the WASP executive in the ferrying division of the ATC.[866]

In November 1942 WAFS took to the air on their first mission, ferrying Piper Cubs from Lock Haven, Pennsylvania, to Mitchell Field, New York. That same day the first WASP class (Class 43-1) graduated.[867]

The WASP program had first begun at Ellington Field at Houston, Texas[868] in August 1942[869] and soon Cochran was overwhelmed with more than twenty thousand applications to the program. At least sixteen of the original twenty-eight members of the WAFS transferred to the WASP,[870] and already had at least five hundred flying hours, exceeding the minimum requirement of three hundred hours for entry into the WASP program.[871] The facilities at Houston proved unsuitable and the first class was delayed until November,[872] but an opening came when the British left their training base at Avenger Field in Sweetwater, Texas, and the WASP program was moved there. The WASP consisted of both flying and non-flying, operational and administrative personnel.[873] The last class of trainees graduated from Avenger Field on December 7, 1944. This was the famous "Lost Class" As a member recounted:

> "...Why they let us graduate nobody knows. They knew we were in primary, that we would be deactivated and there would be no more classes. Yet they let us graduate and get our wings. I will be eternally grateful for that."[874]

As of December 20, 1944 there were 916 female pilots still serving in the AAF:

AAF Headquarters	1
Training Command	620
HQ/ATC	2

---

[866] Craven, W.F. and J.L. Cate. *The Army Air Forces in World War II. Services Around the World, Vol. VII*, p. 529.

[867] Williams, *Women Airforce Service Pilots*, p. 22.

[868] Cochran, *The Stars at Noon*, p. 120.

[869] Correspondence from former Wasp, Mary Lou Colbert Neal, February 1, 1994.

[870] Cochran, *The Stars at Noon*, p. 129.

[871] Correspondence from former Wasp, Mary Lou Colbert Neal, February 1, 1994.

[872] Ibid.

[873] "Personnel, Civilian, Women Airforce Service Pilots," AAF Regulation No. 40-8, Headquarters, Army Air Forces, Washington, April 3, 1944.

[874] Noggle, Anne. *For God, Country, and the Thrill of It. Women Airforce Service Pilots in World War II*, (College Station, Texas: Texas A & M University Press, 1990), p. 14.

Air Transport Command	139
First Air Force	16
Second Air Force	80
Fourth Air Force	37
Weather Wing	11
Proving Ground Command	6
Air Technical Service Command	3
Troop Carrier Command	1 [875]

By the time the WASP was disbanded in December 1944, some 12,650 planes had been delivered at a collective distance of approximately 9,224,000 miles within the time frame of twenty-seven months.[876] 77 different types of aircraft had been flown.

In June 1944 the House Committee on the Civil Service looked into the possibility of militarizing the WASP, an idea which they found to be of no use, since the very existence of the WASP had become superfluous. The committee recommended that it halt any further training or recruiting. The fortunes of war had turned in favor of the Allies, causing a surplus of male pilots. Later, in March 1944, both General Arnold and Jacqueline Cochran were in favor of women pilots being integrated as a branch of the WAC.[877] Their change of heart was probably due to the fact that they both had seen the writing on the wall; the WASP was going to be deactivated, since the Allies were winning the war. The WAC seemed like the only place Cochran could have her women pilots. The political duel between Cochran, Love and Colonel Hobby continued, but women pilots never became a branch of the WAC. Attempts were made to get a bill through Congress which would make the WASP an actual military organization, but all were defeated. As some consolation, former Wasps were offered commissions in the army in 1949. One hundred fifteen women accepted them and some made the army their career. Ironically, they were not allowed to pilot aircraft.

By the time of their deactivation, the WAFS and WASP had lost thirty-eight pilots in flight accidents, the first casualty being Jane Champlin, a Waf, who was killed in a crash at Westbrook, Texas on June 7, 1943.[878] Jacqueline Cochran noted that, because of their civilian status, Wasps, "...didn't even have the right to a military funeral."[879] Often, Cochran had to pay out of her pocket to have the body of a deceased Wasp put in a pine box to be shipped to their next-of-kin. She and many others wanted the WASP to be given military status, and as soon as possible. She demanded that insurance benefits be paid to survivors of deceased Wasps, just as was normally done for regular members of the military. The benefits which were sought, but not secured, for the WASP were: 1) Compensation to

---

[875] Craven, W.F. and J.L. Cate. *The Army Air Forces in World War II, Vol. VII*, p. 536.
[876] Ibid, p. 533.
[877] Scharr, *Sisters in the Sky*, p. 497.
[878] Phyllis J. Read and Bernanrd L. Witlieb., *The Book of Women's Firsts*, (New York: Random House, 1992) p. 87.
[879] Ibid, p. 535.

Jacqueline Cochran wears the Army Air Forces patch in bullion. The ribbon above her wings is for the Distinguished Service Medal, awarded to her personally by General Arnold. (Courtesy: M.L. Bataille, Paris)

families of Wasps killed in the line of duty, 2) medical benefits, 3) civil service job priority, 4) post-war bonuses, and 5) Army Honorable Discharge certificates awarded to Wasps, along with service pins.[880]

It wasn't until 1977 that Congress recognized that the services provided by the WASP during war time equated to military service, making its members eligible for veterans' benefits.[881]

Initially, there was no standard uniform for WFTD trainees. As a former Wasp put it:

> *"Any combination of civilian clothes, except cowboy boots, was allowed."*[882]

When the WFTD and WAFS were merged into the WASP classes at Avenger Field, the girls wore cotton coveralls and the notorious white turbans, known as "Urban's Turbans," for the name of the 318th's commander, Major Robert Urban.[883] The women were required to wear the turbans to keep their hair out of machinery.

WASP trainees wear cotton overalls and the disliked white turbans.

---

[880] Granger, *On Final Approach,* p. 443.
[881] Noggle, Anne. *For God, Country and the Thrill of It,* p. 14.
[882] Ibid, p. 8.
[883] Ibid.

WAFS: Uniforms and Insignia

The first few Wafs were sent by Nancy Love to a depot at Newcastle Army Base to pick up the standard army air corps flight equipment. They were issued wool summer flight suits, the majority of which were too large for most of the women. They also received new goatskin A-2 jackets, flight helmets, goggles and parachutes.[884] The Wafs were instructed to keep their equipment receipts, since items would have to be returned as they wore out and needed replacement. Any piece of equipment that could not be accounted for was paid for by the Waf herself. Parachutes were stenciled with each Waf's name. They were also issued a fleece-lined leather helmet, fur-lined gloves, a leather cold-weather face mask, boots, and fleece-lined jackets and pants.[885]

Wafs wearing leather A-2 jackets with the ATC patch. On the far right are Wafs Florene Miller and Teresa James. (Courtesy: Fred J. Slightham)

After returning to their barracks, they were shocked to see Waf Betty Gillies jump off the truck and begin rubbing her brand new goatskin jacket in the dirt. She stood up, smiled proudly and explained that, "No old pilot would ever wear a shiny new jacket. The only people who wear new looking stuff are people who haven't soloed yet."[886]

The premier WAFS uniform was made for Nancy Love by Carlson's of Wilmington, Delaware for an on-camera interview. The initial result was

---

[884] Scharr, *Sisters in the Sky*, Vol, 1, pp. 71-72.
[885] Ibid, p. 131.
[886] Ibid.

extremely unattractive. The trousers, for example, had been cut in an almost jodhpur style. After several more fittings and alterations, Love had a uniform that would be good enough for the newsreel cameras. Afterwards, she returned the uniform to Carlson's.

Love wanted to get her pilots into uniform before their first mission. She was unable to procure enough olive drab or khaki material to make twenty-eight suits, so a greyish-green wool serge was chosen. It cost each Waf approximately $75.00 for a blouse, skirt and pair of trousers. A white shirtwaist was worn on dress occasions, where a cotton khaki shirt was for regular duty. These shirts were purchased from the Manhattan Company. Wafs weren't allowed to wear typical GI khaki because, as Love explained, they were neither commissioned officers or enlisted men. Their headdress consisted of a piped, greyish-green garrison, or "overseas," cap like that worn by regular officers, but with the curtain fold being on the wearer's left side.

Nancy Love, pilot at left, and Betty (Huyler) Gillies, co-pilot at right, were the first women to fly the Boeing B-17 heavy bomber. They are wearing khaki blouses and trousers.

Brown leather oxfords with a Cuban heel were worn with the uniform, and Wafs carried a brown rectangular leather purse or shoulder bag. The Wafs were required to purchase two uniforms so that they would always have a clean one available.

A gray wool overcoat was ordered, which had a lining that could be buttoned in for cold weather. The coat was double-breasted and had eight pairs of gray plastic buttons. A half belt was sewn on the back of the coat, and a vent flap ran from it to the coat's hem. Most of the girls realized that they wouldn't be able to afford two uniforms, an overcoat, shoes, a purse, shoe polish and the like on a month' salary. "Officers are given a uniform allowance; why aren't we?" was frequently heard. Officers were "government issue" with all its benefits, but the Wafs were civil employees with no benefits. The Wafs went to Carlson's to be fitted for uniforms and the results were hardly satisfactory. The pants were too baggy and the skirts were too big. This was corrected after much complaining. At any rate, they did have their new uniforms in time to wear on their first mission.

The final uniform design consisted of a gray-green gabardine single-breasted blouse with a four gray plastic button closure and four patch pockets. Shoulder straps of the same material were sewn at each shoulder. The blouse had a cloth belt and corresponding loops at the side of the blouse. The silver colored buckle was metal and rectangular. The cuffs of the blouse had a darker stripe of grayish-green mohair, an insigne which normally denoted an army officer, being worn by the ranks of second lieutenant through colonel: Ranks which no Wafs could hold. the wearing of the WAFS uniform caused much confusion. On commercial flights, Wafs were often mistaken for stewardesses. Some even thought they were members of the Mexican Army or senior Girl Scouts.[887] At no time was a tie worn with this uniform. As mentioned previously, the collars of the white or khaki shirts were worn over collar of the uniform blouse. Surprisingly, on November 9, 1942 the Air Force Supply Division declined to officially recognize the WAFS uniform.[888]

Wafs were issued belted blue woolen gabardine flight suits.[889] A round, leather patch with the gray, red, white and blue ATC emblem was sewn to the left breast pocket (cloth patches of similar size may also have been worn). A flight helmet and goggles were worn with the suit while flying.

Wafs wore regular athletic outfits or even flight suits for physical training.[890]

Period photographs show Nancy Love, her assistant, Betty Gillies, and other Wafs wearing khaki shirts, khaki trousers and khaki web belts with standard rectangular brass metal buckles. The Army Air Forces patch

---

[887] Granger, *On Final Approach*, p. 63.
[888] Ibid, p. 64.
[889] Scharr, *Sisters in the Sky*, Vol. I, p. 94.
[890] Granger, *On Final Approach*, p. 100.

Waf Florene Miller wears the WAFS uniform. (Courtesy: Fred J. Slightam)

Cigarette advertisement showing a Waf wearing a khaki flight suit with the ATC emblem. (Courtesy: Peterson Air Force Base Museum)

Note: Both a yellow and a silver patch were worn by the Ferrying Command and the Transport Command.

The Air Forces Ferrying Command patch. On May 1, 1942 all Air Corps units and commands were redesignated "Air Forces." The background color behind the globe is golden-yellow, and the red and blue lines along the upper left form the Morse code letters "AFFC." Prior to this date the Morse code letters spelled "ACFC" (Air Corps Ferrying Command) which was established on May 29, 1941.

was sewn just below the shoulder on the left sleeve and worn unofficially until being authorized by General George on November 9, 1942.[891]

Upon being accepted into the WAFS, the girls were given a pair of wings, which they wore over the flap of the left breast pocket of the gray-

---

[891] Ibid, p. 64.

ish-green blouse or khaki shirt. Photos also show the wings being pinned to the upper left pocket flap of the blouse. These wings, designed by Raymond Lowey,[892] had four rows of feathers which had little detail to them. In the center of the wings was the circular insigne of the Air Corps Ferry Command: A stylized aircraft over a portion of the globe with the letters "ATC" in Morse code along the left side of the round. Below was a scroll with "Civilian Pilot" in raised letters. At the inner portion of the wings on the viewer's left side were the letters, "A.C.," while "F.C." was on the right. These wings had a hinged pin and roll catch fastener. When the WAFS were absorbed into the WASP in 1943, the former WAFS were supposed to wear the new WASP wings, but several period photographs show Ferry Command wings being worn on the left breast of the WASP uniforms by former Wafs.[893]

Manufacturer of wing was Robbins Co., Attleboro, Mass.

Excellent photo of Florene Miller showing the WAFS insignia. (Courtesy: Fred J. Slightham)

[892] Ibid, p. 60.
[893] Scharr, *Sisters in the Sky*, Vol. 2, p. 554.

These wings raised many questions and comments from the public:
"Say, young lady, what are those wings, anyway?"
"Ferry pilot wings."
"Oh. To Staten Island."
"No, I fly planes——I ferry them for the Air Forces."
"Huh? Oh, you mean you work on the planes and they let you wear the wings as a compliment, sort of. That's it."
"No, not exactly. I ferry the planes."
"Oh. You do. All by yourself?"
"Yes."
"Well—who flies the plane?"[894]

Wafs wore a pair of silver, clutch back, wing and propeller devices affixed to each lapel of the blouse. A pair of silver colored metal distinctive insignia (also referred as "DIs") of the ATC were affixed to each shoulder strap.* The silver ATC emblem showed a stylized aircraft upon the upper section of a globe, with latitude and longitude lines. Very often, these distinctive insignia had pin backs, but examples with clutch backs also exist.

The Army Air Forces patch was worn on the upper left sleeve. On the uniform blouse, a grayish-green tab, with "W.A.F.S.," embroidered in ultramarine-blue block letters, was sewn just below the AAF patch. Given the short life span of the WAFS, this patch and tab combination should be considered one of the rarest of the period.

*They could also wear the "d.i.'s" of the units they were attached to, i.e., different commands instead of those of the ATC. Wasps referred to these as "Glamour Buttons."

Rare WAFS tab with an Army Air Corps patch worn by Bernice Batten. (Courtesy: Ed Anderson, Jr.)

The silver wing and propeller insigne was also worn on the wearer's left side of the garrison cap, while a small, cloth or metal version of the ATC patch (or "distinctive insignia") was sometimes worn on the right side. The curtain was probably bordered in silver and black flecked piping.

---

[894] Granger, *On Final Approach*, p. 63.

The first WASP graduates at Ellington Field wear white blouses, tan trousers and unpiped khaki garrison caps. (Courtesy: Ed Anderson, Jr.)

WASP Uniforms and Insignia

The first Wasps turned out to graduate on the grounds of Ellington Field in Houston, Texas, wearing white blouses, tan trousers, known as "generals pants,"[895] brown leather shoes and a khaki garrison cap which had no piping.

Prior to the introduction of the WASP Santiago-blue uniform, graduates assigned to the Air Transport Command-Ferrying Division wore standard Army "pink" trousers, shirtwaists, tie and garrison cap. Khaki items of clothing were worn during the summer. During the winter, Wasps also wore Army olive-drab trousers, shirtwaists, khaki ties and olive-drab garrison caps. The garrison caps had regular Army officer's black and gold piping around the curtain edge.[896]

News of the WASP program circulated widely in the clothing industry with many firms offering to design its uniform. The following companies are know to have produced or submitted prototype uniforms, but the uniform design had to be approved by the Quartermaster Corps before any action could be taken. Among the companies were the Hamilton Tailoring Company,[897] the C.B. Shane Corporation of Chicago, which produced a prototype WASP trench coat,[898] and the Hannes Schneider Sports Company, New York City, which manufactured a few winter parkas. "Saks Fifth Ave., NY" maker/tailor labels have also been observed in WASP uniforms.

---

[895] Conversation with former Wasp, Dorothy Smith Lucas, 1995.

[896] Byrd Howell Granger, *On Final Approach. The Women Airforce Service Pilots of WWII,* (Scottsdale, AZ: Falconer Publishing Company, 1991) p. A-90/E.

[897] Letter, August 6, 1943, from the Hamilton Tailoring Company, Cincinnati, Ohio, to Jacqueline Cochran.

[898] Invoice from the C.B. Shane Corporation, Chicago, Illinois, November 15, 1943, to Jacqueline Cochran. Letter from the C.B. Shane Corporation, January 13, 1944 to Jacqueline Cochran, and letter from Jacqueline Cochran to the C.B. Shane Corporation, February 5, 1944.

Jacqueline Cochran later recounted:

"When it came time to select a uniform for the women pilots, a drive was made to have them use the new blue uniform which had been readied in quantity for the Army Nurse Corps and then changed. (The modified nurse's uniform was to have golden-yellow and ultramarine-blue trimming on the shoulder straps.) Another drive was attempted to have me use an excess amount of material that had been bought for the WAC. In addition to the discarded uniform for the nurses and one I had made from the excess WAC material, I had one designed according to my own ideas with Santiago-blue material, which I knew was a favorite with the Air Force. I presented these three uniforms on live models to General Arnold. My choice was on a beautifully proportioned Greek professional model who had volunteered her services. The other two uniforms were girls I had borrowed from the Quartermaster General's office and they did not have classical physical dimensions to say the least. There was no question of the choice in General Arnold's mind and he was so intrigued with the fashion show and my technique of presentation that he took us all immediately to George C. Marshall's office. General Marshall looked us over carefully and speaking very judiciously said he liked best the uniform I had on. I was not wearing a uniform, but a regular suit and I tried to so explain. He still liked it best and I finally had to tell him how very much more uniforms like it would cost than others."[899]

Professional model Deana Clark wears the proposed Santiago-blue WASP uniform with cut-out cardboard lapel insignia and wings. (Courtesy: U.S. Air Force)

---

[899] Jacqueline Cochran, *The Stars at Noon*, pp. 123-124.

"Economy won Marshall over to his second choice, which was on my Greek model and that was how the choice of the WASP uniform was made."[900]

Cochran had a prototype uniform made at her own expense by Nieman-Marcus of Dallas. The first record found of the WASP Santiago-blue uniform being worn is in a letter dated November 18, 1943 from Cochran to Mr. Theodore Rinis of the Clothing Section of the Office of the Quartermaster General in Washington. In the letter, she thanked him for fitting her uniform and stated:

"Everyone said that it fitted and looked just lovely, and, if it hadn't been for your help and kindness, I would not have had it to wear to the Forum."[901] In all, the development of the WASP uniform cost the Quartermaster General's Office $1,623,190.00.[902]

Again, thanks to Nieman-Marcus of Dallas, Texas, on February 11, 1944[903] the last two classes of Wasps graduated in smartly-fitting uniforms. A Cochran wrote to Stanley Marcus, "If it had not been for your unfailing cooperation we would not have been able to have the last two classes in uniform before they left the school. Neither would it have been possible to have the girls looking so lovely when we had our 'red letter day,' March 11 [1944], when we were honored with the presence of General Arnold and seven of his staff at the school."[904]

Procurement of bulk WASP uniforms was initially a problem, but orders to proceed with the procurement of items of WASP uniform were approved April 14, 1944. First, though, Cochran had to furnish size tariffs, and she was remarkably slow about it:

"A representative of this office had repeatedly contacted by telephone the Office of the Director of Women Pilots since 21. April [1944] in an effort to obtain size tariffs on the five hundred sets of WASP clothing but to date this information has not been made available.

This office desires to again call to your attention the fact that it is impossible to proceed with the procurement of these items until sizes desired...are made available...."[905]

On July 1, 1944 1,600 jackets (i.e. blouses) were ordered.[906] Meanwhile, as of May 1, 1944 the following approved items of uniform were sent to the Commanding General of the Philadelphia Quartermaster Depot to be used as the standard to the procurement of WASP uniforms:

1 duffle bag;
1 field cap, blue poplin;
1 wool knit cap;
1 pair of gloves with woolen inserts;
1 pair of leather shell gloves;
1 pair of wool mitten inserts;
1 pair of deerskin mitten shells;
1 parka;
1 pair of arctic or cold climate overshoes;
1 pair of low overshoes;
1 pair of woolen ski socks;

1 raincoat;
1 trainee and exercise suit;
1 blue cardigan;
1 pair of cotton anklets;
1 pair of wool anklets;
1 pair of leather dress gloves;
1 summer necktie;
1 winter necktie;
1 [blue] winter scarf;
1 blue summer shirt;
1 summer dress white shirt;
1 blue winter shirt;
1 pair of woolen underwear;
1 wool undergarment vest.[907]

When the WASP uniform was finally issued it caused quite a sensation. Margaret Nissen, Uniform Control for United Air Lines, praised the uniform highly, saying that United would like to consider having new uniforms made based on the WASP uniform. Miss Nissen requested photographs of the uniform and promised that the fabric used would be a different color than the WASP uniform and the style would be changed in order that no conflict would arise.[908] Cochran responded to Miss Nissen, saying that the uniform could not be copied, since the WASP wanted to have a distinctive uniform which would not cause them to be confused with any other branch or organization.[909] Miss Nissen accepted Jacqueline's letter gracefully and added, "We girls in the airline industry have great admiration, to say nothing of envy, for the girls in the WASP who have been fortunate enough to qualify and do such a marvelous job for our War Effort [sic]."[910]

---

[900] Ibid, p. 124.
[901] Letter from Jacqueline Cochran to Theodore Rinis, Clothing Section, Office of the Quartermaster General, November 18, 1943.
[902] Letter from Colonel H.R.W. Herwig, Q.M.C., Air Quartermaster, Office of Assistant Chief of Air Staff, M.M.& D., to the Quartermaster General, Washington, D.C., June 19, 1944
[903] Byrd Howell Granger, *On Final Approach. The Women Airforce Service Pilots of WWII*, (Scottsdale, AZ: Falconer Publishing Company, 1991) p. A-80/D.
[904] Letter from Jacqueline Cochran to Stanley Marcus, March 25, 1944.
[905] Letter from Lieutenant Colonel C.D. Garrett to Colonel Van der Lutz, War Department, Assistant Chief of Air Staff, Office of the Air Quartermaster, May 13, 1944, regarding WASP clothing.
[906] Letter from Colonel [name illegible] to Headquarters, Army Air Forces, Attn: Colonel H.R.W. Herwig, Air Quartermaster, July 1, 1944.
[907] Letter from Garrett, Commanding General, May 1, 1944.
[908] Letter from Margaret Nissen, Uniform Control, United Airlines Transportation Corporation, May 27, 1944.
[909] Letter from Jacqueline Cochran to Margaret Nissen, Uniform Control, United Airline Transport Corporation, May 27, 1944.
[910] Letter from Margaret Nissen, United Airline Transport Corporation, to Jacqueline Cochran, Jun 1, 1944.

William Taylor, the president and general manager of *Lineas Aereas Mexicanas, S.A.* wrote:

"Don't you think it would be a very nice 'Good Neighbor' gesture on the part of ...yourself to let us use your uniform design here in Mexico? I would appreciate it tremendously. Our personnel are all Mexican, and the señoritas, who would wear the uniform are persons of exceptionally good standing."[911] He included a swatch of green material with his letter. Cochran replied,

"*Dear Mr. Taylor,*

It distresses me greatly to have to write this letter, since, we are, I can assure you, very honored to know that you like our uniforms so much that you want to use them for you hostesses.

As I wrote Miss Nissen..., it was chosen as much for the reason that it does not resemble any other uniform of the women's services.... I am sure you can readily understand our desire to keep it for our exclusive use.

...Please be assured that we would be delighted to be of assistance to you if we felt we could properly do so.

Sincerely,

Jacqueline Cochran

Director of Women Pilots"[912]

The dress, or walking out uniform consisted of a white or light blue shirt, depending on the occasion, and the Santiago-blue blouse with the three wooden button closure. The winter version of the dress uniform was made of thirteen ounce wool gabardine, while the summer version of the uniform was made of 10-1/2 ounce tropical worsted.[913] The blouse had two breast pocket flaps and two side pocket flaps, all of which were secured by a black wooden button. Wooden buttons were also worn on the shoulder straps.

As late as 1944 documentation exists which discussed changes (which were not implemented) in the WASP uniform. The manner of these changes dealt with ordering new material for the WASP uniform.[914] The only noticeable change or, rather, variation seen on the WASP dress uniform was that some Wasps declined to wear the belt.[915]

Once the Wasps received their uniforms, there seemed to have been many instances of it being worn improperly. Cochran had heard about an

---

[911] Letter from William Taylor, President and General Manager, *Lineas Aereas Mexicanas, S.A.*, to Jacqueline Cochran, June 13, 1944.

[912] Letter of June 29, 1944 from Jacqueline Cochran to William Taylor, President and General Manager, *Lineas Aereas Mexicanas, S.A.*

[913] Erna Risch, *A Wardrobe for Women of the Army: Q.M.C. Historical Studies No. 12*, (Washington, DC: Historical Section, General Administrative Services Division, Office of the Quartermaster General, 1945), p. 150.

[914] Commanding General, Philadelphia Quartermaster Depot, to the Procurement Division, Directive No. 1. P-C-675 (44) (WASP) Misc. Clothing, May 1944.

[915] Conversation with former Wasp, Dorothy Smith Lucas, January 1996.

The Santiago-blue WASP blouse. (Courtesy: Ed Anderson, Jr.)

Jean Babb, class of 43-7, wears the Santiago-blue uniform.

```
                                                      40-9
                                                    8 Pages
                                                     Page 1
AAF REGULATION )              HEADQUARTERS, ARMY AIR FORCES
NO. 40-9       )              WASHINGTON, 14 FEBRUARY 1944
```

PERSONNEL, CIVILIAN

Wearing of the WASP Uniform

1. <u>General</u>. The wearing of the WASP uniform should be a matter of personal pride to all WASP personnel. Uniform clothing, equipment, insignia, and devices are hereby authorized and prescribed for use by WASPs, and WASP personnel are restricted from wearing any other than the regulation uniform, insignia, or devices, or in any way other than hereinafter prescribed. It will be the responsibility of those entrusted with authority to assure compliance with the provisions of this Regulation.

2. <u>Prescribed Uniform</u>:

   a. The WASP dress uniform will consist of the following:

   Jacket
   Skirt
   White shirt
   Black tie
   Beret
   Shoes
   Hose
   Gloves

   (1) The dress jacket and skirt of the uniform should be a matter of pride to every WASP and should be worn at every opportunity. (See exhibit 1.)

   (2) White shirts will be worn for all dress occasions and formal inspections, unless otherwise specified by the commanding officer. (See exhibit 2.) Blue shirts may be worn for operational duty.

   (3) The tie will be tied in a four-in-hand knot placed at the collar opening. (See exhibit 2.) It will be worn at all times for duty at the station to which assigned unless otherwise prescribed by the commanding officer.

   (4) The WASP beret or other appropriate headgear, except flying helmet, will be worn at all ti... except when in a building. It will be worn not more than one inch above the hairline at temples but in no case will it be worn so that an excess of hair appears in front. The insignia will be directly in line with the nose and the blouse of beret tilted to right side toward the back, as shown in exhibit 3. While flying, appropriate headgear for the type of ship being flown (field cap, knitted cap, helmet) will be worn. Headgear need not be worn in transport airplanes. In aircraft with sliding hatch, or in any open airplane, the above-mentioned types of headgear will be worn.

   (5) The service shoe will be worn with slacks at all times and for all formal inspections, whether slacks or skirt is designated, unless otherwise prescribed by the commanding officer. A dress shoe of the following specifications may be worn with skirts on occasions other than formal inspection, if desired:

   Style: Woman's pump or oxford with plain unperforated toe.
   Last: Wall toe.
   Material: ¹Upper - Genuine black calf, or suitable substitute
             leather, that is not shiny.
             Out sole - Six-iron thickness, good quality, vegetable
             tanned sole leather.
             Heel - Shall not be greater than 18/8 (approximately
             2 1/4")

                                                    4-6139,AF

instance where a publicity photographer was to visit the Wasps at Romulus Air Base, Michigan. She immediately sent a letter to Mrs. Esther M. Rathfelder, WASP executive for Operations:

"...A very high percentage of the girls were improperly uniformed, that is, they had no insignia on at all, or they had the insignia on improperly, or were outside without a hat, or had their shirt collars outside the jacket, or had the long jacket on with the slacks. In other words, Public Re-

40-9
8 Pages
Page 2

(6) Hose will be conventional long stockings, inconspicuous, without clocks or decoration of any kind; neutral beige in color; or rayon, silk, or nylon. Hose will be worn with skirt, right side out, with seam straight. Ankle socks will be worn only with exercise clothing, functional clothing, or slacks.

(7) Utility gloves or mittens may be worn with slacks, short jacket, or functional clothing. Dress gloves will be worn with dress uniform and for all formal inspections. The dress glove for summer wear will be of white washable material, buckskin or cotton, plain in design, with no fancy or colored stitching. The length will be not more than two inches beyond the wrist. The cuff will be tucked under the coat sleeve.

(8) Insignia will be worn in accordance with exhibits contained in this Regulation. WASPs will not wear official U.S. Army insignia except with prescribed WASP uniform.

(9) WASP slacks and battle jacket, as well as any functional flying clothing, will be worn for operational duty only and will not be worn for any social occasion. Slacks will not be worn in any public place except when absolutely unavoidable; every effort should be made to avoid wearing these articles into a town, other than for transient purposes. Insignia on battle jacket will be worn as indicated in exhibit 4.

(10) Bag, utility, will be worn on the left side, suspended from the left shoulder except when carrying packages, in which case it may be worn with strap on right shoulder, swung over left hip. It will not be worn for formal inspections. Under no circumstances will articles be carried in the pockets of the dress uniform.

(11) Scarf with overcoat, raincoat, or functional clothing is optional.

(12) Sweaters may be worn under battle jacket or functional clothing, but must not be visible.

(13) Overcoat may be worn with either slacks or dress uniform. It will be as long as the skirt or not more than one inch longer. Belt will not be drawn so tightly as to prevent skirt from hanging evenly. AAF shoulder patch is the only insignia which will be worn on the overcoat.

(14) Raincoat and overshoes may be worn with either dress uniform or slacks when weather conditions make it desirable.

(15) Overcoat, parka type, will be issued only to WASPS in severely cold climates, upon approval of the Commanding General, AAF.

(16) Exercise suit will not be worn except for active exercise.

b. No part of the uniform will be worn with civilian clothing.

c. No pins or other jewelry will be worn exposed upon the uniform by any member of WASP personnel. Bracelets, beads, and earrings will not be worn, and rings must be inconspicuous. Plain, inconspicuous wrist watches or identification bracelets may be worn. No flowers will be worn or carried when in uniform unless expressly approved by the appropriate commanding officer.

d. The uniform to be worn for the season, day, or occasion will be prescribed by the appropriate commanding officer.

3. Wearing of the Uniform. WASP personnel will wear the prescribed uniform at all times, except:

4-6139,AF

lations had to discard practically all of the pictures because the girls were not properly uniformed according to AAF Regulation 40-8. I am simply telling you this because you will be acting squadron leader when ... [the photographer] arrives to take the pictures."[916]

---

[916] Letter from Jacqueline Cochran to Esther M. Rathfelder, WASP Executive for Operations, 552 AAF Base Unit, ATC, New Castle Army Air Base, Wilmington 99, Delaware, June 1, 1944.

40-9
8 Pages
Page 3

a. When on leave in excess of four days spent away from base.

b. When in own home with not more than three guests present in addition to members of family.

c. After duty hours within confines of quarters.

d. When attending mixed social gatherings at which evening or dinner clothes are required, in which case evening or dinner clothes may be worn.

e. When actively engaged in sports, such as tennis, golf, swimming, etc.

f. On other appropriate occasions when prior written permission of the commanding officer and squadron leader has been obtained.

4. **Issue of Clothing and Equipment.** The WASP uniform, insignia, and devices, protective clothing, and equipment which are to be issued in accordance with AAF Regulation 65-23 and will remain the property of the AAF and consist of the following:

Item	Basis of Issue	Item	Basis of Issue
—Bag, duffle	2 ea.	—Jacket, winter, short	2 ea.
—Beret, summer	1 ea.	—Jacket, summer, short	2 ea.
—Beret, winter	1 ea.	Mittens, insert, trigger finger	2 pr.
—Cap, field, blue, poplin	2 ea.	Mittens, shell, trigger finger	1 pr.
Cap, wool, knit	1 ea.	Overshoes, arctic, 4-buckle, women's	1 pr.
—Coverall, work	3 ea.	Overshoes, low, women's	1 pr.
—Distinctive insignia:		—Overcoat, field, trench, WASP	1 ea.
—Shoulder patch, Air Corps (1 for outer garment)	9 ea.	—Overcoat, parka type, WASP	1 ea.
—Beret insignia	1 ea.	Raincoat, WASP	1 ea.
—Lapels, WASP	2 sets	—Slacks, summer	3 pr.
—Lapel wings	2 sets	—Slacks, winter	2 pr.
—Pilot wing	1 ea.	—Skirt, summer	2 ea.
—Flying suits, summer	1 ea.	—Skirt, winter	2 ea.
Flying suits, winter	1 ea.	Socks, wool, ski	3 pr.
Gloves, shell, leather	1 pr.	Sweater, cardigan	1 ea.
Gloves, wool, insert	2 pr.	Suit, exercise, trainee	2 ea.
—Jacket, summer	2 ea.		
—Jacket, winter	2 ea.		

a. The above clothing may be issued to WASP trainees as determined to be required by the commanding officer of the WASP training base. No items which indicate successful completion of flying training will be issued to trainees.

b. In the event of a separation from the organization, each item of clothing and equipment issued will be returned in good condition, less normal wear and tear. Payment will be required for any article of clothing or equipment lost, destroyed, or damaged through carelessness.

5. **Items Available for Purchase.** The following items will be made available for women pilots to be purchased at their own expense, price list covering these items to be made available at a later date:

Item	Basis of Purchase	Item	Basis of Purchase
Anklet, cotton	3 pr.	Shirt, winter	4 ea.
Anklet, wool	3 pr.	—Shirt, dress	3 ea.
—Bag, utility	1 ea.	—Shirt, summer, blue	4 ea.
—Gloves, leather, dress	1 pr.	Shoes, dress, black, low	2 pr.
—Necktie, summer	2 ea.	Stockings, rayon, summer	4 pr.
—Necktie, winter	2 ea.	Underwear, wool	3 suits
Scarf	1 ea.		

4-6139,AF

The beret was designed by John Fredericks and was made of Santiago-blue material. It could be worn with either the blouse or battledress jacket. The beret examined by the author was lined with a purplish-grey material, and exhibited the trademark of the Knox Company of New York in silver leaf.[917]

40-9
8 Pages
Page 4

6. <u>Purchase of Additional Uniforms.</u> A WASP will have the privilege of purchasing uniforms and other items of clothing in addition to those which are issued. A WASP may also purchase regulation material for the purpose of having a uniform made by her own tailor. Clothes made by the women for themselves, made by tailors for them, or received by them from other than official sources will be made from material procured from official sources and will conform in pattern and color to the WASP uniform issued through official sources. The uniform may be fitted by tailors designated for that purpose or by individual or her own tailor. In no event shall the uniform fit so snugly as to cause it to wrinkle. The skirt will be fitted in such a way as to always be free of wrinkles and be long enough to completely cover the knee. The jacket will be buttoned at all times when worn. Under no circumstances will the collar of the shirt be worn outside the jacket, and the shirt will always be tucked inside the skirt or slacks.

  a. WASPs desiring to have shirts made by own tailor may do so, providing fabric for shirt be bleached white, plain weave, closely woven, weighing approximately 4 ounces per square yard. The construction of the fabric will be sufficiently opaque to overcome any tendency for undergarments to be apparent. Style must not deviate from the white shirt, dress, which is available through official channels for purchase.

  b. A Wasp who exercises the privilege of purchasing additional equipment and who at a later date becomes separated from the WASP organization will not be permitted after such separation to wear the following pieces of uniform and insignia purchased by her:
  All headgear
  All insignia and devices
  Jacket
  Short jacket
  Overcoat, field, trench

  c. A WASP at the time of her separation from the organization may sell to another WASP any of the articles purchased by her.

7. <u>Appearance:</u>

  a. Uniforms will be kept scrupulously clean and pressed, with devices and insignia bright and free from tarnish and corrosion.

  b. Neatness and good grooming are of the utmost importance. Slips will not show below the uniform skirt.

  c. The hair will be dressed in such manner as to be no less than 1/2 inch above the collar of the jacket. It must not touch the collar and must be well groomed and neat at all times.

  d. Heavy or conspicuous makeup will not be used.

8. <u>Conduct.</u> WASPs will at all times conduct themselves in a manner befitting the dignity of the uniform. Intoxication or conspicuous and unbecoming conduct will be grounds for immediate dismissal.

By command of General ARNOLD:

BARNEY M. GILES
Major General, United States Army
Chief of Air Staff

OFFICIAL:

THOMAS A. FITZPATRICK
Colonel, AGD
Air Adjutant General

DISTRIBUTION:
"A"

Attachment: 4 Exhibits

4-6139,AF

In May 1944 two approved examples of the WASP beret were sent to the commanding general of the Philadelphia Quartermaster Depot. A

---

917 Beret belonging to former Wasp, Madge Leon Moore, 1995.

letter from Lieutenant Colonel C.D. Garrett dated May 22nd specified that one beret was made for wear in winter while the other, made of tropical worsted material, was for wear in the summer.[918] A packing list from Bolling Field, DC of May 16th stated that one winter and one summer beret were first shipped to Cochran for her approval. Five hundred summer weight berets and five hundred winter weight berets were ordered, ranging in sizes from 21 cm to 23 cm.[919] Five hundred complete uniforms and work clothing were also ordered at this time.

The WASP beret. (Courtesy: Ed Anderson, Jr.)

Interior of the beret, showing the Knox Company trademark. (Courtesy: Ed Anderson, Jr.)

Wasp Dorothy Smith wearing the beret. (Courtesy: Dorothy Ann Smith Lucas)

---

[918] Letter to the Commanding General, PQD, Subject: WASP Clothing items, on behalf of the Quartermaster General, May 22, 1944.

[919] Letter to the commanding general, PQD, Subject: Size Tariff for WASP Clothing, May 15, 1944.

Illustrations from AAF Regulation No. 40-9[920] show both a beret for wear by WASP pilots and another for trainees. The trainee beret was of the same design as the pilot beret, the difference being that the coat of arms of the United States badge was replaced by the gold and silver wing and propeller insigne, like that worn by Army Air Forces cadets on the front of their visored caps. Apparently, this insigne was never actually worn by WASP trainees.

PILOT BERET
(Worn 1 inch above hairline with insignia centered on line with nose)

TRAINEE BERET
(Worn 1 inch above hairline with insignia centered on line with nose)

Cochran informally requested of Colonel Georges F. Doriot, Assistant, Quartermaster Corps, that designs for WASP insignia be drawn up by the Quartermaster.[921] It was important that Colonel Doriot convey to Jacqueline that,

"...the various designs submitted are distinctive and not in conflict with any provision of the National Defense Act pertaining to the wearing of the military uniform."

Doriot went on to say,

"There were also submitted...with your request certain designs which were prepared on existent cap insignia using the official distinguishing symbol of the Coat of Arms of the United States. This office does not recommend the [use of the national arms] for an organization not part of the Army. It does, however, recommend that all symbols adopted for the W.A.S.P. be of distinctive composition."[922]

Despite Doriot's letter, a lead impression of the WASP beret insigne was sent to the Quartermaster General on January 5, 1944.[923] He replied in a letter of January 12, 1944 to the Commanding General of the

---

[920] AAF Regulations, No. 40-9, February 14, 1944.
[921] Memo from Colonel Doriot to Jacqueline Cochran, Army Air Forces, Room 4 D 957, Pentagon Building, Arlington, Virginia, November, November 11, 1943.
[922] Ibid, Subject: Insignia for Women's [sic] Army [sic] Service Pilots.
[923] Registered mail. Subject: Insignia, Caps, WASP, to: The Quartermaster General, Attention: Illegible, Captain Paul E. Walz.

Philadelphia Quartermaster Depot, that the "...sample lead strike of the Insignia, Cap, W.A.S.P. is satisfactory. It is recommended that the die be hardened and this office be furnished twelve samples of the completed insignia...."[924] The Quartermaster General was informed in December 1943 that lead strikes were desired for the "...Insignia, Cap and Collar, WASP."[925]

The finished beret insigne was a smaller gold version of the United States coat of arms. It was secured to the front and center of the WASP beret by a vertical pin.

The obverse and reverse of the beret insigne. (Courtesy: Ed Anderson, Jr.)

The popular battledress jacket was similar in style to the "Ike" jacket of the period, being waist length, and made of Santiago-blue material. It had two patch breast pockets. Though not false pockets, Wasps were not to carry anything in them. Blue plastic buttons were hidden under the front closure flap, as well as under the flaps of the breast pockets. A blue plastic button secured the waist band to itself at the wearer's left side. A blue plastic button was worn at each shoulder strap.

The shoulder straps extended from the shoulder seam of the jacket to the edge of the collar. The portion near the shoulder seam was sewn with the traditional "X" pattern stitching. A distinctive insigne was in the center of each shoulder strap.

The collar was worn open at the top, although it could be closed for cold weather. A gold, clutch-back "W.A.S.P." acronym was worn horizontally on the wearer's right collar flap, while the wing and propeller insigne was affixed horizontally to the left collar flap. (Period photographs show that these insignia were sometimes worn positioned vertically on the collar.)

WASP wings were fastened on the left breast pocket flap or immediately above the upper left pocket flap seam.

The jacket had three darts or pleats just above the waist band, and there were dart or pleats just above each cuff band.

Santiago-blue trousers were worn with the battledress jacket. They were pleated in front and had a zipper on the left side, which is traditional construction for women's trousers. Five cloth belt loops were sewn at even intervals at the waistband of the trousers, which was secured at the top of the zipper by a blue plastic button.

924 Letter from Colonel Doriot to the Commanding General, PQMD, January 12, 1944.
925 Letter from Captain Paul Densen to the Quartermaster General, December 10, 1943.

WASP trousers.
(Courtesy: Dorothy Smith Lucas)

Battledress jacket worn by Wasp Dorothy Ann Smith. Note the post-war addition of the American Campaign and World War II Victory Medal ribbons. (Courtesy: Dorothy Smith Lucas)

The beret or other appropriate headdress (such as the blue flight or utility cap) was worn with the battledress jacket and trousers. This uniform was popular among the Wasps, who often wore it while on ferrying missions.[926]

Imagine the disappointment of the graduating class of December 18, 1943 when Mrs. Cliff Deaton, 318th AAFTED at Sweetwater, Texas received a telegram from Cochran dated December 1, 1943 with the news that it would be impossible to obtain slacks and battle jackets for the class that was to graduate in December.[927]

Photographs show Wasps wearing khaki (or tan) and olive-drab shirtwaists, trousers, ties and overseas caps while on duty. Wasps also wore the blue trousers with the light blue shirtwaist. The black tie was optional. When the shirtwaist was worn without the blouse or battledress jacket, the gold "W.A.S.P." insigne was affixed to the right collar. The wing and propeller insigne was worn on the left collar. Wings were worn above the left breast pocket.[928]

SHIRT (BLOUSE) BLUE OR WHITE
(Insigne worn only when not wearing dress jacket or battle jacket)

Cochran was notified by a letter from Brigadier General M.G. White of the Pentagon that the Wasps had been given permission to wear the shoulder sleeve insigne of the Army Air Forces,[929] the insigne being an ultramarine-blue circular patch with a white star with a red center being flanked on each side by golden-yellow wings. Fifteen of these patches, hand embroidered in gold and silver bullion,[930] were sent via special delivery to the Quartermaster General, Washington, DC, to the attention of a Captain Altenbush from Lieutenant E.A. Kostopoulos, Quartermaster Corps, on January 29, 1944.[931] The letter stated that it was "imperative that these patches be handled in such manner as to reach Miss Jacqueline Cochran by 1300, 16 November 1943...."[932] A sample of uniform fabric of the WASP uniform was submitted to the Philadelphia Quartermaster Department,[933] probably to assure that the colors of the patch matched the San-

Wasp Madge Leon wears the patch of the Army Air Forces on the upper left sleeve of her blouse. (Courtesy: Madge Leon Moore)

---

[926] Conversations with former Wasps, Dorothy Smith Lucas and Madge Leon Moore, 1995.

[927] War Department telegram from Jacqueline Cochran to Mrs. Cliff Deaton, 318th AATED, Avenger Field, Sweetwater, Texas, December 1, 1943.

[928] Army Air Forces Regulation 40-9, p. 6.

[929] Letter from Jacqueline Cochran to Brigadier General M.G. White, November 24, 1943.

[930] Letter from Captain R.R. Walton, War Department, Office of the Quartermaster General, to the commanding general of the Philadelphia Quartermaster Depot, to the attention of Lieutenant Emanuel Kostopoulos, November 13, 1943.

[931] Letter, special delivery, from Research and Development, 400.11, PQRM, January 29, 1944.

[932] Letter from Captain R.R. Walton to Lieutenant Emanuel Kostopoulos, November 13, 1943.

[933] Ibid.

tiago-blue WASP uniform. The sample Army Air Forces patches were delivered by messenger to Cochran on November 16, 1943, "...prior to the hour set by the office."[934] (Despite the issuance of these patches, a period photograph of Wasp Lois E. Brook shows her wearing the dress WASP uniform with a Third Air Force patch sewn to the upper left sleeve of the blouse.[935])*

As late as May 1944 approved samples of the following items were sent to the commanding general of the Quartermaster Depot:

Insignia, Beret   Insignia, Lapel, wings
Insignia, Lapel, WASP   Insignia, Pilot
Insignia, Cap, Cadet,*   Insignia, Shoulder Sleeve, AAF[936]
*(*See also, Beret, Summer, Winter, and Trainee)*

The C.B. Shane Company designed and manufactured the WASP trench coat. It was double-breasted with four pairs of dark plastic buttons. The trench coat was made of neutral gabardine. A cloth belt with a dark, possibly plastic, rectangular buckle, was worn about the waist, secured by cloth belt loops. The blue lining could be removed from the coat. The sleeve had a decorative half-belt near each cuff. The cloth belts were secured at the sleeve edge by a dark plastic button. These belts are thought to have been merely decorative. the Army Air Forces patch was sewn to the upper left sleeve of the trench coat.

*Wasps were allowed to wear the patch of the unit they were assigned to. Brook's last posting was at Camp Davis AAF, North Carolina, under command of the Third Air Force.

This trench coat was produced under the "Season Skipper" brand name. Also shown is the shell liner tag.

WASP double-breasted trench coat. (Courtesy: Ed Anderson, Jr.)

---

[934] Message from Lieutenant E. A. Kostopoulus for the commanding general, November 6, 1943.

[935] Scharr, *Sisters in the Sky*, Vol. II, p. 563.

[936] Letter from Lieutenant C.D. Garrett to the commanding general, Philadelphia Quartermaster Depot, May 3, 1944.

Hannes Schneider Sports Company produced a parka-style trench coat in limited quantities for wear by Wasps serving in very cold climates.[937]

This Santiago-blue, parka-style trench coat was lined and considered excellent for high altitude flight. It was issued to Joanne Trebtoske, 43/4, in the fall of 1944. (Courtesy: Ed Anderson, Jr.)

Cardigan sweaters were issued to Wasps from existing stocks and were dyed blue to match the WASP uniform.

A cotton uniform dress was under consideration of being changed to a seersucker-like material. It would be less expensive and better looking than the dress worn previously, and probably, in very limited quantities. Star-Maid Dresses of New York City sent a cotton dress, size twelve to Cochran.

"At Major Klein's request, this dress was especially made in our sample room."[938] Star-Maid then offered to make any necessary alterations.

---

[937] Risch, *A Wardrobe for Women of the Army, Historical Studies No. 12*, p. 151

[938] Letter from Henry Silverstein of Star-Maid Dresses, New York, New York, to Jacqueline Cochran, June 30, 1944.

Eight Wasps stationed at Newcastle Army Air Base were shown the new dress, which they liked. A request was made that the skirt be given a little more flare and be made of cotton twill or summer weight chambray.[939] On July 1, 1943 Colonel H.R.W. Herwig was notified that the dress prototype submitted by Star-Maid via Major Klein had been approved and that 3,200 units had been ordered. In the summer of 1943, a dress (and beret) made of light-weight, blue-striped material, was obtained in limited quantities for WASP, mainly those who were stationed in the deep southern United States.[940]

It was decided that the following items of clothing be issued to Wasps, depending on their training status, when they arrived at Avenger Field:[941]

Olive-drab coveralls with a cloth belt and with or without patch pockets, waist and leg pockets. The cloth belt had a metal rectangular buckle;
Field cap;
Exercise suit;
Rain coat;
High or low overshoes, depending on the season;
Fifinella shoulder patch;
Gloves or mittens to be worn while flying;
Knit cap;
Cardigan;
Gloves or mittens for formations;
Ski socks.**[942]
**The last three items were issued during the cold weather season.

After a probationary period of two weeks, the following uniform items were issued to trainees. The weight of the material depended on the season:
Santiago-blue battledress jacket;
Skirt;
Beret;
Trench Coat;
Necessary insignia.[943]
Slacks were issued after the primary phase of training had been completed. In the interim, the trainees had to provide their own clothing.

---

[939] Letter from Esther M. Rathfelder, WASP Executive for Operations, 2nd Ferrying Group (552 AAF Base Unit), Ferrying Division/ATC, Newcastle Army Air Base, Wilmington 99, Delaware, to Jacqueline Cochran, Headquarters, WASP, Pentagon Building, Washington, DC, no date. Subject: Summer uniform dress for WASP.

[940] Risch, *A Wardrobe for Women of the Army, Historical Studies No. 12*, p. 154.

[941] Letter, special delivery, from Research and Development, 400.1141, PRQM, January 29, 1944.

[942] Risch, *Wardrobe*, pp. 151-154.

[943] Letter from Mrs. Cliff Deaton, Chief Establishment Officer, Headquarters, 318th Army Airforces [sic] Training Detachment, to Jacqueline Cochran, no date.

It was mandatory that Wasps purchase their own shoes and anklets and, after the probationary period, the following:
Work, (khaki) and dress (white) shirts;
Black ties;
Stockings;
Gloves;
Black utility bag;
Scarf.[944]

Photographs show Wasps also wearing an olive-drab uniform, consisting of trousers, shirt and overseas cap with officer's gold and black piping. The tie could either be of olive-drab or tan.

These Wasps wear olive-drab shirts, trousers and tan ties.

As late as 1944 prototype uniforms were being submitted to Cochran. The Hannes Schneider company of New York shipped one navy-blue jacket, size 16, and one Aspen blue jacket, size 14, in late January.

The WASP suit, or coveralls, were designed by Federeic J. Dormer, and were of the conventional one-piece style with a drop seat. Patch pockets were sewn below the knee of the coveralls, and two patch pockets were sewn at the waist.[945] In addition, Hannes Schneider sent two prototype "two-piece, intermediate pile-lined flying suits."[946] Initially, the Wasps were issued Army Air Forces flight suits, which were notoriously oversized. The Wasps referred to them as "Zoot Suits."[947]

In October 1943 the company of Deitsch, Wersba & Cobbola, Inc., of New York City, sent what was described as "experimental clothing" in

---

[944] Ibid.
[945] Risch, *Wardrobe*, p. 154.
[946] Letter from Hannes Schneider Company to Jacqueline Cochran, January 22, 1944.
[947] Conversation with former Wasps Madge Leon Moore, 1995 and Yvonne Wood, 1998.

Santiago-blue, one-piece flight suit with drop seat. (Courtesy: Ed Anderson, Jr.)

WASP trainees Helen Dettweiler, Florence Anageros and Dale Dailey studying radial aircraft engines. They are wearing the olive-drab coveralls with cloth belt.

the form of "WASP Uniforms." Exactly which uniforms were shipped could not be determined from the order.[948]

Wasps were issued standard Army Air Forces goatskin A-2 jackets, fleece-lined leather pants and fleece-lined leather B-3 jackets and other pieces of standard flight equipment. A leather name tag was sometimes worn on the left breast of the fleece-lined jacket. A round cloth or leather patch with the figure of Fifinella, the "good" little gremlin and WASP mascot, was stitched to the left breast of the A-2 jacket, below the name tag.

These Wasps wear the leather A-2 jacket with the Fifinella patch sewn to the left side. The Wasp, second from left, wears a B-3 jacket. (Courtesy: Smithsonian Institution)

Maggie Callahan and Jean C. Parker (far right)) wear the A-2 leather jacket with leather Fifinella patch.

---

[948] Army Service Forces, Philadelphia Quartermaster Depot, 2800 South 20th Street, Philadelphia 45, PA. From: W.E. Gibbs, Lieutenant, QMC.

Detail of the embroidered Fifinella patch. (Courtesy: Betty Williamson Shipley)

A-2 jacket worn by Betty Williamson Shipley. It was given to her by her husband, F.M. Shipley. (Courtesy: Betty Williamson Shipley)

Specification tag in the neck of the jacket. (Courtesy: Betty Williamson Shipley)

An example of a hand-painted leather Fifinella patch worn by Rene Nielson (43-3). (Courtesy: Ed Anderson, Jr.)

Rene Nielson's (44/3) A-2 jacket with a leather patch. (Courtesy: Ed Anderson, Jr.)

Pat Gibson's A-2 (44-4) leather jacket with leather name tag and embroidered patch. (Courtesy: Ed Anderson,)

Left: Williamson was in 44-6. It is not known why she was wearing the 319th patch which is associated with only the 43/1 & 2 classes.

Assorted leather jacket patches. (Courtesy: Ed Anderson, Jr.)

Gayle Snell. (44-9).

Nancy Featherhoff (43-6).

Della Gremling. (44-4).

By April 18, 1944 the Procurement Division, Clothing Branch, had not received approved samples of such items as rayon stockings, dress black shoes and the utility bag, which had been authorized for procurement from ASF on April 18, 1944.[949] Three days later the Military Planning Division, Research & Development Branch sent the following reply to the Procurement Division:

---

[949] Letter, special delivery from Research and Development, PQMD, 400.1141 PQRM, January 29, 1944.

B-16, Jacket, Flying, Intermediate WASP.
(Courtesy: Ed Anderson, Jr.)

A-12 Trousers, Flying, Intermediate WASP. (Courtesy: Ed Anderson, Jr.)

"1. In reference to attached memorandum from your division dated 22. May 1944, the following information is furnished:

    a. 2 [sic] pairs, Stockings, Rayon, Summer, WASP are being sent to your division this date.

    b. 2 [sic] Bags, Utility, WASP, are also being sent to you this date. These bags represent the design, color, etc., however the leather is to have a [crack] resistant finish.

    c. As for Shoes, Dress, Black, the Office of the Director of Women Pilots has disapproved the present shoe and has requested that a study be made to develop a more satisfactory shoe. Samples cannot be furnished to you until approval is received from the Director of Women Pilots."[950]

The low cut, black dress shoes proved to be of poor quality. Colonel H.R.W. Herwig of the Quartermaster Corps, Air Quartermaster, suggested that further study be devoted to finding appropriate footwear for the WASP.

Through a friend of Cochran's, Harold Volk of Volk Brothers Company in Dallas, the British shoe manufacturer, Walker, rushed a sample pair of shoes to her to inspect. these had the cross-over strap, and were referred to as the "monk type."[951] This shoe had a light weight sole, which Mr. Volk assured Cochran could be made heavier if she wished.

Instead of sending two pairs of shoes to be worn by two models, oddly enough, he sent "...two samples—one for the right foot and one for the left foot so that your model can wear them at the same time for comparison."

The other shoe was made of brown unlined bucko leather, and was sold under the label of "British Walkers." Volk Brothers carried this shoe in black calfskin with a slightly higher heel.

The problem with the monk-type shoe was that it was not usually carried in the inventories of most retailers, and had to specially manufactured after obtaining permission from the War Production Board via Mr. Lawrence Sheppard, who was the director of the Leather Shoe Branch.[952]

The advantage of the unlined shoe was that Volk Brothers kept it in stock, therefore it could be readily available for the Wasps. Of the two shoes submitted to her, Cochran liked the monk-type. Since these would primarily be used as dress shoes there was no need to have them made with heavier soles. The shoes were to be sent to the office of the Quartermaster General for final approval.

In her letter, Cochran amusingly remarked, "The only complaint I have is that I don't know where we can find a model who can fit into a size four shoe! Don't you know that Washington girls have big feet?"[953]

The shoes were officially rejected by the Office of the Director of Women Pilots. At this time [May 26, 1944], samples could not yet be sent to the Procurement Division without Cochran's approval.[954] A memorandum from the Air Quartermaster in Washington requested he be provided with reasons why the low, black shoe wasn't satisfactory for the WASP.[955]

---

[950] Letter from Captain R.R. Walton, War Department, Office of the Quartermaster General, to the commanding general of the Philadelphia Quartermaster Depot, to the attention of Lieutenant Emanuel Kostopoulos, November 13, 1943.
[951] Letter from Harold Volk to Jacqueline Cochran, August 1, 1943.
[952] Ibid, pp. 1-2.
[953] Letter from Jacqueline Cochran to Harold Volk, August 20, 1943.
[954] War Department Transmittal Sheet, Army Service Forces, from the Quartermaster General, to the Procurement Division, Clothing Branch, Regarding WASP Clothing.
[955] Ibid.

Cochran finally approved a shoe pattern, called "Shank's mare," but it was never ordered for the WASP.[956] They wore instead a low-top, black leather shoes with the battledress jacket and trousers, but a black oxford (pump) was worn with the dress blouse and skirt.[957]

Wasps wore standard neutral colored hosiery, made of rayon, silk or nylon.[958]

The black leather utility bag was rectangular in shape and had a shoulder strap. It was worn from the left shoulder and was not to be carried at formal occasions.

The proposed WASP summer uniform and black utility bag.

Black leather WASP utility bag with round closing clasp. (Courtesy: Ed Anderson, Jr.)

A month before the official establishment of the WASP, Lieutenant Colonel W. Randolph Lovelace, II, acting chief of Aero Medical Laboratory for the Army Medical Corps, a winner of the Collier Trophy for his research into the effects of altitude on pilots, sent two anthropologists to Sweetwater to measure the trainees so that goggles, flying helmets and masks could be properly designed for the women.[959] New information which would assist in the design of better bail-out oxygen equipment was gleaned from Colonel Lovelace's WASP study.[960]

It appears that goggles were procured for the Wasps through channels a Wright Field, Ohio. Cochran had been trying to get supplies of gog-

---

[956] Erna Risch, *A Wardrobe for Women of the Army: Q.M.C. Historical Studies No. 12*, (Washington, DC: Historical Section, General Administrative Services Division, Office of the Quartermaster General, 1945), p. 153.
[957] AFFREG, No. 40-9, p. 1.
[958] Ibid.
[959] Letter from Lieutenant Colonel W. Randolph Lovelace, II, Medical Corps, Acting Chief, Aeromedical Laboratory, July 8, 1943.
[960] Ibid.

gles for three months with no results.⁹⁶¹ The Quartermaster's office approved the purchase of Ray-Ban goggles from the Bausch and Lomb Optical Company, but they refused to sell the goggles to the WASP, since they felt the organization "...was not a qualified government agency."⁹⁶²

Five hundred black wooden buttons, mounted on cards just as commercial ones are, were ordered to be sold to the Wasps. Coming up with the buttons proved to be of no consequence, but only two hundred blue plastic rectangular buckles for wear on the Santiago-blue cloth belt could be procured at that time.⁹⁶³

The sizes of the buttons worn on the dress blouse were: Three buttons, 34 ligne, and six buttons, 30 ligne.⁹⁶⁴ Five hundred sets of extra buckles and buttons were procured in 1944 to be sold as replacements were needed.⁹⁶⁵

The design of a light-weight, summer WASP hat had not been approved as of July 1, 1944. The field cap was a short visored, "baseball"-style cap and was favored by Wasps for wear with the battledress jacket and

Betty J. (Hanson) Erenberg and Shirley Haugan wear the battledress jacket and trousers with the blue utility cap. (Courtesy: Smithsonian Institution)

---

⁹⁶¹ Letter from Nora T. McSweeny to Mrs. Cliff Deaton, April 27, 1944.
⁹⁶² Interdepartmental memo from H. R. Shaffer to Mrs. Cliff Deaton, February 12, 1944.
⁹⁶³ Memo from Lieutenant Colonel C.D. Garret, the War Department. Subject: Buttons and Buckles for WASP Uniforms, May 15, 1944.
⁹⁶⁴ Memo from Colonel H.R.W. Herwig, QMC, Air Quartermaster, Office/Assistant Chief of Air Staff to Quartermaster General, Headquarters, Army Air Forces, May 12, 1944.
⁹⁶⁵ Memo from Lieutenant Colonel C.D. Garrett to the War Department, A SW, OQMG, Washington, DC, Subject: Buttons and Buckles for WASP Uniforms, May 15, 1944.

Santiago-blue flight and/or utility cap made by Knox of New York. Note it has folding ear flaps for colder conditions. (Courtesy: Ed Anderson, Jr.)

trousers. Some Wasps pinned the small Fifinella emblem on the front of the cap.[966]

The much disliked turban was worn with the athletic suit or coveralls. When the Wasps were told they would no longer be required to wear the turban, they built a bonfire and burned them.[967]

In 1944, Miss Billy Russy of Knox Hats sent two examples of garrison caps to Cochran for her consideration.[968] Cochran liked the samples that Knox had provided and she further requested that an example of the cap similar to that worn by members of the Red Cross be submitted to her.[969] But, a garrison cap was never produced for the WASP. Period photos do show Wasps wearing the army officer's garrison cap with gold and black piping with the wing and propeller insigne pinned to the left side flap.

A round white patch with the blue border encircling a blue wasp exists. "W.A.S.P." is embroidered in yellow thread. This patch has been attributed to the Women Airforce Service Pilots, but a period newspaper article and photo shows members of a civilian volunteer group, also known as "Wasps," wearing a piped garrison cap with this style of patch sewn to the left curtain of the cap. (see "Women's Ambulance Safety Patrol," p. 304)[970]

---

[966] Conversation with former Wasps, Dorothy Smith Lucas and Madge Leon Moore, 1995.

[967] Vera S. Williams, WASPs: Women Airforce Service Pilots of World War II, (Osceola, Wisconsin: Motorbooks International, 1994), p. 23.

[968] Letter from Billy Russy of Knox Hats to Jacqueline Cochran.

[969] Letter from Billy Russy of Knox Hats to Jacqueline Cochran, 1944.

[970] Document, George Petersen.

A pair of collar insignia using the initials W.A.S.P. were designed to be worn on the collars of WASP uniforms. The initial strike of the insigne disclosed that, "...the period after the letter "P" is too large and should be changed to conform more nearly to the size of the other periods. Furthermore, if the letters are examined under a magnifying glass, it will be noted that the edges of some of the letters, particularly in the case of the letter "S," are rough and should be smoothed out before hardening."[971]

The finished product was a gold, clutch-back W.A.S.P. insigne which was worn in pairs on the collar of the four-pocket dress blouse.

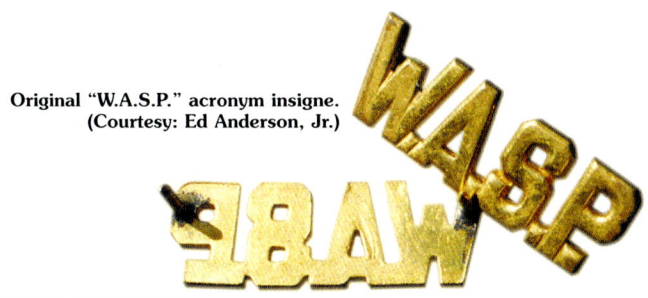

Original "W.A.S.P." acronym insigne.
(Courtesy: Ed Anderson, Jr.)

Insignia belonging to Wasp Betty Williamson Shipley. (Courtesy: Betty Williamson Shipley)

The wing and propeller insigne was of the same style as that worn by officers and cadets of the Army Air Corps/Army Air Forces, consisting of a silver propeller superimposed on a pair of horizontal gold wings. These insignia were worn in pairs on the lapels of the four-pocket dress blouse. Only one WASP insigne was worn on the right collar of the battledress jacket, while the wing and propeller insigne was worn on the left collar. Insignia were likewise worn on shirt collars when worn without the blouse or jacket.

On November 18, 1944, the Heraldic Section of the Office of the Quartermaster General received an urgent order for the manufacturing of one thousand W.A.S.P. service pins, which were to be worn on civilian

---

[971] Letter from Colonel Doriot, January 5, 1944.

clothing.⁹⁷² These new pins were to be a half inch in diameter. The letter included the design of the new pin, and mentioned that the "...center be made of blue enamel, the wings of silver, the letters WASP in silver, and the circle (or outer rim) be made of a yellow gold colored metal, with the United States Army Air Forces in suitable blue lettering." [sic] General Arnold gave approval to the new pin.

One has to question why a new pin was ordered when the WASP was very soon to be demobilized.⁹⁷³ Perhaps it was believed that Congress would pass the bill militarizing the WASP. The former may have been closer to the truth, since a transmittal sheet stated "...Inasmuch as the Air Forces desired that 1,000 of these pins be made available by 20 December 1944 [sic], it is requested that this matter be expedited."⁹⁷⁴ The use of the words, "United States Army Air Forces" was quickly challenged, since the Wasps were still civil servants.⁹⁷⁵ On the same day Colonel Doriot sent a letter to the commanding general of the Philadelphia Quartermaster Depot, describing in detail the new pin: ".....Attention is invited to enclosed design of a lapel pin which it is desired be manufactured with a ball-shaped safety pin and catch. The entire design is to be made 1/2" diameter, silver base metal, with the impression of the WASP Aviation Badge impressed below the enameled surface. The letters W.A.S.P. are to be in silver while the designation 'United States Army Air Forces' is to be in blue enamel as well as the circular section of the lapel pin."⁹⁷⁶

WASP service lapel pin. The design of this silver and blue enameled pin was approved by order of the Secretary of War on November 20, 1944. On December 18, 1,000 of these 1/2-inch diameter pins were delivered to the AAF Headquarters for distribution to the Wasps on December 20, 1944.

Not only did Doriot request one thousand of these pins be delivered to USAAF headquarters by December 18th, he furthermore stated that Air Force funds would pay for the pins. Doriot requested that two lead strikes be furnished to his office for approval. He added that, "this pin was approved by order of the Secretary of War, this date [November 20, 1944]."⁹⁷⁷

The original drawing was to be returned to Doriot's office. He requested six of the lapel pins be furnished to his office, in addition to the one thousand ordered.⁹⁷⁸ Eight days later Doriot sent a letter to the War Department, requesting he be advised of the status of the new pins.⁹⁷⁹ The Research and Development Division of the Quartermaster Depot informed the Quartermaster General on December 1, 1944 that the American Insignia Company of New York had been contracted to produce the pins. "Production of die has been completed and delivery of the completed order

(1,010) at the Depot on or before 14. December 1944 has been promised."[980] Four strikes of the new service pin were sent special delivery to the Heraldic Section of the Quartermaster Corps by Captain Walz on December 7, 1944. A thousand of these new pins were delivered by Colonel Hopping to Colonel Van der Lutz on December 16, 1944. Seven

> **WAR DEPARTMENT**
> HEADQUARTERS OF THE ARMY AIR FORCES
> WASHINGTON
>
> FEB 1 0 1945
>
> Miss Laurine Y. Nielsen
> 303 East Main Street
> Klamath Falls, Oregon
>
> Dear Miss Nielsen:-
>
> It is a pleasure to send you with this letter the Certificate of Honorable Service and Service Pin earned by you as a member of the WASP.
>
> May I take this opportunity to thank you for the fine contribution you have made to the WASP organization, to the Army Air Forces and to the war effort. I have considered it a great privilege to be associated with such a fine group of girls, and an honor to have been Director of the WASP.
>
> Hearty good wishes to you for the future.
>
> Sincerely,
>
> JACQUELINE COCHRAN
>
>
>
> 2 Incls
> cbf
> pin

Transmittal letter signed by Jacqueline Cochran with a WASP service pin. (Courtesy: Ed Anderson, Jr.)

---

[972] Letter from W.R. McReynolds, Brigadier General, U.S.A., Air Quartermaster, to Arthur E. Dubois, Office of the Quartermaster General, Heraldic Section.
[973] Letter of November 18, 1944 from Colonel William F. [Illegible].
[974] Transmittal Sheet, Assistant Chief of Statt, G-1, from Colonel C.C. Hixon, General Staff Corps and Major C.S. Alston, November 20, 1944.
[975] Letter from Colonel Doriot to Military Personnel Division, Army Service Forces, Washington, DC, November 20, 1944.
[976] Ibid.
[977] Ibid.
[978] Army Service Forces, Immediate Action, Office of the Quartermaster General, Washington, DC, from Colonel Georges F. Doriot, QMC, to: Commanding General, PQMD. Subject: Service Pin for WASP Personnel, November 20, 1944.
[979] War Department, November 28, 1944.
[980] Letter from Captain Paul E. Walz.

of the pins were filed away in the Heraldic Section of the OQMG.[981] A notation of January 1, 1945 read, "Drawing, Wasp pin removed to Heraldic file."[982]

For a fee of $1.00 Walt Disney gave license to the WASP to wear his charactature of the "good" little gremlin named Fifinella. She was often referred to by the Wasps as "Fifi." A "good" gremlin was supposed to protect the Wasps from the "bad" gremlins. These "bad" gremlins were first noted by RAF pilots who told tales of gremlins causing problems with their aircraft. Gremlins were defined as "...mythical rogues of the air," and "...[imps] of bad luck to whom disasters are attributed in the roaring kingdom of the war-time sky." According to pilot lore, "only pilots and navigators and air gunners and people who fly can see those things."[983] The official image of Fifinella was described in the license as: "A design of Fifinella wearing goggles and wings, jumping into space."[984]

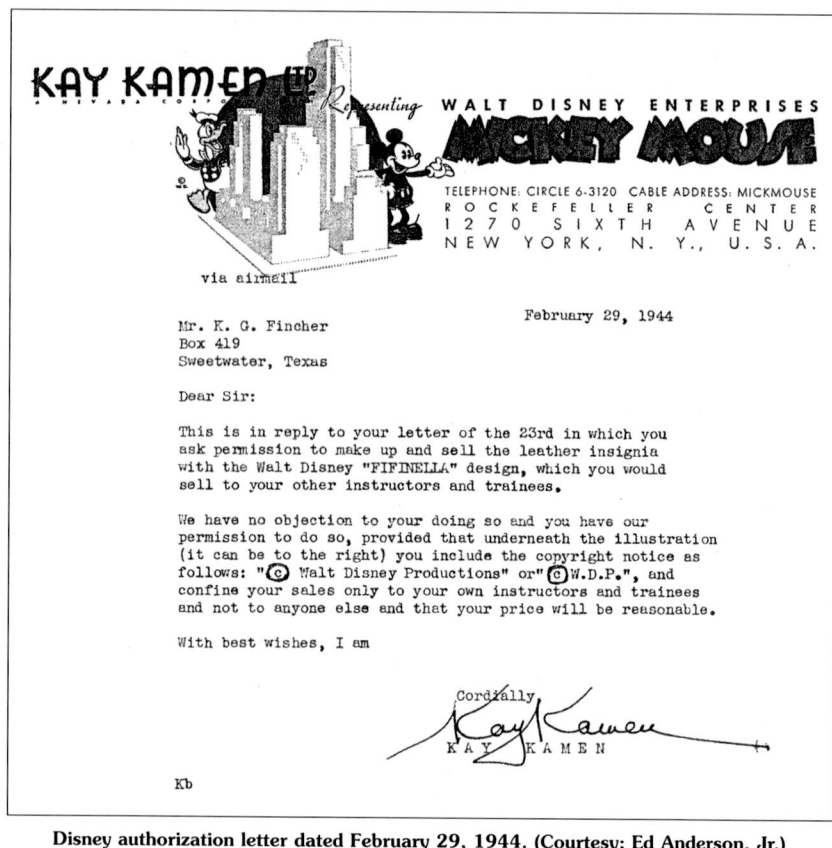

Disney authorization letter dated February 29, 1944. (Courtesy: Ed Anderson, Jr.)

---

[981] Ibid, December 15, 1944.

[982] Message from Lieutenant E.A. Kostopoulus, November, 6, 1943.

[983] Walton Rawls, *Disney dons Dogtags. The Best of Disney Military Insignia from World War II,* (New York: The Abbeville Publishing Group, 1992) p. 29.

[984] License from Walt Disney Productions, January 12, 1944.

A prototype of the Fifinella shoulder patch was sent to the Commanding General, Army Service Forces, in January 1944. Twelve thousand Fifinella patches were ordered by Colonel William F. McKee.[985] The resulting patch was an ultramarine-blue circle with a full color, machine-embroidered figure of Fifinella. The image of Fifinella was worn on patches made of cloth or leather on the leather flight jacket, and while this ultramarine-blue Fifinella patch was possibly issued, it was never worn by the Wasps.

Fifinella patch with requested "©W.D.P." copyright noted. (Courtesy: Ed Anderson, Jr.)

Machine-embroidered Fifinella patch on a ultramarine-blue circle. (Courtesy: Ed Anderson, Jr.)

Two variations of the patch for 318th AAFFTD (Army Air Forces Flying Training Detachment.) The patch at left has a red background and the one below has a smaller red circle on a white background. (Courtesy: Ed Anderson, Jr.)

[985] Letter from Colonel McKee, January 19, 1944.

As on the previous page, but for the 319th AAFFTD. Both patches have been observed in period photos on shirt sleeves and scarfs. (Courtesy: Smithsonian Air and Space Museum)

Fifinella patch with a dark blue wool background. (Courtesy: Ed Anderson, Jr.)

Unknown class.

Fifinella, the "good little gremlin" designed for the WASP by Walt Disney. This is a luggage sticker. (Courtesy: Institute of Texan Cultures, San Antonio, TX)

Perhaps naively the Wasps in the first class thought that since they had been through all the cadet flight school courses that they would be awarded regular army air force pilot's wings. The commanding general of the Gulf Coast Training Center sent word that wings would only be awarded to military pilots. "Graduates will not receive any wings."[986]

The first graduating class of twenty-three Wasps did not have the Santiago-blue uniform, and turned out for the ceremonies at Ellington Field

---

[986] Granger, *On Final Approach*, p. 112.

at Houston, Texas in 1943[987] wearing white shirts, khaki trousers with khaki web belts, and khaki garrison caps. It had become evident that the wings Cochran had ordered would not be ready on time for graduation. She hurriedly purchased twenty-three pairs of standard pilot's wings and had the shield in the center cut down and covered with a shield bearing the designation, "W 1" and "319th" on a scroll above. (Cochran personally paid for all the wings for the classes of 43-1 through 43-7). Five types of variations of this design were awarded to the classes of 43-1 through 43-7.[988] These wings had the hinged pin and roll catch fastener. Several variations of this design of class wings exist. A unique pair of bullion class wings embroidered upon a brownish cloth backing were observed in a private collection during this research, but their origin is unknown.

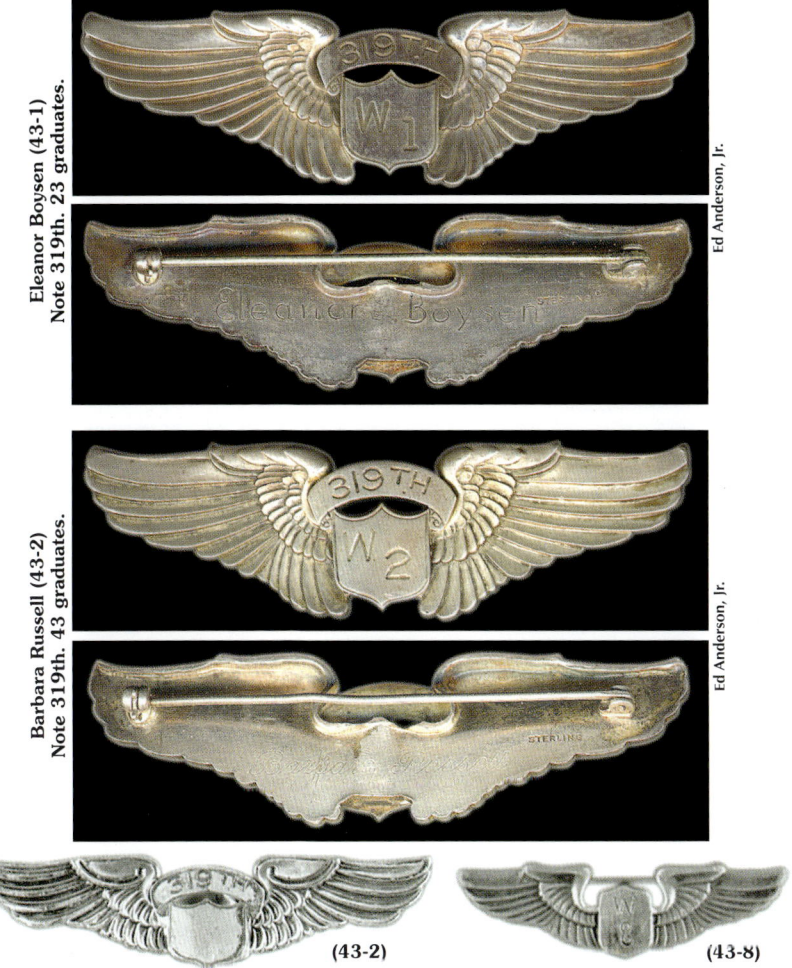

(43-2) (43-8)

Miniature WASP wings. The one at left belonged to Carol C. Filmore and the one at right belonged to Jocelyn Moore. (Courtesy: Ed Anderson, Jr.)

---

[987] Scharr, *Sisters in the Sky*, Vol. 1, p. 422.
[988] Granger, *On Final Approach*, plate A-67/C-A, 69/C.

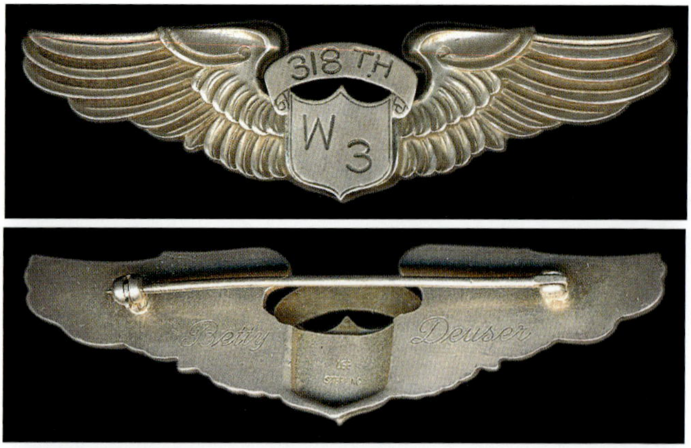

Ed Anderson, Jr.

Betty Deuser (43-3)
Note 318th. 112 graduates.

Ed Anderson, Jr.

Helen Calhoun (43-4)
Note 318th. 38 graduates.

Wasp Constance Liewellyn wears a class wing presented to her after graduating at Liberty Field, Camp Stewart, Georgia.

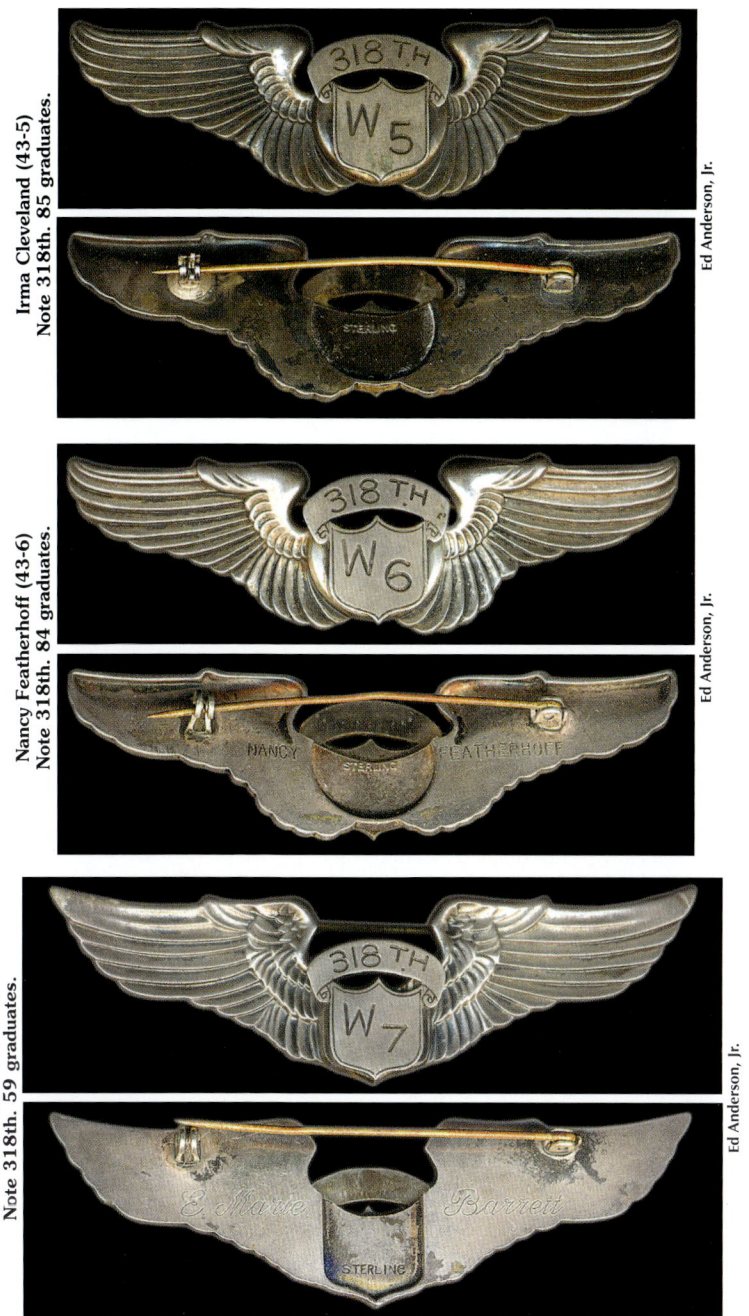

Mary Lou Colbert (later, Neale) was presented her wings by her father, Rear Admiral L.C. Colbert, at her 1943 graduation.[989] She holds the distinction of being the first woman to join the WASP.[990]

---

[989] Letter from former Wasp, Mary Lou Colbert Neale, February 1, 1994.
[990] Letter of March 31, 1977 from Mary Lou Colbert Neale.

Wasp Mary Lou Colbert receives her wings from her father, Rear Admiral L.C. Colbert, Director of the Coast and Geodetic Survey, as Jacqueline Cochran looks on. Colbert was in the first class of WASP trainees to graduate, 1943. (Courtesy: Mary Lou Colbert Neale)

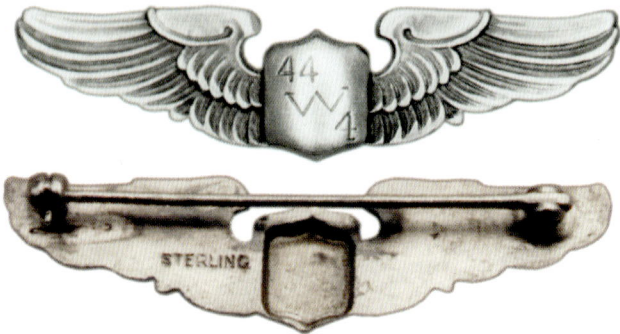

Madge Leon's wings, awarded to the WASP class of 44-4. (Courtesy: Madge Leon Moore)

Ten drawings of the WASP wings designed by the Quartermaster Corps were submitted to the commanding general of the Quartermaster Depot by Colonel Doriot in December 1943.[991] Doriot requested that a lead strike of the new wings be sent to his office for approval prior to hardening the die. Doriot's office was not pleased with the resulting strike; it did not conform to the submitted drawing.

> "The wings have not been correctly spaced and several portions of the strike are not in conformity with the design; also the diamond is set too far forward. It is requested that corrections be made so that the badge will be in conformity with the design as shown on the drawing, and that a new lead strike be furnished this office. Care should be exercised to see that the strikes submitted to this office are not bent as the designs are liable to be distorted and difficult to check."[992]

A new lead strike was submitted to Colonel Doriot in January 1944. It was "...satisfactory with the exception that the portions of the wing indi-

---

[991] Ibid, December 2, 1943.
[992] Letter from Colonel Doriot to the Commanding General, PQMD, December 7, 1943.

cated on the enclosed drawing should be modeled more smoothly instead of so pronounced."[993] It was specified that the wings would be "...unnumbered and undated...."[994]

The second style WASP wings featured the heraldic form of shield for women, i.e., a lozenge. The class of 43-8 of December 17, 1943 was the first to be in line to be awarded the new wings, which did not arrive on time. A supply of AMICO wings was found. To make the lozenge shaped shield in the center, the center shield of the pilot's wings was partially removed and the new WASP lozenge was superimposed upon it.[995] A design for the WASP wings was presented to Colonel Doriot. He stated that a sketch of pilot's wings, which was, "...the silhouette of the Air Corps Aviation [badge] with the addition of a lozenge in the center.... This office does not recommend the addition of these...symbols for an organization [which is] not a part of the Army. It does, however, recommend that all symbols adopted for the WASP be of distinctive composition."[996]

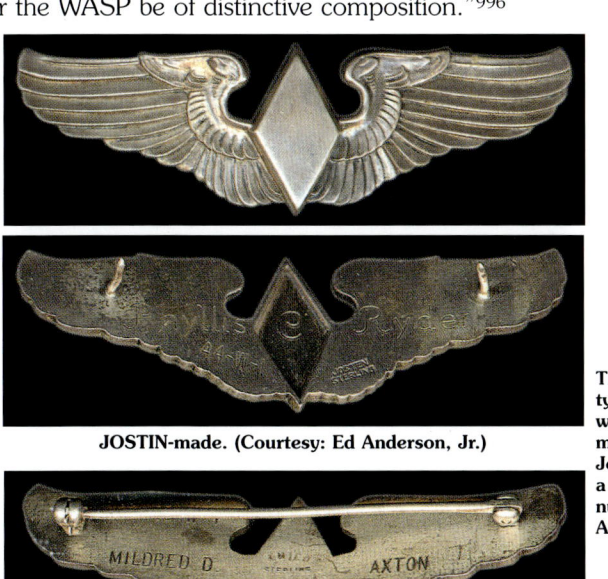

JOSTIN-made. (Courtesy: Ed Anderson, Jr.)

AMICO-made. (Courtesy: Ed Anderson, Jr.)

The majority of WASP wings was made by Josten, and a small number by Amico.

On April 11, 1944, a check in the amount of $5.28 was issued to the base quartermaster at Bolling Field, DC, from Cecelia Edwards as payment for six pairs of WASP wings. One pair was shipped directly to Carol Webb, WASP, Staff Pilot, Randolph Field, Texas. The remaining five pairs

---

[993] Ibid, January 5, 1944.
[994] Synopsis, from the Quartermaster General to the Commanding General, QMD, PA, January 20, 1944.
[995] Granger, *On Final Approach,* plate A-69-C.
[996] Memo from Colonel Doriot, November 11, 1943.

The recipient of this JOSTIN-made wing had the clutch posts removed and a standard pin and roll catch attached. (Courtesy: Ed Anderson, Jr.)

of wings were sent to Jacqueline Cochran at Room 3D-1045 at the Pentagon.[997]

A directive from the office of the quartermaster general assured that "supply will not be effected [sic] of the WASP wings requested on the enclosed order form the 33rd Ferrying Group Exchange, Fairfax Field, Kansas...."[998]

The second pattern WASP wings were secured to clothing with two barbs and corresponding clutches or a straight pin and roll catch, proven by a memo of December 1, 1944 from the Office of the Quartermaster General, requesting that it be provided with wings which had a pin on a hinge and roll catch fastening device.[999] The existence of pin-back WASP wings is borne out by examples in the possession of former Wasps.

Mary Lou Colbert Neale wears the second pattern WASP wings. (Courtesy: Mary Lou Colbert Neale)

[997] Letter from Cecelia Edward to Private Ross, c/o Base Quartermaster, Bolling Field, DC, April 11, 1944.

[998] Index sheet from Air Service Forces, Office of the Quartermaster General, Philadelphia Quartermaster Depot, May 6, 1944.

[999] Ibid.

Miscellaneous WASP-Related Items
All items in this section are courtesy of Ed Anderson, Jr.

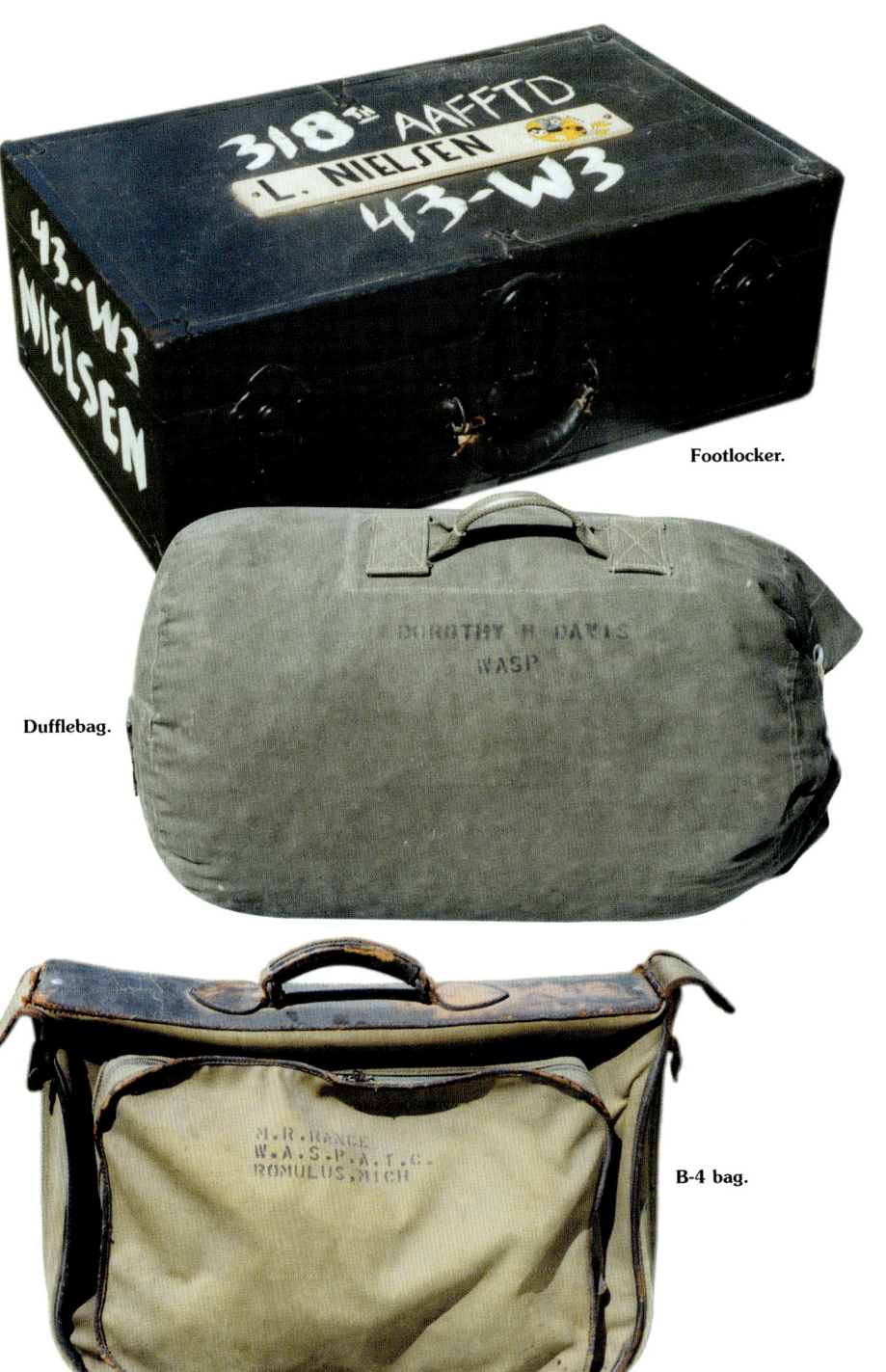

Footlocker.

Dufflebag.

B-4 bag.

This clipboard was strapped to the leg for note-taking while in flight. It was made at Avenger Field and was smaller for Wasps.

Air Transport Command identification badges (6th Ferrying Command at Long Beach, California) similar to those worn by Wasps and other personnel.

1. Identification tags will be worn by WASPs at all times. They may be temporarily removed only as the necessity of personal hygiene may require. These tags will be worn suspended from the neck, underneath the clothing, so that neither the cord nor the tags will be visible. The tags will be made up as follows:

    (1) First line - name of wearer.

    (2) Second line - CAA license number, record of Tetanus immunization and blood type.

    (3) Third and fourth lines blank.

    (4) Fifth line - the letters WASP and letter indicating religion of wearer.

    (5) Example:

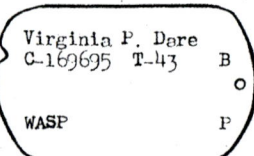

Identification tag variations.

Evelyn Trammell's bracelet presented to her upon soloing on August 22, 1940.

Irma Cleveland's identification crash bracelet and tag. The reverse is engraved "Skies Full of Happiness."

Dottie Davis' wing bracelet (44-10) and small engraved airplane given to her at the time of her solo flight (June 12, 1944).

Hand-embroidered WASP wing on leather for wear on a flying jacket.

Enamelled pin normally worn on the flight and/or utility cap. The far right example was made by JAYCO (J.J. Sweeny Co.)

THE AVENGER
"We live in the wind and sand . . . and our eyes are on the stars"

VOL. 1   AVENGER FIELD, SWEETWATER, TEXAS, THURSDAY, SEPTEMBER 2, 1943   NO. 4

318th GRADUATES LARGEST CLASS

Out In The Blue
By B. J. Welz

What will we do when we graduate? What kind of planes will we fly? Where will we live? These and many other similar questions are asked daily by Avengerettes eager to get to work for Uncle Sam.
Lovelle Richards, a member of the first class and now based with the Sixth Ferrying Group in Long Beach, reports some interesting highlights. The girls based at Long Beach live in barracks and enjoy the facilities of the officer's club. They do their own laundry and are required to keep their barracks up to military standards. These hard-working members of the Air Corps are on duty seven days a week from eight until

Maj. Gen. Brandt Addresses 43W-4

The morning of August 7, 1943, saw one hundred and twelve members of class 43-W-4 receive their wings. The largest class graduated thus far was addressed by Maj. Gen. Gerald C. Brandt, Commanding General of Gulf Coast Training Center. Visitors thronged the field and classes W-5, -6, -7, -8, led by Group Commander Margery Sanford, passed in review, marching to the music of the Midland Army Air Base Band.
Miss Jacqueline Cochran, Director of the Women's Pilot Training Program, expressed again her pride in the fact that her faith in the feasibility of such a program

Gold cap badge worn by male flight instructor Jerry Boxberger at Avenger Field.

Silver cap badge and wings worn by Civilian Flight Instructor Jerry Boxberger while at Avenger Field.

WASP song book.

217

The 318th
Army Air Forces Flying Training Detachment
announces
the Graduation of Class 43-W-4
Saturday, August 7, 1943
Avenger Field, Sweetwater, Texas

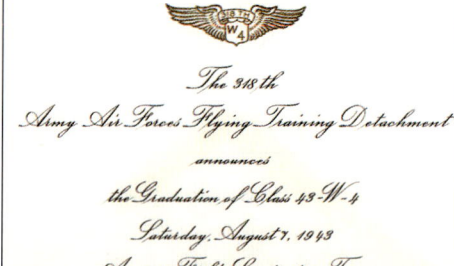

Announcement for the graduation of Class 43-W-4 on August 7, 1943.

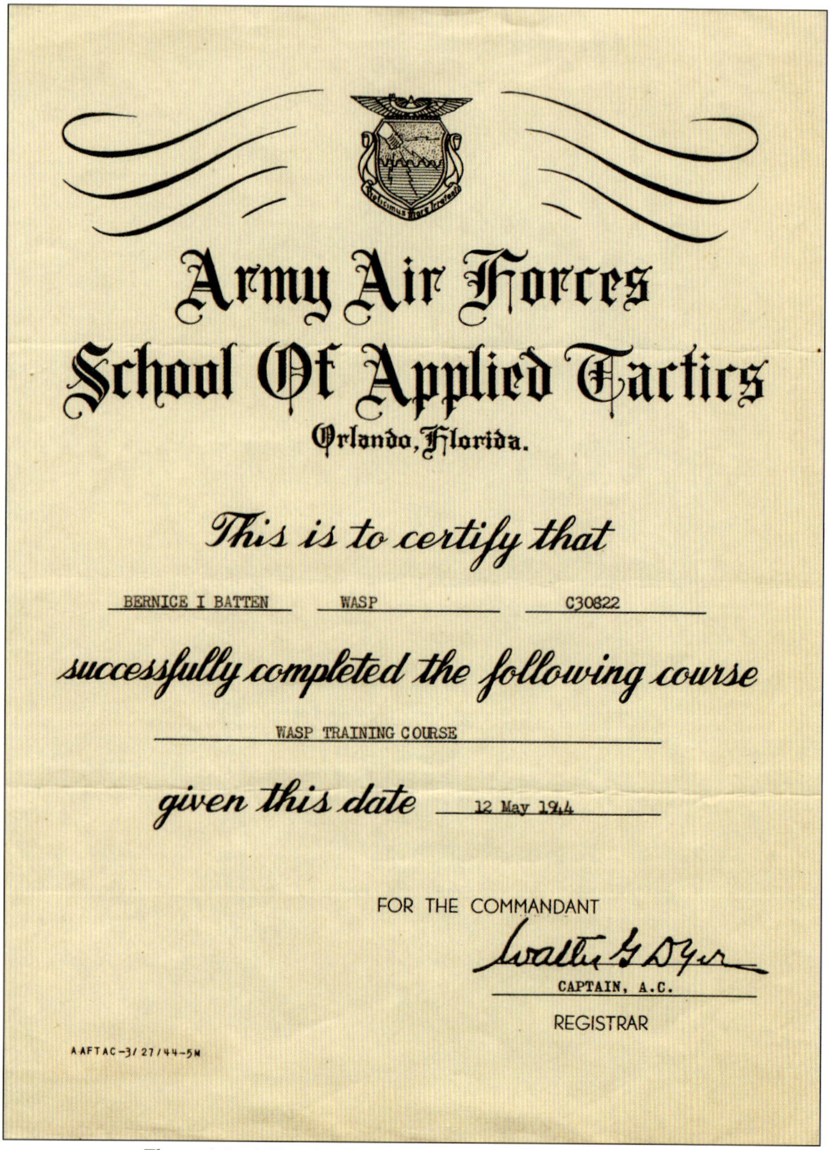

Army Air Forces
School Of Applied Tactics
Orlando, Florida.

This is to certify that

BERNICE I BATTEN WASP C30822

successfully completed the following course

WASP TRAINING COURSE

given this date 12 May 1944

FOR THE COMMANDANT

Walter G Dyer
CAPTAIN, A.C.
REGISTRAR

AAFTAC-3/27/44-5M

The recipient, Bernice Batten, was one of the original WAFS.

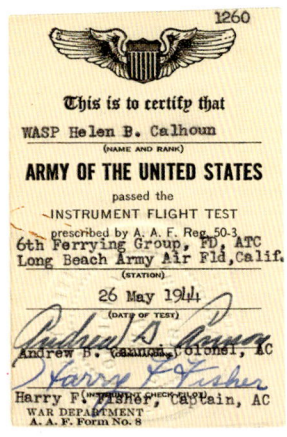
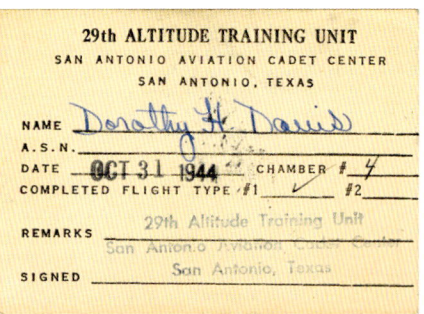

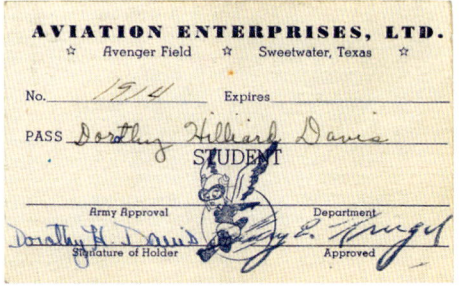
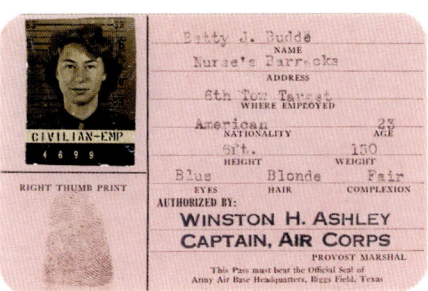
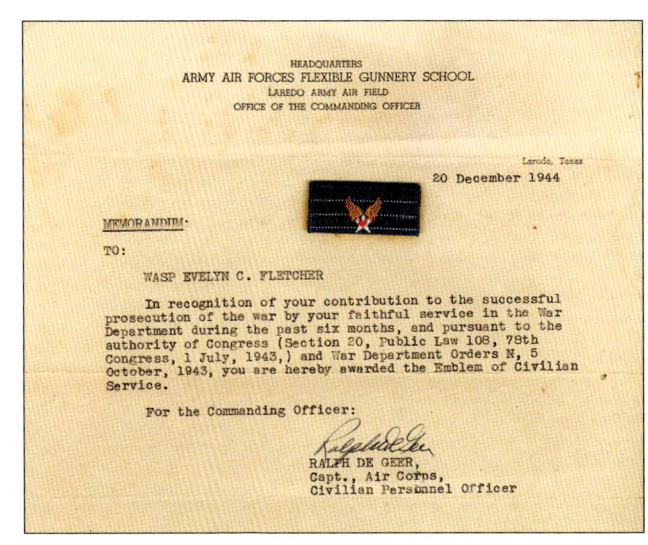

Honorable Discharge

from the Armed Forces of the United States of America

This is to certify that

EVELYN C. FLETCHER 113-05-7356 Women's Air Force Service Pilots

was Honorably Discharged from the

United States Air Force

on the 20th day of December 1944. This certificate is awarded as a testimonial of Honest and Faithful Service

JAMES C. O'NEAL, MAJOR, USAF
AFMPC, RANDOLPH AFB, TEXAS

DD FORM 256 AF
1 NOV 51

THIS IS AN IMPORTANT RECORD — SAFEGUARD IT!

CERTIFICATE OF HONORABLE SERVICE

WITH THE ARMY AIR FORCES

This is to certify that _____ has successfully completed the prescribed training for Women Air Force Service Pilots, comparable to the course given Aviation Cadets, and has faithfully and loyally served the Army Air Forces as a Woman Air Force Service Pilot (WASP) for a period of ___ months. As a volunteer she has helped establish the capacity of women as non-combat military pilots. Her services have been of great value to the Army Air Forces in World War II.

COMMANDING GENERAL, ARMY AIR FORCES

DIRECTOR OF WOMEN PILOTS

Note: This document was sent with a transmittal letter and discharge pin.

WASP Class Books

43-W6, W7

43 (class year)/W1, W2, W3 classes (W=women).

43-W4, W5

43-W8 and 44-W1.

44-W2.

44-W3.

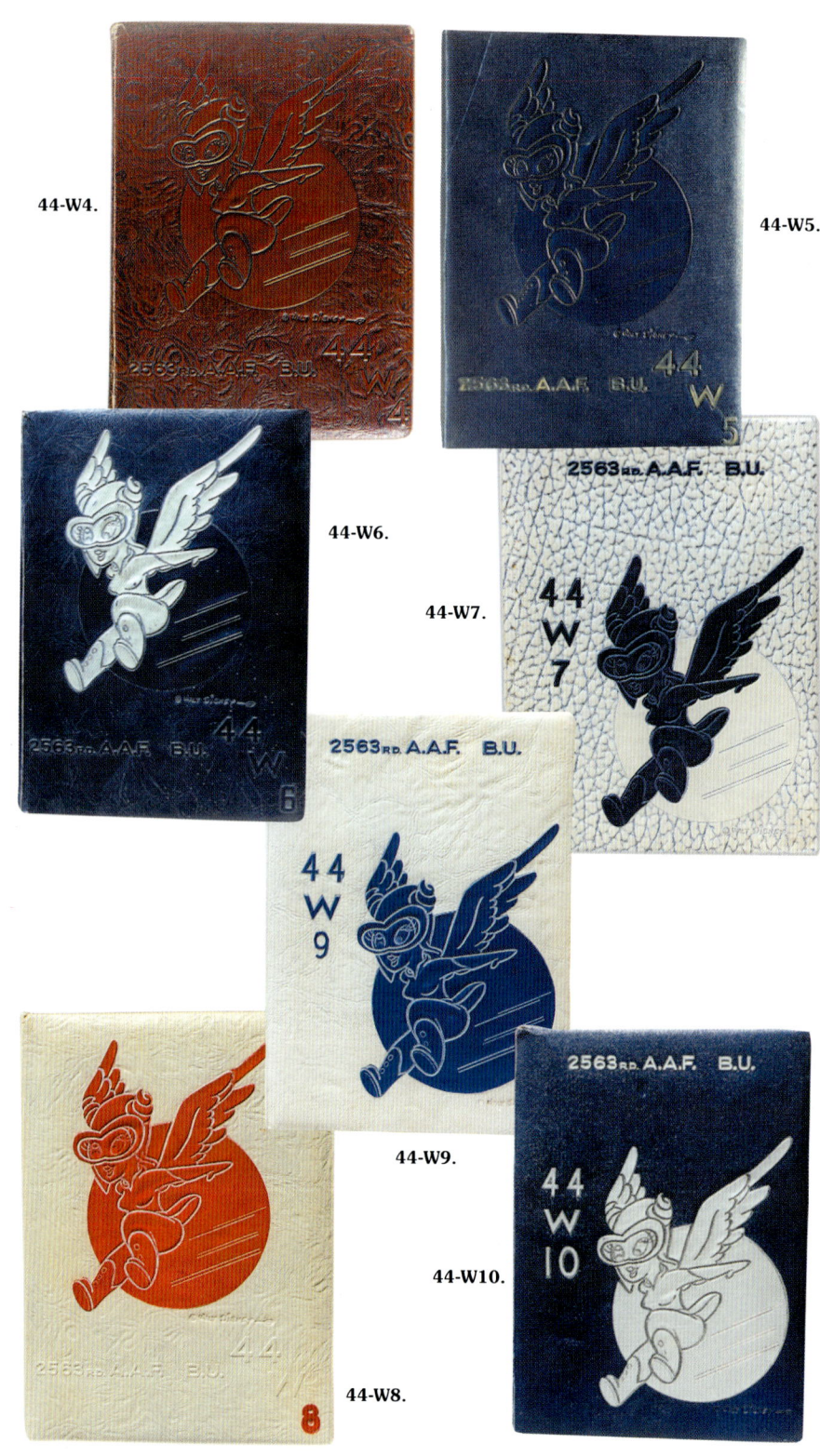

44-W4.
44-W5.
44-W6.
44-W7.
44-W9.
44-W8.
44-W10.

Wasps Killed During World War II

Champlin, Jane
Clarke, Susan P.
Davis, Margie L.
Dussaq, Katherine
Edwards, Marjorie D.
Erickson, Elizabeth
Fort, Cornelia
Grimes, Frances F.
Hartson, Mary
Keene, Edith
Lawrence, Kathryn B.
Lee, Hazel Ah Ying
Loop, Paula
Lovejoy, Alice
McDonald, Lea Ola
Martin, Peggy
Moffatt, Virginia
Moses, Beverly
Nichols, Dorothy

Norbeck, Jeanne L.
Oldenburg, Margaret C.
Rawlinson, Mabel
Roberts, Gleanna
Robinson, Marie Mitchell
Scott, Betty
Scott, Dorothy
Seip, Margaret J.
Severson, Helen Jo
Sharon, Ethel Marie
Sharp, Evelyn
Silver, Gertrude Thompkins
Stine, Betty P.
Toevs, Marion
Trebing, Mary E.
Webster, Mary L.
Welz, Bonnie Jean
Wood, Betty Taylor

Women in the United States Air Force,
(WAF—Post World War II)
Air Force Nurse Corps
and
Air Force Women's Medical Specialist Corps

Waf wearing the transitional USAF uniform, consisting of a khaki WAC uniform garrison cap, blouse, shirtwaist and tie. The blouse has the gold USAF buttons, gold "U.S." in a circle and winged propeller in a circle collar insignia, and USAF sergeant's chevrons and Army Air Forces shoulder patch. Her cap is piped in the WAC colors of old gold and moss-green.

Prior to the passage of the National Security Act, which made the Air Force a seperate branch of service on September 18, 1947, the plan was to train Wacs and Wafs together. However, with the creation of the United States Air Force, it decided to train the Wafs itself.[1000] Colonel Geraldine P. May was appointed as the director of the Women in the Air Force.

Colonel Geraldine P. May, Director, Women in the Air Force.

WAF officers and enlisted women, wearing the old WWII uniforms and Army Air Force sleeve patch, gaze up at the winged insigne of the 7239th WAF Squadron.

Women enlistees received basic training at Lackland Air Force Base, Texas. The first group was the 3741st WAF Training Squadron. They enlisted first as privates (later, as "WAF Airmen") for periods of three to six years. The first woman to enlist in the United States Air Force was Staff Sergeant and former "Air Wac" Esther Blake (July 1948).[1001] The period publication, "Woman Veteran" names Mary Irene "Jane" Webster as the first Waf, enlisting at Bolling Air Force Base in September 1948. At least one former Wasp, Hazel J. Raines, joined the WAF Reserve in 1950 as a Second Lieutenant.[1002] The WAF Officer Candidate School was also locat-

---

[1000] Betty J. Morden, *The Women's Army Corps, 1945-1978* (Washington, DC: Center of Military History, United States Army, 1990), p. 74.

[1001] WIMSA 1998 Calendar, see "March."

[1002] Dorothy Tuttle, "First WAF Mobilization Assignment," *Woman Veteran,* Vol. IV, No. 3 (March 1950): p. 3.

The US Air Forces' first WAF, Mary Irene "Jane" Webster receives a salute from her father, Major Daniel C. Webster. Her mother, Ann Webster is on the right. Waf Webster was sworn into the USAF at Bolling Air Force Base, Washington, DC, September 1948. (Courtesy: *Woman Veteran*)

Former WASP Hazel J. Raines became a second lieutenant in the WAF. (Courtesy: *Woman Veteran*)

ed at Lackland Air Force Base.[1003] In 1950, British Squadron Leader (the equivalent of a major) Joyce Borlase came to Lackland to serve as an assistant to the chief of military training in the USAF Officer Candidate School, and as the director of the military training of Air Force women. Borlase was formerly in charge of training women of the Women of the Royal Air Force (WRAF) during World War II.[1004] However, women were not integrated into the Air Force with the passage of the Women's Armed Services Integration Act of 1948. While it had specific articles dealing with branches of service, for example, Title I concerned the Army, Title II, the Navy and Marine Corps, the Air Force did not follow suit until November.[1005] Many saw no need for women in the new Air Force, especially enlisted women. For a time it was hoped that the only women in the Air Force would be officers. Some in the Air Force saw the acronym "WAF" as standing for "Women's Air Force," when it actually referred to "Women in the Air Force." "WAF" sounded to some like a corps, and the Air Force wanted nothing to do with corps. However, some military men did recognize the capabilities of women. General Curtis LeMay said, "I don't want a bunch

---

[1003] PIO, Sixth Army Recruiting Service, "WAC & WAF Enlistments in the Regular Army & Regular Air Force," *Your Key to the Future in the Women's Army Corps and the Women in the Air Force,* ca. 1953: pp. 2 and 7.

[1004] Dorothy Tuttle, "British Leaders trains American Wafs," *Woman Veteran,* Vol. IV, No. 6 (June 1950): p. 5.

[1005] Unless otherwise stated, information about women in the USAF was obtained from the book by Maj. Gen. Jeanne Holm, USAF (Ret.), *Women in the Military. An Unfinished Revolution.* Revised Edition. (Novato, CA: Presidio, 1992) p. 115.

of green kids here. You send me people who can run that switchboard...and who can do the job ready-made and I'll take any number of them. I don't care whether they're men, women, or children. I've ...got a job to do here at SAC."[1006] Still, the infant WAF was at best a token organization. It barely survived through the Korean War. By the 1960's, women in the military in general had been reduced to what were called "typewriter soldiers." By 1965, with little or no support from the Air Force, the number of enlisted women in the Air Force dropped to 4,700.[1007] Emphasis was placed on quality and not quantity, but the emphasis soon became more or less a beauty contest, affecting all the women's services. A board of senior Marine Corps officers reported that,

"In accordance with the Commandant's desire, [women Marines] must be the most attractive and useful women in the four line services. Within a ...group of enlisted women, there is room for none but the truly elite."[1008]

The Air Force picked up on this idea and told the commander of its Recruiting Service to provide a "better looking WAF." Appearance became the primary concern for women wanting to join the Air Force. Four photographs were taken of each aspirant Waf: full-face, side, front, and back. Training in the field was no longer done, but women were given instruction on how to apply make-up properly.[1009] Gone were the days when women worked as drivers, mechanics, control tower operators and flight stewards. By 1958, women in the Air Force were no longer allowed to serve in areas such as control tower operations, meteorology, intelligence and the like, but were relegated to desk jobs.[1010] They were no longer trained for maximum fitness, but now to maintain an attractive figure. Extreme hairstyles were not permitted, of course, but too-short hairstyles suggested lesbianism, so much emphasis was put on hair style.

The Air Force Nurse Corps was established on July 1, 1949. Some army nurses transferred to the new corps. The first chief of the corps was Colonel Verna Zeller. E. Ann Hoefly, who was the fifth chief of the corps, later became the first to be promoted to Brigadier General in 1971.[1011]

Members had to be graduate registered nurses. They served in Air Force hospitals at air bases all around the world. They also served as flight nurses aboard Air Force aircraft.[1012] In June 1950, the Air Force and the Army offered regular commissions to women who had previously served in

---

[1006] Ibid, p. 172.
[1007] Ibid, pp. 176-177, and p. 174.
[1008] Ibid, pp. 180-181.
[1009] Ibid, p. 181.
[1010] Ibid, p. 184.
[1011] WIMSA Bulletin. "Special Drive to Honor Service Directors & Corps Chiefs," p. 4.
[1012] United States Department of Defense, "Make Your Choice...Pick 1 of 9," It's a Big Decision. You'll be Glad You Joined, ca. 1950: p. 6.

the Army or Army Air Forces as nurses, physical and occupational therapists and dietitians.[1013]

The Air Force Medical Specialist Corps was created in 1949. Wafs in this area of service worked in USAF hospitals in the United States and overseas as physical and occupational therapists and dietitians.[1014] It later merged with the Biomedical Corps. So far, there have been no women appointed to the position of Chief.[1015] Its members served as dietitians and physical and occupational therapists in Air Force hospitals at home and abroad.[1016]

Not all Air Force nurses worked as flight nurses. Many were stationed at hospitals in Thailand and Vietnam. Air Force nurses serving in Vietnam were stationed at Tan Son Nhut Airbase—Saigon, Da Nang Airbase and Cam Ranh Bay Airbase. Flight nurses flew with patients evacuated from one hospital to another. Some flew evacuation flights from Japan to the United States. The Air Force's workhorse cargo planes, the C-123's and C-130s, were converted to carry patients. The C-9's were the only planes which were specifically built and equipped to carry patients.[1017]

In April 1949 it was announced that until the new WAF uniform was developed, women officers and enlisted women would wear the World War II Army style uniform. The officer's uniform consisted of a winter blouse, made of olive-drab (Army shade no. 51) elastique or barathea material. Optionally, they could wear this blouse made of covert wool, in olive-drab Army shade number 37, or of wool serge, of olive-drab Army shade number 33.

The WAF officer uniform of this time had simulated bodice pockets with flaps that had gold buttons, and two side welted pockets. The blouse, in fact, was identical to that worn by Army nurses during World War II.

Enlisted Wafs' uniform was like that worn by Wacs during the war.

During the summer, WAF officers wore a similar uniform, but it was made of tropical worsted or gabardine khaki (Army shade no. 61). The sleeve braid was of khaki Army shade number 5 mohair. Enlisted women wore the basic WAC-style blouse. Tailored blouses were identical to those worn by officers, without the sleeve braid. A photograph taken in spring 1950 shows Lieutenant Colonels Miriam E. Perry, Chief of the Air Force Women's Medical Specialist Corps and acting chief of the Air Force Nurses, Verena M. Zeller wearing this uniform with the Army Air Forces patch on their upper left sleeve, even though USAF Chief of Staff General Hoyt S. Vandenberg is wearing the new blue Air Force uniform.[1018]

[1013] Dorothy Tuttle, "Regular Army Commissions Available for Medical Women," *Woman Veteran*, Vol. IV, No. 6 (June 1950): p. 3.

[1014] Government pamphelt, "It's a Big Decision. You'll be Glad You Joined." Circa 1950's, p. 6.

[1015] WIMSA Bulletin. "Special Drive to Honor Service Directors & Corps Chiefs," pp. 4-5.

[1016] Ibid.

[1017] Elizabeth Norman, *Women at War. The Story of Fifty Military Nurses Who Served in Vietnam* (Philadelphia: The University of Pennsylvania Press, 1990) pp. 85-86.

[1018] Photograph shown in "Congratulations for the Chiefs!," *Woman Veteran*, Vol. IV, No. 4, April 1950, p. 5

Officers and enlisted women could purchase the winter jacket, which was similar in style to the "Ike" jacket. It was single-breasted with a concealed three-button front and made of covert wool material, olive-drab (Army shade no. 37), wool serge, olive-drab (Army shade no. 33), or elastique or barathea wool, olive-drab (Army shade no. 51). Enlisted women wore smaller versions of the new Air Force chevrons for enlisted men, consisting of gray thread chevrons on blue backing with a gray thread star in the center. The patch of their assignment was sewn to the upper left sleeve.

The cut of the jacket was altered to allow an easy fit over the bust. The shoulders of the jacket were padded to produce a square, trim line. A band, 1 3/4" wide, fitted around the waist and fastened three inches to the left of the center of the jacket by means of a metal gripper or snap. To fit a woman's figure, the fullness of the jacket was worked into the band by two flat darts on each side of the front. Two flat, shorter darts were incorporated on the back of the jacket. To keep the jacket in place, a button hole tab was sewn into the interior of the back waistband. The skirt or trousers were secured to the jacket with corresponding buttons on their waistbands.

There were two pleated patch pockets with flaps and buttons on the bodice of the jacket. Under the flaps were fly tabs. The edges of the pockets and flaps were slightly rounded. The flaps were slightly scalloped, having a slight point in the center. An interior pocket was sewn into the lining on the right side.[1019]

Enlisted women had the option to purchase this jacket, but it was not a required item of uniform for them. Their jackets could be made of covert wool, olive drab (Army shade no. 37) or olive-drab (Army shade no. 33)

This WAF staff sergeant wears the "Ike" jacket. Note the bullion "USAF in Europe" patch on her sleeve.

[1019] Air Force Letter (AL) 35-48, "Military Personnel, Uniforms for the WAF." Washington, DC: April 8, 1949, pp. 1-3.

serge wool.[1020] An enlisted woman's jacket was observed during this research which has a three-button, concealed closure and two scalloped pocket flaps with gold Army buttons. The waistband fastened with two snaps and two pairs of hook and eyes.

WAF "Ike" jacket with gold US Army buttons and USAF insignia. (Photo by Ronda Shell)

Officers had the option of purchasing a summer "Ike" jacket, made of tropical worsted or gabardine khaki (Army shade no. 61). It was also available to enlisted women, but only as an optional purchase item.

The required officer's winter barathea or elastique skirt was olive-drab Army color number 54. Optional materials were covert wool (Army shade no. 37), wool serge (Army shade no. 33), or barathea or elastique in Army shade number 51. It had a 1 1/4" waistband and closed on the left side.

Enlisted Wafs wore the skirt made of covert wool, Army shade number 37. A skirt made of wool serge, Army shade number 33, could be worn, if the skirt of shade number 37 was not available.

Officers and enlisted women were required to have a summer skirt. Officer's skirts were made of tropical worsted or gabardine khaki material (Army shade no. 61). Enlisted women wore tropical worsted skirts. Gabardine skirts were an optional purchase item.

Olive-drab (Army shade no. 51) slacks could be worn with the M-1943 field jacket or the M-1943 field jacket liner. The slacks had no cuffs, but sufficient material was left to allow for hemming. There were two slash pockets at each side, and the slacks closed at the left side.

Officers wore a plain or twill weave olive-drab (Army shade no. 51) worsted shirtwaist, which had a basic stand-and-fall collar with a six-button closure and one plastic button at the neck. There were two bodice pockets with flaps with matching buttons. Enlisted women wore issue shirtwaists.

The shirtwaist was available in summer weight material, of khaki (Army shade no. 1) or gabardine (Army shade 61). The necktie for officers and enlisted women was made of khaki cotton mohair (Army shade no. 5).

The winter garrison cap for officers was like that worn during World War II by Army nurses. It was made of elastique or barathea olive-drab wool (Army shade no. 51). The curtain was piped in gold and black-flecked pip-

---

[1020] AFL 35-48, April 8, 1949, No. 2, p. 3.

ing. It was also available in olive-drab covert wool (Army shade no. 37) or of olive-drab serge (Army shade no. 33). These last two items were optional.

Enlisted Wafs wore a similar cap, first with moss green and old gold WAC piping and then, supposedly finished with ultramarine-blue and orange-gold woven piping, or possibly the later horizontal-striped piping.

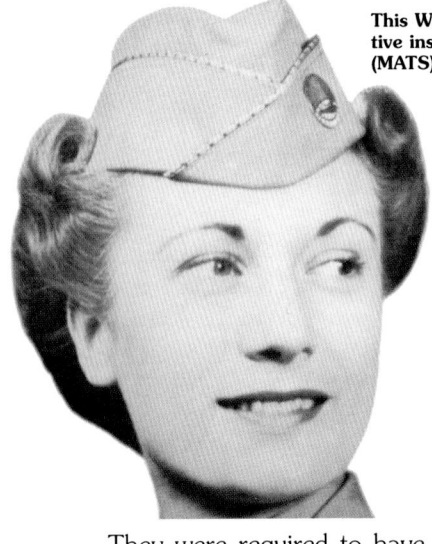

This Waf wears the WAC garrison cap with the distinctive insigne of the Military Air Transport Service (MATS) on its left side, 1950.

Officers and enlisted women also wore a summer version of the garrison cap. Officer's caps were made of tropical worsted or gabardine, Army shade no. 61 and was identical to the winter garrison cap.

Enlisted women wore the same cap, except with enlisted piping.

Women officers were permitted to purchase a cotton, poplin or twill overcoat with a removable lining and hood. It was like that worn by WAC officers.

They were required to have the double-breasted, olive-drab (Army shade no. 52) wool ulster overcoat, made of doeskin, beaver, melton or kersey. They could also have the cloth coat, made of olive-drab (Army shade no. 51) elastique or barathea. The former was very much like the second pattern WAC officer's overcoat.

A short overcoat was also manufactured, which was like the Army male officer's mackinaw, the difference being that the closure was reversed to conform with normal women's clothing construction.

Women officers could purchase a double-breasted coat of "commercial design", having a half-belt or all-around belt. The color had to be similar to Army shade number 54.

Raincoats were required for officers and enlisted women. It was a water repellent commercial coat. Officer's coats had shoulder straps. Enlisted women wore issued raincoats.

Additional items were required as part of the uniform. Only a vague description of the early WAF bag was discovered. Regulations did indicate that it had a removable shoulder strap, and was to be worn with the strap over the right shoulder, extending across the chest and resting on the left side, WAC-style. The shape and exact color of the utility bag isn't known.

Similarly, leather women's dress gloves were required by the uniform regulations, but not described. Cotton dress gloves and olive-drab woolen gloves were required.

Regulations also required that Wafs have the chamois-colored WAC dress scarf as part of their kit.

Regarding insignia, this period in Air Force uniform history is very interesting, and sometimes vague.

Prior to 1949 members of the new Air Force wore standard gold Army buttons. Regulations of April 1949 indicate that "...Air Force gold buttons will replace Army gold buttons where applicable. Replacement will be made on a station basis when available. (Required)"[1021]

It also indicates that Wafs held Warrant Officer ranks. They were "authorized to wear insignia identical to that prescribed for Air Force Commissioned officers. Rank insignia will remain as currently prescribed by AFL 37-5,"[1022] i.e., gold US Army insignia.

Officers could wear their insignia in miniature on the collar of the shirtwaist, when the blouse wasn't worn.

Enlisted women wore " 'U.S.' collar insignia, lapel insignia, chevrons, and gold buttons, as authorized by AFL 39-25."[1023] At least by May 1950, new enlisted collar insignia was designed for women and men. It consisted of a gold "U.S." cut-out within a cut-out gold circle for wear on the right collar. A gold wing and propeller in a cut-out gold circle was worn on the left collar. At least one period photograph shows Wafs stationed at the 3742nd WAF Training Squadron at Lackland Air Force Base wearing this insignia on the closed collars of their khaki shirtwaists. They are also wearing khaki ties tucked in under the second waist button with the Army Air Forces patch on their upper left sleeve.[1024] This insignia was also shown being worn on the four-pocket World War II enlisted woman's blouse by Waf Private, First Class Delores Troy. Though referred to as "Private, First Class, she is wearing the USAF chevron and star on the uniform blouse along with the old Army Air Forces patch. The "U.S." and winged propeller in a cut-out circle insignia are also found in silver, presumably indicating their wear on the new blue Air Force uniforms.

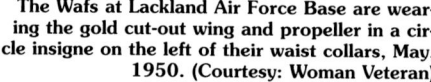
The Wafs at Lackland Air Force Base are wearing the gold cut-out wing and propeller in a circle insigne on the left of their waist collars, May, 1950. (Courtesy: Woman Veteran)

[1021] AFL 35-48, Item u. (1), p. 7, April 8, 1949.
[1022] Ibid.
[1023] Ibid.
[1024] USAF photograph in *Woman Veteran,* May 1950, Vol. IV, No. 5, p. 3.

Gold metal USAF collar insignia.

Waf Private First Class Delores Troy.
(Courtesy: Woman Veteran)

This Waf wears crew member wings and the distinctive insignia of the Military Air Transport Service (MATS) on the lapels of her blouse, June, 1950.

Authorized combinations of the WAF winter service uniforms items.

By November 1950, the United States Air Force had its distinctive uniforms. The Wafs winter uniform consisted of a fully-lined, single-breasted blouse made of 12-12.5 oz. wool serge of blue, shade 84 material. (Wool standard weave 12-12.5 oz. gabardine material, blue, shade 84, was optional.) The front of the uniform was secured by four USAF silver colored, oxidized metal buttons, 30 ligne. Welts simulated breast pockets, while there were two side pockets with semi-scalloped flaps. The open collar had rounded ends and wide lapels. Officer's wore oxidized silver "U.S." insignia on their collars; enlisted women wore oxidized silver "U.S." cut-out insignia in a circle on their collars. Insignia could also be made of silver bullion embroiderey.[1025] A light blue (shade 126) oxford cloth shirtwaist was worn under the jacket, or with the skirt.[1026] The unique collar had Air Force blue trim (shade 83), also called "undertabs,"[1027] so no tie was worn. A white long sleeve rayon shirtwaist with these "undertabs" was also available. When worn without the blouse, officers wore their rank insignia pinned to both sides of the collar.

Shirtwaist.

Enlisted "U.S." collar insigne worked in silver bullion embroidery.

Enlisted oxidized silver "U.S." collar insigne.

The new USAF WAF blue uniform. (Photo by Ronda Sheel)

[1025] AFR 35-14, p. 12.
[1026] Ibid, p. 9.
[1027] Ibid, p. 9.

This USAF flight nurse wears the WAF blue uniform, light blue shirtwaist and the WWII pattern Army flight nurse wings.

WAF enlisted woman's light blue (left) and khaki shirtwaist (below, left) with integral blue collar tabs.

WAF enlisted woman's flight jacket and trousers (Photo by Ronda Sheel)

The five-gore skirt (three gores in front; two in the back) was made of material matching the blouse. It had a waistband of self material, and a waist band lining tab and button, a placket with slide fastener and interior button and loop. There were two kick pleats in the two gores.

Officers and enlisted women could wear a blue (shade 84) flight jacket and matching trousers with the semi-stiff garrison cap. The jacket had a full lining and was single-breasted with a zipper closure. The waist band fastened on the left side. The open collar and lapels were of the same design as worn on the winter uniform blouse, with shoulder straps and false welted breast pockets. The flight jacket could be worn with matching slacks or a skirt. During the summer, the flight uniform consisted of blue trousers which had a tab and button at the cuffs, for a tight fit at the ankle, a light blue short sleeve shirtwaist with open collar and a pocket on the left breast, (this waist was also worn as an exercise uniform.) and the semi-stiff flight cap. The trousers worn during the 1960's and 1970's had a slash pocket on each side and were pleated and did not have the buttons and tabs. They closed on the left side with a blue button on the waistband and a zipper.

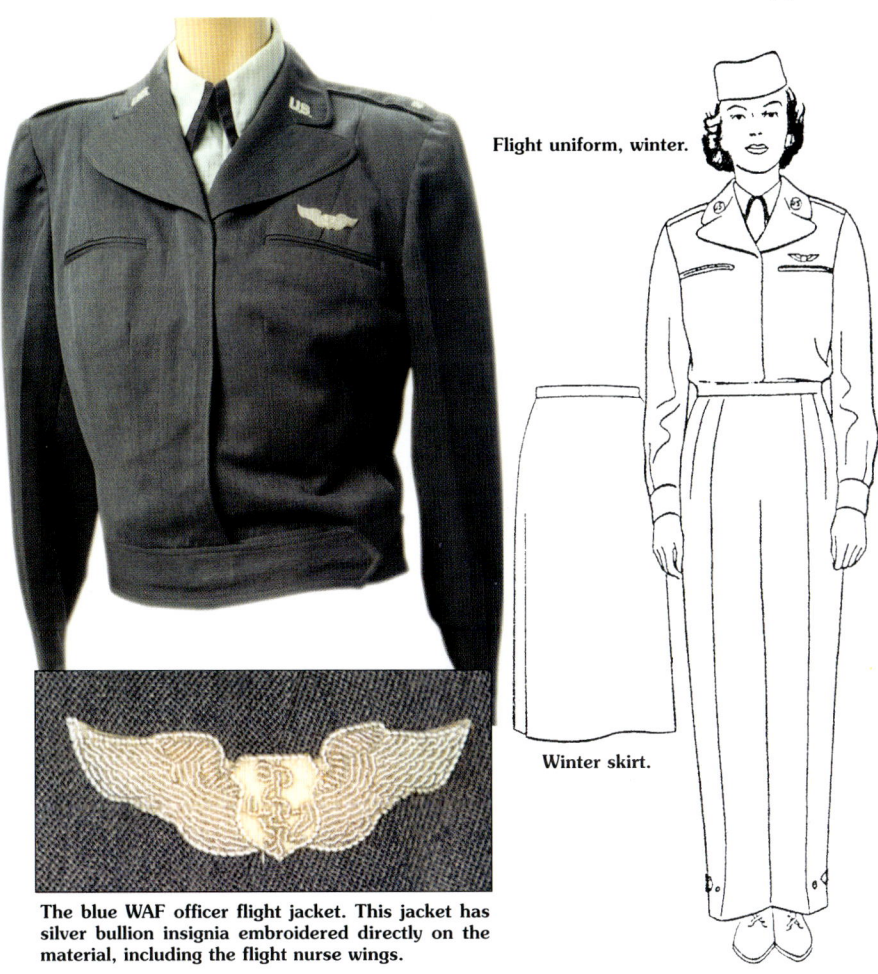

Flight uniform, winter.

Winter skirt.

The blue WAF officer flight jacket. This jacket has silver bullion insignia embroidered directly on the material, including the flight nurse wings.

If a Waf had served with a unit during World War II, she was permitted to wear its patch on her upper left sleeve. World War II overseas service chevrons, World War II overseas service bars and federal service stripes were of silver colored thread on a blue backing. They were sewn to lower left sleeve. Waf aides wore a silver-colored rayon or metallic aiguillette with a knot and one metal needle. It attached to the uniform under the left shoulder strap, near the shoulder seam. Regulations from 1950 illustrate a woman's blouse with the distinctive insignia of an aide worn on the blouse lapels. Additionally, an illustration from these regulations shows the manner of wearing the French and Belgian Fourragere and the House of Orange lanyard from the Netherlands from the left shoulder strap of a woman's blouse.

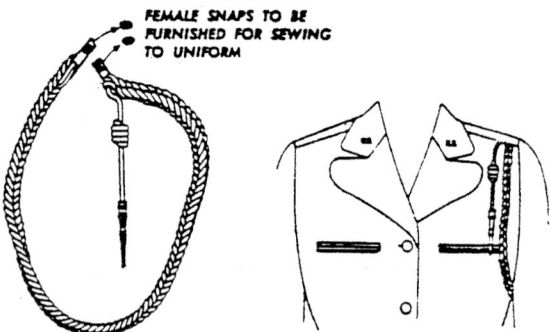

Flight uniform, summer.

Aides and attachés were distinguished by aiguillettes of silver-color rayon or metallic-type cord worn with the service uniform.

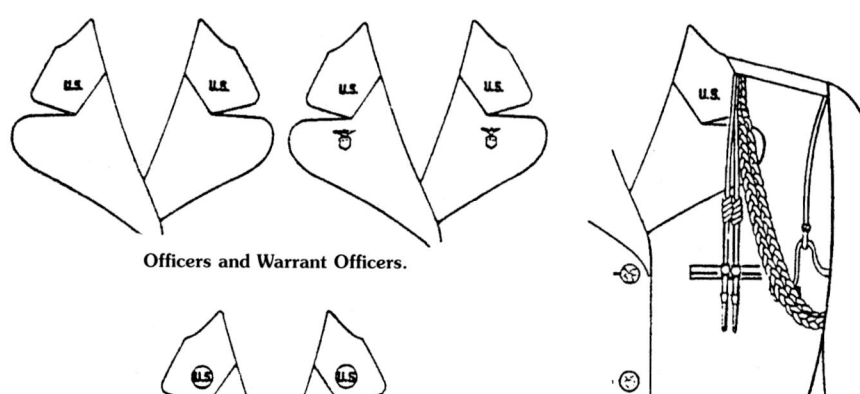

Officers and Warrant Officers.

Enlisted women.

Arrangement of foreign awards and fourragere. French and Belgian fourragere and Netherlands orange lanyard shown.

238

The summer uniform was identical in style to the winter uniform, but was made of 8-12 oz all white wool or wool combination fabrics. Officers wore a blue mohair stripe near each sleeve cuff. The summer skirt of the same color material, but had four gores and was cut on the bias of the material. It had a two-ply waistband, buttonhole and button, placket with slide fastener, two loops for suspending the skirt on a rack, and a hook and eye closure. It also had two side seam pockets. The wear of this uniform was optional.

Air Force "suntan" officer's blouse with thread ribbons. It is dated 1957.

Left: the summer cord uniform.
Right: the white uniform.

Rare example of the white WAF uniform, dated 1953. The skirt has two kick pleats on the reverse. (Photo by Ronda Sheel)

Female USAF Identification Tags
(Courtesy: Steve Rohde)

```
"KLEINER MAC II"
CAPT G.E.McMANIMIE
    AL 80040
```

M-1940: Type 3. This tag was made before transferring into the USAF and carries the old Army serial number with "A" prefix. The "AL" prefix—WAF officer. Note that originally her serial number was "L 80040."

```
GRIFFITH ETHEL E
AA 8203950
T52        B NEG

              P
```

M-1940: Type 3. This Korean War period tag is for an enlisted WAF. During WWII her serial number was "A 203950." "AA" prefix—USAF enlisted WAF.

```
THOMPSON, MARY L
AR 147
T-53       A NEG

              P
```

M-1940: Type 2. Korean War period. "AR" prefix—Hospital Dietitian. Thompson retired in May 1961 as a major.

```
DILLINGER, ALTA F
AN 2243807
T 53       A POS
RH POS
              P
```

M-1940: Type 2. Korean War period. "AN" prefix—USAF Nurse.

```
BALDWIN, NANCY A
AL 215315
T51        O

              C
```

M-1940: Type 1. Korean War period. "AL" prefix—WAF officer.

M-1940: Type 3. Late 1950s period. "W" suffix—WAF officer. Regular USAF commission.

```
CALDWELL, LUCILLE
21233W
T57        O NEG

CATHOLIC
```

M-1940: Type 2. Mid 1950s period. "AM" prefix—Physical Therapist.

```
FORTUNE, MARTHA J
AM 2261718
T58       B POS

              C
```

M-1960: "FR" prefix—Regular female officer/warrant officer on active duty. This prefix plus serial number was used from 1965-1969. It was replaced in July 1969 by the Social Security number.

M-1960: As above, but "FV" prefix followed by seven digits—Reserve female officer/warrant officer on active duty.

241

Wafs could wear a summer blouse, Air Force tan (shade 1193), skirt in tan (shade 1192), shirtwaist in tan (shade 1505), and blue service hat with tan (shade 1193) top. This uniform was equivalent to the men's summer service uniform, and was worn as late as 1965.[1028] The neck tab color was blue.

A special summer blouse and skirt was made of cotton cord material, with narrow white, black and wale-blue stripes, shade 166. The blouse of this uniform differed from the standard uniform blouse in that it was shorter and had no lining.

The USAF WAF officer (center) wears the two-piece summer uniform. (Courtesy: Alice Strong Barber)

This popular summer uniform consisted of a single-breasted top and skirt, made of the previously mentioned stripe cotton cord (white, black and wale blue). It had short sleeves with peaked cuffs, each secured with a 20 ligne USAF button. The edges of the collar and lapels were slightly rounded. There were two simulated welted breast pockets. The matching four-gored skirt was cut on the bias, and had a two-ply waistband, hook and eye, placket with slide fastener, button and buttonhole, and two loops for hanging the skirt on a rack. There was a pocket at each side seam.[1029] Enlisted women wore rank chevrons on each sleeve, while officers wore their rank

---

[1028] *The Air Officer's Guide* (1965), pp. 77-78.

[1029] Air Force Regulation (AFR) 35-14, "Military Personnel: Service and Dress Uniform for Air force Personnel," November 15, 1950, p. 10.

Specification label inside of the top.

Far right: The special summer cord uniform. (Photo by Ronda Sheel)

insignia pinned in normal position on the shoulder straps.

This uniform was worn until being replaced in 1966 by a blue and white pinstripe corded uniform, consisting of a top and skirt. It was similar in style as the green and white cord uniform worn by members of the army. The collar, shoulder straps and cuff upturns of the USAF summer uniform were piped in dark blue material. Enlisted women wore their rank insignia sewn to the sleeves. Officers wore their rank insignia pinned in the appropriate position on the shoulder straps. Enlisted women wore a pair of oxidized-silver "U.S." in a circle insignia on their collar, while officers wore the oxidized silver "U.S." insignia. Two false breast pockets were at the bodice and the blouse closed with four removable USAF buttons.

New uniforms for women of the Air Force (L to R): blue raincoat and hood, enlisted woman corded summer uniform, officers' all-white uniform, officers' blue winter uniform, and the enlisted woman blue overcoat. (Courtesy: Woman Veteran)

OTS "trainee" or "OT" Kipgen wears the summer corded uniform in 1966. Note the addition of "OT Major" shoulder boards. (Courtesy: Ken Lazier)

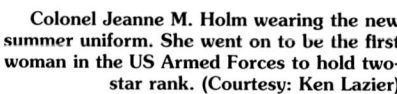

Colonel Jeanne M. Holm wearing the new summer uniform. She went on to be the first woman in the US Armed Forces to hold two-star rank. (Courtesy: Ken Lazier)

The garrison cap (also referred to as a "flight cap") was formed or semi-stiff, did not fold flat, and had no curtain. Most caps were lined in black. Officer's wore a rank insigne attached to the forward left section of the cap. There was no piping on the cap. As a period recruiting pamphlet stated, " 'Perky' best describes the new flight cap."[1030]

The use of the flight cap was to be phased out by 1975, being replaced by the blue furfelt beret.[1031]

Semi-stiff WAFs garrison cap.
(Photo by Ronda Sheel)

WAF captain (center) wearing the semi-stiff garrison cap with the cord uniform. (Courtesy: Alice Strong Barber)

Markings inside the garrison cap illustrated here.

The service hat had a blue (shade 84) wool serge frame whose brim was multi-stitched and upturned. The crown cover of the hat was removable and available in three colors: white—the most widely worn; gray wool (shade 167) to be worn with the winter uniform and; blue, white and black cord, to be worn with the summer uniform. The crown of the first pattern hat had a lower profile than later ones. Enlisted women wore this hat with a removable blue band, upon which fastened an oxidized-silver enlisted woman's screwback badge. Company grade officer's wore the USAF coat-of-arms insigne in the center of the removable hat band, either in oxidized-silver metal or silver bullion embroidery. Field grade officers wore the same hat, but with the addition of silver bullion clouds, arrows and lightning bolts on either side of the coat-of-arms.

[1030] United States Air Force, "Uniforms," Smartest Woman of the Year! ca. 1950: p. 16.
[1031] AFR 35-10, Required and Optional Uniforms for Women, Chapter 4, February 25, 1975, p. 4-3.

Major Elizabeth J. Strippy wears the semstiff garrison cap with her flight jacket. (Courtesy: Ken Lazier)

Half Way

The company grade and field grade cap in wear. Colonel Holm is at right. (Courtesy: Ken Lazier)

Early WAF officer's hat with the low crown. (Courtesy: Alice Strong Barber)

Enlisted woman's hat. (Photo by Ronda Sheel)

Field grade officer's hat. (Photo by Ronda Sheel)

Company grade officer's hat. (Photo by Ronda Sheel)

During the 1950's and 1960's, Wafs wore gray (shade 163) cotton gloves with the winter service uniform. Black leather gloves could be worn as well. White cotton gloves could be worn with the summer uniform. A gray scarf, which matched the gloves, was an optional part of the winter uniform.

Accessories like the handbag and shoes were of smooth black leather. The handbag had a shoulder strap, and was made of calf. The flap closed with a metal fastener, embossed with a round USAF coat-of-arms button in oxidized silver. It was worn from the left shoulder, except when in formation when it was not.

Handbag.

Smooth black leather shoes or pumps, with a closed heel and toe, completed the uniform. White pumps were worn with the summer uniforms.

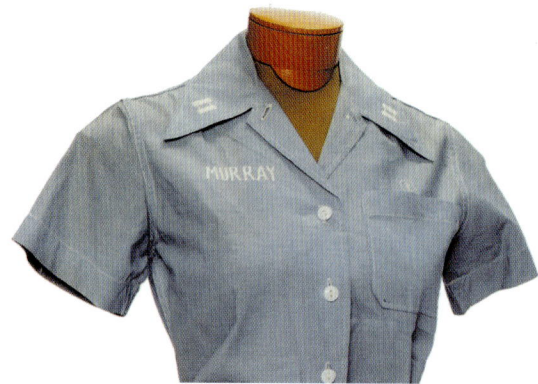

Light blue Air Force nurse's exercise shirt with the rank insignia, name and nurse's shield embroidered directly to the material in white thread. (Photo by Ronda Sheel)

The exercise uniform consisted of a light blue chambray short-sleeved shirtwaist and a flared skirt which buttoned down the front. The waist had one pocket on the left breast. A light blue denim billed cap was worn with the uniform. By 1954, light blue denim shirts, denim slacks and a hip-length dark blue denim coat were added.[1032]

WAF exercise uniform combination.

Waf officers who served in the Women's Medical Specialist Corps and nurses wore a white ward uniform dress with a white hospital duty cap. Miniature rank insignia were pinned to each side of the collar. A blue (shade 158) velvet ribbon, 1/4" in width, was worn a half inch from the upper part of the cap.[1033] They also wore a small antiqued-silver shield, having a serpent on a staff, surmounted by the letters, "MS." It was worn above the bodice pocket or above any ribbons. The first badge had no insigne at its top; the second level of this badge had a star at the top; the highest level of this badge had a star on a ribbon at its top. When the Women's Medical Service Corps merged with the Biomedical Science Corps, the "MS" designation was replaced with an "S."[1034]

Air Force nurses wore a similar badge, but with a lighted lamp behind the serpent and staff. This badge was approved in 1972 and came in three grades: USAF nurse—serpent and staff upon a lighted lamp, no in-

---

[1032] USAF Publication, *The WAF Wardrobe,* ca. late 1950s, p. 87.
[1033] AF 35-14, p. 19 and p. 22.
[1034] Lt. Col. Anthony Aldebol, USAF (Ret.), *Army Air Force and United States Air Force Decorations, Medals, Ribbons, Badges and Insignia, 1941-1997.* (Fountain Inn, SC: MOA Press, 1997), p. 40.

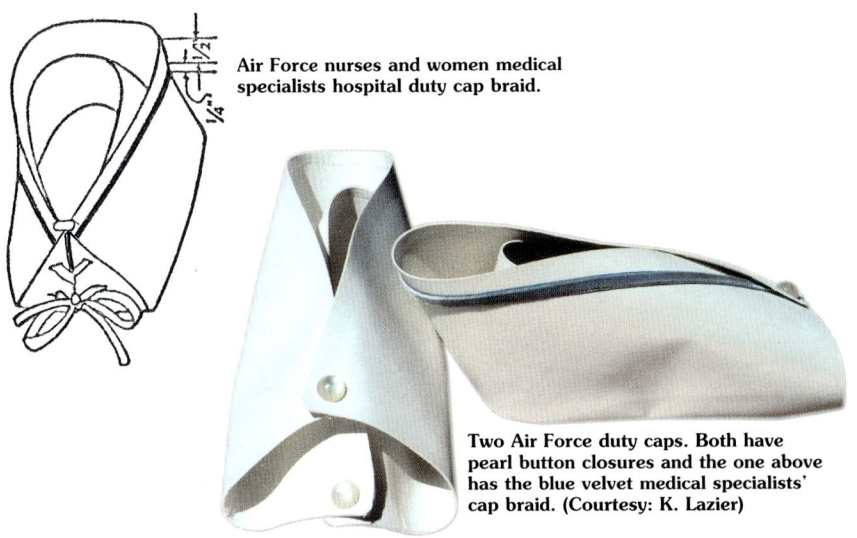

Air Force nurses and women medical specialists hospital duty cap braid.

Two Air Force duty caps. Both have pearl button closures and the one above has the blue velvet medical specialists' cap braid. (Courtesy: K. Lazier)

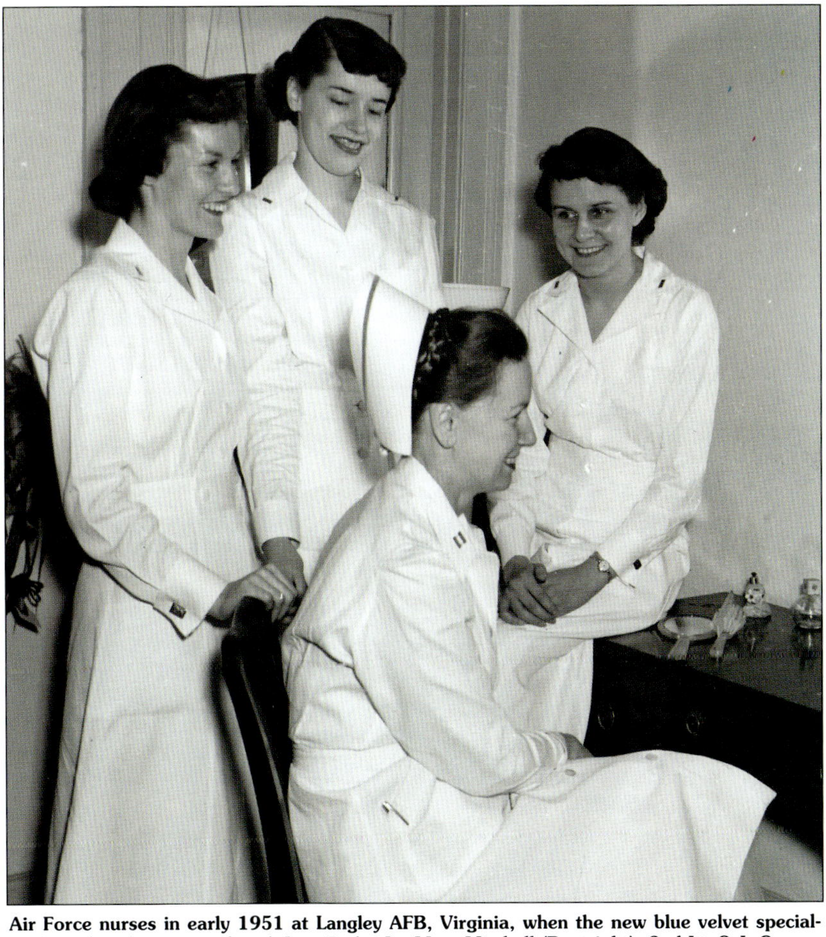

Air Force nurses in early 1951 at Langley AFB, Virginia, when the new blue velvet specialists' cap braid was introduced. L to R: 1st Lt. Mary Mitchell (Boatright), 2nd Lt. S.J. Conroy (Williams), unknown, and Capt. Rice. (Courtesy: Col. Mary Boatright).

Air Force nurse's badge in silver (left) and hand-embroidered wire (right) for wear on the blue uniform.

As above, but with added star for a senior nurse. (All courtesy: Ken Lazier)

As above, but with a star on a billowing ribbon for chief nurse.

Note positioning of the senior flight nurse wings, chief nurse insigne, and hand-embroidered ribbon set which denotes service in the Vietnam War. The Air Medal ribbon is second from the left, top row.

signe at the top; senior nurse-as before, but with a star at the top of the badge, and: chief nurse-as before, but with a star on a billowing ribbon at the top.[1035]

Members of the Air Force Nurse Corps were required to be registered graduate nurses. They served at USAF medical facilities all over the world. Members were authorized their own pattern of wings by October 1968. The wings measured two inches in width and had prongs and clutches for fastening to the uniform. They were of silver-plated copper based alloy. The finish was "aged" or slightly oxidized. Wings of sterling silver could be privately purchased.[1036] Flight nurses wings had a shield in the

1st Lieutenant Doris M. Abbott, USAF Nurse Corps, wearing the nurse's badge in March of 1965. (Courtesy: Ken Lazier)

[1035] Aldebol, p. 40.
[1036] Russell J. Huff, *A Salute to America's Wings. A Complete Study of the Military Wings of America* (Bradenton, FL: Sunshine Press, 1993), p. 70.

center which had a serpent and staff superimposed over a lighted lamp." The Senior Flight Nurse wings had a star at the top of the shield; a Chief Flight Nurse had the star upon a billowing ribbon.[1037]

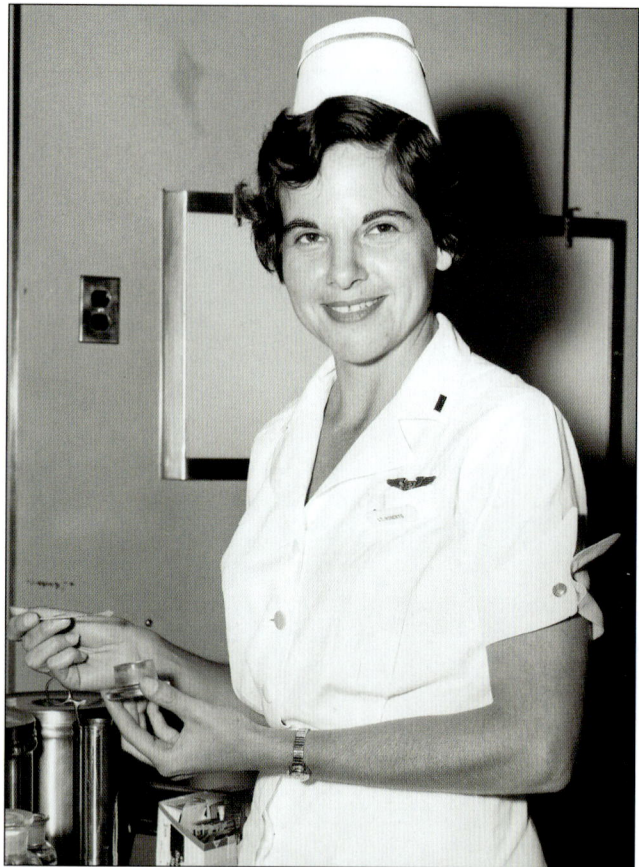

1st Lt. Charlotte Roberts wears the flight nurse wings on her ward uniform at Whiteman AFB in 1961. (Courtesy: Charlotte Roberts)

Standard 2" silver flight nurse wings. (Courtesy: Ken Lazier)

Hand-embroidered version.

Note: The lighted lamp on these badges represents the lamp of Florence Nightingale.

As above, but directly embroidered in white cotton on the light blue, short-sleeve exercise shirtwaist. (Courtesy: Ken Lazier)

[1037] Ibid, p. 71.

The flight nurses at right and left are wearing flight uniforms. Note their utility shirts have embroidered ranks, wings and names. (Courtesy: Judith A. Wolfard).

Flight nurse course diploma for graduating at Gunter AFB, Alabama, on August 4, 1951. (Courtesy: Mary J. Wathen)

Three variations of the 1453rd Aeromedical Evacuation Squadron, to which a number of Air Force flight nurses were assigned. It was initially a naval evacuation squadron. (Courtesy: Charlotte Roberts)

Enlarged photo of the senior flight nurse wings.

Chief flight nurse wings.

This lieutenant colonel's white summer uniform has a 3" flight nurse wing as illustrated in the August 22, 1963 dress regulations.

Unpiped garrison cap.

    A garrison cap which folded flat was introduced at an undetermined time, being made of blue (shade 84) material. At first, the cap had no piping for all ranks. Later, general officers wore silver piping around the curtain edge; other officers wore silver piping with blue flecking and enlisted women wore blue cord piping.
    Wafs serving in Vietnam wore the same olive-green 100% cotton fatigue blouse and slacks as Army nurses and Wacs. Subdued rank insignia were worn on the collar and a white or subdued name tape was sewn over the right bodice pocket. The subdued "U.S. Air Force" tape was sewn over the left bodice pocket. The olive-green slacks had a cargo pocket on the

255

front of each leg, and fastened on each side with three olive-green buttons. A matching small-brimmed "boonie" hat or officer's "baseball" cap could be worn with the uniform, along with women's black combat boots.

WAF nurse's olive-green fatigue shirt. The captain's bars and nurse's name are embroidered in black thread directly to the material. Upon closer examination of the shirt interior, it shows that the subdued "U.S. Air Force" tape has been sewn over an embroidered USAF nurse's shield. (Photo by Ronda Sheel)

Captains Lorraine Klinghoffer, Louise Nichols and Joanne Meier are the first female flight nurses assigned to the 903rd Aeromedical Evacuation Squadron headquartered at Tan Son Nhut AB, RVN, August 1967.

Prior to 1975, Wafs wore a black informal uniform which was identical in style to the blue service uniform. It was worn with a white shirtwaist and black necktab.[1038]

Summer and winter mess dress uniforms were in wear by 1965. The winter uniform consisted of a black wool polyester blend or mohair wool short jacket, with three small USAF buttons slanted on each side of the front. Slip-on black backed shoulder boards were worn, attached through loops on the jacket. Black mohair officer's stripes, measuring one-half inch in width, were sewn on the lower section of both sleeves. A white shirtwaist

---

[1038] AFR 35-10, Required and Optional Uniforms for Women, Chapter 4, p. 35-10, February 25, 1975.

1st Lt. Doris M. Abbott, USAF Nurse Corps, wears the winter mess dress uniform in March of 1965. (Courtesy: Ken Lazier)

The white summer mess dress uniform in wear. (Courtesy: Ken Lazier)

Note the comparative size difference between a male (top) and female (bottom) slip-on shoulder board. (Courtesy: Ken Lazier)

Actual size.

Officer's dress cape. Note collar tabs with captain's rank insignia.

Mess dress uniform (officer).

with three pleated ruffles on each side of the opening was worn under the jacket. The waist closed with small pearl buttons. A black, crescent-shaped necktab was worn under the collar. Other parts of this uniform were a matching black cummerbund, black suede pumps, black fabric or suede handbag and white gloves.

The summer version of the mess dress uniform was identical in design, but made of white polyester/viscose. The white pumps were made of white fabric or leather.

The wear of miniature medals and insignia with these uniforms was manditory.

The dress cape was made of black wool gabardine and was lined in oyster-white satin. Rank insignia was worn on the collar tabs.[1039]

Director, Women in the Air Force
  Colonel Geraldine P. May
Chiefs of the Air Force Nurse Corps
  Colonel Marina Zeller, 1956-1959;

[1039] All information about the mess dress uniforms was found in *The Air Officer's Guide,* 1965, pp. 76 and 78.

Colonel Frances Ley, 1956-1960;
Colonel Dorothy Zeller, 1960-1963;
Colonel Ethel Kovach, 1963-1968;
Brigadier General E. Ann Hoefly, 1968-1974.[1040]
Chiefs of the Air Force Women's Medical Specialist Corps
Lieutenant Colonel Miriam E. Perry, 1950[1041]

Vietnam War period USAF officer's "party suit." (Photo by Ronda Sheel)

USAF "Thunderbirds" shirt and ascot; worn by Staff Sergeant Bonnie Krzysiak, administration.

[1040] WIMSA Bulletin, "Drive to Honor Directors," p. 5.
[1041] Dorothy Tuttle, "Congratulations for the Chiefs!," *Woman Veteran*, Vol. IV, No. 4. (April 1950): p. 5.

Women Ordnance Workers
(WOWs—World War II)

Women ordnance workers, or "Wows," were civilian employees of the Army Ordnance Department. Workers in the Philadelphia Ordnance District Headquarters designed a uniform for women ordnance workers in 1942.[1042] They wore olive-drab elastique or khaki wool gabardine uniforms that were almost identical to the WAC uniform, except for insignia and the detachable shoulder straps. The public often mistook these women for Wacs. Wows wore the patch of the depot they were assigned to, or a round white felt patch with the ordnance flaming bomb insigne embroidered in "ordnance red", eight stars surrounded the bomb and were embroidered in blue silk, and the patch had a blue silk border.[1043] An Army ordnance officer's gold flaming bomb insigne was attached to the left lapel of the blouse and sometimes on the forward section of the left curtain of the garrison cap.

Ordnance worker's patch.
(Courtesy: Phil & Linda Darling)

Khaki version of the Ordnance worker's uniform. (Courtesy: Phil & Linda Darling, photo by Ronda Sheel)

[1042] US Army Signal Corps photograph caption, SC 130479, March 1942.

[1043] Ibid.

Miss Catherine McCaughey, wearing her new uniform, designed and adopted by girls employed in the Philadelphia Ordnance District Headquarters, Philadelphia, PA, "makes-up" on her way to luncheon. Her khaki uniform and matching cap are wool gabardine. Shoulder, sleeve and front buttons are Army type. Sleeve insignia is the Ordnance bomb embroidered in Ordnance red in the center of a white felt background, encircled by embroidered blue silk stars, with a blue silk embroidered border. March 11, 1942. (Courtesy: National Archives)

Olive-drab elastique blouse worn by Women Ordnance Worker's (WOWs). Note the Army Ordnance officer's insignia attached to the lapel. (Photo by Ronda Sheel)

Removable shoulder strap on the olive-drab elastique blouse. The faux army buttons are the shankless type.

Olive-drab elastique garrison cap with an Army Ordnance officer's insigne attached to the forward curtain. (Photo by Ronda Sheel)

The garrison cap was patterned like that worn by Army men, some with the addition of "ordnance red grograin ribbon."[1044]

The overcoat matched the uniform color and was double-breasted with a double inverted, pleated split in the back with two buttons.[1045]

Some Wows in the Ninth Service Command wore khaki garrison caps, skirts and shirts with officer's or enlisted men's insignia, which was against the law. The ordnance depot ordered the removal of all Army insignia from their uniforms, but Wows were allowed to retain the clothing.

Perhaps the woman ordnance worker was more readily characterized by Norman Rockwell's painting of "Rosie the Riveter." She is shown wearing heavy denim bibbed overalls, leather shoes, shirt with the sleeves rolled up, goggles and face mask. Wows were also provided with the "WOW bandanna," designed by the Ordnance Department. It could be obtained in either "Ordnance white" with a print of red flaming ordnance bombs or in "Ordnance red" with the print scheme reversed.[1046]

WOW, Inc. was founded in Chicago, Illinois, and had as its uniform "a trim Air Force Blue uniform, with patch pockets, brown leather belt and open white neck [blouse]...(and) an overseas cap." The WOW insigne was a gold shield with stylized initials "WOW" arranged vertically in the center, upon crossed cannon. Wings with "USA" in the center were at the top.[1047]

Right: A "Rosie the Riveter" poster.

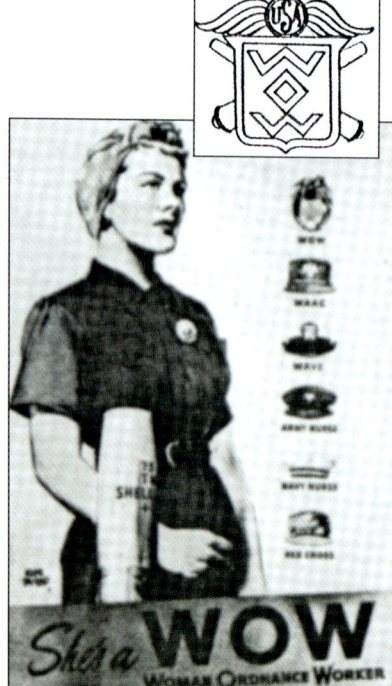

[1044] US Army Signal Corps photograph caption, SC 130476, March 1942.

[1045] Ibid.

[1046] George A. Rosecrans, "A Salute to the Ordnance Women of World War II," *The Ordnance Magazine*, Spring 1984: pp. 10-11.

[1047] Charles H. Bogart, "She's a WOW," *Trading Post*, October-December 1984: p. 14.

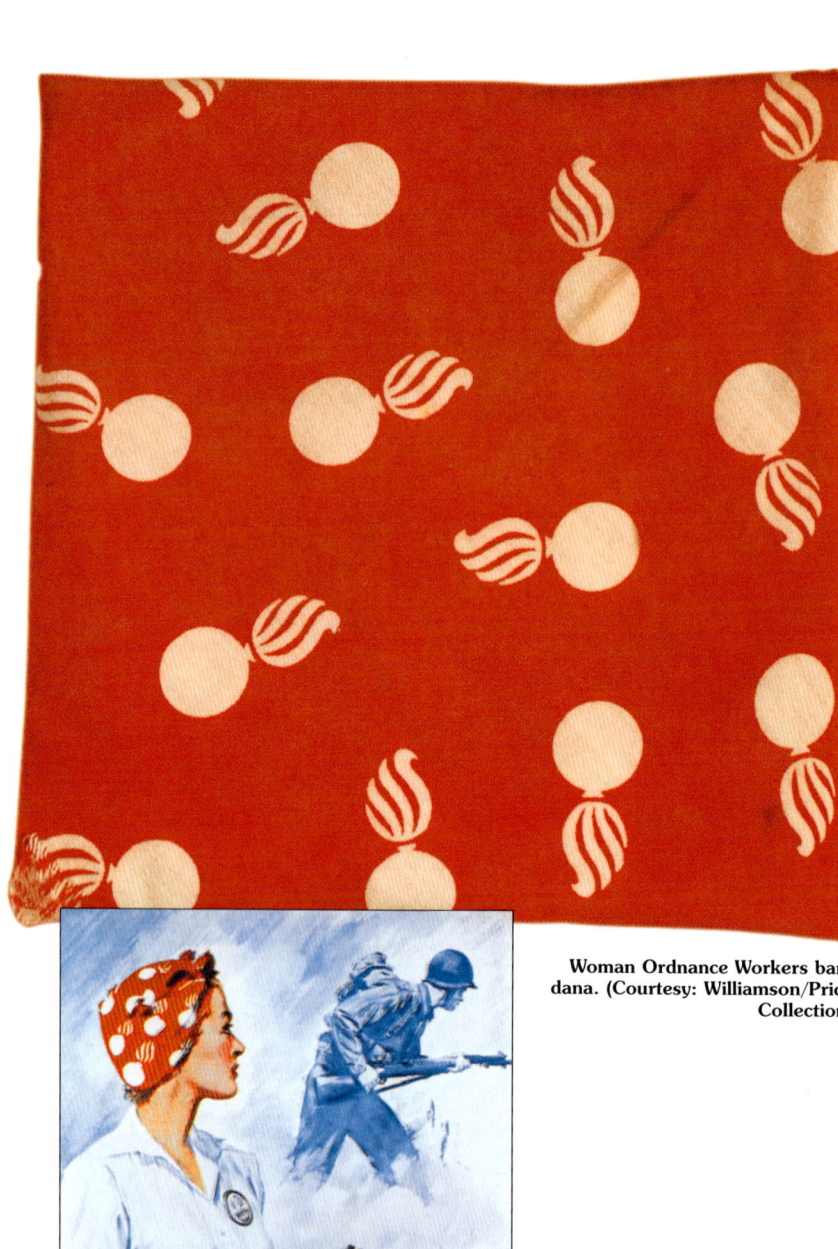

Woman Ordnance Workers bandana. (Courtesy: Williamson/Price Collection)

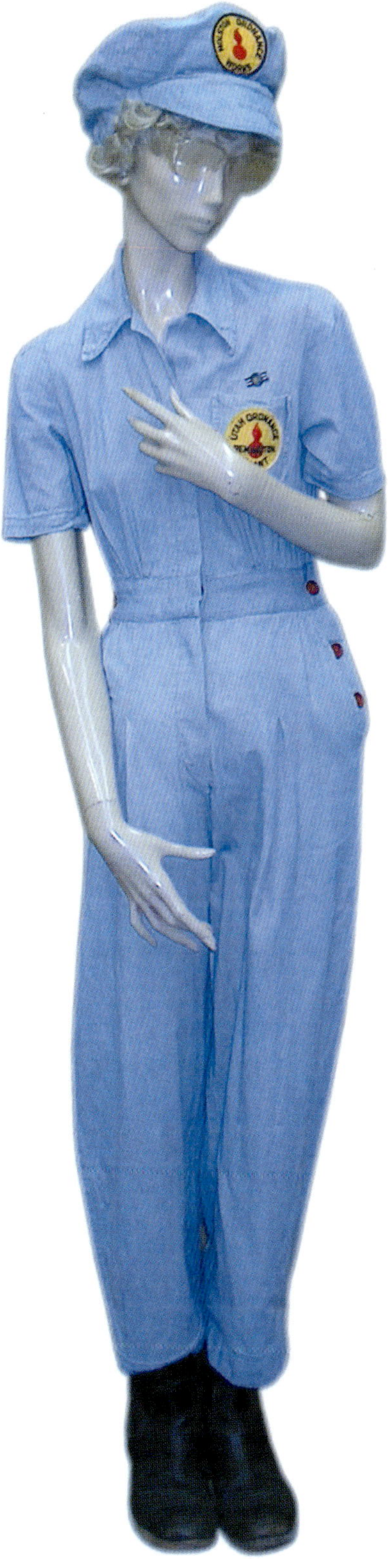

Women Ordnance Worker's jumpsuit. (Courtesy: John Mull)

Red side buttons for drop-seat closure.

Women Ordnance Worker's cap with "U.S. Gov't. Property" stamp and "Holston Ordnance Works" patch. (Courtesy: John Mull)

War worker's patches for various ordnance and arsenal sites. (Courtesy: Phil & Linda Darling)

A selection of ordnance patches. (Courtesy: Phil & Linda Darling)

Unidentified worker's shirtwaist.
(Courtesy: Al Schell)

Women's Overseas Hospital of the U.S.A.
(World War I)

With America's entry into World War I a New York hospital, the New York Infirmary for Women and Children, sent a medical mobile care unit to France, complete with a full staff, including female doctors. Its director was Caroline Finley. While rather plentiful, these *bona fide* physicians had been repeatedly turned down for service in the ranks of the army's medical corps. Members of the Women's Overseas Hospital offered their services to the war effort, but were turned down by the government. The French, however, welcomed them. More than five hundred refugees were cared for by the W.O.H. at Labouheyre, France.[1048]

Dr. Finley and about thirty others formed a splinter group that went to work in French hospitals alongside French physicians. In the interim, the direction of the WOH was given to Mrs. Raymond Brown, who was appointed General Director in France of the Women's Overseas Hospital. The organization was disbanded in 1920.[1049]

These women were uniformed, but the only description of them found was that they were dressed "in khaki and puttees...like real men...about thirty of them."[1050]

Women's Unit of the Jewish Welfare Board
(See, "The Jewish Welfare Board," p. 319, Vol. 1)

[1048] Schneider, *Into the Breach,* p. 90.
[1049] Ibid, p. 90.
[1050] Ibid, p. 90.

Women War Correspondents
(World War I, World War II, the Korean and Vietnam War)

Peggy Hull Deuell (1889-1967). This photo was taken during her first assignment covering the Texas-Mexico border problems with Pancho Villa in 1916. The uniform was borrowed from the Ohio National Guard. (Courtesy: Otto Spronk photo coll.)

Peggy Hull Deuell's correspondent's pass for the Siberia Expedition in 1918. (Courtesy: Otto Spronk photo coll.)

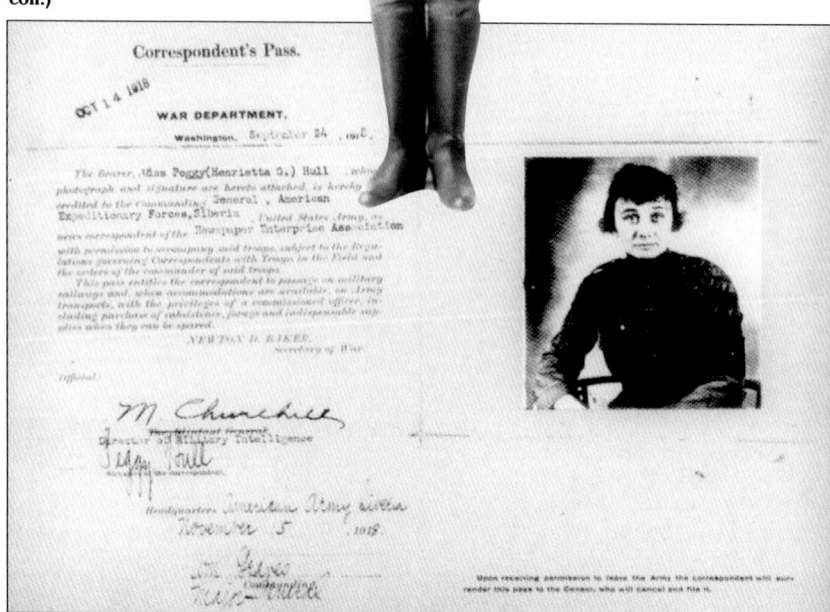

Ruth Cowan is geared-out for battlefield reporting with all the necessary military equipment. The "C" armband indicates a war correspondent. No other insignia were worn. (Courtesy: Otto Spronk photo coll.)

The "C" armband was initially the only insigne to be worn by female correspondents as shown on this bookcover on the life of the famous war photographer, Dickey Chapelle. (The book was published by Ballentine Books of New York in 1992.) (Courtesy: Otto Spronk photo coll.)

Note: Dickey Chapelle was killed while on patrol with U.S. Marines near DaNang, Vietnam, in November 1965.

In October 1943, Lieutenant General Jacob L. Devers, commander of the US forces in the European Theater of Operations (ETO), ordered that women war correspondents would now wear a khaki beret, instead of the standard service cap [i.e., "garrison cap."] The reason for this order is that eight women had signed a petition requesting the change. Devers reasoned that, "if eight women can agree on any one hat, they ought to have it."[1051]

Helen Kirkpatrik in 1942. She is wearing the U.S. Army woman's officer uniform with a dark green patch with gold lettering on her beret. Note that the patch is padded and the lettering is hand-embroidered gold wire. (Courtesy: Otto Spronk photo coll.)

U.S. War Correspondent patch worn on the garrison cap. It has orange-yellow embroidery on a dark green base. (Courtesy: Otto Spronk photo coll.)

Women correspondents in London, 1942. Left to right: Mary Welsh, Dixie Tighe, Kathleen Harriman, Helen Kirkpatrick, Lee Miller, and Tania Long. They wear army uniforms with the officer's "U.S." on the garrison cap, and the "C" armband. Note that some wear the male officer's style self belt with buckle. (Courtesy: Otto Spronk photo coll.)

[1051] "Eight Women Agree on a Hat; To Devers That's News," *The New York Times* October 22, 1943: p. 15.

The men's style officer's garrison cap remained, however, as the staple of the uniform worn by female war correspondents. It had the round "U.S. War Correspondent" patch in yellow thread, sewn to the left forward curtain of the cap.

France, 1944. Left to right: Ruth Cowan (AP), Sonia Tomara (*New York Herald Trib.*), Rosette Hargrove (Newspaper Enterprise Assn.), and Betty Knox (*Evening Standard*, UK). Ruth Cowan has a cloth war correspondent's patch glued to the front of her helmet.

Virginia Irwin in Berlin, 1945. She is wearing the beret with the round war correspondent patch, and a square war correspondent shoulder patch on her raincoat. (Courtesy: Otto Spronk photo coll.)

Female correspondents wore officers' uniforms, for example, the olive-drab elastique blouse with gold metal "U.S." insignia pinned near each end of the collar. The "U.S. War Correspondent" patch was sewn to the upper left sleeve of the blouse. "War Correspondent" was machine-embroidered in yellow thread upon matching wool and sewn just above the left breast pocket. The rest of their wardrobe was standard WAC or ANC issue with the "U.S. War Correspondent" insigne added. Plain olive-drab plastic buttons were worn on the blouse or the standard US Army buttons were covered with self material.

Civilian employee of the U.S. War Department patch (blue triangle on tan base cloth). It has been observed being worn by female war correspondents. (Courtesy: Otto Spronk photo coll.)

As above, but for war correspondents. (Courtesy: Otto Spronk photo coll.)

As above, but for radio commentators. (Courtesy: Otto Spronk photo coll.)

Sonia Tomara in 1942. She is wearing the officer's piped garrison cap with the dark green war correspondent's patch. Above the left blouse is the yellow on black "War Correspondent" stripe.

[War Correspondent patch image]

Narrow "War Correspondent" patch sometimes sewn just above the left bodice pocket of the blouse (yellow on black, olive-drab or tan).

"Official U.S. War Correspondent" patch (yellow cotton thread embroidery on black base cloth).

"Official U.S. War Photographer" patch (yellow on black). (Courtesy: Otto Spronk photo coll.)

"Official U.S. Army Photographer's" patch (hand-embroidered gold wire on a ribbed black cloth). (Courtesy: Otto Spronk photo coll.)

As above, but orange-yellow machine-embroidery on a black base cloth. It has been observed sewn on an armband. (Courtesy: Otto Spronk photo coll.)

"U.S. War Correspondent" patch (black cotton thread embroidery on brown felt-like cloth). (Courtesy: Otto Spronk photo coll.)

Some correspondents wore slip-on "U.S. War Correspondent" loops on the shoulder straps of their uniform.

Tropical slip-on loop for the epaulets (blue lettering on a khaki base cloth). (Courtesy: Otto Spronk photo coll.)

WAAC officer's blouse with blue on tan war correspondent shoulder patch. Unique on this blouse are the embroidered blue on tan lapel diamonds with the "U.S." showing through. (Courtesy: Otto Spronk photo coll.)

Shoulder patch for war correspondents with the publication "The Stars and Stripes" (yellow embroidery on black cloth base). (Courtesy: Otto Spronk photo coll.)

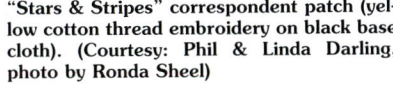

"Stars & Stripes" correspondent patch (yellow cotton thread embroidery on black base cloth). (Courtesy: Phil & Linda Darling, photo by Ronda Sheel)

Female war correspondent's olive-drab elastique blouse. The gilt U.S. Army buttons have been covered with self material. (Courtesy: Phil & Linda Darling, photo by Ronda Sheel)

"Pacific Stars and Stripes" war correspondent's patch. The first edition of the "Pacific" version was published on October 3, 1945 and covered the post-war period, Korea and Vietnam. Red/white/blue embroidery on a blue ribbed base material. (Courtesy: Otto Spronk photo coll.)

As above, but in hand-embroidered wire. (Courtesy: Otto Spronk photo coll.)

"Yank Correspondent" patch (orange on a tan base cloth with "Correspondent" in yellow thread). (Courtesy: Otto Spronk photo coll.)

Navy war correspondent collar insignia. The anchor is gilt and the "C" is silver colored. (Courtesy: Otto Spronk photo coll.)

Navy war correspondent patches. Left: gold wire hand-embroidery and right: yellow cotton embroidery on a black cloth base. (Courtesy: Otto Spronk photo coll.)

U.S. Marine Corps war correspondent stripe (red lettering on a black base cloth). (Courtesy: Otto Spronk photo coll.)

Metal war correspondent's badge. It has been observed worn as a cap insigne as well as a breast insigne by U.S. and British war correspondents during the World War II and Korea periods. (Courtesy: Otto Spronk photo coll.)

Metal "U.S. War Correspondent" badge similar in design to the previously illustrated one. (Courtesy: Ed Anderson, Jr.)

Shelley Smith Mydans, *Life* correspondent.

China/Burma/India World War II war correspondent shoulder patches. Left: fully machine-woven version (red/white/blue with an olive-drab edging). Below: multi-piece construction with embroidered lettering. (Courtesy: Otto Spronk photo coll.)

Note: all the illustrated insignia in this section were worn by both male and female war correspondents and photographers.

Epaulet slip-on for "Allied War Correspondents" wearing the British uniform in World War II. Gold wire hand-embroidery on a dark green base cloth. (Courtesy: Otto Spronk photo coll.)

"C" war correspondent's patch worn on the garrison cap while wearing the British uniform in World War II. (Courtesy: Otto Spronk photo coll.)

As above, but for "Foreign War Correspondents" wearing the British uniform. (Courtesy: Otto Spronk photo coll.)

As above, but "C" and background in gold wire for wear on the British visored cap. (Courtesy: Otto Spronk photo coll.)

Asian-made "Official U.S. Army Photographer" patch (yellow-orange machine-embroidery on a black base material). (Courtesy: Otto Spronk photo coll.)

United Nations arm patch for war correspondents. It was worn by correspondents from all allied nations covering the Korean War (white and blue "terry cloth" texture). (Courtesy: Otto Spronk photo coll.)

"American Forces Korea Network/radio and TV" patch (white on a black base cloth, A.F.K.N. Radio/TV lettering done in red thread). (Courtesy: Otto Spronk photo coll.)

"American Forces Network Europe" radio and TV patch (white and blue embroidery on a red base cloth). (Courtesy: Otto Spronk photo coll.)

Following is a partial listing of famous female war correspondents in World War I and II.

World War I:
Peggy Hull,
Gertrude Atherton,
Rheta Dorr, *New York Evening Mail & Evening Post*,
Sophie Treadwell, *The San Francisco Bulletin*,
Ellen Lame,
Medallion Dotty,
Winifred Sweet Black,
Helen Johns Kirtland, *Leslie's Weekly*,
Sigrid Schultz, *Chicago Tribune*,
Anna Steese Richardson, *McCall's*,

World War II:
Therese Bonney
Margaret Bourke-White;
Iris Carpenter, *Boston Globe*,
Ruth Cowan, *The Associated Press*,
Gladys Rockmore Davis, *Life*,
Peggy (Henrietta G.) Hull Deuell, Lawrence, Kansas,
Janet Flanner, *The New Yorker*,
Rosette Hargrove, *Newspaper Enterprise Association*,
Helen Kirkpatrick,
Betty Knox, *England's Evening Standard*,
Erica Mann, *Liberty Magazine*,
Lee Miller, *Vogue*,
Sonia Tomara, *New York Herald Tribune*,[1052]

World War II was covered by a total of 127 female war correspondents and war photographers.

[1052] Frederick K. Voss, *"Reporting the War. The Journalistic Coverage of World War II."* (Washington, DC: Smithsonian Institution Press, 1994) pp. 81-82, and 194-195.

Lee Miller, *Vogue*. (Courtesy: George A. Petersen)

Margaret Bourke-White has a hot drink on board a rescuing destroyer, with Lord David Herbert, transport radio officer. (Courtesy: George A. Petersen)

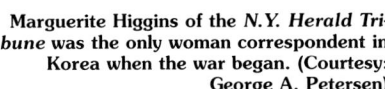

Marguerite Higgins of the *N.Y. Herald Tribune* was the only woman correspondent in Korea when the war began. (Courtesy: George A. Petersen)

Women War Department Civilian Employees
(Uniformed)

Civilian women serving with the War Department wore the same uniform described before, but with lapel insignia consisting of inverted khaki triangles with "US" embroidered in the center in blue thread. A square khaki patch with embroidered with a blue upright triangle in the center and a khaki "US" in the center was worn on the upper left sleeve of the blouse.

Variation of the insigne worn on the lapels and garrison cap curtain by civilian women (and men) who served with the US War Department. The patch is made of silver wire embroidery with a medium blue thread "US" and a darker blue border.

Bullion version of the civilian US War Department employee patch.

Olive-drab elastique blouse worn by a civilian working for the US War Department. (Photo by Ronda Sheel)

Unusual woman's battledress jacket with kelly-green shoulder straps. Note the civilian employee of the US War Department patch on the left sleeve and on the garrison cap. The form of the cap is the standard woman's style. The crown of this example is kelly-green, matching the shoulder straps on the jacket. (Photo by Ronda Sheel)

Anne M. O'Malley of New York City wears the uniform of a civilian employed by the US War Department. It includes the small khaki triangles with blue embroidery on the lapels of the blouse and one on the left forward section of the garrison cap. This photo was taken in Berlin in 1946.

Metal blue and tan lapel and garrison cap triangles worn by civilian employees of the US War Department. (Courtesy: Ed Anderson, Jr.)

Anne M. O'Malley's uniform insignia. Top: small triangles, worn on the lapels of the uniform blouse and on the forward section of the garrison cap curtain. The larger patch at the bottom was probably worn on the left sleeve. Its triangular shape is contrary to the standard rectangular patch worn by War Department civilian employees. The lapel patches measure approximately 1.5"x1.75", whereas the larger patch measures 3.25"x3".

Women War Workers
(World War II)

Women working in the aircraft industry in California during World War II were fitted with what was called, "Flying Fortress Fashions." (Douglas, Lockheed, and Boeing factories had approved the outfits for their female employees.) They were designed by Murial King, who had created fashions for Ginger Rogers, Katherine Hepburn and Margaret Sullivan.

King's fashions for war workers had a distinct "flight" theme, including lines in her clothes which suggested "wings." She also designed divisional insignia of unknown design to be worn on the left collars of the outfits. King suggested that workers should wear hash marks to denote length of service on the left sleeve of their uniforms below the company logo.

King created a wardrobe of twelve items, including Celanese suits for office workers, heavy duty coveralls, slacks, work aprons, overalls, skirts, shirts and dresses. The color of the material was "flight blue."

Fabrics were chosen for their durability. Celanes, a materiel with a tight weave that resembled sharkskin, was selected to be used for the uniforms worn by office workers. Celanese fabric was named, "Fortress fabric," and was used in the making of the work jacket, dress, dress skirt, shirt, a tailored shirt and blouse, apron and pants. Sanforized cotton was used to make clothing for heavy work: A bench apron, overalls, jacket, pants, shirts and overalls.

King later worked to design a combination lunch box and beauty kit, along with becoming safety headwear and shoes.[1053]

Women war workers wore a variety of clothing, along with identification badges and in some cases, the patch of the company they worked for.

Pratt & Whitney worker's identification badge. The yellow horizontal bar at the bottom indicated the person's type of work. Note the Pratt & Whitney length-of-service pins attached to the leather tab. (Phil & Linda Darling)

A lathe worker in California in 1942 wears a slack suit and bandanna.

Label inside a pair of navy blue coveralls. (Courtesy: Phil & Linda Darling)

1053 Virginia Pope, "Wardrobes Ready for War Workers," *The New York Times,* April 26, 1943: p. 16.

Consolidated Aircraft worker's patch. (Courtesy: Phil & Linda Darling)

Anita Carlson wears the Consolidated Aircraft Corporation patch on the left sleeve of her uniform. (Courtesy: Olio's)

A supervisor in a plant in Texas which produced aircraft for the Navy (L) wears what appears to be a khaki uniform and dark tie. She also wears a miniature set of USN aviator's wings over a winged patch, the center of which reads, "We keep them flying." Below this patch is her identification badge. (Courtesy: Franklin D. Roosevelt Library)

Gold and white production pins. These pins were also made in silver and white.

Monsanto Chemical workers wearing the company uniform.

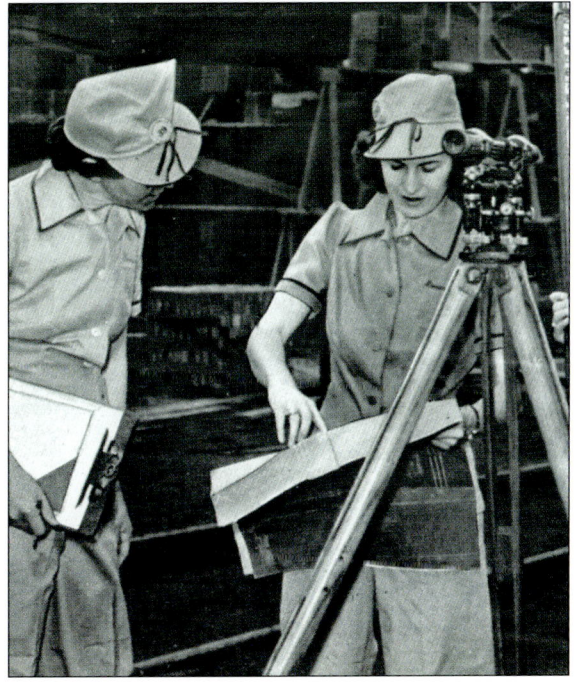

Joe Stone

HAWTHORNE CLUB

D. A. MOORE, PRESIDENT
J. H. SWARD, VICE-PRESIDENT
ELIZABETH MATUSZ, VICE-PRESIDENT
G. F. BARTIZAL, TREASURER

E. L. F. HEINRICH, EXECUTIVE SECRETARY

HAWTHORNE STATION   CHICAGO, ILL.

TELEPHONE
LAWNDALE 5000
EXTENSION 3903

December 1943

Name: Anna H. Forst   Dept. 2546

Your Officers and Directors of the Hawthorne Club have asked your supervisor to give you the attached insignia. We hope you will wear it and keep it as a symbol of your contribution to the National War Effort.

It seemed to us that the members of the Hawthorne Club would be glad to have an emblem to show their friends and associates that they are important members of our Country's "Arsenal of Communications."

We are, therefore, happy to present you with this insignia, not merely as a present-day gift, but as something you may prize in future years as an evidence of the important part you played in World War No. 2.

D. A. MOORE, President

Supervisor

A Western Electric War Worker insigne and transmittal letter presented by the Hawthorne Club of Chicago in December 1943. (Courtesy: Joe Stone)

Women's Air Reserve
(W.A.R.)

When the Betsy Ross Corporation was formed in the early 1930s a number of women fliers immediately joined, but it did not have sustaining power. Shortly thereafter another and better organization was established in the New York area called the Womens Aeronautical Air Force. Once again, after an energetic start, interest lagged. Finally, in 1933, a group of west coast women formed a new organization under the direction of Florence "Pancho" Barnes and registered it as the Women's Air Reserve (W.A.R.). As of January 1934 it had 46 members. Its purpose was to aid during disasters, especially with medical attention. The group consisted of doctors, nurses, fliers and parachutists who could go directly by air to the scene of the disaster and air-drop medication and first aid equipment to survivors.

The W.A.R. met once a week and studied first aid under the direction of Dr. Emma McNair Kittridge, and on the first Sunday of each month

Colonel Florence Barnes, Captain Nancy Chaffee, Captain Bobbi Trout and Lieutenant Violet Neill while attending the Cleveland Air Races in early September 1934.

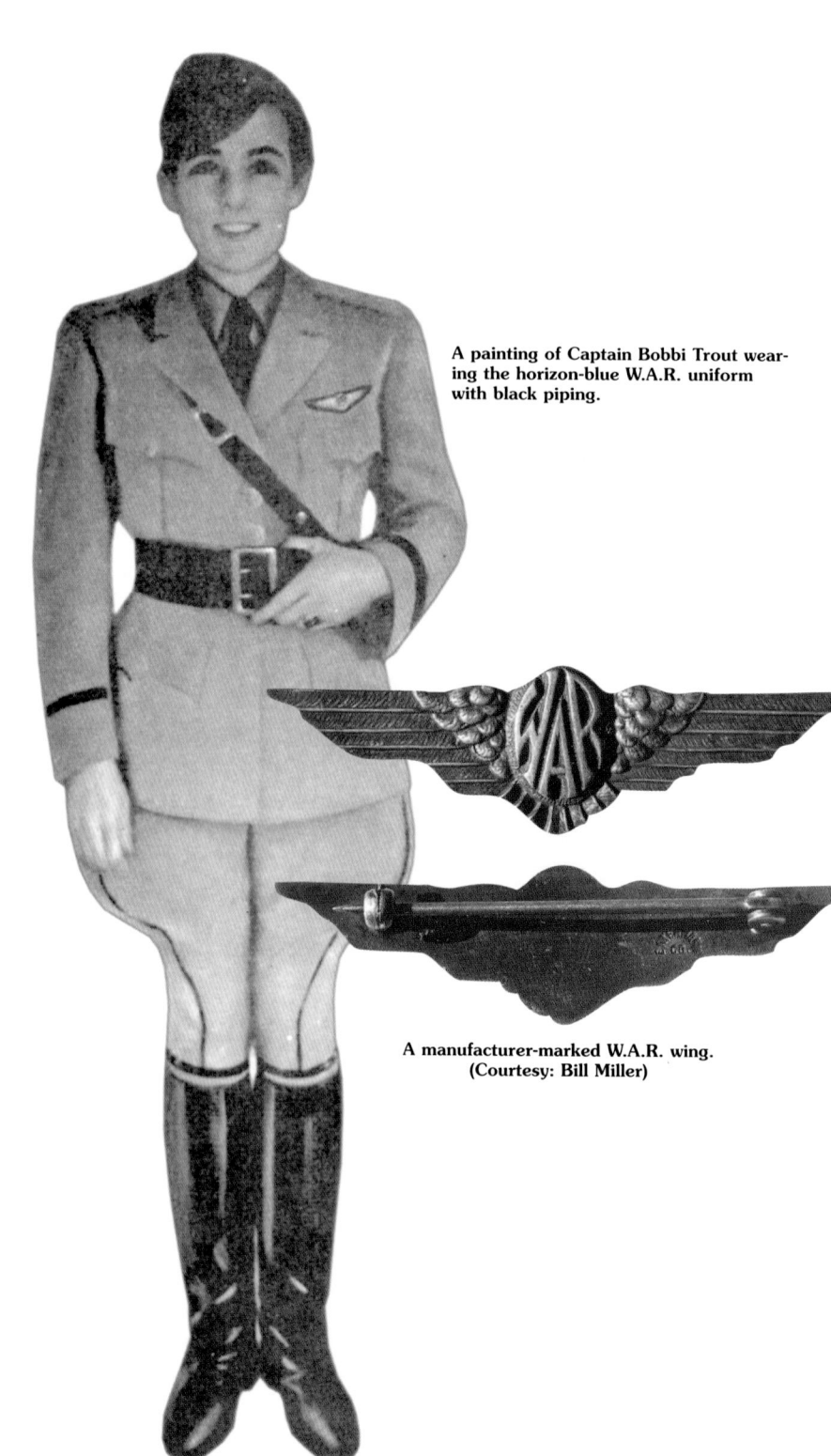

A painting of Captain Bobbi Trout wearing the horizon-blue W.A.R. uniform with black piping.

A manufacturer-marked W.A.R. wing. (Courtesy: Bill Miller)

drilled on the Army Parade Grounds at Long Beach, Alhambra Airport or Mines Field. Their preamble read in part: "The primary object of this organization shall be to train women pilots in practical mechanics, as pertaining to any skilled workmanship, academic work, and in flying so that they may be qualified and available for military or civic service in these United States of America in any national or civil emergency."

Horizon-blue jackets and breeches were worn with black berets, belts, ties and puttees or riding boots. The breeches were piped in black and the jacket sleeves had black military-style officers' stripes. The women also conferred unofficial military ranks on themselves.

As war loomed on the horizon, the government studied the feasibility of forming an auxiliary organization of women pilots for the ferrying of certain categories of airplanes. W.A.R. members soon found themselves involved in various aspects of the aviation industry, the Civil Air Patrol or the Air Corps Ferrying Command.

The W.A.R. wing. It has been determined from period photos that most members wore an embroidered version. Also, the central oval surrounding the "WAR" letters appears to be absent and the letters are more horizontal.

Mrs. Paul Mantz takes an emergency call during a drill.

The ranks on the shoulder straps are evident in this newspaper photo.

All information on the W.A.R. was documented in "Just Plane Crazy: Biography of Bobbi Trout" by Donna Veca and Skip Massio, and published by Osborne Publishers in 1987.

Women's Ambulance and Defense Corps of America
(WADCA)
(World War II)

The WADCA or, more commonly, the "WADC", was created in November 1940 in Los Angeles, California. The national commander was Victoria Brown. Members were required to take standard and advanced first aid and infantry drill courses. Some optional courses included army first aid, home nursing, nutrition, litter drill, chemical warfare, ambulance and heavy vehicle driving and rescue squad.[1054]

WADCA members participated in Red Cross First Aid classes and handled sandbags and cement, visited veteran's hospital wards, sold War Bonds, worked in canteens and served as chauffeurs and ambulance drives. As actress and WADCA Staff Sergeant Marsha Hunt explained:

"Having a station wagon at the time, I enlisted it along with me for service. ...My wagon and I would help evacuate the San Fernando Valley. Just where to, I don't think we were ever told. But we were ready."[1055]

The WADCA uniform consisted of a khaki, four-pocket blouse and a skirt with a kick pleat. Some WADCA uniforms observed were made of light olive material. The single-breasted blouse was closed by four plain russet brown plastic buttons. The flaps of the pleated patch breast pockets and side pockets were fastened with these buttons, as were the shoulder shoulder straps. Officers wore rank insignia on their shoulder straps and mohair cuff stripes on the sleeves of their blouses. Their rank insignia consisted of a series of plain circular metal badges. Auxilaries wore their rank insignia on both sleeves of the blouse and short jacket. The latter was similar to the blouse, but had no lower portion. It closed with six russet brown buttons and had a wide band at the bottom and two pleated patch pockets with scalloped flaps at the bodice. A skirt, and possibly trousers, were worn with this short jacket. A matching khaki shirtwaist and dark tie were worn with both uniforms. Common to the uniforms observed during this research was the presence of a white cloth name tag sewn inside the blouse, along with a tag printed in brown with a facsimile WADCA insigne, stating that the material of the uniform was made specifically for the WADCA uniform.

The WADCA garrison cap was cut in the style of an army officer's cap, with the same type curtain. Auxiliaries' caps had no piping, but offi-

---

[1054] Christy Fox, "Presenting the W.A.D.C.A." *The Los Angeles Times,* April 4, 1943, Women's Section ed., sec. Archives, Clubs, Features, page numbers unknown.

[1055] Marsha Hunt, *The Way We Wore. Styles of the 1930's and 40's and Our World Since Then,* (Fallbrook, CA: Fallbrook Publishing, 1993) p. 280.

National WADCA commanders meet in the San Francisco Bay area in January 1944. Seated, left to right: National Adjutant Betty Yohalem, Capt. Norma Bailey (San Francisco) and Capt. Vivian Gilmore (San Francisco). Standing, left to right: Commander Jean Giles, Commander Gladys Carter (probably from Elmira, New York) and Commander Bette Martell. Gladys Carter wears the rare WADCA blue uniform. (Courtesy: Steve Johnson)

WADCA officer's uniform. Note the WADCA emblem on the car door.

Typical khaki WADCA blouse and skirt.

Round silver-colored rank insigne on a shoulder strap.

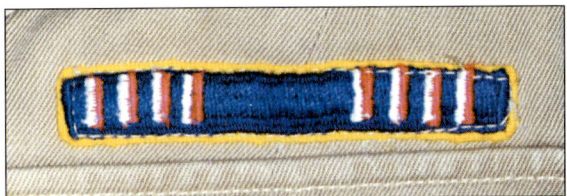

Detail of the thread ribbon bar. (Courtesy: Phil & Linda Darling)

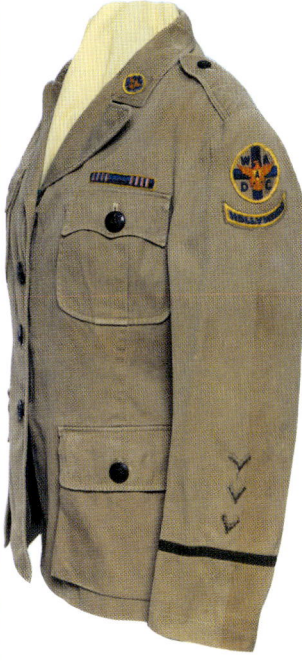

WADCA officer's blouse with the "Hollywood" tab. Note the olive-drab mohair cuff stripe, which does not encircle the sleeve, and the three chevrons. The thread ribbon bar is embroidered directly above the left breast pocket. Its significance is not known. (Courtesy: Phil & Linda Darling)

This WADCA auxiliary wears rank chevrons on her sleeves, one service chevron on the lower left sleeve, and no tab under the WADCA patch. (Courtesy: Smithsonian Institution)

WADCA auxiliaries' short khaki jacket. The "Inglewood" tab is just under the WADCA patch. The collar insignia are the embroidered kind. (Photo by Mark Riese)

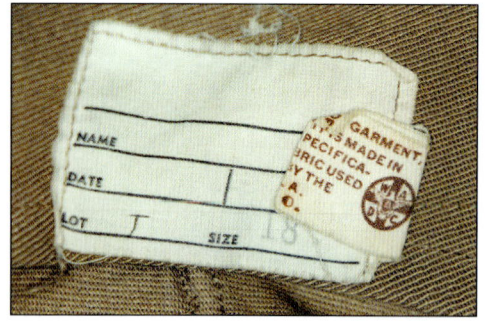

Name tag and special WADCA tag.

cers' caps were piped around the curtain, possibly in black silk with gold flecking. The WADCA patch was sewn to the left forward section of the curtian. Some auxiliaries and officers wore a brown leather belt, with or without the cross strap.

WADCA officer's cap.
(Courtesy: George A. Petersen)

Auxiliarie's garrison cap. (Photo by Ronda Sheel)

WADCA cavalry unit members wore khaki trousers and shirtwaists, ties and web belts with gold rectangular buckles and khaki garrison caps. WADCA discs were worn on the collar of the waists. The round WADCA patch with "Cavalry" tab were worn on the left sleeve of the shirt. One period photograph shows a mounted color guard with the United States flag and a special WADCA cavalry flag. The private in the photograph is saluting with a Patton sabre.

Insignia consisted of screw-back, gold metal collar discs, some of which were slightly domed while others were flat. They were embossd with the initials, "WADC", a blue enamel cross and a red enamel eagle with wings spread. A gold shield was upon its chest with a black "A" in the center. Cloth embroidered versions of the collar disc were also worn. The main

Mounted WADCA members. (Courtesy: George Petersen)

Domed WADCA collar insigne.

color difference between the two styles of collar insignia was that the embroidered one had a gold thread border.

The WADCA patch was worn on the upper left sleeve of the blouse. It was circular, with the same color scheme of the cloth collar discs. An arched tab with the town name or unit designation was worn about a half inch below the patch. The tabs were embroidered upon a khaki backing, with the name embroidered in blue thread and the tab edged with golden yellow thread.

Known WADCA patch tabs:
ACME Unit;
Alhambra;
Arcadia;
Auxiliary;
Baldwin Park;
Barstow;
Canoga Park;
Cavalry;
El Monte;
El Sereno;
Elmira, New York;
Florence Firestone;
Garfield;
Glendale;
Gloria Gardens;
Hollywood;

Standard WADCA patch with the "Hollywood" tab below. (Courtesy: Patt Anthony)

(L to R) Standard WADCA patch; oversized WADCA patch with a white backing. Also note the unusual positioning of the letters; unheard of WADCA patch with a blue backing, and different color scheme. (Courtesy: Patt Anthony)

Huntington Park;
Inglewood;
Junior;
LACGH (Los Angeles County General Hospital);
Las Vegas;
Los Angeles;
Lynwood;
Montebello;
North Long Beach;
Oakland;
Reno;
Rosemead;
San Fernando;
Shafter;
Stockton;
Temple City;
Van Nuys;
WASCO;
West Hollywood.[1056]

Trimmed WADCA tabs.
(Courtesy: Patt Anthony)

[1056] Information compiled and provided by F. Patt Anthony.

- CANOGA PARK
- CAVALRY
- EL MONTE
- EL SERENO
- ELMIRA NEW YORK
- FLORENCE FIRESTONE
- GARFIELD
- GLENDALE
- GLORIA GARDENS
- HOLLYWOOD
- HUNTINGTON PARK
- INGLEWOOD

- JUNIOR
- L.A.C.G.H.
- LAS VEGAS
- LOS ANGELES
- LYNWOOD
- MONTEBELLO
- NORTH LONG BEACH
- OAKLAND
- ROSEMEAD
- SAN FERNANDO
- SHAFTER
- STOCKTON

Small, khaki or light olive colored length-of-service chevrons were sewn to the lower left sleeve of the uniform blouse. The points of the chevrons faced the edge of the cuff.

Matchbook cover showing a Disney-designed WADCA mascot. (Courtesy: Sylvia Leasure)

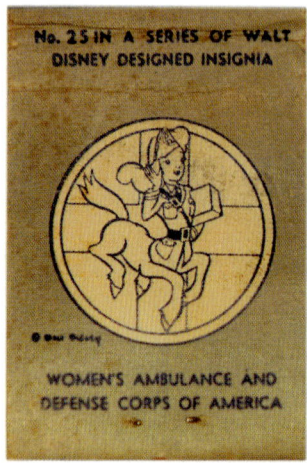

Women's Ambulance Safety Patrol
(WASP—World War II)

Established in 1940 in Illinois with eight members, these "Wasps" were a group of women volunteers who learned ambulance driving, how to take apart and reassemble an engine, map reading, military drill and first aid. By the time the United States had entered World War II, there were two hundred members. The WASP was supervised by Lieutenant Colonel William Nichol.[1057]

[1057] "They're WASPS, but They Stop War's Sting!," *Chicago Herald-American,* August 11, 2nd Front Page edition, p. 13.

Period photographs show these women wearing a white shirtwaist, dark tie, tucked-in military style, a dark skirt, dark garrison cap with colored piping with the W.A.S.P. patch sewn to the left side, above the curtain of the cap.

WASP (i.e., "Women's Ambulance Safety Patrol") patch. (Courtesy: Phil & Linda Darling)

WASP members at work. Note the wasp on their patch is a different configuration. (Courtesy: George Petersen)

Women's Army Auxiliary Corps
(WAAC)
Women's Army Corps
(WAC)
(World War II-1973)

The Women's Army Auxiliary Corps (WAAC) was established by an Act of Congress (Public Law 554—77th Congress) and approved on May 11, 1942.[1058] President Franklin D. Roosevelt signed the Women's Army Auxiliary Corps Bill on May 15th, and Oveta Culp Hobby became its director on May 16th. She served as director until July 11,

---

[1058] United States Army, *The Officer's Guide,* (Washington, DC, 1942) p. 51.

Colonel Oveta Culp Hobby. (Courtesy: National Archives)

1945.[1059] Though the WAAC served alongside the army, it was not a part of it. The first WAAC training camp was at Ft. Des Moines, Iowa. The WAAC became the Women's Army Corps, an actual part of the United States Army, on July 1, 1943. The first woman to join was Mrs. Elsie M. Clark, a grandmother.[1060]

The first class of officer candidates consisted of 440 women, forty of whom were black.[1061] This class trained four weeks and were given their commissions on August 29, 1942. They were referred to as the "Pioneer 440."[1062] The ship carrying the first WAAC officers overseas was sunk. They were rescued by a British destroyer. These women were assigned to General Eisenhower's headquarters in North Africa. At the same time,

---

[1059] Bettie J. Morden, *The Woman's Army Corps, 1945-1978*, (Washington, DC: Center of Military History, United States Army, 1990), p. ii.

[1060] Unknown period newspaper item.

[1061] Mattie E. Treadwell, *The Women's Army Corps*, (Washington, DC: Office of the Chief of Military History, 1953.) p. 590.

[1062] "We're in this War, Too," pp. 30-31.

WAAC color guard, Ft. Des Moines, Iowa.

Waac Frances Dupree Harris stands behind the training center sign at Ft. Des Moines, Iowa. (Courtesy: Frances Dupree Harris)

WAC training center sign.

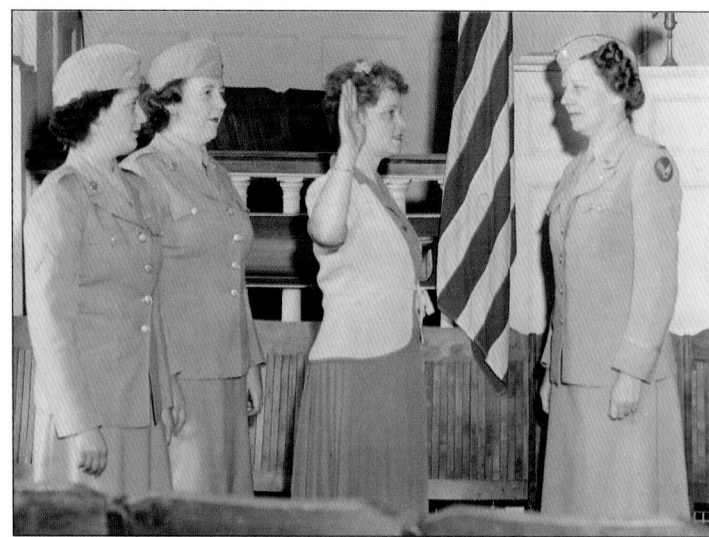

A girl from Bath, Maine, is sworn into the WAC at the Bath City Hall. (Courtesy: Fred W. Elwell)

Waacs were serving in England.[1063] The first WAAC unit sent to overseas was the 149th WAAC Headquarters, which landed in Algiers on January 27, 1943. Among these women the first Hispanic Waac, Carmen Contreras-Bozak. Japanese-American Wacs served as interpreters, interrogators and written language translators.[1064]

During World War II 140,000 women served in the WAAC/WAC, more than 5,000 of them were sent to the Pacific Theater of Operations, to places like New Guinea, Manilla, Leyte and Hollandia.[1065] They also served in the European Theater of Operations, New Caledonia, India, North Africa and Egypt. Said one stateside Wac, Corporal Sara Sykes, "We practically drool when we hear of someone going overseas."[1066] The Waacs proved to be up to their mission. In England, Colonel Hobby saw smart, competent Waacs, who were up early every morning, dressed in maroon robes with their boyfriends' patches sewn to them, hitting the cold showers. Most of these Waacs were on duty at General Eisenhower's headquarters and at Eighth Air Force installations. They faced occasional air raids, and learned to deal with them, sometimes without losing much sleep. The drill was to hustle out of the barrack, crouch in a trench until the "all clear" was sounded, and then climb back into their cots without actually waking up. The popular greeting changed from, "What's cooking?" to "Nervous in the service?" By 1944, there were 1,170 Wacs in the ETO.[1067] Sixteen Wacs received the Purple Heart for wounds they obtained while London was being bombed; 565 Wacs received the Bronze Star and

---

[1063] LaVerne Bradley, "Women in Uniform," *The National Geographic Magazine,* October 1943: p. 447.
[1064] WIMSA Calendar, 1997, see "April" and "July."
[1065] Ibid, see "September."
[1066] Army & Navy. "Hobby's Army," *Time,* January 17, 1944: p. 58.
[1067] Ibid, p. 57.

sixty-two were awarded the Legion of Merit.[1068] Wacs who served with the 9th Bombardment Division were allowed to wear six battle stars on their ETO ribbons for campains in Normandy, the Ardennes, Northern France, Central Europe, the Rhineland and the Air Offensive over Europe.[1069] General Carl A. "Tooey" Spaatz, Commander of the USSTAF, awarded the Wacs of the 302nd Transport Wing a commendation:

> "Under the weight of [German Field Marshal] von Rundstedt's smashing counter-offensive Allied lines bent, curved back, but held. Calls swamped rear echelons for supplies, men. Wacs of the 302nd Transport Wing met the challenge. From 1630 hours, December 24, [1944], until 1430 hours, Christmas Day, they worked feverishly to help get the needed reinforcements and materiel to the the front."[1070]

A contingent of sixty-two Wacs were assigned to the OSS (Office of Strategic Services) in London in 1943. It was Wac Sergeant Majorie Wells of Logan, Ohio, serving at General Eisenhower's Forward Headquarters, who typed the official cable announcing to the world Germany's unconditional surrender. Sergeant Wells stated:

> "We [Wacs] were too tired to get excited. I finished the necessary number of copies about 0530 and went home to catch some sleep. My roommate, Sergeant Katherine Ruch,...didn't believe me when I told her the news."[1071]

It was Wacs from the 3341st Signal Service Battalion who manned the telephones at the Potsdam Conference in July 1945. The 7708th WAC Detachment served with the War Crimes Group in Germany in 1946.[1072] In response to the infamous smear campaign, the origins of which are still a mystery, one WAC left this poem in her scrapbook:

"Buzz Buzz Buzz Buzz
Yes Brother sure I've heard
All your filthy rumors
And I don't believe a word.
Just who are those heroines
These women without shame
Well listen to me mister and
I'll proudly tell their names.
They're my mother and my sister
My girl friend and my wife
The kind of American women
I've respected all my life.

She's the next door neighbor's daughter
She's the girl from down the street
She the girl of American girlhood
And by gosh she can't be beat.
I won't say they're all perfect
There may be things you can't condone
Be he who's sinless among us
Let that fellow throw the stone.
And if sometime their conduct
Isn't all your fancy points
Would you want girls on the firing line
To act as plastic saints.

[1068] Philip R. Smith, Jr., "Women in Army Service," *Army Digest,* February 1969: p. 16.
[1069] LTC Anna W. Wilson, WAC Staff Inspector, *The WAC.* (Paris: The Orientation Branch, Information and Education Division, Hq., USFET, Immediate Post-World War II), pp. 3-4.
[1070] Ibid, p. 26.
[1071] Ibid, p. 2.
[1072] WIMSA 1998 Calendar, see "January."

Would you put them in a prison
Where they'd never have no fun
Would you put them in a convent
As they do the holy ones

Sure go out and spread your filth
With smirking silly smile
Then click your heels together
And give a Nazi 'Heil.'[1073]

G.I.'s in England, and probably elsewhere, were known to harrass some Wacs terribly. One Wac remembered on outings to London,

> "Wherever we went there was a chorus of wolf calls and whistles. It got tiresome. ...GI's [walked] behind us talking in loud voices about our legs, our breasts, and how we would be in bed. More than once they told us that [Wacs] were overseas to sleep with the men—that was [our] mission!"[1074]

However, other GIs appreciated the presence of the Wacs. One often visited them, "because we were like the women he knew back home, well-mannered and not swearing all the time."[1075]

The title, "Air Waac" (changed to "Air Wac" after the integration of the corps into the regular army) was coined by Army Air Force recruiters in order to increase enrollment. While the designation, "Air Wac" was officially disapproved of by the War Department, it was very popular and was used throughout the war, even on recruiting posters. By 1945 there were more than 7,300 Air Wacs serving overseas and 32,000 serving in the United States. They were assembled into companies and assigned to air bases and fields. They proudly wore Army Air Forces patches and the AAF enlisted pattern collar disc. Officer's wore the winged propeller insignia on

"Air Waac" Frances Dupree (Harris) wears the Pallas Athene collar disc and a bullion Army Air Forces patch on the upper left sleeve of her blouse. Harris served at the Santa Ana Army Air Base in California. (Courtesy: Frances Dupree Harris)

Army Air Forces metal identification badge for "Air Waac" Frances Dupree (Harris). (Courtesy: Frances Dupree Harris)

[1073] Found in the scrapbook of Pvt. Ada O'Dell, WAC Detachment, Ft. Slocum, New York.
[1074] Elizabeth P. McIntosh, *Sisterhood of Spies,* (Annapolis, Maryland: Naval Institute Press, 1998) p. 90.
[1075] Ibid.

Left: Elaine M. Winchell after receiving her commission in the WAAC.

Below: Elaine M. Winchell as a "Air WAAC" officer. (Courtesy: Candace St. Lawrence)

Elaine M. Winchell married Capt. John St. Lawrence on October 21, 1945. She joined the WAAC on December 17, 1942, and was honorably discharged on June 22, 1943 to accept a commission in the U.S. Army. (Courtesy: Candace St. Lawrence)

United States of America

Certification of Military Service

This certifies that Elaine M. Winchell
L 903 519

was a member of the Army of the United States
from June 23, 1943
to December 13, 1945
Service was terminated by Honorable Relief From Active Duty
Last Grade, Rank, or Rating First Lieutenant
Active Service Dates Same as above

Prior Active Service: Women's Army Auxiliary Corps, service number A 903 519, from December 17, 1942; honorably discharged on June 22, 1943 to accept commission in the Army of the United States.

Army Air Corps/Army Air Forces enlisted collar insigne, worn also by "Air Wacs."

AAC/AAF officer's collar insignia.

the lapels of their uniforms. Air Wacs served as clerical workers, communications, in control towers, and as aircraft mechanics, among other jobs. Some served aboard aircraft as radio operators (as noncombatants). At least twenty Air Wacs received a pair of Air Crew member wings.[1076] In 1946, many Wacs were trained at the ATC Flight Traffic Technician's School at Morrison Field, West Palm Beach, Florida, to serve aboard planes with the Air Transport Command, the "biggest airline in existance." They drew flight pay and were awarded Army Air Force Air Crew Member wings.[1077] Several Wacs served aboard planes as photographers, radio operators and

Air crew member wings.

These Wacs, wearing "Mae West" life vests, are undergoing training at the Air Transport Command (ATC) Flight Traffic Technician's school at Morrison Field, Florida. Graduates became flight traffic clerks and served aboard ATC aircraft, qualifying them to wear silver Army Air Forces crew member wings. (Courtesy: George Petersen)

[1076] Gordon Rottman and Francis Chin, Elite Series: US Army Air Force: 2. (London, England: Osprey, 1994) p. 28.
[1077] "Members of WAC Fly with the ATC, Wear Wings," WAC News Letter, Vol. 2, No. 3. (January 1946): p. 3.

mechanics. A few Air Medals were awarded to Wacs, one to a Wac detailed in India for her work in mapping the "Hump." Another Wac received the Air Medal posthumously. She was serving aboard a plane used for aerial broadcasting when it crashed.[1078] (After the end of World War II, some Air Wacs were made members of the United States Air Force in 1948, and were designated, "Wafs." ("Women in the United States Air Force.")

WAC members contributed to many of the achievements of World War II. Members detailed at Los Alamos and Pasco were especially proud the day atomic bombs were dropped on Hiroshima and Nagasaki. The feeling was that Wacs who worked on the Manhattan Project (or the atomic bomb project) had done more than any to shorten the war and spare the lives of American soldiers. It was dubbed, "our day," and selected WAC units were awarded the Meritorious Unit Service Award. One WAC officer received the Legion of Merit and twenty Wacs were awarded the Army Commendation Ribbon.[1079]

General Eisenhower sent a telegram to Colonel Hobby on May 14, 1945, the WAC's third anniversary. It read,

"During the time I have had Wacs under my command, they have met every test and task assigned them. I have seen them work in Africa, Italy, England, here in France—at Army installations throughout the European Theater. Their contrubution in efficiency, skill, spirit, and determination is immeasurable. In three years the Women's Army Corps has built for itself an impressive record of conduct and of service, and given the womanhood of America every right to be proud of their accomplishments."[1080]

Medal of Saint Geneviev of Paris, patron saint of the WAC.

WAAC service medal and miniature version.

[1078] Mattie E. Treadwell, United States Army in World War II. Special Studies: "The Women's Army Corps." (Washington, DC: Office of the Chief of Military History, Department of the Army, 1954) p. 286.
[1079] Ibid, pp.328-329.
[1080] Lt.Col. Wilson, *The WAC*. (Paris, Immediate post-World War II publication), pp. 30-31.

Wacs served with distinction during the Korean and Vietnam wars. A handful of women served with combat units in Vietnam. Communication Specialist Donna Loring was assigned to the 44th Signal Battalion at Long Binh and was under fire during the Tet Offensive. She and 100 other women slept in wooden huts, unarmed and protected by only one GI with an M-16.[1081]

During the time of organizing the WAAC, Colonel Hobby had the only WAAC uniform in existence. "She had to take an electric fan and an electric iron on her travels so that she could wash it out every night."[1082]

A reporter for *"Newsweek,"* posing as a recruit, went through the clothing line and was issued articles of uniform. "Though I felt strait-jacketed in my uniform, I discovered that the regular Waacs love them."[1083] At first, and to the relief of everyone, it was announced that the Army would not design the WAAC uniform. That assignment was given to Dorothy Shaver, who was vice president of Lord & Taylor of Manhattan.[1084] Colonel Hobby assisted with the creation of the WAAC uniform. However, the design of the uniform eventually became the responsibility of men in the Quartermaster Corps, who tried to design a WAAC uniform based on men's standard sizes, such as 42 long, 42 short, etc., whereas women's sizes were entirely different. The result was a stiff and masculine looking uniform. Finally, a Women's Clothing Section was created within the Research and Development Branch, Military Planning Division, which was located in New York, instead of Philadelphia. Ira Markwett, Captain R.H. Barmon and Maxine Spengler were appoint to this new department.[1085]

However, procurement was initially a problem, with many Waacs going through basic training without uniforms. Those who did have uniforms sometimes had the "wrong" ones. The 42nd WAAC Post Headquarters Company from Daytona Beach, Florida, arrived at Fort Dix, New Jersey in a blinding snowstorm wearing summer-weight uniforms. Equally distressing was that Waacs stationed in the desert southwest had to wear long sleeve shirts and woolen anklets. Colonel Hobby had to repeatedly request that an overcoat be provided for the Waacs and, while she was in England, the commandant of Fort Des Moines, Colonel Hoag, pleaded for shipments of gloves, wool lined trousers, wool underwear, and the like, to "properly protect and safeguard [the] health of this command." He was ignored.[1086] The whole problem of supply to the WAAC can be traced to the

---

[1081] Barbara Walsh, "Women of Valor," *Maine Sunday Telegram,* July 4, 1999, Coast Edition edition, pp. 1A and 10A.

[1082] Helen Rogan, Mixed Company. *Women in the Modern Army.* (New York: G.P. Putnam's Sons, 1981) p. 130.

[1083] Weatherford, *American Women and World War II* , p. 48.

[1084] Ibid.

[1085] Unless otherwise noted, the majority of information contained herein was found in the book by Erna Risch, *A Wardrobe for Women of the Army.* (Washington, DC: Office of the Quartermaster General, 1945) pp.25-26.

[1086] Mattie E. Treadwell, United States Army in World War II. Special Studies: "The Women's

seemingly lack of interest on behalf of the Quartermaster Corps of the Army, the Requirements Division and the Services of Supply. (One ingenious WAC serving in the South Pacific prepared herself a bridal gown by using a parachute canopy, which had been given to her by a member of an airborne unit near her. She made a veil from khaki mosquito netting, bleached white.)[1087]

The WAAC winter uniform consisted of a blouse and skirt of dark olive drab 12 oz. covert wool cloth, the color having been decided on March 11, 1942. Officers' uniforms could be made of dark or light olive-drab, whereas the uniforms worn by enlisted women were made of olive-drab or light olive-drab material. Khaki cotton was chosen to be used in the manufacturing of officer and enlisted rank's summer uniform.

The first WAAC officer's blouse had a four-button front closure, two pocket flaps with buttons on the bodice and two slash pockets on the lower sides.

In March 1942, in order to conserve metal it was decided that olive-drab plastic buttons would be used on the uniform, instead of standard metal ones. These buttons were embossed with the WAAC eagle (see section about headdress.) Enlisted women did not received gold buttons embossed with the coat-of-arms of the Army of the United States, until the summer of 1944.

WAAC olive-drab plastic button.

The lower sleeves of the blouse had officer's mohair cuff braid. Rank was worn on the shoulders on sewn-on passants, of the same material as the uniform. These were replaced by shoulder straps when the WAAC became part of the Army, but the blouse with passants was worn until supplies were exhausted.

A cloth belt was included on the premier WAAC uniform, designed by Maria Krum (March 25, 1942), but it was soon eliminated, since it was pointed out by Colonel Grice that it clashed with the uniform. After meeting with designer Philip Mangone on April 27, Colonel Hobby decided that a belt would be an asset to the WAAC uniform, and give it a military flair. The first Waacs to receive this uniform were stationed at Ft. Des Moines, Iowa. It was noted that some Waacs pulled the belt too tight, ruining the line of the blouse. The belt was eliminated in October.

Army Corps." (Washington, DC: Office of the Chief of Military History, Department of the Army, 1954) pp. 151-152.
[1087] Helen Rogan, Mixed Company. *Women in the Modern Army.* (New York: G.P. Putnam's Sons, 1981) p. 137.

This WAAC officer models the belted blouse and "pink" skirt. (Courtesy: National Archives)

Enlisted version of the WAAC uniform with the belted blouse. (Courtesy: National Archives)

A close-up of the passant with rank insignia. (Courtesy: Ed Anderson, Jr.)

The second pattern WAAC uniform was like the first, without the belt, but the passants remained at the shoulders of the uniform blouse.

Second pattern WAAC uniform without belt. (Courtesy: Noelle Young)

Winter uniform with passants. (Courtesy: Ed Anderson, Jr.)

These two WAAC "Junior Leaders," i.e., corporals, wear the second pattern winter uniform with the olive-drab buttons. Both are "Air Waacs" and the one at right wears distinctive insignia on the lapels of her blouse. (Courtesy: Marshall University)

Though not found in regulations, it appears that WAAC/WAC trainees at times wore a khaki blouse with plain brown buttons. (Courtesy: National Archives)

Colonel Hobby wearing the belted khaki summer uniform.

Second pattern WAAC uniform without cloth belt. (Courtesy: Noelle Young)

These Waacs wear the khaki belted uniform with no insignia, probably indicating that they are recruits.

Khaki version of the second pattern WAAC uniform.

Second pattern WAAC officer's khaki blouse with passants at the shoulders and plastic buttons embossed with the WAAC eagle. Though not present, WAAC officer's "Pallas Athene" insignia would have been worn on the lapels. This uniform belonged to Ruth A. Shaver who enlisted in the WAAC on Nov. 4, 1942. She became a captain and spent 20 months in Europe as an assistant intelligence officer and a member of the French Intelligence section of the Psychological Warfare Division, SHAEF. Shaver was awarded the Bronze Star and Legion of Honor before her discharge in 1947. (Courtesy: Greensboro Historical Museum, Greensboro, North Carolina, photo by Patt Anthony)

US Army Signal Corps Lieutenant Jimmie Dollahite wears the second pattern uniform. While the belt was no longer worn, the passants remained, May 13, 1943.

WAAC officer ranks and their military equivalent:
- Director — Colonel
- Assistant Director — Lieutenant Colonel

Field Director	Major
First Officer	Captain
Second Officer	First Lieutenant
Third Officer	Second Lieutenant[1088]

WAAC enlisted ranks and their equivalent:

Chief Leader	Master Sergeant
Technical Leader	Technical Sergeant
First Leader	First Sergeant
Staff Leader	Staff Sergeant
Leader	Sergeant
Junior Leader	Corporal
Auxiliary First Class	Private First Class
Auxiliary	Private[1089]

The profile of the Greek goddess of war, Pallas Athene, was approved as the branch insigne of the WAAC on June 26, 1942. On March 25, 1942, old gold and moss-tone green were chosen as the official branch colors of the WAAC.

The head of the Greek goddess of war, Pallas Athene, the WAAC/WAC branch-of-service insignia. (Courtesy: National Archives)

WAAC/WAC guidon. (Courtesy: US Army Museum, Ft. Sam Houston)

Small WAAC pin, probably for wear on civilian clothing, with chain and year "42."

WAAC rings, showing the profile of Pallas Athene. (Courtesy: Sylvia Leasure and Noelle Young)

[1088] Mary Steele Ross, *American Women in Uniform*. (Garden City, NJ: Garden City Publishing Co., Inc., 1943) p. 61.

[1089] Ibid, pp. 61-62.

WAAC pledge pin. (Courtesy: John Mull)

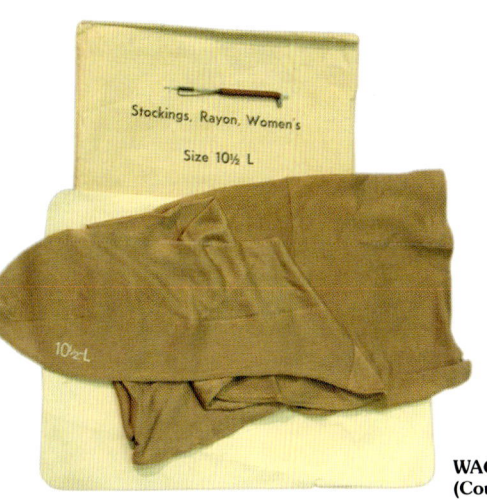

WAC hose and darning hook. (Courtesy: John Mull)

WAC guidon. (Courtesy: John Mull)

WAC/ANC folding slippers. (Courtesy: John Mull)

This 1943 dated photo, taken in Des Moines, Iowa, shows two ladies assigned to the 7th Service Command. Note the differences in the two uniforms and unit patches (left is later with thick rays and right is earlier with narrow rays. (Courtesy: John Mull)

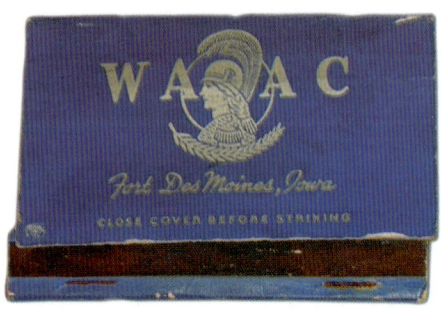

WAAC matchbook. (Courtesy: John Mull)

WAC matchbook cover. (Courtesy: John Mull)

Souvenir postcard set depicting W.A.A.C. activities. (Courtesy: Noelle Young)

Blue felt souvenir WAAC pennant. (Courtesy: Noelle Young)

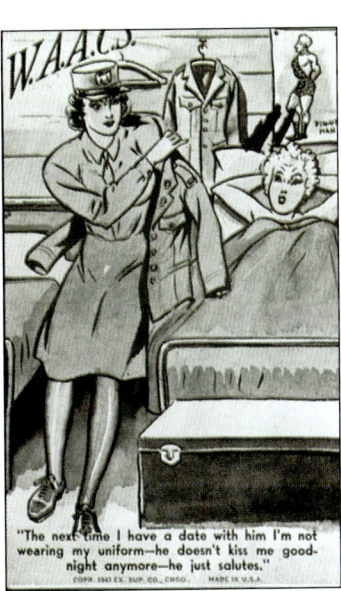

Maroon pocket-size patch for the WAACS. (Courtesy: Noelle Young)

Humorous W.A.A.C.S. postcard. (Courtesy: Noelle Young)

Souvenir W.A.C. t-shirt purchased at Ft. Des Moines, Iowa. (Courtesy: Noelle Young)

A Halco-made WAAC play suit consists of a cap, blouse, skirt and simulated leather purse and belt. At right is a detailed photo of the "Jr. WAAC" patch. (Courtesy: Noelle Young)

WAAC identification bracelet.

WAAC officers wore the standard rank insignia worn by regular army officers and enlisted women wore standard army chevrons. Since it was unlawful for any person not a member of the United States Army to wear its uniform or any distinctive part of it, it was necessary for enlisted Waacs to wear a old-gold tab embroidered with "W.A.A.C" in moss-tone thread directly under their chevrons.

Above: Fully embroidered "WAAC" tab. Right: On golden-yellow felt. (Courtesy: Noelle Young)

A detachment of Waacs arrive in England, July 19, 1943. Note that the WAAC Private First Class wears the "WAAC" tab beneath her chevron. (Courtesy: National Archives)

WAAC-inspired compacts. The finish of the one at left is green enamel and the one at right is blue enamel.

WAC-related compacts.
(Courtesy: Noelle Young)

WWII WAC Identification Tags
(Courtesy: Steve Rohde)

```
LOU EMMA CANFIELD
L-800019  T42-45   A
MRS.C.Z.CANFIELD
GEORGE WEST
TEXAS           P
```

M-1940: Steel, Type 1. WAC officer with an Army of the United States (AUS) commission. The T42 date probably indicates an original WAAC officer. "L" prefix—WAC officer. Next-of-kin name and address.

M-1940: Steel, Type 2. Tag issued in 1944. No next-of-kin.

```
TER HAAR, DOROTHY
L-116060  T43-44   O

                   P
```

```
MABEL V GIBSON
A-906371   T43 44   A
MRS EDITH M PULLEY
125 N 4TH ST
CORVALLIS ORE     P
```

M-1940: Brass, Type 1. "A" prefix—Army enlisted female.

M-1940: Brass, Type 1. First tag issued in Feb. 1943 in Des Moines, Iowa.

```
EVELYN M. SIEMS
A 202182   T43      O
CHARLOTTE M. SIEMS
88-18 150 STREET
JAMAICA, N. Y.
```

```
EVELYN M. SIEMS
A-202182  T43 44  O

                  P
```

M-1940: Steel, Type 2. Second tag issued in Feb. 1944 at Ft. Ogolthorp, Georgia. No next-of-kin.

M-1940: Steel, Type 1. This next-of-kin tag has "J" for Jewish religion.

```
CARLYN R SAIDEL
A-201108   T43    B
SOPHIA S FELDMAN
30 W 54TH ST
NEW YORK N Y     J
```

M-1940: Steel, Type 2. This tag was issued in the 9th Corps area.

Hand-knitted identification tag bag worn by WAC Dorothy Elrod.

Identification tag worn by Mrs. Ruth B. Yost, a civilian female working for the U.S. Army during World War II.

```
  GINGER
M. V. GIBESON
WAC DET T.P.S.
FT. BENNING, GA.
```

Left and below: Identification tags for M.V. Gibeson's dog, "Ginger." The pet was obviously moved from coast to coast. The "T.P.S." designation at left is for The Parachute School.

```
EMMA ROHDE
A-609255 T44    O


                C
```

Identification tag worn by Emma Rohde who enlisted at age 49 on August 16, 1944. She had three sons also in the service during World War II.

331

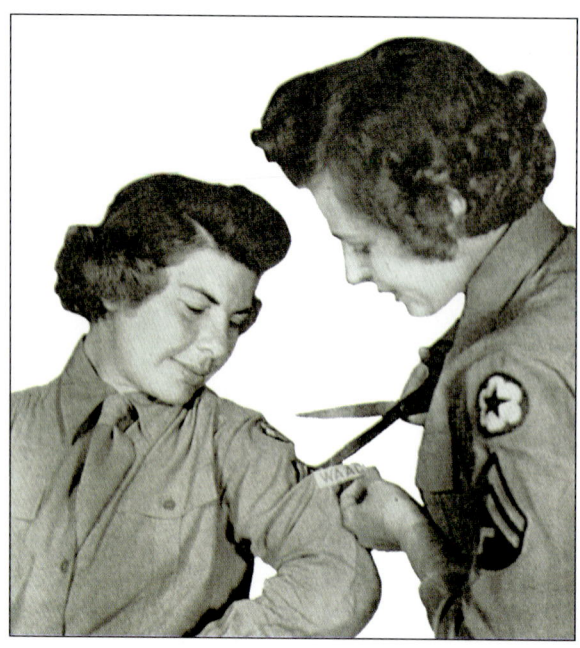

A Waac has the "W.A.A.C." tabs removed from the sleeves of her shirtwaist, signifying the absorption of the WAAC into the US Army, thus becoming one of its branches, i.e., the WAC. (Courtesy: George Petersen)

Enlisted members of the WAAC wore the standard Army "U.S." gold, clutch-back disc on the right collar of the uniform blouse and waist, while a gold disc bearing the left profile image of Pallas Athene was worn on the left collar. Officers wore the cut-out profile image of Pallas Athene on their lapels. and the left side of their shirtwaist collars. It was to be worn in like manner after the WAAC became the Women's Army Corps, unless the wearer was detailed to a branch-of-service, such as the Army Air Forces or signal corps, at which time the appropriate branch insignia would be worn (e.g., a wing and propeller for the Army Air Forces and crossed signal flags for the signal corps.) Wacs were not permitted to wear the insignia of the infantry, field artillery, coast artillery, tank destroyer units, cavalry and armored center units.[1090]

WAAC/WAC enlisted woman's collar disc.

WAAC and WAC officer's lapel insigne.

[1090] AR 600-37,

The WAC officer on the right wears the lapel insignia of an infantry officer indicating service at the Infantry School at Ft. Benning, Georgia (this was not according to regulations).

Captain Jane S. Humboldt Heald, WAC recruiting officer, wears the dark olive-drab shirtwaist and khaki tie with her new captain's bars pinned on the right side of the collar and the Pallas Athene insigne on the left. November 20, 1944.

Waacs wore a shirtwaist of 4-1/2 oz., plain weave cotton with a matching khaki necktie. They were also provided with an olive-drab shirtwaist. During the summer months, Waac drivers wore a two piece herringbone twill suit, as well as khaki slacks and shirts (provided in 1944).

These Washington D.C. Waacs wear the khaki shirtwaist, tie, skirt and "Hobby hat."

Olive-drab wool shirtwaist worn with dark olive-drab tie. (Courtesy: National Archives)

"Air Wac" olive-drab wool shirtwaist. (Courtesy: Frances Dupree Harris)

Herringbone twill shirtwaist and trousers. (Courtesy: National Archives)

The WAAC service shoe was a brown leather oxford made by Marshall, Meadows & Stewart, Inc. At this time (May 1942), plans for galoshes, moccasin-style bedroom slippers and athletic shoes were submitted to the General Staff for approval.

WAAC/WAC brown service shoes. The shoe at far left has an issue rubber overshoe. (Courtesy: Noelle Young)

Waac Margaret Bliss Lane puts a shine on her shoes. She was the daughter of the US Ambassador to Columbia, Arthur Bliss Lane. Ft. Des Moines, Iowa, February 19, 1943. (Courtesy: National Archives)

When the Women's Army Auxiliary Corps (WAAC) became the Women's Army Corps (WAC) in 1943, it's members were then a bona fide part of the United States Army, and had the right to wear its uniforms and insignia. The plastic uniform buttons were replaced with standard gold ones, embossed with the Great Seal of the United States. The WAAC hat insignia were replace by standard officer's and enlisted men's insignia.

The winter service uniform for WAC officers and warrant officers consisted of an olive-drab women officer's wool garrison cap with officer piping, olive-drab blouse or field jacket. The only difference in this uniform from the previous one was that the passants were replaced with shoulder straps. A khaki shirtwaist and necktie were worn, along with a matching wool skirt or matching slacks (when authorized). This uniform was also worn in khaki by officers and enlisted women, and was available for wear in white with white accessories, but may have been restricted to Wacs in the Washington, DC area.

Knox Division, Hat Corporation of America (hereafter referred to as "Knox Hats"), Dobbs, and the Stetson Hat Company began submitting competing designs for the designs of the WAAC hat and garrison cap in March of 1942. In the end, the headgear designed by Knox Hats was chosen, which was the famous "Hobby Hat;" a cloth-brimmed hat, made of

Enlisted WAC winter uniform worn by Sgt. Frances Dupree Harris. Note the chamois scarf and Army Air Corps patch. (Courtesy: Francis Dupree Harris)

WAC officer's winter uniform. (Photo by Marc Riese)

WAC officer trousers. Same style was also available in tan (or pinks). (Photo by Mark Riese)

The rare WAC white uniform. (Courtesy. National Archives)

WAC officer Gloria Pickett (left) wears the winter "pinks & greens" while Bettejane Greer wears the officer's khaki summer uniform. (Courtesy: National Archives)

The new summer officer's uniform including garrison cap, chamois gloves and scarf. (Courtesy: National Archives)

Enlisted WAC's khaki uniform blouse. (Courtesy: US Army Museum, Ft. Sam Houston)

This summer blouse, which belonged to "Air Wac" Sgt. Frances Dupree Harris, has the Pallas Athene collar disc instead of the standard "U.S." disc. Top: Wedding photo of Jesse and Frances Dupree Harris showing her wearing this bouse. (Courtesy: Frances Dupree Harris)

WAAC identification tag.
(Courtesy: Ed Anderson, Jr.)

This WAAC summer officer's blouse is a transition item. Note it still retains the passants instead of having shoulder straps, but has gold army officer's buttons authorized in 1943. (Courtesy: Noelle Young)

This WAAC member wears a summer uniform without any insignia of any kind on the blouse or cap. (Courtesy: Noelle Young)

The unique, jeweler-cast WAAC hat badge attributed to Colonel Hobby. (Courtesy: National Archives)

WAAC officer's hat insigne.

khaki twill, with semi-stiff top and sides. According to Colonel Hobby's specifications, the hat was to be the same for officers and enlisted women, differing only in the type of insigne worn on the front. The Heraldic Section had provided Colonel Hobby with a few pencil sketches of a hat insigne to be used by WAAC officers. She took the sketches to a New York jeweler, who produced a gold, hand cut eagle, which Colonel Hobby wore herself. An impression of Hobby's insigne was made for the Heraldic Section, and it became the standard hat insigne for WAAC officers, and the central design of the hat device for enlisted women. It was also the design used on initial WAAC buttons. The hat had a matching cloth chin strap, which was secured at each side by a small, olive-brab plastic button embossed with the WAAC eagle. These chin strap buttons were worn by both officers and enlisted women on their khaki or olive-drab hats.

WAAC officer's hat insinge.

Lt. Nell E.J. Farnham. (Courtesy: Al Schell)

Chocolate-brown WAAC hat with officer's eagle insigne. (Courtesy: Noelle Young)

Interior label for the above hat. (Courtesy: Noelle Young)

WAAC enlisted woman's first pattern hat insigne.

WAAC enlisted woman's winter "Hobby hat." (Courtesy: National Archives)

Tan summer WAAC hat with first pattern enlisted woman's insignia. (Courtesy: Noelle Young)

Interior label for the above hat. (Courtesy: Noelle Young)

Enlisted Wacs wearing the first pattern (type 1) "Hobby hat" and insignia. (Courtesy: National Archives)

WAAC type 1 "Hobby hat." modified by replacing the olive-drab plastic chin strap buttons with gold US Army buttons. The WAAC officer's hat insigne has been replaced with the regular army officer's insigne. (Photo by Ronda Sheel)

WAC officer's winter hat with a US Army officer's hat badge. (Courtesy: National Archives)

WAC enlisted woman's winter hat with the US Army enlisted hat badge and gilt Army chin strap buttons. This hat was made by Stetson. (Courtesy: Museum, Peterson Air Force Base)

The Knox and Dobbs hats came under criticism; the Stetson model proved to be superior construction. The hair oil shield in the Knox hat was made of cellophane and tended to crack. Sweat caused the hats made by Knox and Dobbs to pucker. The style of the cap made it impractical to launder and ship. Knox Hats was appointed to produce an improved "Hobby Hat." The improvements were: 1) the cloth visor would be made twice as thick and heavy by using vulcanized fiber, which could withstand dry cleaning; 2) the weight of the inner lining which stiffened the crown top was increased; 3) the old pleated lining was replaced with a fitted lining, which could easily be reblocked; 4) the haircloth weight used to stiffen the sides of the hat was increased to increase the rigidity of the hat.[1091] Wearing of the Hobby hat was authorized only for dress occasions. In the summer of 1943, however, WAAC officers were issued a tropical worsted hat to go with the tropical worsted uniform.

A summer fatigue hat was to be worn on duty. It was very unpopular, and by early 1943, many people requested that a garrison cap be designed for the WAAC, which became the Women's Army Corps, or WAC, on the first of July.

WAAC fatigue hat. (Courtesy: National Archives)

The WAC garrison cap was designed by in 1944 by Knox Hats. A wool covert cap was made for the winter uniform, a tropical worsted khaki cap was provided to be worn with the tropical worsted khaki uniform, a shantung cap for the summer and winter off-duty dress, and a cotton cap for wear with the summer work uniform. Officer's caps were piped along the curtain with gold and black piping. Rank insigne was worn on the forward section of the left curtain. Enlisted women's caps were piped in old gold with moss-tone green flecking. Sometimes, a distinctive insigne was pinned to the left forward section of the curtain on the garrison caps worn by enlisted women.

Shantung enlisted woman's garrison cap. (Courtesy: George A. Petersen)

[1091] *Wardrobe*, pp. 156-157.

WAC officer's winter garrison cap.

WAC private Louise E. Segedy wears the winter WAC garrison cap. The old gold and moss-green piping is evident.

WAC officer's summer garrison cap.

WAC enlisted woman's winter garrison cap. (Photo by Ronda Sheel)

Major Charity Adams, commanding officer of the 6888th Central Postal Directory Battalion in England, reviews her troops, February 1945. She and Captain Abbie Campbell (behind Adams) wear the WAC officer's garrison cap. The other women wear the enlisted garrison cap.

WAC khaki summer garrison cap. (Photo by Ronda Sheel)

WAC summer garrison cap in the style worn by men. (Photo by Ronda Sheel)

This WAC sergeant wears an unpiped, men's style garrison cap.

Wacs also wore an off-duty dress, availible in two fabrics. They were designed by the Quartermaster Corps, so that Wacs could have a "graceful, comfortable dress for their hours off duty." Previous designs based on afternoon civilian dresses were rejected by Wacs. They stated: "We are soldiers. We want to look like soldiers." The dresses were designed for the Wac's social time, to be worn on dates, to receptions and dances, in theaters and restaurants and while on furlough. The winter dress was made of all wool "Horizon Tan" crêpe. The color was chosen because it blended well with the standard overcoat and other pieces of uniform. The summer dress was made of all viscose rayon shantung in a color called "Military-Beige."

Officer's off-duty dress with wide sleeves and matching garrison cap, 1944.

Corporal Frances Harris wears the off-duty dress while on leave. She also wears the chamois scarf. (Courtesy: Frances Dupree Harris)

These off-duty dresses were of the shirtdress style, with wide shoulders and a slender waist, enhanced by a narrow tailored self belt with a cloth-covered buckle. It had long, loose fitting sleeves with turn back cuffs. The sleeves of the summer dress could be modified by cutting them off and hemming them to a point just above the elbow, depending on the wearer's preference. The skirt of the dress had six gores, and the dress had a fly front with a zipper closure. There were two shield-shaped pocket with flaps that buttoned on the bodice. The pointed shirt-style collar could be worn either open or closed. Either way, the "U.S." monogram for officers or disc for enlisted women was worn on the right collar, while the branch-of-service insigne was worn on the left collar.

Mother and daughter Wacs! Private Cleo Yoont (left) and daughter Avis Larsen wear the off-duty dress with the olive-drab garrison cap.

The design of the dresses was the same for officers and enlisted women. The latter wore their rank stripes embroidered upon the same material as the dresses. The colors of these dresses were carefully chosen to go well with all skin types.

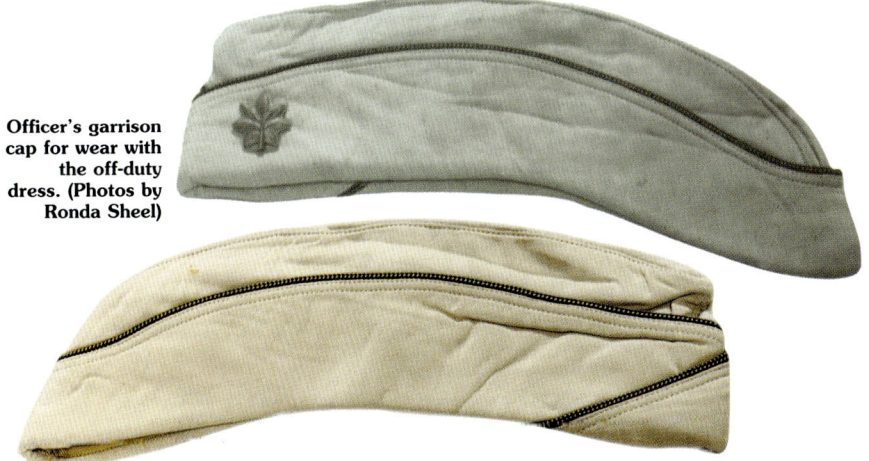

Officer's garrison cap for wear with the off-duty dress. (Photos by Ronda Sheel)

Accessories were made for both dresses. A matching garrison cap, made of rayon shantung, was of the same material as the dress, but the olive-drab garrison cap could be worn as well. Officer's caps had their normal piping, as did the caps for enlisted women. Wacs were to wear brown, commercially designed shoes with closed toe with the heel no higher than 2-1/4 inches. A simple brown, untrimmed handbag, without a shoulder strap, and of commercial design was carried with the dress. Wacs could wear standard cotton chamois gloves.

WAC officer's field jacket. (Courtesy: US Army Museum, Ft. Sam Houston)

Officers wore their winter garrison cap with the winter dress, made of wool barathea and enlistees wore their winter garrison cap, made of olive drab covert wool. Wacs could carry the previously described handbag or the regulation WAC utility bag with the dress, and regulation gloves.[1092]

In 1944 the women's field jacket was approved for wear by WAC members. It was a short jacket, made of 14 oz. covert wool material in olive-drab shade number 37. The jacket was single-breasted with a concealed button front, with a convertible collar and lapels. It had no pockets on the front, but there was an interior pocket. It was designed to fit well over the wearer's bust and shoulders. There was a 2" waistband of self material which extended around the jacket and closed on the left side with a button and hidden buttonhole. A snap was sewn approximately an inch above the top of the waistband. Two front pleats in the front and four in the back allowed the jacket to blouse attractively. The collar measured about 1 3/4" wide at the center back and about 2-1/2" at the end, or notch. Shoulder straps of self material were sewn at the shoulders and slightly forward, the points of which reached under the collar. Each shoulder strap had a single gold Army button. The sleeves had 2" cuffs of self material which closed with a single button and button hole. Officers and enlisted women wore their standard insignia on this jacket.[1093]

In 1944, it was realized that a warm and comfortable uniform was needed for the conditions overseas. This uniform would serve as both a duty uniform and one for dress. It was approved for Wacs and Nurses serving in the European Theater of Operations on July 28, 1944 by the Chief Surgeon in the Theater. This new uniform consisted of a battledress jacket, skirt, trousers and garrison cap. Supplying them (and Army Nurses) with it presented a problem. Production quotas of the uniforms could not be met in the United States. It was found that some of these uniforms could be produced in England and Ireland, with the United States providing the materials to be used. This was discussed with Major General W.W. Richard, Director of Clothing and Stores of the British War Office. The firm chosen to do production in England was Debenhams, Ltd., but their production number

---

[1092] "Special for Women's Editors," Facts about the new WAC Off-Duty Dress, War Department, Bureau of Public Relations, Washington, DC, May 8, 1944.

[1093] War Department Circular No. 12, Washington, DC: January 9, 1945, pp. 2-4.

WAC Tech. Corporal Jean Darling (L) and Technical Sergeant Dorothy Arnold return to the United States in 1946. Note that both women are not wearing ties and that both are wearing SHAEF patch distinctive insignia on the lapels of their battledress jackets and on the curtain of their garrison caps. (Courtesy: George Petersen)

Enlisted battledress jacket. (Courtesy: John Angolia)

WAC Captain Kaye Summersby, aide to General Eisenhower, in the battledress uniform. (Courtesy: Eisenhower Library)

A winter battlejacket worn by an "Air Wac."

Medals and insignia worn by Sgt. Emma Rohde. (Courtesy: Steve Rohde)

estimates were very low. However, in a letter from General R.M. Littlejohn, USA, to Colonel Cohen, USA, of August 9, 1944, Littlejohn wrote Cohen,

> "The question of providing a limited number of garments for WACs [sic] and nurses is an emergency due to the fact that production in the States had not been forthcoming and to the fact that women on the Far Shore must be furnished a suitable garment.... To meet this current emergency you are authorized to confirm the agreement with Debenhams."[1094]

While waiting for production to catch up with demand, Wacs were authorized to report to the London Sales Store where they would be given a receipt, entitling them to go to Debenhams to be measured for uniforms. Estimated time of receipt of the new uniform was three weeks. Samples of this uniform were sent by General Littlejohn to the Office of the Quartermaster General in the United States.

Ireland committed to providing the following items of uniform for the WAC only four weeks from their reception of cloth:

50,000 jackets, field, wool women's at the expected monthly rate of 2,000 per week; 75,000 skirts, field, wool, at the expected delivery rate of 3,000 per week; 75,000 slacks, field, wool, at the expected delivery rate of 3,000 per week; 200,000 caps, garrison, at the expected delivery rate of 6,000 per week.[1095]

Happily, the Irish-made uniforms were well made. Consequently, England committed to manufacture 6,000 jackets, skirts and slacks for enlisted Wacs, and 4,000 for officers by late November or early December 1944. 50,000 battledress jacket uniforms (jacket, skirt and trousers) were prescribed for WAC members as well as Army nurses. It took 20,000 yards of material to make them, and an additional 9,000 yards of material was needed to manufacture 50,000 garrison caps. This uniform was available for purchase at continental sales stores, and by October 2, 1944, 200 of these uniforms were shipped by air to the sales store in Paris.[1096]

Wacs serving as cooks or bakers wore a white, bloused cook's cap, a white dress and white apron and, when needed, white cotton work gloves.[1097]

Wacs serving in hospitals wore the WAC hospital dress. Those who were volunteer nurse's aides could wear the Red Cross nurses' aide uniform while on duty.

A herringbone twill one-piece exercise suit was worn during physical activities. Anklets were worn with appropriate shoes.

[1094] Burns, p. 13.

[1095] Prepared under the direction of Captain Robert W. Burns, Chief, Historical Records Branch, OCQM, European Theater, History of Nurses and WAC Uniforms in the European Theater, 1942-1945, no date, p. 25.

[1096] Burns, p. 27.

[1097] George A. Petersen, ed., *WWII US Army Regulations for the Service and Field Uniforms: Clothing, Headdress, Insignia, Medals and Equipment, Enlisted and Officers, Male and Female Personnel.* (Springfield, VA: National Capital Historical Sales, Inc., no date), AR 600-37, 12-14, p. 8.

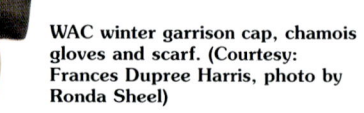

WAC winter garrison cap, chamois gloves and scarf. (Courtesy: Frances Dupree Harris, photo by Ronda Sheel)

Custom-made summer battledress jacket. (Courtesy: Noelle Young)

WAC hospital dress. (Courtesy: National Archives)

WAAC officers wore a double-breasted wool overcoat which had two rows of eight plastic buttons. Each was embossed with the WAAC eagle. There were two welted pockets on each side of the coat. The cuffs were belted and rank was worn on the passants. WAC officers wore the same overcoat, but with shoulder straps instead of passants.

Corporal Ethel "Penny" Anderson wears the yellow scarf. (Courtesy: J.R. Angolia)

WAAC officer's overcoat. (Photo by Mark Riese)

WAC officer's field overcoat.
(Photo by Mark Riese)

It was a common practice for Wacs who collected military patches to sew them to the overcoat liner, which was then used as a robe. (Courtesy: Frank Robertson)

WAC officers wearing the field overcoat.

WAC officers wore a field overcoat while on duty with troops. It was double-breasted and of elastique or barathea Army olive-drab shade 51. It was belted, had shoulder straps and a removable hood, as well as a liner which buttoned in. It closed with five pairs of large, olive-drab buttons. Two diagonal hanging pockets were at each side of the coat, and the sleeve cuffs were belted.[1098]

Left: WAC overcoat. (Courtesy: Frances Dupree Harris)

Right: Reverse of the overcoat. (Courtesy: Frances Dupree Harris)

Enlisted women wore a olive-drab wool double-breasted overcoat. There were no passants or shoulder straps at the shoulders. The cuffs were belted and a self-belt was on the reverse. Olive-drab plastic buttons embossed with the WAAC eagle were first worn on the coat, being replaced by gold US Army buttons after becoming the WAC. Rank chevrons were worn on the sleeves. Unit patches, when authorized, were worn on the upper left sleeve at the shoulder.

WAAC overcoat for enlisted women. (Courtesy: National Archives)

[1098] Ibid, AR 600-37, 20-21, p. 12.

The utility overcoat was made of tackle twill cloth, and had a lining which buttoned inside the coat, a reverse flap and removable hood. It was also water repellent.

The utility coat with removable hood being worn in the field. (Courtesy: Noelle Young)

A short field jacket was worn by officers and enlisted women. It had four pockets with flaps, shoulder straps, and a drawstring waist that adjusted inside. This jacket was also worn by Army nurses.

WAC field jacket. (Courtesy: National Archives)

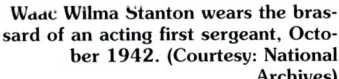

Felt on felt WAAC brassard. gold lettering on green felt, with green felt tie strings.

Newly-arrived recruits being marched away from the railway station at Ft. Des Moines, 1942. Note that their escorts wear the WAAC belted uniform with a brassard as the only insigne. (Courtesy: National Archives)

Waac Wilma Stanton wears the brassard of an acting first sergeant, October 1942. (Courtesy: National Archives)

WAC military policewoman, 1944. (Courtesy: National Archives)

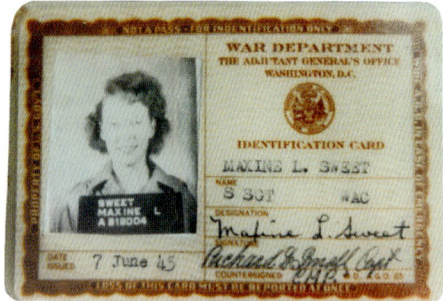

WAC War Department identification card.

Non-commissioned officer's club membership card to a WAC.

WAAC/WAC metal frame name tag.

WAC installation ID button.

WAAC enrollee pinback. (Courtesy: John Mull)

Wacs wore two standard Army identification tags, suspended from the neck by a 25 inch metal chain of heat-resistant, non-corrosive and non-toxic metal. The top tag was worn 2-1/2 inches above the lower tag which was normally suspended from a small second chain.[1099]

The first utility bag approved for the WAAC was to made of imitation leather, which was not only unattractive, but unacceptable, since its finish cracked and peeled. In 1942, Mrs. A.A. Lentz, Colonel Hobby's assistant, presented a utility bag designed by Richard Koret, Inc. It was styled in the familiar "mail pouch" form, and made of calfskin. The Quartermaster General rejected this bag as being too expensive, and was manufactured

[1099] AR 600-37, Section IV, Miscellaneous, 42. (George A. Petersen, ed.).

from a critical war material. Another, almost identical bag, was submitted by Lesco Limited, but it was made of sealskin. A large supply of sealskin, water buffalo and goatskin was found, thus the WAAC could have its utility bag. It had a russet brown, natural hide finish and was lined in olive material. The center of the interior of the bag was divided, and this was partitioned to have four extra compartments. The flap of the bag had a male snap which fastened into the corresponding female snap on the bag. (The underside of the flap of a WAAC/WAC utility bag observed during this research was stamped in black ink, "B-2790.") The matching leather shoulder strap could be removed by unsnapping the ends of the strap. The strap length was adjustable, having a black metal sliding buckle.

WAAC officer with utility bag. (Courtesy: National Archives)

WAAC/WAC utility bag. (Photo by Ronda Sheel)

WAAC officer's with non-standard utility bags. (Courtesy: National Archives)

Originally, the bag was to be carried from the right shoulder, with the strap extending across the chest and resting on the left side. This was unsatisfactory, so it was ordered that the bag be carried from the left shoulder. This was a problem, as well, since the strap tended to slip from the shoulder, so Waacs were again ordered to carry the utility bag from the right shoulder and across the chest.

The Waacs arrive in England outfitted with web belt, gas mask bag and leather utility bag. (Courtesy: National Archives)

These Wacs are carrying a variant utility bag.

Variation WAC utility bag. (Courtesy: Greensboro Historical Museum; photo by Patt Anthony)

During World War II, the WAAC/WAC uniform was copied by several organizations. Some civilian secretaries who worked for the Army bought olive-drab blouses with gold buttons and wore them with officer's "pink" shirts. Female secretaries at Valley Forge Military Academy in Pennsylvania wore a uniform which was almost identical to the one worn by WAAC members, right down to the "Hobby Hat." WAAC Headquarters complained to the school, which responded that their uniform had its differences. The skirt had a pleat, and the buttons bore the crest of the Academy, as did the hat. Some stores on the east coast offered a "Junior WAAC uniform," which they described as "an exact copy of the real WAAC uniform."[1100] Colonel Hobby had proposed in 1942 that an order be issued so that, "no organization or group of women employed by the American forces...wear a uniform or parts of a uniform which are of a color or a pattern which would cause them to be confused with members of the WAAC."[1101] Despite Colonel Hobby's protests, WAAC officer uniforms would continue to be sold to any civilian women who were going overseas.

Members of the USO, female correspondents, movie stars, Congresswomen and women of society went overseas as soon as the war in Europe was over. The Army felt it was necessary for their safety that these women be allowed to wear some sort of uniform. It was decided that they would wear enlisted and officer WAC uniforms, to the outrage of the WAC. They felt they had worked hard and earned the privilege to wear the uniform, and that it would be a disgrace for civilian women to wear it, and rightfully so. It was believed that this practice would "react to the serious detriment of the morale of the women who have served the Army well and faithfully under the rigorous conditions of overseas life...."

Colonel Hobby finally conceded the wear of WAC uniforms, provided that civilians wear conspicuous colored shoulder straps, sleeve braid and cap crowns, plus the blue coat worn by Army Hostesses and Librarians. But it was too late. Already, hundreds of WAC uniforms had been sold to civilians. The entire cast of "Panama Hattie" was outfitted in WAC uniforms. The result was the deflation of the Wacs' pride and espirit de corps. They now felt they "...had been hooked as sentimental suckers by a government that penalized enlisted service and handsomely rewarded those who stifled their patriotic fervor until the danger [of war] was over." Many members of the WAC were justifiably angered and demonstrated as much by refusing civilian jobs in the Army offered to them after the war.[1102]

Honorably discharged, enlisted women were permitted to keep the following items:

1 barrack bag;
1 WAC utility bag (purse);
1 set of collar insignia;
1 set of sewn on rank and other sleeve insignia;
1 WAC enlisted women's overcoat of any style;
1 yellow scarf, if the overcoat is kept;
1 complete uniform, all parts of matching color and material (i.e., 1 blouse, 1 skirt, 1 garrison cap, 2 wool or cotton shirtwaists.);

[1100] Mattie E. Treadwell, United States Army in World War II. Special Studies: "The Women's Army Corps." (Washington, DC: Office of the Chief of Military History, Department of the Army, 1954) p. 199.
[1101] Ibid, p. 400.
[1102] Ibid, pp. 400-402.

All gloves, identification tags, anklets, shoes, stockings, neckties, underwear, towels and toiletries.[1103]

Enlisted women who were discharged in order to accept commissions or be appointed as warrant officers could keep everything except their enlisted blouse, skirt, overcoat and garrison cap.[1104]

After World War II, Wacs and Army nurses wore the same uniform until the "Hattie Carnegie" uniform was created in 1950. Beginning in 1947, enlisted women wore two "U.S." flat or domed collar discs on their collars, and two flat or domed discs with the branch-of-service insigne on them on their lapels.[1105] A branch-of-service disc was also worn by enlisted women on the left forward curtain of the garrison cap.

The second director of the WAC was Colonel Westray Battle Boyce Long[1106] (July 12, 1945-March 4, 1947[1107]). With the coming war in

This post-WWII "Air Wac" wears the Pallas Athene disc on her garrison cap.

Post-WWII Wac with collar discs on the collar and lapels of her uniform blouse.

[1103] AR 615-40, c 1, Washington, DC, February 1, 1945. (Petersen, George, ed. *"World War II US Army Regulations for the Service and Field Uniforms: Clothing, Headgear, Insignia, Medals, and Equipment Enlisted and Officer, Male and Female Personnel."*)
[1104] Ibid.
[1105] William K. Emerson, *Encyclopedia of United States Army Insignia and Uniforms*. (Norman, Oklahoma: University of Oklahoma Press, 1996), p. 516.
[1106] Charlotte Palmer Seeley, *American Women and the US Armed Forces*. (Washington, DC: The National Archives Trust Fund Board, 1992) p. 167.
[1107] Bettie J. Morden, *The Women's Army Corps, 1945-1978*. (Washington, DC: Center of Military History, 1990), p. ii.

The modeling of the new woman's Army uniforms designed by Hattie Carnegie. (Courtesy: National Archives)

Korea, all female former members of the WAC, WAVES, SPARS, Army and Navy Nurse Corps, WAFS and WMSC were recalled to active duty. The first WAC Reserve Officer to be called up was Captain Grace I. Butler, who had served with the First Airborne Army during World War II. She was the daughter of an active duty Army colonel and a former World War I Army nurse.[1108] In 1950, two bills were put before Congress that would authorize directors of women's military organizations to be a Brigadier General and Rear Admiral.[1109] Fort McClellan, Alabama, became WAC headquarters in 1954. It was commanded by a female general.[1110] The Women's Army Corps Training Center and Officer Candidate School was opened at Fort Lee, Virginia on October 4, 1948. It was commanded by Lieutenant Colonel Elizabeth C. Smith. The first basic WAC company graduated there on December 10, 1948, and the first class of Regular Army Officer Candidates graduated on April 1, 1949. The first ever bivouac training for women started there on October 31, 1949[1111] The WAC band, called the 14th Army Band, was formed at Fort Lee, Virginia and made its

---

[1108] Dorothy Tuttle, "WAC Veteran Volunteers to Serve Again," *Woman Veteran*, Vol. IV, No. 6 (June 1950): p. 1.

[1109] Dorothy Tuttle, "Keeping up with Congress," *Woman Veteran*, Vol. IV, No. 7 (July 1950): p. 8.

[1110] Helen Rogan, *Mixed Company. Women in the Modern Army*. (New York: G.P. Putnam's Sons, 1981) p. 30.

[1111] Brochure, "Women's Army Corps Training Center, Fort Lee, Virginia," February 1953, p. 3.

debut on March 31, 1951. It was the only band of its kind at the time.[1112] Personnel at the Training Center wore name tags while on duty. Celluloid tags were worn above the left pocket of the uniform blouse or shirtwaist, when the latter was worn an as outer garment. Leather name tags were buttoned to the left pocket of the blouse or shirtwaist:

1) Basic and Specialist Trainees: Celluloid name tag with last name typewritten in capital letters on a white background.
2) Officer Candidates: Leather name tag with last name printed in black on a white background;
3) Assigned Enlisted Personnel: Leather name tag with last name printed in black on a light blue background;
4) Commissioned Personnel and Warrant Officers: Leather name tag with last name printed in black on a pink background.[1113]

During World War II, a detachment of Wacs served at the Parachute School at Fort Benning, Georgia. Some worked in the motor pool as drivers, secretaries, stock and mail clerks, and subsistence noncommissioned officers. Others trained and worked as parachute packers, or "riggers."

WAC detachment at the Parachute School, Ft. Benning, Georgia, WWII.

The fundamentals of packing the B-7 chest parachute and the T-5 parachute were learned during the first week at rigger's school. Thirty-two Wacs worked in the schools' regular packing section and fifty-five packed parachutes in the school's maintenance section. The second week, Wacs were taught to sew chutes on a machine or by hand, and by the third week, how to pack trays and mend harnesses. By the fourth week, students repaired parachute canopies. The last week, students finished their instruction in the packing of all types of parachutes. Each parachute was carefully inspected before being issued.

[1112] Ibid, p. 4.

[1113] "Administrative Regulations, Headquarters, Women's Army Corps Training Center, Camp Lee, Virginia," June 1, 1949, p. 8.

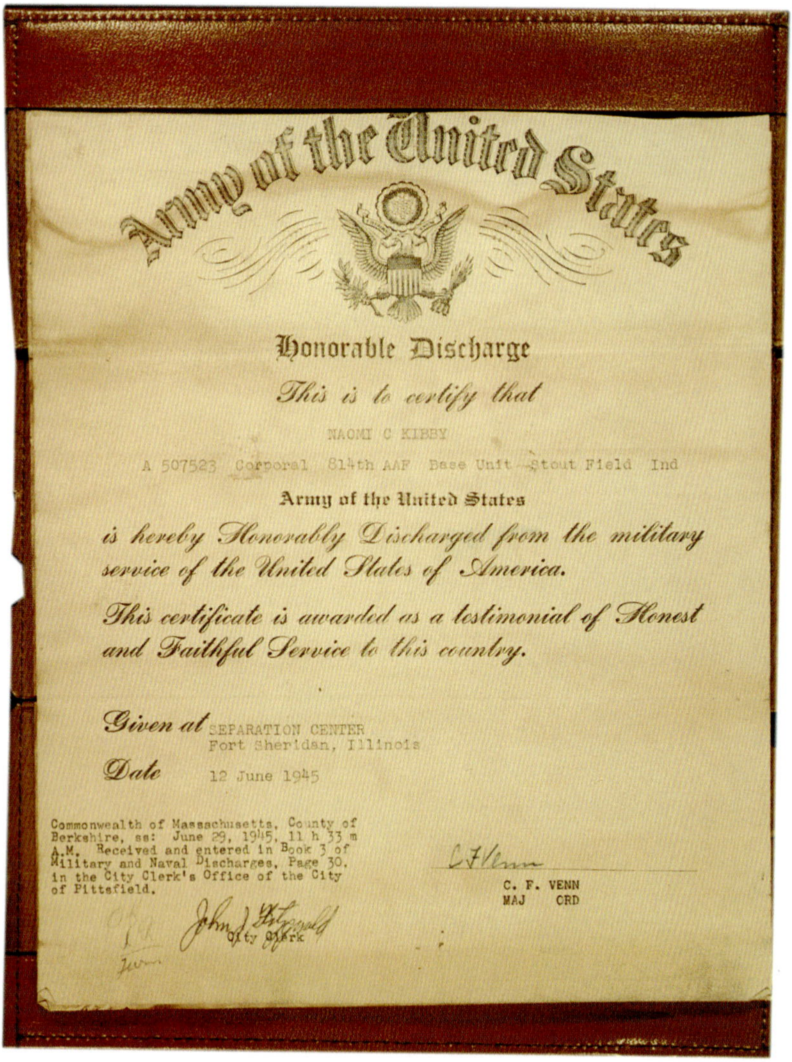

Army of the United States

Honorable Discharge

This is to certify that

NAOMI C KIBBY

A 507523 Corporal 814th AAF Base Unit Stout Field Ind

Army of the United States

is hereby Honorably Discharged from the military service of the United States of America.

This certificate is awarded as a testimonial of Honest and Faithful Service to this country.

Given at SEPARATION CENTER
Fort Sheridan, Illinois

Date 12 June 1945

Commonwealth of Massachusetts, County of Berkshire, ss: June 29, 1945, 11 h 33 m A.M. Received and entered in Book 3 of Military and Naval Discharges, Page 30, in the City Clerk's Office of the City of Pittsfield.

City Clerk

C. F. VENN
MAJ ORD

Honorable discharge document in leather folder presented to "Air Wac" Corporal Naomi C. Kibby, 814th AAF Base Unit, Stout Field, Indiana.

Korean War and Post Korean War Period WAC Identification Tags

(Courtesy: Steve Rohde)

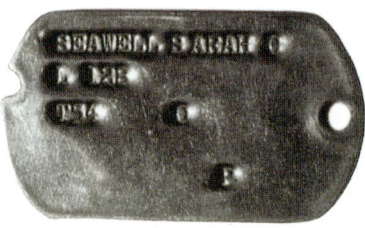

M-1940: Type 3, WAC officer. "L" prefix—WAC officer, Regular Army commission.

M-1940: Type 3-B, WAC officer. Wehrle served in WWII as an enlisted WAC and was commissioned as a 1st Lt. in 1954. Note religion is spelled out.

```
HARRISON PATRICIA A
   WR-8604602    O
T50         C
```

M-1940: Type 3-A. This lady enlisted in the WAC in late 1943/early 1944. She served in WWII, then went into the U.S. Army Reserves, and was recalled for the Korean War. "WR" prefix—WAC EM Reserves.

M-1940: Steel, Type 3-A. Note the new "WA" prefix—WAC EM Regular Active Army which was authorized in 1949.

```
CORBAN, EDNA M.
WA8109860
T-51      A

                    P
```

```
LORRAINE,
RUBY M
WA8406660
T59      A
PROT
```

M-1940: Type 3-B. This tag has an abbreviated religion designation.

M-1940: Type 4. This tag has no "T" date and has the religion spelled out.

```
MCBREARTY,
BRENDA A
WA822090986
O
ROMAN CATHOLIC
```

```
SANTISTEVAN, G.
WA8603814
T-51     A

         C
```

M-1940: Type 3-A. The second digit of the number designates 6th Corps area.

Note:
With the adoption of the double letter prefix for the WAC, the number "8" was also added in front of all World War II WAC serial numbers. The second digit now indicated the corps or service command site.

WAC rigger Private Mary Johnson Hill (Cedartown, GA), affixes a yellow tag to a parachute indicating that it needs to be repaired. The Parachute School, Ft. Benning.

Paratroopers packed their own parachutes for their first five jumps; after that, they were packed by the parachute school's riggers.

Qualified rigger's wings were not awarded until "Graduation Day." That day, a Wac packed twelve parachutes and boarded a C-47 transport with twelve paratroopers. It was a time of great tension. She would only get her silver jump wings with the "R" if all the parachutes she had packed opened. The paratroopers wore an emergency parachute on their chest to be used if the main chute failed to open. Qualified WAC riggers wore the silver paratroop jump wings with an "R" in the center of the parachute on an infantry-blue oval, sewn over the left breast pocket of the uniform blouse. All members of the Parachute School wore the Airborne Command patch on the upper left sleeve, and the round, infantry-blue patch embroidered with a white parachute and white border on the left curtain of their garrison caps.

WAC rigger Private Eleanor M. Mason had a pet squirrel named Boots. He supposedly won his "wings" as a jumper during a parachute drop at Lawson Field.**

(**Information obtained from the November and December 1944 and the January 1945 issues of *Army Life* magazine.)

With the passage of the Women's Armed Services Integration Act of 1948, work began on a standardized uniform for all female members of the United States Army: the Women's Army Corps, the Army Nurse Corps

Private, First Class Mattie Lee Turner, Dillon, South Carolina, wears the wings of a qualified parachute rigger on an infantry-blue oval, Ft. Benning, Georgia. Note also the Airborne Command patch on her left sleeve and the round airborne patch on her garrison cap.

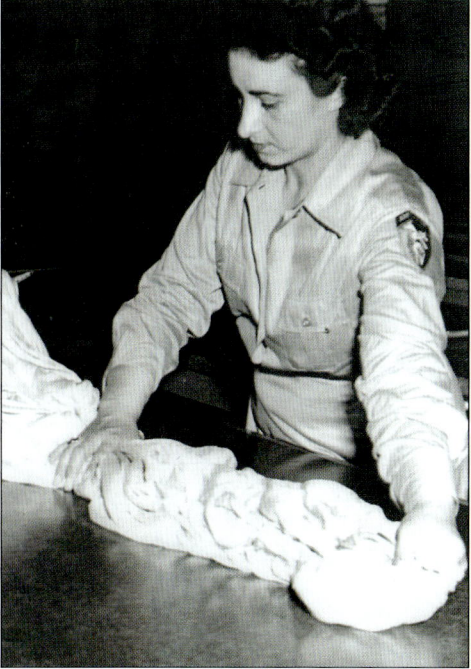

Private Edna V. Stone of the WAC Detachment packs a parachute at the Parachute School at Ft. Benning. Note the Airborne Command patch on her left sleeve. June 1, 1944.

Sterling silver, pin-back qualified parachute rigger jump wings and oval, Airborne Command patch.

and the Women's Medical Specialist Corps. The only difference in these new uniforms would be the branch-of-service insignia.

A committee was appointed by the Quartermaster General in 1949 to oversee the development of new uniforms. All members were civilians and leaders in the fashion world. Sitting on the committee were Edna Woolman Chase, Editor-in-Chief of *Vogue* magazine, Tobe Coller Davis, a fashion merchandise consultant, Eleanor Lambert, fashion publicist, Mary

Brooks Picken, authority on advertising and home economics, Dorothy Shaver, president of Lord & Taylor of New York (she had previously consulted on uniforms for the Quartermaster General during the Second World War), and Mrs. Carmel Snow, Editor of *Harper's Bazaar*.[1114] Fashion designer Hattie Carnegie was chosen to design the new uniforms.

On February 23, 1950, the uniforms designed by Carnegie were publicly shown at a special preview at the headquarters of the First Army at Governors Island, New York.[1115] This uniform was discontinued for wear on October 1, 1964.[1116]

The new wardrobe for Army enlisted women and officers consisted of the wool duty uniform, made of hard finished taupe worsted serge. The blouse was single-breasted and had a nipped-in waistline and softly rounded hipline. There were two crescent welt pockets at the sides of the blouse, and two non-functional verticle crescent pockets just above the waist of the blouse. These were fitted very close to the center of the blouse, i.e. at each side of the opening. The blouse was worn buttoned completely, accenting the collar with its fashionable rounded corners. The top edge of the blouse opening was held in place by a taupe thread loop, which attached over a corresponding taupe plastic button sewn under the collar. Since this loop often broke, it is not uncommon to find it replaced on some uniforms with a snap. Shoulder straps had a smaller antique bronze button near the point. The blouse closed with five antique bronze buttons, embossed with the conventional army coat-of-arms.

The matching five-gore taupe skirt was slightly flared with double darts in front. The hem line was adjusted to the fashion of the time.

Taupe plastic button and loop under the blouse collar.

[1114] Colonel Robert S. Anderson, MC, USA, editor-in-chief, *Army Medical Specialist Corps*. (Washington, DC: Office of the Surgeon General, Department of the Army, 1968) p. 359f.
[1115] Ibid, p. 361.
[1116] *The Officer's Guide*. (Washington, DC: The National Service Publishing Company, 1961), p. 145.

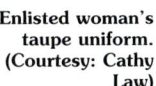

Officer's "Hattie Carnegie" taupe uniform. (Courtesy: Alice Strong Barber; photo by Mark Riese)

Enlisted woman's taupe uniform. (Courtesy: Cathy Law)

Antique bronze buttons.

Officers wore taupe mohair cuff braid on each sleeve. Length of service hash marks were smaller than their World War II counterparts on male uniforms, measuring only 7/8" by 1/8".[1117] They were worn on the left sleeve, just above the cuff braid; World War II service bars were worn on the right sleeve. The color of these hash marks and bars was changed from gold to chamois on a taupe cloth backing.

Chamois WWII service bars and officer's mohair cuff stripe.

[1117] Hill, p. 106.

Officers wore a gold "U.S." insigne on the right collar, with the branch-of-service insigne worn on the right (e.g., the WAC officer's Pallas Athene insigne, Army nurse's caduceus, or Women's Medical Specialist Corps caduceus). Rank was worn at the shoulder edge of each shoulder strap, 2" from the shoulder seam.

WAC officer's collar insigne machine-embroidered to a piece of taupe cloth.

Enlisted women wore a gold disc with the "U.S." initials on the right collar and a disc with their branch-of-service insigne on the left collar. Their insignia of rank were made in a reduced size and of the new chamois color thread upon a taupe backing.

Master Sergeant Lois Burdock wears the taupe uniform, June 22, 1953. She is standing beside Brigadier General Edward Danforth.

Private First Class chevron, chamois on taupe.

Staff Sergeant chevron, chamois on taupe.

Unit patches were sewn to the upper left sleeve of the blouse. A patch denoting the wearer's previous unit assignment overseas could be sewn to the right shoulder. As stated in a 1949 WAC publication:

> "Individuals assigned to United States Army units during World War I between 6 April 1917 and 11 November 1918, or World War II between 7 December 1941 and 2 September 1945, all dates inclusive are authorized to wear shoulder sleeve insignia on the right shoulder, in the same relative position as the sleeve insignia of their present assignment unit of left shoulder, or an organization to which they were assigned while serving overseas."[1118]

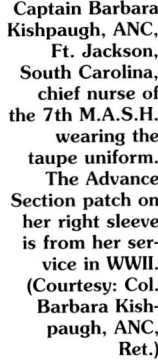

Captain Barbara Kishpaugh, ANC, Ft. Jackson, South Carolina, chief nurse of the 7th M.A.S.H. wearing the taupe uniform. The Advance Section patch on her right sleeve is from her service in WWII. (Courtesy: Col. Barbara Kishpaugh, ANC, Ret.)

The overcoat was made of matching taupe material, being double-breasted with four pairs of larger antique gold embossed buttons. It had a large collar with rounded ends. Pockets which resembled those worn on the blouse, were at each side of the coat. A larger version of the taupe thread loop and taupe plastic button could be used to close the collar completely. Smaller antique bronze buttons were secured on the shoulder straps.

Rank insignia and patches were worn on the coat by enlisted personnel and officers as prescribed in regulations. The back of the coat was

---

[1118] "Administrative Regulations, Headquarters, Women's Army Corps Training Center, Camp Lee, Virginia," June 1, 1949, p. 7.

Taupe WAC enlisted woman's overcoat. (Photo by Mark Riese)

pleated, with a half-belt secured with two larger antique bronze buttons. A liner could be buttoned inside the coat.

Women were issued a taupe nylon or rayon raincoat, single-breasted with a belt and a composition buckle. It had a flared shape and was loose-fitting. The front closed with seven buttons. The crescent welt pockets had both inside and outside openings. A hood buttoned in around the collar and had a drawstring for adjustment.

The new headdress consisted of a smart-looking taupe hat with a brim, which turned up slightly and was stitched on the left side. (The width of the brim, at the center of the hat, measured approximately 2-1/4".) The back brim was about 2-1/2" wide at the center and folded flat against the back of the crown of the hat. The left side of this brim formed a belt, which reached under the front brim up-turn, across the front on the hat, passing through a cloth loop, and ending in a point under the back flap. The interior was lined in a slightly darker taupe satin or silk, and had a taupe grosgrain sweatband. Some hats had only a size label sewn to the right of the center back seam, while others had a large, white specification tag, sewn to the underside of the grosgrain band. It was printed in black letters. For example:

Officer's taupe hat with antique bronze insigne.

"Hat, Wool, Taupe, Women's Size 21-1/2, Dunhill Hat Corp., Cont. QM # 28253, dated June 13-1952, Spec. #10874A (Q.M.C.), Pattern Date-8-27-51, Stock No. 73-H-56321-50, 100% Wool, Exclusive of Ornamentation, N.Y.Q.M.P.A., Inspector."[1119]

Privately purchased hats probably existed.

Enlisted women wore an antique bronze, pin-back Army coat-of-arms in a circle, off center of the cap and to the right; officers wore an antique bronze, small Army officer's insigne, which measured 1 5/8" tall,[1120] attached just off center and to the right. Hats observed during this research had an "X" stitch in the center of the front grosgrain sweat band to assure proper placement on the head.

Enlisted woman's taupe hat with pin-back antique bronze device. (Photo by Ronda Sheel)

The garrison cap was identical for all ranks; officers did not wear piping along the curtain. This cap was made of taupe (shade no. 121) wool and lined in a slightly darker taupe silk or satin. A small white size tag was sewn near the back interior of the right side. The tag observed in this research read: "Designed to fit a 21 Headsize." Some caps also had a large specification tag sewn just forward of the size tag. This tag measured approximately 3" x 1-1/2" and read:

"Cap, Wool, Taupe, Shade-121, Women's, M. Tannenbaum, Dated 10, Feb. 1951, Q.M. 10570-01-11731, Spec No. MIL-C-10804, Pat. Date-22, Dec. 1950, 21, Stock No.73-C-64850-10, N.Y.Q.P.A., 100% Wool, Exclusive of Ornamentation, Inspector."

Taupe garrison cap.
(Photo by Ronda Sheel)

[1119] Hat in author's collection.
[1120] Hill, p. 106.

Officers wore a rank insigne pinned to the left forward section of the cap curtain and, when necessary, enlisted women wore a distinctive device.

A taupe field jacket was issued for wear with a taupe skirt or taupe slacks. Its design was very much like the blouse, having the same shoulder straps and collar with rounded ends. It was single-breasted, closing with five antique bronze Army buttons. There were two smaller antique bronze Army buttons at the shoulder straps. Like the blouse, there was a taupe string loop and button to close the neck completely.

A crescent pocket was positioned on each side of the center opening, just above the lower fourth button. The waistband was of self material and of two pieces. The end of the front band fastened on the wearer's left side with two snaps in a horizontal line. The two pieces of the band fastened at each side of the jacket with two antique bronze Army buttons, which allowed adjustments for comfort. The cuffs of the jacket closed with a smaller antique bronze embossed button. Rank and branch-of-service insignia and patches were worn as previously described.

Enlisted taupe field jacket and skirt. (Photo by Mark Riese)

Summer beige-taupe dress and garrison cap. (Photo by Ronda Sheel)

WAC School distinctive insignia (DI). Probably worn by instructors and administrators of training from 1953 to 1959 when Wacs were officially mustered into the Regular Army. (Courtesy: John Mull)

These members of the Women's Medical Specialist Corps (center) wearing the summer beige-taupe chambray dress and garrison cap. (Courtesy: Alice Strong Barber)

Officers and enlisted women were provided with a short sleeve summer dress made of beige-taupe (taupe shade 124) cotton chambray broadcloth. The dress had a tailored waist and flowing skirt. Like the blouse, it had the collar with rounded ends, shoulder straps, but with no buttons (the ends of the shoulder straps were simply tacked down), and crescent pockets at the side and just above the waistline. It closed with five removable antique bronze buttons. The top of the closure had a taupe thread loop and corresponding button under the collar. The collar could be worn open or closed. A white specification tag, printed in black ink, was sewn inside of the dress on the left side of the bodice. It read:

"Dress, Cotton, Taupe, Shade—124, Women's, Size 10 S, The Ward-Stilton Co., 29. Feb. 52, QM-24847, MIL-D-10677A (QMC), 55-D-3150-80, Pattern Date 2 July 51, N.Y.Q.M.P.A."

A white size tag was also sewn into the neck seam. Shoulder pads of self material were attached to the dress with snaps.

A stiffened self-cloth belt with an antique bronze buckle was held at the waist by a thread loop at each side of the dress.

For officers, rank insigne was pinned to the right collar and branch-of-service insigne pinned to the left collar. Enlisted women wore their standard gold collar insignia, as previously described. Chevrons were worn on the sleeves.

The unpiped garrison cap worn by all ranks was of the same material as the dress. Officers wore a rank insigne on the left forward section of the cap curtain.

The white uniform was of the same style as the taupe blouse, skirt and service hat, but it was made of white Palm Beach material, with matching white accessories. White oxfords, of commercial design, with closed heel and toe were worn with this uniform. The heel could be no lower than

The beige-taupe garrison cap. (Photo by Ronda Sheel)

1-1/2", and could of brown or white leather. White dull finish leather or fabric pumps, with a maximum heel height of 3", were also worn with the white uniform. The heel could also be white or brown.[1121]

The white leather shoulder bag prescribed for this uniform was identical to the café brown shoulder bag.)[1122]

The white shirtwaist was made of nylon, rayon or silk. It had French cuffs, which required antique bronze or gold cuff links.[1123]

White cotton knit or nylon gloves were worn with this uniform.

The white "Hattie Carnegie" uniform worn by a lieutenant in the Woman's Medical Specialist Corps. (Courtesy: William Emerson)

White version of the Hattie Carnegie uniform.

The shoulder bag was made of café brown calf with an expandable gussett bottom. The leather shoulder strap was adjustable, but could not be removed. The bag was lined in dark chocolate brown and had a center partition. The back section had a welted zippered compartment. The front of the partition had two horizontal cloth pockets, one above the other. The short flap fastened with a antique gold button snap, embossed with the coat-of-arms of the Army. Unique to this shoulder bag was a small wallet (or "passport pocket"),[1124] whose flap extended to the outside of the purse, giving the appearance of another pocket on the front of the purse. It also had an antique gold button snap. When undone, this wallet pulled from the purse, revealing three horizontal cloth compartments, one above the other. This wallet was held in place by a matching piece of chocolate-colored lining material and could not be removed from the bag. The shoulder bag was carried by all ranks. The use of this shoulder bag was discontinued in 1962.

The café brown shoulder bag. (Photo by Ronda Sheel)

While the Carnegie uniform was stylish, it had several drawbacks, and was overall disliked. Once, while in a hospital, General Eisenhower confided to an Army nurse that he preferred the women's uniforms from World War II.[1125] The close fit of the collar and lines of the uniform were uncomfortable, and the material was too warm for most climates, and not warm enough for others. The only time this uniform was worn in Korea was when officers arrived in country and when they departed. The rest of the time, they wore World War II vintage field uniforms.[1126]

[1121] SR 600-37-2, July 17, 1951, Hill, p. 113.

[1122] Document entitled, "New Uniforms for Army Women," p. 2.

[1123] SR 600-37-2, July 17, 1951, Hill, p. 113.

[1124] Hill, p. 109.

[1125] Anecdote from Colonel Barbara Kishpaugh, ANC.

[1126] Unless otherwise noted, all information about women's Army uniforms from the "light taupe" to the new green uniform was found in the book by Shelby L. Stanton, *US Army Uniforms of the Korean War*, (Harrisburg, PA: Stackpole Books, 1992) p. 119.

Fatigue hat worn by Major, and later General Anna Mae Hays. (Courtesy: US Army Medical Department Museum)

Theater-made patch worn on the fatigue uniform by Major Neva Rohr during the Korean War.

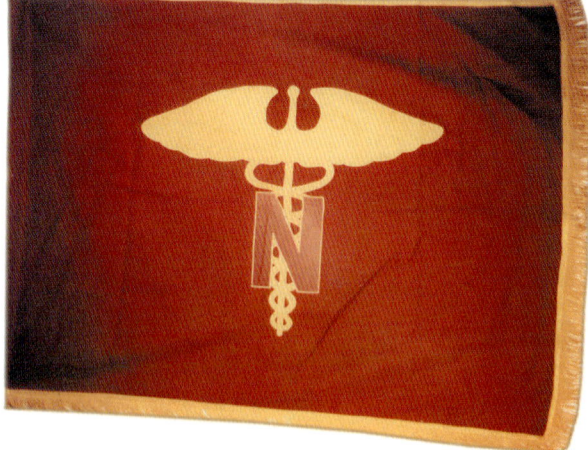

Flag which belonged to Major, and later General Anna Mae Hays. (Courtesy: AMEDD Museum, Ft. Sam Houston)

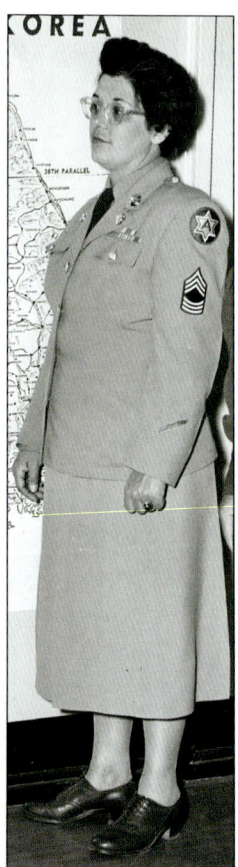

WAC Master Sergeant wearing the enlisted summer "light taupe" or "beige" uniform with a tie instead of the neck tab.

In May 1954 the Army issued a summer uniform, which was first designated the "light taupe" uniform, but this was soon changed to the "beige" uniform. It was made of wool gabardine in light beige (shade no. 146) or tropical worsted material and eventually became known as the "silver taupe" uniform. The blouse was worn with a matching skirt, a tan shirtwaist and caf -brown cotton, silk or rayon neck tab.[1127] The collar was always worn open.

[1127] Hill, p. 119.

In the 1960's this uniform was also manufactured in lightweight polyester/wool gabardine or polyester/wool tropical. The blouse was single-breasted and closed with four buttons. (The uniform was first issued with antique bronze buttons, but these were replaced with gold Army buttons in January 1961.) There were no bodice pockets or flaps, but there were two crescent welted side pockets. Shoulder straps of self material were at the shoulders, each secured with a smaller antique bronze button. The collar was rounded and worn open with lapels. Officers wore light taupe (shade no. 145) mohair cuff braid.

LTC Mildred Turner, former chief nurse of the 251st Station Hospital, South Pacific, 1944-1945, wearing the "silver taupe" uniform. (Courtesy: US Army Medical Department Museum)

The "light taupe" or "silver taupe" blouse with antique bronze buttons. Note the thread ribbons on the bodice and the two bars for a year's service overseas during WWII, and the Meritorious Unit Citation Patch on the left sleeve. (Photo by Mark Riese)

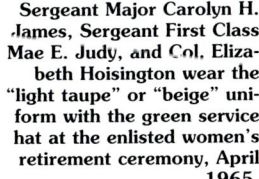

Sergeant Major Carolyn H. James, Sergeant First Class Mae E. Judy, and Col. Elizabeth Hoisington wear the "light taupe" or "beige" uniform with the green service hat at the enlisted women's retirement ceremony, April 1965.

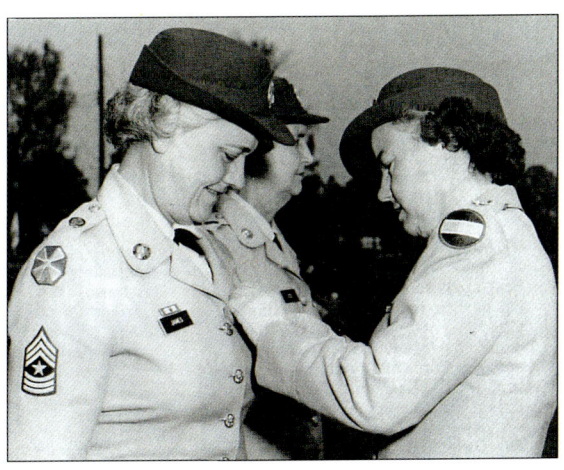

The tan (shade no. 130) shirtwaist was made of cotton. The brown neck tab was worn at the center of the closed collar. The tab was worn whether or not the blouse was worn.

The style and form of the service hat and garrison cap was the same as worn with the Carnegie uniform.

This uniform was so popular that it remained in Army stocks until July 1968.

Officer's "silver taupe" blouse.

The beige uniform, June 1963. (Courtesy: William Emerson)

M-1960: Type 1A. Note the "WA" prefix—WAC EM in the Regular Active Army.

M-1960: Type 3. Note this second set of tags carries the lady's Social Security number.

The café-brown shoulder bag was carried with this uniform, and café-brown pumps or oxfords were worn with appropriate hosiery. Women could wear gray-beige (shade no. 270) cotton or nylon gloves.

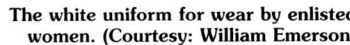
The white uniform for wear by enlisted women. (Courtesy: William Emerson)

Major Barbara Kishpaugh, ANC wearing the "silver taupe" uniform blouse with correct shirtwaist and neck tab, April 17, 1964. (Courtesy: Colonel Barbara Kishpaugh, ANC (Ret.)

The white uniform of 1959 consisted of a white blouse with the slanted, crescent side pockets, open collar and had a four gold embossed button closure. It was made of cotton twill or polyester/rayon gabardine weave material. The blouse was worn with a matching white skirt, hat and a shirtwaist with a black tab. Officer's white ribbed cotton braid was worn on each cuff, three inches from the edge of the sleeve.

Army officers white hat with removable band embroidered with gold bullion laurel leaves.

The first hat worn with the white uniform was of the Carnegie style, with the left brim turned up slightly, and a curtain strap which terminated on the right side under a self loop. The chief difference was that the US Army coat-of-arms insigne was positioned in the center of the hat. Officer's and enlisted women wore their hat insignia in gold metal. This hat style was discontinued in June 1969. In 1962, the more familiar hat with the uniform brim was introduced.

The white purse was made of leather or fabric, the material of which matched the shoes. It was of commercial design, being the clutch or envelope style. A shoulder chain was optional. White kid, doeskin, cotton/nylon or leather gloves were worn, as were white leather or cloth shoes, with heels measuring 1-1/2 " to 3". The fabric shoes were only to be worn after duty hours.[1128]

White U.S. Army purse. the specification tag inside is dated 1963.

Café-brown shoulder bag with antique-gold button snaps and attached white change purse.

[1128] Hill, pp. 121-122.

With the introduction of the new Army green uniform, the color for leather accessories was changed from brown to black. The café-brown women's accessories were completely replaced with black shoulder bags and shoes by August 1962.

The first black Army shoulder bag issued for wear with the new green uniform was the same style as the café-brown one.

Army purse carried from 1959-1965. This purse belonged to Army nurse Major Leontina M. Savage.

Army purse carried from 1966-1968.

Army purse, ca. 1969. (Photo by Ronda Sheel)

Post-1969 army purse.

By July 1, 1960 the chamois on taupe material enlisted insignia of grade was changed to goldenlite on the new Army green uniform material. The Army allowed remaining stocks of the chamoise on taupe insignia to be used for one year before becoming obsolete.

Having been approved for purchase by officers in 1957, the green winter uniform became standard for both officers and enlisted women on October 1, 1962. This uniform matched that worn by male members of the United States Army. Oddly enough, Wacs and Army nurses arrived in Vietnam wearing this uniform, heels and all, while male soldiers arrived in combat uniforms.[1129]

It featured a green wool serge or wool gabardine, single-breasted blouse (shade no. 44) with a four-button front, open rounded collar with lapels, shoulder straps of self material, and matching skirt. There were two slanted, crescent side pockets. A lightweight green uniform, made of blended lightweight polyester/wool gabardine or polyester/tropical wool, was produced in Army green (shade no. 344). Officers wore black ribbed mohair cuff braid, 1/2 inch in width. Women general officers wore 1" black ribbed cuff braid. (Anna Mae Hays, ANC, was the first female general officer.) For a short time, a green version of the Carnegie service hat was worn with this uniform, before being replaced with the new hat in 1962. Company grade officers wore a removable hat band which had a single gold stripe at the bottom edge.

Field Grade officers wore a matching band embroidered with gold bullion oak leaves. The officer's hat device was affixed to the center of the band. The hat bands were held in place by an elastic strap in the back, which was covered by the upturn in the rear of the hat. This hat wasn't available to enlisted women until 1964.

Captain Barbara Kishpaugh wearing the new green winter uniform, 1961. (Courtesy: Colonel Barbara Kishpaugh, ANC (Ret.))

[1129] Elizabeth M. Norman, *Women at War. The Story of Fifty Military Nurses Who Served in Vietnam*, (Philadelphia: University of Pennsylvania Press, 1990) p. 18.

Brigadier General Elizabeth Hoisington's green winter uniform. She was promoted just moments after General Hays was, and thus became the second female general in US history.

The first female officer to make the rank of general was Anna Mae Hays, ANC. This photo was taken at the Pentagon in September of 1973. Hays, to the right of General Westmoreland, has just been awarded the Distinguished Service Medal. Note the wide mohair cuff braid on her uniform blouse.

Field Grade officer's hat with tarnished gold bullion embroidery on the removable band.

Company grade officer's hat. (Photo by Ronda Sheel)

Typical Army women's hat box. (Photo by Ronda Sheel)

The company grade officer's service hat being worn. (Courtesy: William Emerson)

Brigadier General Elizabeth P. Hoisington wears the white uniform at her retirement ceremony, July 30, 1971. Note that she has been awarded the Distinguished Service Medal. (Courtesy: US Army)

A tan (shade no. 130) shirtwaist was worn with a removable black neck tab. This waist was replaced in 1967 by one made of a polyester/cotton blend. It had short sleeves and a six button closure and was of tan (shade no. 446) material. The white shirtwaist was introduced in 1972. It was worn with a black neck tab. All of these shirtwaists had Peter Pan collars which closed at the top with a thread loop over a corresponding button, sewn under the left collar.

The Hot Weather Field Uniform was officially introduced in 1969, but nurses serving in Vietnam had been wearing it since 1968. Faded uniforms indicated many washings, i.e., that the wearer was a "seasoned veteran" of the war; bright, newly-issued uniforms indicated someone who had just arrived in the country. These nurses were considered to be untried, while the one's wearing the faded uniforms commanded the most respect.[1130]

Herringbone twill shirt of the type worn by Army Nurses or WACs. This example has an embroidered nurse's caduceus on the left collar. Note the absence of the pocket on the left sleeve. (Photo by Ronda Sheel)

Army nurses hot weather poplin shirt. Note the pocket on the upper left sleeve, The patch is the subdued version of the US Army Vietnam patch. (Photo by Ronda Sheel)

It consisted of a loose-fitting poplin shirt of olive-green 107 and was worn tucked into the matching slacks or outside them (coat style). The collar was worn buttoned or open, and a matching flap buttoned under the opening of the collar. A white "T" shirt was worn underneath. The shirt had two patch pockets with flaps, and the buttons were visible. The flaps had finished holes to accommodate writing implements.

[1130] Ibid, p. 20.

The shirt closed with five green plastic buttons. A patch pocket was sewn to the left sleeve and the cuffs had buttons. The sleeves could be folded up just above the wearer's elbows.

Officer's rank insigne was worn on the right collar, while the branch-of-service insigne was worn on the left collar. Both insignia were usually embroidered in black thread. A name tape was worn over the right bodice pocket and a "US Army" tape was worn over the left..

The slacks buttoned on each side and had two cargo pockets. Black leather service boots or black leather oxfords were worn with the uniform.

The man's utility cap or the much favored small brimmed fatigue hat could be worn with the uniform.

The much-favored short-brimmed hat, Vietnam, 1971. (Courtesy: Col. Barbara Kishpaugh, ANC (Ret.))

Lieutenant Diane Kiser, ANC (center) wearing the herringbone twill shirt and trousers in Vietnam, 1968. Note the white name tapes. (Courtesy: Diane Kiser)

Nurses wore a maroon scarf with this uniform when authorized to do so. High russet leather shoes and a field cap completed the summer field uniform.[1131]

At first, Army women wore white name tapes over their right pockets and the gold on black "U.S. Army" tape over their left pockets. This changed to black on green tapes over both pockets. Insignia went from metal to black and brown (for the ranks of second lieutenant and major) embroidery. Most all of the insignia worn on this uniform became the subdued type.

Additionally, overshoes, commonly called "rubbers" in black or brown rubber coated cotton were issued to women, and gray or black overshoes were also permitted. Women could purchase commercial galoshes or boots in black or brown color, but in July 1962, only the black galoshes were authorized. Women also wore black leather mildew resistance service

---
[1131] Hill, p. 128.

Major Barbara Gray was the first Army Medical Specialist Corps member to serve in Vietnam, 93rd Evacuation Hospital. (Courtesy: US Army Center of Military History)

Nurses wearing subdued insignia, except for the metal distinctive insignia worn by the nurse on the right. (Courtesy: Col. Barbara Kishpaugh, ANC (Ret.))

boots, black oxfords, men's socks with cushioned soles, and high black plain overshoes styled like boots.[1132]

Army nurses continued to wear the white ward uniform with a high, stiff hat.

Army nurses in Vietnam, 1970, wearing combination combat boots. (Courtesy: Col. Barbara Kishpaugh, ANC (Ret.))

The army nurse captain wearing the white ward uniform. (Courtesy: US Army)

---

394 [1132] Hill, p. 131.

Jacket liner worn as a coat. (Photo by Ronda Sheel)

A tan opaque raincoat with detachable hood could be purchased at Post Exchanges. It had a self belt with a Lucite buckle and a matching carrying case.[1133]

In 1966, green (Army shade 274) raincoat was introduced. It was double-breasted with shoulder straps, side slash pockets, a self belt and removable havelock. Officer's wore rank insignia on the shoulder straps. A gray-beige (Army shade no. 273) acrylic scarf could be worn with the raincoat. It was folded in half and crossed at the center from left to right.

In 1969 officers were authorized a overcoat of wool gabardine (Army green shade 44), which was double-breasted with vertical side pockets and shoulder straps. It had a removable liner. Rank insignia were worn on the shoulder straps.[1134]

An unattractive Cold Weather Field Uniform was introduced in May 1969 and consisted of an olive-green (Army shade 108) blouse of heavy wool serge. It was single-breasted and closed with four gold embossed buttons. No cuff braid was authorized. The blouse had four patch pockets with flaps. A tan (Army shade 446) shirtwaist was worn with a black neck tab. Rank and branch-of-service insignia were worn on this uniform per regulations. The uniform had a matching skirt and slacks. The legs of the slacks bloused when worn with women's black leather service boots. There was also an unpiped matching garrison cap. Regulations indicate that the man's olive-green (Army shade 106) utility cap could be worn with this uniform when it was worn with slacks.[1135]

The cold weather field uniform and garrison cap. (Photo by Mark Riese)

[1133] Hill, p. 120.
[1134] Hill, p. 136.
[1135] Hill, p. 137.

A wool flannel shirtwaist, olive-green 108, had two patch breast pockets and a patch pocket on the left sleeve. The collar could be worn open or closed and officers wore their rank insigne on the right collar and the branch-of-service insignia on the left collar. Enlisted women wore their rank on the sleeves. The shirtwaist was worn tucked into the match wool serge slacks, with the collar open or closed. The women's olive-green 108 garrison cap or the men's olive-green 106 utility cap were worn with this uniform.[1136]

The green and white cord striped summer blouse, skirt and garrison cap were worn by both enlisted women and officers. All ranks used four gold US Army removable buttons for closure. Enlisted women wore gold on green chevrons on each of the sleeves and the appropriate discs on the collar. A black plastic name tag with white letters was worn over the right bodice. Ribbons were worn over the left breast. While this uniform blouse had no shoulder straps, rank insignia was pinned in the appropriate location on the shoulders by officers. The gold "U.S." insigne was worn on the right collar and the branch-of-service insigne on the right collar. Apparently, no patches were worn on this uniform. The uniform was piped in green cord around the collar, the sleeve cuffs and the leading edge of the curtain of the garrison cap. Officers wore the same cap as enlisted women, but with a rank insigne attached to the left forward section of the curtain.

This officer wears the cord uniform with a "US Army Vietnam" patch in a hanger suspended from her collar.

General Anna Mae Hays' cord uniform.

[1136] Hill, p. 138.

WAC detachment in Vietnam. Note the ascots with the "US Army Vietnam" logo being worn. (Courtesy: US Army)

The training duty uniform, worn here by a drill sergeant, indicated by the distinctive hat. (Courtesy: US Army)

The green cord garrison cap was the same style for officers and enlisted women. (Photo by Ronda Sheel)

Specification label inside the green cord garrison cap.

Beginning in 1971, enlisted women wore a training duty uniform consisting of a light green, short sleeve shirtwaist with metal rank insignia on the collar. A black and white plastic nametag was worn on the right bodice. The waist tucked into darker green cotton shorts, over which was worn a matching short skirt. White cotton anklets were worn with white tennis shoes or black low shoes. The green cord garrison cap was worn with this uniform. Army female drill sergeants wore a distinctive high-crowned, brimmed canvas hat with a cloth chin strap. The left side of the brim was turned up and the dress enlisted hat device was on the front center. This hat was also worn by drill sergeant's with the green and white cord uniform and fatigues.

The Army introduced a blue semi-dress uniform for officers, warrant officers and enlisted women on June 13, 1957.[1137] It was identical in style to the light taupe uniform.

The full uniform consisted of an Army Blue (shade 150) fingertip length wool cape (optional), black collar tab, miniature or full size medals, decorations or ribbons, white cotton gloves, a black leather envelope-style handbag, Army Blue wool service hat, appropriate insignia, wool taupe overcoat, tan rayon scarf, white shirtwaist, dress black leather oxfords or black leather pumps, nylon taupe or neutral stockings, and the Army Blue blouse and skirt. Badges, insignia and rank insignia as authorized, were part of this uniform.

This uniform was authorized to be worn off-duty by all ranks at official functions, or while on recruiting duty. It was not permitted to be worn as a duty uniform.

Enlisted woman in the Army blue uniform (1957-present), a wool barathea material, worn with black accessories. This uniform was also worn by officers. (Courtesy: US Army)

Army enlisted woman's blue uniform.

[1137] Unless otherwise noted, all information about the 1957 Army Blue uniform for women is from SR 600-37-2, C 7, "Personnel, Service Uniform for Women Army Personnel," Washington, DC: June 13, 1957.

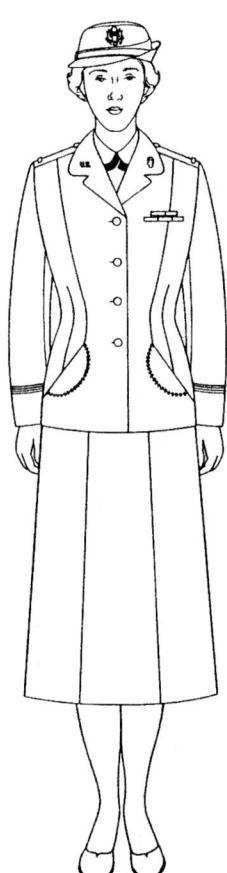

Army blue uniform, officers.

The blouse was made of Army Blue (shade no. 150, the same color as the cape) wool barathea cloth, 12-14 oz., or 12-14 oz. blue broadcloth, and was single-breasted with a four gold Army button closure. The blouse was fully lined in black satin. The blouse had shoulder straps of self material, with a smaller gold Army button near the end. Enlisted women wore shoulder straps which had rounded ends, and were piped in gold colored rayon or rayon cord edge braid, 1/8" wide. A smaller gold Army button was worn near the edge of both shoulder straps. The blouse had a welted pocket on each lower side. A matching Army Blue skirt was worn with the uniform. The white shirtwaist was worn with a black tab made of eight ounce tropical worsted.

(L to R) The officer's blue semi-dress uniform with shoulder straps, enlisted woman's green uniform, officer's evening dress uniform, officer's green uniform, enlisted woman's blue semi-dress uniform. (Courtesy: William Emerson)

Officers wore, in lieu of mohair cuff braid, two 1/4" wide two vellum gold brocade or gold colored rayon or nylon stripes, sewn with a 1/4" space between them, and over a silk stripe in the wearer's branch-of-service color. The distance between the edge of the sleeve cuff and the bottom stripe was three inches. Warrant officers did not wear these stripes:

Army Nurse Corps and Army Medical Specialist Corps—
Maroon silk stripe, Army shade number 65017;

Women's Army Corps—Moss-green silk stripe, Army shade number 65022.[1138]

Enlisted women wore a one-eighth wide gold colored nylon or rayon soutach (Russian) braid stripe on their cuffs, three inches from the edge of the end of the sleeve. Officers and warrant officers wore their rank insignia on the shoulder straps of the uniform blouse. Enlisted women wore insignia that was gold in color on Army Blue cloth backings. It was smaller than those chevrons worn by men, but when women's chevrons for the blue uniform were not available, enlisted women were permitted to wear the men's insignia of grade for the blue uniform.[1139]

The Army Blue (shade no. 150) hat was designed like the wool taupe hat with the exceptions that the inverted pleat in the middle was omitted and the crown was more rounded and lower in depth. A metal grommet was provided in front of the hat for screw-post officers and enlisted women's insignia, which were gold in color.

Warrant officers and company grade officers wore a single half inch gold two vellum bullion brocade, gold rayon braid or gold nylon stripe, which was sewn to the lower edge of the brim and extended from under the left brim upturn, through the cloth loop and ended under the back upturned brim. Field grade officers wore a spray of gold bullion laurel leaves embroidered upon the brim of the hat, with a space of at least 1-1/2" separating them.[1140]

The hat worn by enlisted women had only the gold army coat-of-arms in a circle insigne as ornamentation.

Officers wore a small, gold, usually screw-post Army coat-of-arms insigne on their hats, while warrant officers wore their distinctive hat insigne. Enlisted women wore the Army coat-of-arms in a circle on their hats. Hat insignia were worn centered on the front of the hats, midway between the top of the curtain strap and the top of the crown.

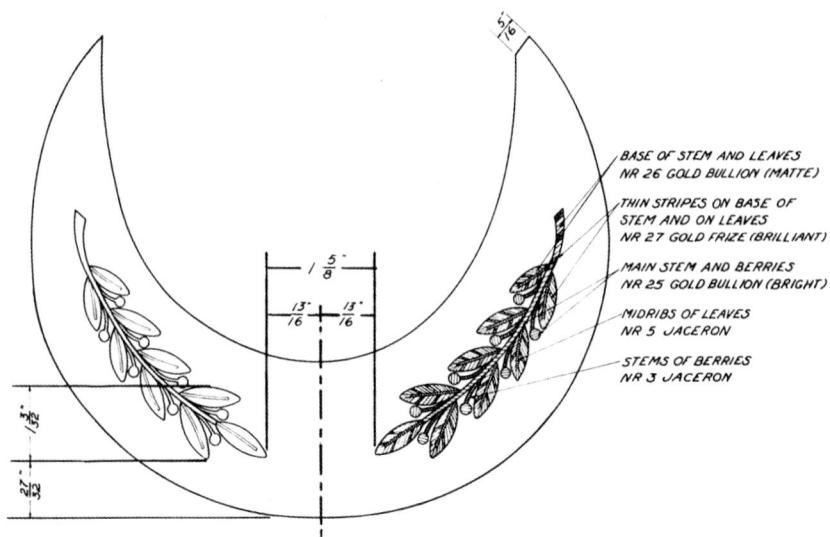

Field grade officers hat brim embroidery pattern.

Example of the Carnegie-style "army-green" hat, circa 1957.

Light taupe hat, of the style worn by the officer on p. 383. (Courtesy: George A. Petersen.)

Carnegie-style dress blue hat, company grade officer. (Courtesy: George A. Petersen)

Carnegie style dress blue cap, field grade. (Courtesy: George A. Petersen)

Army blue hat, field grade officers.

Army blue hat, company grade officers and warrant officers.

Army blue hat, enlisted women.

Officers wore a gold "U.S." on the right collar, centered 1" from the lower edge. The branch-of-service insigne was worn on the left collar in the same position as the "U.S." insigne.

The Army Blue (shade no. 150) wool cape was made of 12-14 oz. wool barathea or broadcloth and was lined in gold (Army shade no. 175) synthetic satin material. This item was optional, and the taupe overcoat could be worn in its place.

The "dress blue" uniform was modified around 1960, when the color was changed to Army Blue shade number 450, and made of lightweight 9.5 oz. polyester/wool gabardine weave or 9 oz. polyester/tropical wool. On October 1, 1960, the shoulder straps were replaced with passants, curved to fit over the shoulders. These insignia gave the uniform a traditional element, along with its "federal blue" color, since passants had been worn by Federal troops from the Civil War and on officer's blue sack coats just before World War I. Passants consisted of a rectangular strap with a thick gold trim border. The center of the passant was in the branch-of-service color. The wearer's rank insignia was embroidered near each end of the interior rectangle, over the branch-of-service color. Full colonels had only a single eagle insigne embroidered in the center of the passant. Passants were attached to the blouse at each shoulder by either being sewn on, or by snaps, metal hooks and eyelets, which made them easy to remove when the blouse was dry cleaned. The branch-of-service colors for women matched the sleeve braid service color, i.e. maroon for members of the Army Medical Department and moss-green for members of the Women's Army Corps. (Passants with a maroon interior had a narrow white border along the edge of the rectangle.)

[1138] SR 600-37-2, C 7, June 13, 1957, p. 3.
[1139] SR 600-37-2, C 7, p. 4.
[1140] SR 600-37-2, C 7, June 13, 1957, p. 2.

Army nurse's blue blouse with removable passants.

Major Barbara Kishpaugh wearing the new dress blue uniform with passants, instead of shoulder straps, 1966. (Courtesy: Col. Barbara Kishpaugh, ANC (Ret.))

WAC major's passant made by Gemsco.

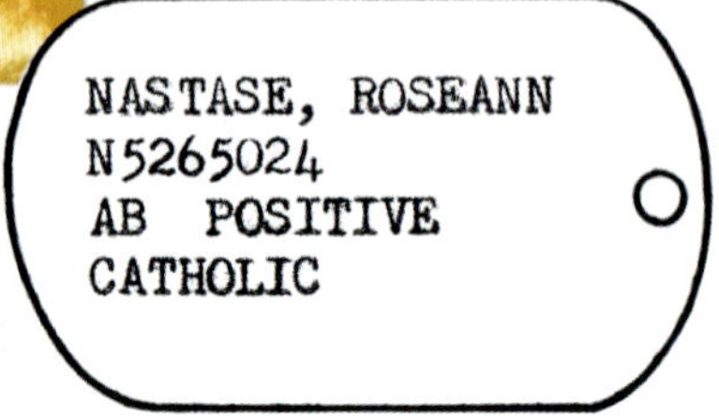

M-1960 identification tag for a Vietnam-era Army nurse with "N" prefix to the (AUS) serial number, plus blood type and religion.

Enlisted women's uniforms retained the shoulder straps with rounded ends.

The cape lining color defined the wearer's branch-of-service; maroon for the Army Medical Department and old gold for members of the WAC.[1141]

WAC officer and Army nurses and officers of the Medical Specialist Corps could wear a white synthetic scarf of commercial design with the overcoat or raincoat when the Army Blue uniform was in wear.[1142]

In 1969, the Army authorized a black mess uniform, for wear year-round at formal social or official functions. It had a black (Army shade 149) polyester/wool or wool tropical jacket with black (Army shade 332) mohair officer's cuff stripes on each sleeve. The shoulder boards were removable and had a gold 3/8" wide gold brocade border with the field in the wearer's branch-of-service color. Rank insignia were embroidered in gold or silver bullion upon the field. Miniature decorations were worn centered on the left side of the jacket.

WAC officer's shoulder board for wear on the mess dress jacket with rank of colonel.

A matching three gore skirt was worn as part of the black mess uniform, along with a white polyester/cotton broadcloth blouse with two sets of ruffles on each side of the button closure. The collar of the blouse was rounded; a black removable necktab was worn under it. The matching black cummerbund fastened just above the skirt zipper (on the left side.)

Black fabric pumps and a matching envelope or clutch purse, with or without shoulder chain, as well as white cloth or leather gloves were also authorized for this uniform.[1143]

Brigadier General Mildred Bailey, director of WAC, 1971-1975, wears the black mess uniform. (Courtesy: US Army)

[1141] Shelby L. Stanton, *US Army Uniforms of the Cold War, 1948-1973,* (Mechanicsburg, PA: Stackpole Books, 1994) p. 211.
[1142] Hill, p. 123.
[1143] Hill. p. 145.

WAC officer's dress blue uniform.

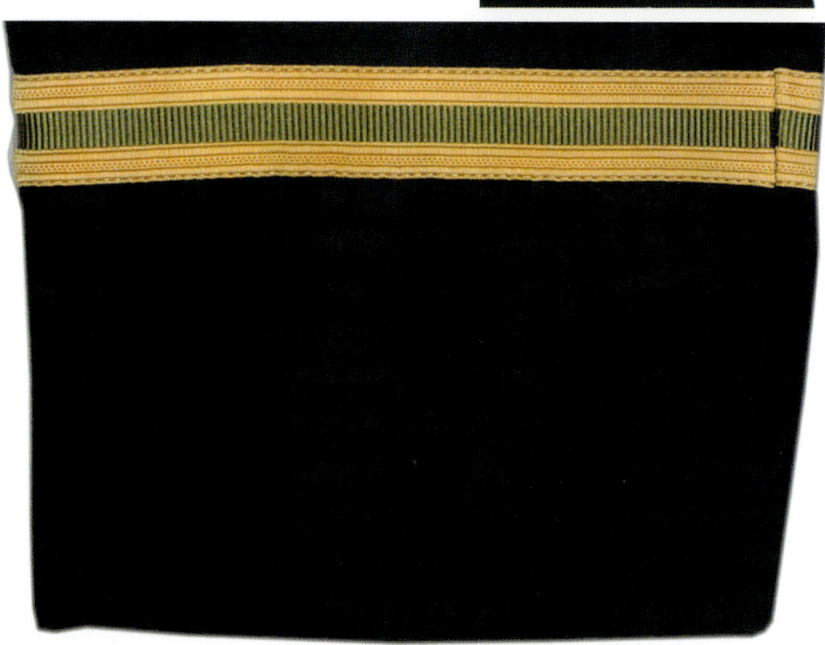

Detail of the moss-green and old gold sleeve stripe worn on the dress blue uniform blouse by WAC officers.

Female officer's white mess dress jacket.

Female officer's shoulder board for wear with the mess dress uniform. The braid of gold borders the maroon central color which indicates the wearer served in the Army Medical Department. (Courtesy: K. Lazier)

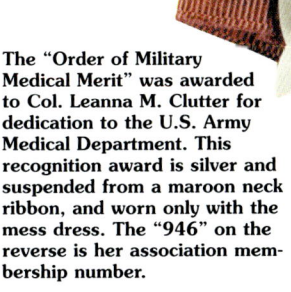

The "Order of Military Medical Merit" was awarded to Col. Leanna M. Clutter for dedication to the U.S. Army Medical Department. This recognition award is silver and suspended from a maroon neck ribbon, and worn only with the mess dress. The "946" on the reverse is her association membership number.

WAC passants from colonel to lieutenant (gold or silver on moss-green). (Courtesy: John Mull)

A white mess jacket, worn with a black skirt, black cummerbund, ruffled shirt, black neck tab and shoulder boards was authorized for wear by female officers in 1967. A white skirt and cummerbund could also be worn with white pumps and gloves.

The white mess uniform. (Courtesy: US Army)

General Bailey models the all-white mess uniform. (Courtesy: William Emerson)

A formal evening dress uniform was authorized for wear by female Army officers in 1959.[1144] Another source lists the period of wear of this uniform from 1952 to 1969.[1145] It was an optional item of uniform, and very few of these uniforms probably exist.

It consisted of a short wool broadcloth midnight blue (Army shade No. 176) short, princess cut jacket with long tapered sleeves, roll collar with open neckline, having hook-and-eye fasteners at the waist. The collar was embroidered with gold bullion laurel leaf pattern. A tab extended out from

---

[1144] AR 670-30, October 20, 1959, Hill.
[1145] Bettie J. Morder, *The Women's Army Corps, 1945-1978*, (Washington, DC: Center of Military History, United States Army, 1990), color plate caption.

The formal evening dress for wear by officers, 1952-1969. The WAC insigne is just visible on the tab below the left collar. (Courtesy: US Army)

Col. Barbara Jane Smith wears the formal evening dress without insignia on the tabs below the collar, 1956. (Courtesy: William Emerson)

Evening dress uniform with jacket.

under each side of the collar. An officer's "U.S." insigne was worn on the right tab, while the branch insigne was worn on the right. Each sleeve had a gold lace trefoil above a horizontal gold lace. The width of the lace was a quarter inch. The height of the sleeve ornamentation was about 5 7/8 inches. The wearer's rank insigne was embroidered in bullion a quarter of an inch above the horizontal braid.

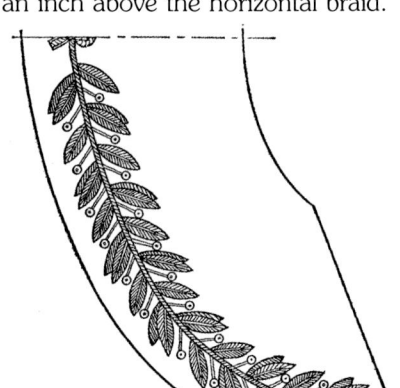

Detail of collar embroidery.

Detail of the sleeve trefoil.

The long skirt was of the same material as the jacket and had five gores. It was straight in front but flared in the back, giving the impression of a train. It fastened on the left side, at the waistband. A short skirt of the same material was authorized for wear with this uniform in 1966.

A white silk twill shirtwaist with a Peter Pan collar was worn under the jacket. It had short sleeves and fastened with six gold US Army buttons. The buttonholes on the shirtwaist were piped and vertical.

A midnight blue (Army shade No. 196) silk faille or rayon twill cummerbund was worn about the waist. It had double pleats in front but was plain in the back. It fasted on the left side with a zipper.

A midnight blue (Army shade No. 176) wool broadcloth headband. It came to a point in the center and tapered down the sides. Gold bullion laurel leaves were embroidered on each side in a graduated pattern.[1146]

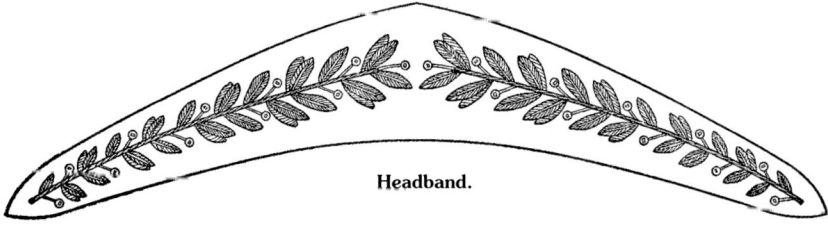

Headband.

A matching cape with gold rayon lining and gold bullion passants with embroidered rank insignia could also be worn with this uniform.

Miniature medals were worn on the left breast of the jacket.

[1146] AR 670-30, August 1966, Hill.

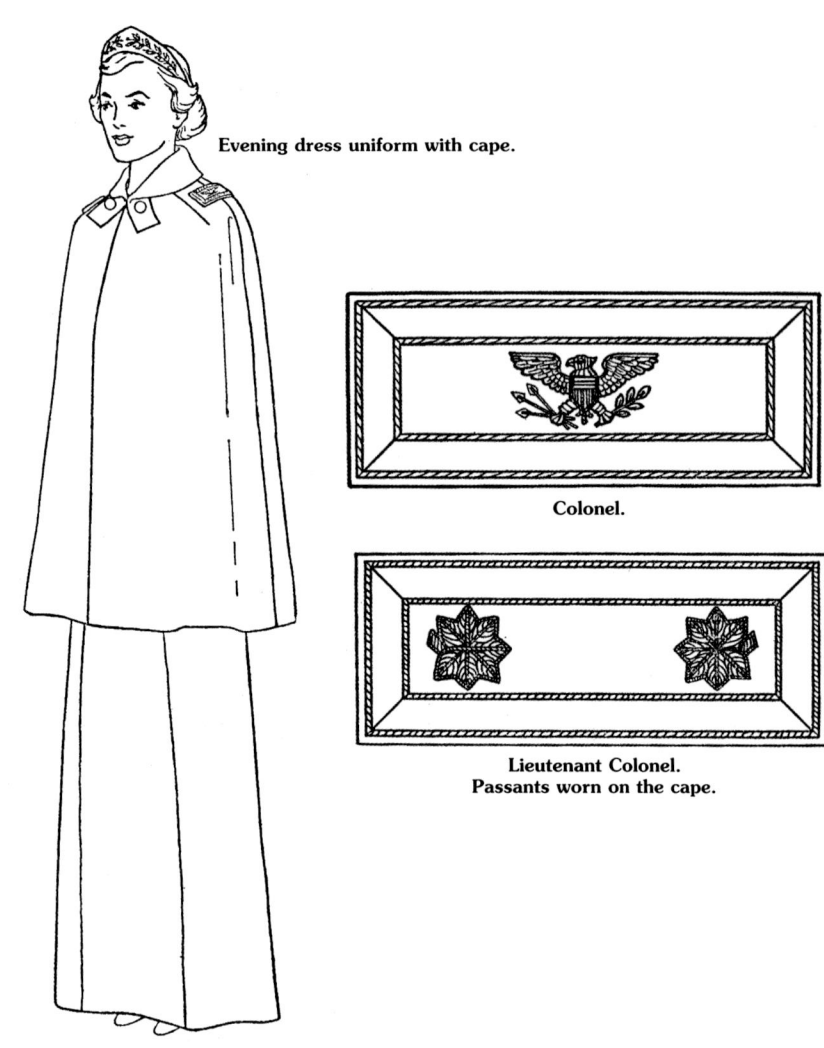

Evening dress uniform with cape.

Colonel.

Lieutenant Colonel.
Passants worn on the cape.

Director of the WAAC
Colonel Oveta Culp Hobby, 1942—1943
Directors of the WAC
Colonel Oveta Culp Hobby, 1943—1945;
Colonel Westray Battle Boyce Long, 1945-1947;
Colonel Mary A. Hallaren, 1947-1953;
Colonel Irene O. Galloway, 1953-1957;
Colonel Mary L. M. Rasmuson, 1957-1962;
Colonel Emily C. Gorman, 1962-1966;
Brigadier General Elizabeth P. Hoisington, 1966-1971;
Brigadier General Mildred I.C. Bailey, 1971-1975;
Brigadier General Mary E. Clarke, 1975-1978.[1147]

[1147] Bettie J. Morden, *The Women's Army Corps, 1945-1978*, (Washington, DC: Center of Military History, United States Army, 1990), p. ii.

Women's Land Army of America
(WLAA—World War I)
(World War II)

Women's Land Army of the U. S. Crop Corps
(World War II)

Mrs. Henry Wade Rogers was the chairman of the Woman's Land Army of America during World War I. By April of 1918, it had chapters in eighteen states.[1148] The New York State chapter incorporated in May.[1149] The WLAA was created in response to President Woodrow Wilson's appeal for the greater production of food for the nation,[1150] and probably worked in conjunction with the United States Food Administration. With a large number of male farmers serving in the armed forces, it was up to the women to plant and harvest crops.

Generally, "farmerettes," as these women came to be known, wore straw brimmed hats, blue jeans and shirts and canvas puttees. Many of the members were college girls who worked during the summer[1151] when school wasn't in session.

Bronze hat badge for wear by members of the Woman's Land Army of America. (Courtesy: Keith Ness)

[1148] "Land Army Praised. President Writes in Appreciation of Women's Farm Work," *The New York Times*, April 11, 1918, sec. 15: p. 4.

[1149] "Woman's Land Army Incorporated," *The New York Times*, April 25, 1918: p. 24:3.

[1150] "Land Army Incorporates. Will Aim to Supply Woman Farm Workers for New York State," *The New York Times*, May 24, 1918.

[1151] "Barnard Girls For Farms. 150 Have Applied for Training with Mount Kisco Unit," *The New York Times*, April 23, 1918: p. 11.

Sun bonnet worn by a member of the Woman's Land Army of Ohio during World War I. (Courtesy: NSCDA Coll.–NMAH/Smithsonian)

Women's Land Army, New Jersey Division, patch. (Courtesy: Phil & Linda Darling)

During World War II, volunteers were again urgently needed to harvest the nation's crops. Members of the 50,000 strong Women's Land Army helped bring in everything from corn in Minnesota to peaches in Georgia. The official "uniform" worn by these girls were dark blue overalls with gathered cuffs, a light blue, long-sleeved shirtwaist and a dark blue and light blue cap. The complete ensemble cost each girl $6.20. The WLA insigne was worn on the hat, overalls, and on a brassard, which was an optional purchase. The color of the insignia is not confirmed, but a period pamphlet states that, "...After a year's service, members will be eligible to wear the insignia with 'WLA' in white letters on a red background." Girls could also buy a dark blue jacket and a light blue shirtwaist with short

World War II Women's Land Army uniform. Note the patch on the overalls and on the front of the hat. (Courtesy: Phil & Linda Darling)

sleeves. Uniform items were purchased through the National Committee on Boys and Girls Club Work.[1152]

Some period photographs show these girls wearing bluejeans, shirts and turbans, and one photograph shows a girl wearing a brassard with "WLA" on her upper left arm. Other photographs show girls wearing bibbed overalls with a shirt and matching jacket. The WLA insigne is visible on the top center of the bib. These girls also wore a unique form of headdress, which seems to have be a canvas-like visored hat with a front upturn, and what appears to be a white mesh top. The WLA patch was sewn to the front of the cap.[1153]

Two World War II posters urging people to "Work on a farm...this summer" and the "join the Women's Land Army." (Courtesy: Charles B. Oellig)

[1152] Women's Land Army of the US Crop Corps Needs Workers (Washington, DC: Extension Service, United States Department of Agriculture, July 1943). Uniforms and visored hats were made by the Knox Hat Corporation.

[1153] Cover of "*Click*" magazine, September 1943.

Yeomen (F): United States Naval Reserve (F)
(World War I)

During World War I women were permitted to join the United States Naval Reserve (F) and were classified as Yeomen (Female)" or "Yeomen (F)." But they were popularly referred to as "Yeomanettes." Some 13,000[1154] of them served stateside during the war, performing mostly clerical duties. The first woman to join the Naval Reserve was Mary Stella Dahm, who enlisted on April 2, 1917 and was assigned to the Bureau of Identification.[1155] Twin sisters Genevieve and Lucille Baker are thought to be the first Yeomen (F) to serve in the United States Coast Guard. Fifty-seven Yeomen (F) died in 1918 during the influenza epidemic.[1156]

Women serving as Yeomen (F) were provided with tailor-made uniforms. Bids were taken from tailors to win the government contract for the following items of clothing: 1,000 blue serge coats and skirts, 2,000 drill white coats and skirt, 2,000 additional drill cloth skirts, 3,000 shirtwaists made of beachcloth or something similar, 1,000 hats made of navy-blue felt, and 1,000 white rough straw hats. The uniforms were made in standard sizes and issued as such, with the government providing the majority of the materials used.

The Norfolk-style navy-blue or white bleached drill single-breasted coats were made to slightly fit the figure of the woman, with the sleeves reaching the wearer's knuckles. The front of the coats were closed with four standard gold navy buttons with three gold navy buttons at each sleeve cuff. Patch pockets with flaps were sewn to the skirt of the coat, at the hips. The bottoms of the pockets were slightly rounded. The top of the pocket was to align with the fourth button. The navy-blue coat was lined in dark blue sateen, while the white coat was lined in skeleton.

Two inch wide bands ran from the shoulder of the coat, in both the front and back and on each side, with loops incorporated to make room for the cloth belt. (This giving the coat its distinctive Norfolk styling.) The belt, 1 3/4" wide, was secured in the front by a gold navy button.

[1154] Breach, p. 8.
[1155] "Woman in Naval Reserve," *The New York Times,* April 3, 1917.
[1156] WIMSA Calender, 1996, see, "July."

A proud Yeomanette poses in her blue uniform. (Courtesy: Roger Bender)

The blue Norfolk blouse worn by Yeomen (F). (Photo by Ronda Sheel)

Sleeve rate for a Yeoman First-Class. The eagle and specialty mark are embroidered in white thread. (Courtesy: Greensboro Historical Museum, photo by Patt Anthony)

Excellent study of the white Norfolk-style blouse and straw hat worn by Yeomanettes. (Courtesy: Mrs. Elizabeth Milano Collection)

Chief Yeoman (F) Lassie Kelly wears the White Norfolk uniform. (Courtesy: U.S. Naval Historical Center)

The white Norfolk blouse. (Photo by Ronda Sheel)

Detail of the skirt of the Yeoman (female) uniform, showing the patch pockets sewn to the skirt front. This was a feature common to many women's uniform skirts of the period. (Courtesy: Greensboro Historical Museum, photo by Patt Anthony)

The long skirts were made of navy-blue serge or white drill, were tailored and full at the hem. There was "...a placket fastened with invisible snappers...." and two patch pockets with flaps and gold buttons on the front of the skirt. The hem of the skirts measured four inches above the wearer's ankle.

The shirtwaist were made with all flat seams. The long sleeves were "...set plain into the arm hole..." and slightly gathered at the cuff, which fastened with two buttons. The collar was worn open and over the collar of the coat. A patch pocket was at the left side and the shirtwaist closed with plain pearl buttons.

Women wore either a navy-blue felt or a white rough or smooth straw hat. The hat brims measured 2-3/4" wide and the crowns were 3-3/4" at the top and 6-3/4" at the bottom. A satin or silk tally reading "Naval Reserve" or "U.S. Navy" was worn around the bottom of the brim.[1157] The rough straw white hat had a black leather chin strap. Women with the rank of chief petty officer wore a metal fouled anchor with the initials, "U.S.N." on the front of their hat.

Chief Yeoman (F) Margaret Mary Fitzgerald wears the "US Navy" tally on her hat. (Courtesy: U.S. Naval Historical Center)

[1157] "Uniforms for Navy Girls," *The New York Times*, June 19, 1917: p. 19:2.

Chief Yeoman (F) Estelle Exner wears a navy blue straw hat with the metal "U.S.N." and anchor badge.

Yeoman (F) Ora L. Hirsch Merritt wears the "Naval Reserve" tally on the straw hat. (Courtesy: U.S. Naval Historical Center)

This Yeomanette wears the hat using the chinstrap. (Courtesy: Niles Laughner)

Chief Yeoman (F) Daisy May Pratt (Erd) wears the white rough straw hat. (Courtesy: U.S. Naval Historical Center)

These Yeomen (F) wear men's middies and "Donald Duck" style hats, which was not according to regulations. (Courtesy: National Archives)

WWI "Yeomanette." Note the designation "U.S.N.R.F." on the tally of her hat. It appears to be done in a thick, possibly bullion, embroidery. (Courtesy: Daniel J. Miller)

This Yeomanette identification tag lists both the date of birth and the date of enlistment. (Courtesy: John Mull)

The rating patch was sewn to the upper left sleeve.

Black low shoes were worn with both uniforms.

Some Yeomen (F) in the Washington, DC area took to wearing navy-blue middies (or "jumpers") with a black sailor's tie and long skirt. Their rank patch was sewn to the left sleeve. Along with this, they wore the familiar "Donald Duck" sailor's hat. This uniform was unofficial.[1158]

Photograph showing a Yeoman (F) wearing a cape. (Courtesy: Roger Bender)

Chief Yeoman Daisy May Pratt (Erd) wears a non-regulation jumper, 1918. See page 421. (Courtesy: U.S. Naval Historical Center)

"Yeomanette Battalion" patch, worn on the left sleeve of the blouse, above the rate. Purpose unknown. (Courtesy: Michael von Deckbar)

[1158] Note on photograph made by the Naval Historical Center, Photographic Section, of Yeoman (F) Daisy May Pratt Erd.

Yeoman (F) were not supposed to serve outside the U.S., however, this woman is wearing at least one French medal.

Young Men's Christian Association

(YMCA—World War I)

The first woman to go overseas for the YMCA was Mrs. Vincent Astor. She Arrived in France in June 1917 and operated the first "Y" canteen at Brest. It was created for American sailors. Mrs. Theodore Roosevelt, Jr. opened the first "Y" canteen in Paris in July.[1159] These so-called "huts," or canteens, were meant to bring a touch of the typical American home to the homesick American soldier. Every effort was made to get male and female "Y" workers attached to combat divisions, but it was not an easy feat. Rather than going through official army channels,

---

[1159] Frederick Harris, Managing Editor, Service with Fighting Men (New York: Association Press, 1922) p. 56.

men and women found ways to get to the divisions where they set up the canteens in dugouts or any available sheltered space. Some of these were well-stocked with cigarettes, canned peaches, pineapples, chewing gum and such. These dugout huts were so close to the enemy lines that at some times hot chocolate could not be served to the troops during the day, for fear of the Germans seeing the steam rising from the hot cooking pots. Qualifications for workers were that they be of excellent character, strong, sensible, loyal to the rules of the YMCA, and have interest in spiritual matters. Workers baked pies, served innumerable cups of hot coffee, mended uniforms, hung mistletoe at Christmas time, washed dishes, scrubbed floors and planned diversions. "It is not too much to say that the success or failure of such a hut as a source of military energy and morale is altogether a matter of the personality of its workers," one contemporary wrote.[1160]

YMCA workers were affliliated with the US Army's Services of Supply, which oversaw a long list of activities: Construction of railways, roads, docks, care and transportation of soldiers and animals, operation of telegraph and telephone lines, hospitalization of the sick and wounded, care of welfare projects and leave areas, embarkation of US troops to the United States, and many other details. The Services of Supply was headquartered in Tours and its Advance Section was the area of active military operations. The District of Paris was a seperate section. The hub of all distrubution of supplies and services was the Intermediate Section, which was in central France. The principal mission of the Services of Supply was the shipment of soldiers and goods to the Advance Section. "Napoleon spoke about an army moving on its stomach; the American Army in France moved over the bent backs of the Services of Supply."[1161]

Canteen life proved to be quite different from what many women expected:

> 'We started with splendid plans to run a sort of quick lunch restaurant with ham and eggs, omelets, hot chocolate, steak, French fried potatoes, chops, etc., I laugh when I think of it. We got up at six and tried to start the fire. French coal is about half slate and you can't depend on it a minute. ...We also had a balky little charcoal burner and my sterno.... The boys drank eighty gallons of chocolate and milk. Our canteen, though too small, is better than many, for we have floors, a few little heating stoves, and best of all, electric lights. Near Argonne, we could not serve hot drinks...because the Germans could see the smoke. We slept in dugouts most of the time.'[1162]

When the chairman of the War Work Coucil toured YMCA installations in 1918 he was so impressed with the women's work that he insist-

---

[1160] "Uniforms for Navy Girls," *The New York Times*, June 19, 1917: p. 19:2. p. 4.
[1161] Frederick Harris, Managing Editor, *Service with Fighting Men* (New York: Association Press, 1922), pp. 139-140.
[1162] Ibid, p. 136.

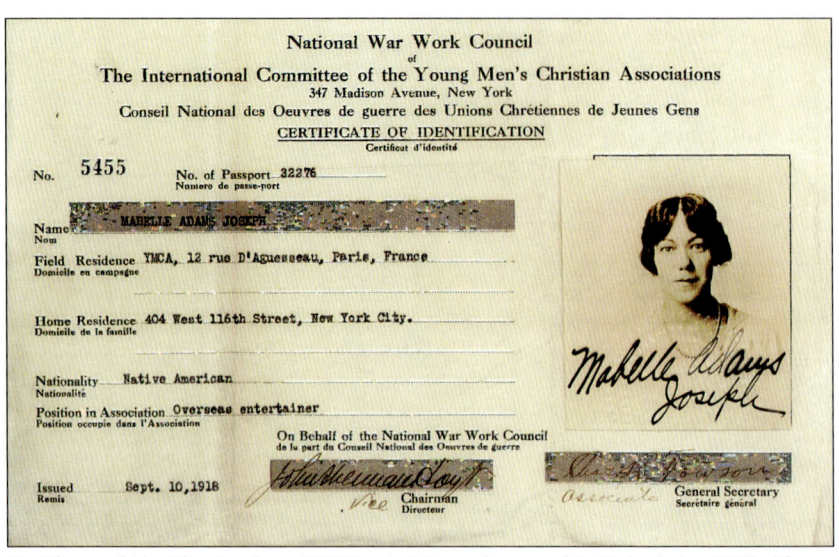

Certificate of identification for a YMCA entertainer who served in Paris during WWI. Of particular interest is that this woman's nationality is noted as "Native American." (Courtesy: Duane Netzly)

ed that they no longer be referred to simply as "canteen workers," but that they be called "secretaries."[1163]

The YMCA also provided equipment for sports, educational programs, Bible study groups, reading materials, and motion picture shows and live theater. Live theater was the most challenging endeavor of the YMCA services. Costuming had to be procured, sets constructed, actors found and time set aside for rehearsals. Theatrical productions were held in what the YMCA called "play factories."[1164] In April 1918, YMCA authorities and other workers met with General Pershing to chart a course of future theatrical performances which were deemed essential in maintaining high moral among the troops of the AEF. The result was the creation of the YMCA Overseas Theater League, which shortly became the Over There Theater League headed by George M. Cohan with Winthrop Ames as its Executive Director.

Though probably limited to the work of male YMCA secretaries, the Honey Bee Club is worth mentioning. Outdoor religious services had become difficult to conduct in the AEF, since a gathering of a large group was an attractive target for the enemy. The members of the YMCA had to limit their religious ministry to small Bible study groups and to one-on-one contact. A special Bible study group was born among the black soldiers assigned to perhaps the worst assignment in the AEF: Graves Registration. Working in Brest, a YMCA secretary used the illustration of the turkey buzzard and the honey bee during one of his talks. The idea of the Honey Bee club was born there, among some four hundred American soldiers. A spe-

---

[1163] Ibid, p. 61.
[1164] Ibid, p. 175.

cial badge was designed for the club, and classes that dealt specifially with the parables of Jesus were organized. The Honey Bee badge came to be highly regarded and was permitted to be worn on the military uniform. The commander of the 802nd Pioneer Infantry restricted the wearing of this badge to men who had a clean record and were of good repute. Military police were ordered to treat this insigne as a badge of honor, and allowed the wearer to pass without question. So highly was the Honey Bee badge regarded that if the wearer happened to commit an offense, the badge was removed from his uniform during a military formation. A total of 21,550 Honey Bee Club badges were awarded to soldiers in the AEF.[1165]

Some restrictions applied to female volunteers for the YMCA. The acceptable ages for workers was from twenty-five to forty-five years old. No women whose parents were born in Austria, Bulgaria, Germany or Turkey could serve. Women whose husbands were born in these countries were exempt as well. In addition to other restrictions, women who were Canadian or British citizens were not allowed to be sent to France.[1166]

But of all the societies that served overseas during World War I, the YMCA received the most criticism. The saying, "that damn Y" was common; cigarettes bought at the YMCA, some soldiers found out, contained a card that said the cigarettes were a gift.[1167] This was explained through a letter of October 23, 1918 from First Lieutenant C.P. Haffley, QMC, US Army to the YMCA, 3rd Division, APO 740, AEF:

"1. Through an error of the Supply Division at Gièvres, this commissary received several cases of Piedmont cigarets [sic], each carton of which contained a return post card stating that these cigarets [sic] were a gift from 'The New York Sun Tobacco Fund.'

2. These cigarets [sic] were sold to you in case lots before this was discovered, there being no marks on the cases to indicate that this was gift tobacco. This matter has been taken up by this commissary with the Supply Depot at Gièvres, and in all probability these cigarets [sic] will be replaced."[1168]

It was also said that its prices at YMCA facilities were too high and that it was trying to profit from the war, which was incorrect. The YMCA canteen service did free many American soldiers, who would have otherwise been running the canteens themselves, to concern themselves with the war. While some of the male YMCA workers were not well prepared for canteen service, the women of the YMCA were highly praised. "Their work is beyond praise, and the *'Stars and Stripes'*...in a glowing editorial recently

---

[1165] Ibid, p. 610.
[1166] Women's Overseas Service, General Information, ca. 1918, p. 5.
[1167] Edward M. Coffman, *The War to end all Wars. The American Military Experience in WWI.* (Madison, Wisconsin: The University of Wisconsin Press, 1980) p. 78.
[1168] Harris, p. 555.

referred to them as 100% efficient."[1169] Private Raymond Curtis, Truck Co. D, 103d Ammunition Train wrote of the YMCA on April 21, 1918:

> "No one who is not a soldier in this camp can really know what the Army [YMCA] means to us boys in camp—it is home, club, church, and all. We would certainly be lost without it."[1170]

YMCA Canteen Workers Mary Sweeney, Bernetta Adams Miller (wounded while overseas) and YMCA volunteers Mary Arrowsmith and Getrude Ely all received the French Croix de Guerre.[1171] General Pershing himself had requested that the YMCA run the post exchanges in France.[1172]

One of the mainstays of the Women's Bureau was to hold dances for the soldiers and, of course, they had to supply dance partners. The idea of "flying squadrons,"—groups of women who traveled—with chaperons—

YMCA "Les Foyers du Soldat" Christmas card.

from hut to hut to dance with the men. However, it took intricate planning to assure the safety of the girls and these squadrons didn't last very long.[1173]

YMCA women were joined with French women in running canteens called *Les Foyers du Soldat, Union Franco-Américaines.* These were often set up in towns which had been destroyed. American women work-

---

[1169] Raymond B. Fosdick, Chairman of the Commission on Training Camp Activities, War Department, Report to the Secretary of War on the Activities of Welfare Organizations serving with the A.E.F. (Washington, DC: The War Department, 1919) p. 5.

[1170] *Service With Fighting Men,* p. 637.

[1171] WIMSA Calendar, 1996, see, "December."

[1172] *The War to end all Wars,* p. 78.

[1173] Harris, p. 63.

ing with the *Foyers du Soldat* had to be able to speak and understand French and have a knowledge of the French way of life. Only seventy-nine YMCA women qualified for this service. One American *Foyer* directrice, Marian Crandall, was killed while on duty at Ste. Menehould. She was buried with French military honors in France, her coffin draped with the French tricolor.[1174]

In August 1918, five YMCA women went to Italy. Their chief achievement was the opening of homes of Americans living in Italy to AEF soldiers. YMCA facilities were located at Bologna, Fiume, Trenso, Milan, Treviso and, until 1919, in Trieste, Rome, Florence, Genoa and Venice. The only American Army regiment to serve in Italy was the 332nd Infantry Regiment, so the YMCA served mainly ambulance drivers and US Navy sailors. Also, there were some 400 men in aviation units stationed at Foggia. American YMCA huts were also established in Great Britain; in London was the Eagle Hut, and in Edinburgh was St. Andrew's Hut.[1175] The YMCA also served in Russia.

In August 1917 the YMCA asked Mrs. Theodore Roosevelt, Jr. to come up with a design for a uniform to be worn by its women workers but its final design had not been decided by November 7, 1917. In a letter to the General Quartermaster, E.C. Carter assured him that, "information as to what we decide finally to prescribe in this regard will be forwarded to you

Detail of a collar insigne. (Courtesy. NSCDA Coll.-NMAH/Smithsonian)

WWI YMCA blouse with an overseas service chevron on the lower left sleeve. (Courtesy: NSCDA Coll.-NMAH/Smithsonian)

[1174] Harris, p. 350.
[1175] Ibid, pp. 64, 82 and 92.

Prohibited from serving with the U.S. Army as a physician, Marguerite Standish Crockett, MD, bought an automobile, shipped it to Italy where she drove it in an ambulance service. In 1917, the YMCA invited her to work in canteens in France. She wears the horizon blue hat, but with bow in front. Note the physician's caducei, worn on the collar of her uniform, in lieu of the "U.S." patches. (Courtesy: YMCA of the USA Archives, University of Minnesota Libraries)

in a few days."[1176] Mrs. Roosevelt "...chose a gray whipcord jacket and skirt. Period YMCA booklets describe the color of the uniform as "gray-green,"[1177] which at least two surviving examples confirm. However, a period manuscript, circa 1918, describes the color as gray.[1178] The jacket was single-breasted with a two-button closure. There were no bodice pockets, but the jacket had large side pockets, unpleated with flaps that buttoned. The cuffs of the sleeves had four buttons. The collar was "horizon-blue" with a pair of "U.S." initials in a red-edged inverted triangle insignia, embroidered in scarlet silk, sewn on each side of the collar. The Y.M.C.A. inverted triangle patch was sewn midway between the shoulder and elbow of the right sleeve of the jacket. Some period photographs show a second patch with wording sewn underneath the triangle patch. Some of them

---

[1176] *Service With Fighting Men*, p. 500.
[1177] YMCA booklets, "Women's Overseas Section, Preliminary Information," ca. 1918, p. 15, and "Women's Overseas Service, General Information," ca. 1918, p. 5.
[1178] Elsie C. Meade, *A Woman's War* (ca. 1918) p. 48.

Example of a WWI YMCA dress. It is made of the same material as the two-piece uniform and has the light blue collar.

Detail of the patches on the mid-right sleeve.

Below: Detail of the Camp Pontanezen patch on the upper left sleeve. A port of debarkation in France, Camp Pontanezen was so muddy that wooden footboards were put down. This is depicted in the design of the patch.

This YMCA woman wears a Polish style cap and insigne.

YMCA women were issued a cape of matching material with a distinctive "horizon-blue" collar.

"Instead of an overcoat we copied an Italian officer's cape which Prince d'Undine had given to Cobina Wright. ...Long and circular, it proved far better than an overcoat, as we could roll up in it when sleeping in camp or on unheated trains.[1183]

Y.M.C.A. canteen, or "hut," workers wore a gray double-breasted, belted, cotton overdress which was worn over regular clothing. It had a large powder blue or white roll collar. The coif with a "horizon-blue" band and white batiste drape had the Y.M.C.A. insigne sewn to its center. Canteen workers could also wear an apron over their clothing. The Y.M.C.A. brassard or patch was worn on the left arm, just above the elbow.

Period photos show that some YMCA workers wore a small silver bullion triangle midway between the shoulder and elbow of the blouse or tunic sleeve. The purpose of this insigne isn't know, but period photos and surviving men's tunics show this insigne worn on the lower left sleeve in pairs, perhaps as a indication of length-of-service. However, since other period photographs show female YMCA workers wearing downward-point-

Small cloisonné and brass YMCA insigne, worn by a few women on the bands of their hats.

Seven women who served with the U.S. Army First Division (L to R): Gertrude Ely, Mary N., Arrowsmith, Ethel Torrance (?), Francis Gulick, Lillian Jones, Elizabeth Dunlop, and Elizabeth Abbe. Note that Ely and Arrowsmith are wearing the French Croix de Guerre, a ribbon bar and Army infantry officer's collar insignia. All the women are wearing the patch of the First Division on their uniforms. Two of the women wear the small enamel YMCA pin on their hats. (Courtesy: YMCA of the USA Archives, University of Minnesota Libraries)

[1183] Dorothy & Carl J. Schneider, *Into the Breach*, p. 127.

ing chevrons to denote length-of-service, the purpose of this emblem is doubly confusing.

YMCA workers were not permitted to wear their uniform until time of embarkation for France. The official uniform was procured from Best & Company of New York, but only after the YMCA placed a written order with the company. After their time or service, volunteers could either keep their uniform and pay the YMCA $125.00 for it, or return it to the Women's Uniform Department.[1184]

The uniform consisted of the following items:
1 Grey-green whipcord coat and skirt suit, with extra suit;
2 Hat, summer and winter weight;
3 Heavy green cap or coat;
4 Four shirt waists [sic] with detachable collars;
5 One tie.[1185]

[1184] Women's Overseas Section, Preliminary Information, ca. 1918, p. 15.
[1185] Ibid, p. 15.

"Amazing Grace" Cleveland Porter served with the YMCA in Rome, supervising work in twenty Italian Army hospitals as the "directress of service of recreation." Note her three Italian medals and her YMCA sleeve patch, which seems to be a variation. (Courtesy: YMCA of the USA Archives, University of Minnesota Libraries)

Hazel Belle Nielson wears a non-regulation and, apparently "horizon-blue" garrison cap with piping and a bronze "U.S." officer's insigne. Note also the "Services of Supply" patch on her upper sleeve.

Gertrude Ely (R) wears the brimmed hat with the bow in back, while Mary Arrowsmith (L) wears the bow in front with the YMCA patch sewn to it. (Courtesy: YMCA of the USA Archives, University of Minnesota Libraries)

Patch worn on the left sleeve.

Service apron of YMCA canteen workers abroad.

This woman wears the belted cotton "over-dress" with a YMCA patch on the right sleeve. The coif band is horizon-blue with a white veil. A small YMCA emblem is sewn to the front. (Courtesy: National Archives)

Felt YMCA emblem for wear on the coif. some canteen workers wore these on the collars of their white duty uniforms.

441

YMCA brassard. (Courtesy: Duane Netzly)

The YMCA apron and brassard. (Courtesy: National Archives)

YMCA coif. (Courtesy: YMCA of the USA Archives, University of Minnesota Libraries)

YMCA chauffeur and friend at Aix-Les-Bains, France. Note the unusual hat she is wearing. The colors of it and her overcoat are not known. Of interest is the "U.S." cypher on the shoulder strap (no doubt worn in pairs) and the "Motor Dept. YMCA" patch on the coat sleeve. (Courtesy: YMCA of the USA Archives, University of Minnesota Libraries)

A YMCA woman wearing an unusual coat with a tab embroidered with the word, "Entertainment," sewn under the YMCA sleeve patch. Paris, 1919. (Courtesy: Richard L. Gilbert)

This YMCA woman wears the inverted triangle insigne on her left sleeve. Paris, WWI.

Additionally, workers carried with them to France a U.S. passport, instructions pertaining to obtaining a French visa and war zone pass, steamship ticket order, uniform order, baggage labels, identification certificate, French money for traveling expenses, and a YMCA "expense blank," for those workers whose expenses, all or part, were being paid by the YMCA.[1186]

---

444   [1186] Women's Overseas Section, Preliminary Information, ca. 1918, p. 16.

LIST OF WORLD WAR I YMCA CANTEENS

Areas	Towns	Date Opened	Date Closed	YMCA Women Personnel
1) Savoie:	Aix Les Bains;	Feb. 15, 1918	June 1, 1919	44
	Chambéry;	"	"	"
	Challes Les Eaux	"	"	"
2) Brittany:	St. Malo;	Aug. 25, 1918	June 15, 1919	24
	Dinard;	"	"	"
	Paramé;	"	"	"
	St. Servan.	Feb. 1, 1919	June 1, 1919	"
3) Auvergne:	La Bourboule,	Sept. 5, 1918	Jan. 15, 1919	28
	Mont Dore	"	"	"
4) Dauphiné:	Grenoble	Sept. 25, 1918	May 6, 1919	36
	Uriage Les Bains	"	"	"
	Allevard	"	"	"
5) Nancy:	Nancy	Sept. 1, 1918	Feb. 20, 1919	14
6) Ardéche:	Vals Les Bains	Nov. 1, 1918	April 25, 1919	10
7) Hérault:	Lamalou Les Bains	Nov. 15, 1918	April 27, 1919	13
8) Gard:	Nimes	Dec. 15, 1918	April 20, 1919	6
9) Riviera:	Nice	Dec. 1, 1918	May 27, 1919	49
	Cannes	"	May 1, 1919	24
	Menton	"	May 10, 1919	25
	Monte Carlo	Jan. 1, 1919	May 15, 1919	25
10) Pyrénées:	Luchon	Dec. 1, 1918	May 10, 1919	15
	Cauterets	"	May 20, 1919	16
	Eaux-Bonnes	Dec. 10, 1918	April 19, 1919	11
	Pau	March 15, 1919	June1, 1919	4
11) Alpine:	Chamonix	Jan. 1, 1919	May 5, 1919	22
	St. Gervais	"	"	"
	Le Fayet	Jan. 20, 1919	"	"
12) Annécy:	Annécy	Jan. 10, 1919	May 20, 1919	19
13) Rhine Valley Areas:	Koblenz	"	May 7, 1919	66
	Neuwied	"	"	"
	Tréves	Jan. 20, 1919	"	"
	Andernach	Jan. 25, 1919	"	"
	Neuenahr	Feb. 10, 1919	"	"
14) Biarritz:	Biarritz	Feb. 15, 1919	June 15, 1919	19
15) ValenÁay:	ValenÁay	Nov. 1, 1918	July 1, 1919	0
16) St. Nazaire:	Ste. Marguerite	Aug, 15, 1918	May 1, 1919	3
17) Brest:	Trez-Hir	Sept. 1, 1918	"	0
18) Lyons:	Lyons	Nov. 1, 1918	July 1, 1919	4
19) Paris:	Paris Division	"	Feb. 15, 1919	NA.[1187]

[1187] Frederick Harris, Managing Editor, *Service With the Fighting Men. An Account of the Work of the American Young Men's Christian Associations in the World War,* Vol. II (New York: Associated Press, 1922) plate xvi.

Young Women's Christian Association

(YWCA—World War I)

The Young Women's' Christian Association had the unique tasks of seeing to the needs of American women serving overseas, providing French women who worked in war production with rooms where they could rest and relax, and accomodations for women visiting posts in the United States, and by the end of World War I, a YWCA "Hostess House" could be found at most military installations in America. Helen A. Davis was the Secretary of this organization.and Katherine Scott was the YWCA War Work Field Secretary.[1188] (The YWCA was not affiliated with the YMCA.) Some 350 YWCA volunteers served in Europe during World War I, while others set up hostess houses near military forts in the United States. These houses provided lodging for women visiting friends or relatives in the services. In Paris, the "YW" ran the luxurious Hotel Petrograd, which had many amenities, including a restaurant, baths with hot water, steam heat and 250 rooms. It was open to women of all nationalities.

YW women found places of "escape" wherever possible. A Miss Russell commandeered quarters in a bombed-out French village where American women serving as telephone operators with the US Army Signal Corps could do their work for the advance on St. Mihiel.

The YWCA provided dormitories for exhausted French munitions workers and provided nurseries for their children. They established classes in sewing, typewriting, stenography, singing and taught English.

Along with the seemingly endless line of refugees and war workers, a new phenomenon arose: War brides. The YWCA became the organization which helped these foreign women set up housekeeping by finding them apartments, and helped them with the paperwork needed for them to go with their husbands to America. One barracks housed not only French war brides, but "...eight Russian girls, one Egyptian, one Algerian, and one Alsatian..."[1189]

During the war, the YWCA had established centers in Russia, Italy, Belgium, France, Czechoslovakia, Poland, Rumania.[1190]

The descriptions of their uniforms is quite sparse, citing only that "the 'domestic' uniform is a dark blue cloth and the one for work 'overseas'

[1188] Charlotte Palmer Seeley, ed., *American Women and the US Armed Forces* (Washington, DC: National Archives Trust Fund Board, 1992) p. 175, No. 165.32.

[1189] Dorothy and Carl J. Schneider, Into the Breach. *American Women Overseas in World War I* (New York: Viking Penguin, 1991) pp. 139-141.

[1190] Ibid, p. 148.

A rare photo of the YWCA uniform being worn. Mrs. Josephus Daniels stands third from the left.

YWCA grey on black cloth sleeve patch. This same insigne was worn on the tricorn hat. (Courtesy: NSCDA Coll.–NMAH/Smithsonian)

YWCA women's blouse. (Courtesy: NSCDA Coll.–NMAH/Smithsonian)

is similar, but lighter in color." The outdoor uniforms are described as, being worn "...both overseas and at home (which were designed by Mrs. Harold Irving Pratt of New York), the similar uniform worn in home service and camp work; also the attractive blue apron and cap of the Canteen Service, and finally, the business women's dress for office work overseas."[1191]

[1191] Report of the Committee on Relics, 1922, p. 11.

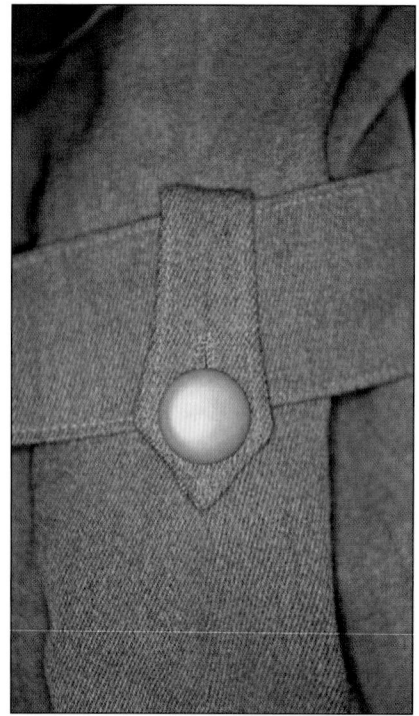
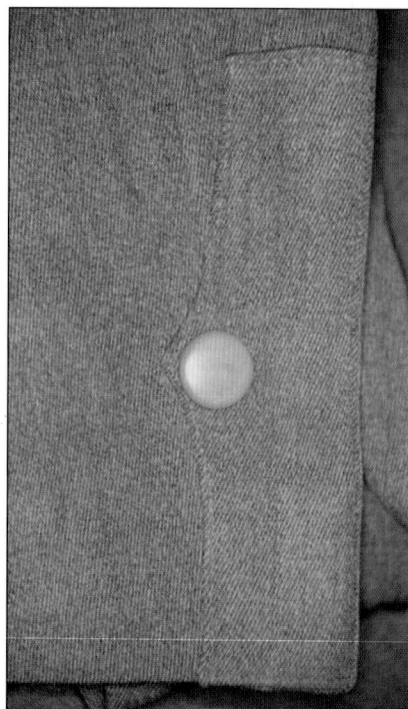

Detail of one of the belt loops. (Courtesy: NSCDA Coll.–NMAH/Smithsonian)

Detail of the sleeve cuff. (Courtesy: NSCDA Coll.–NMAH/Smithsonian)

Overseas workers wore a steel-gray serge[1192] (actually a light greyish-blue) blouse and skirt. The shirtwaist was white with a fly collar. A black bow tie was worn about the neck. The blouse buttons were grey-green in color. The blouse had two patch pockets at the lower sides with scalloped flaps. The self belt secured with two buttons, was held in place by two buttoned, pointed loops at each side of the blouse. It closed with three buttons. A scalloped cuff ornamentation was on each sleeve, with one of these buttons in the center. The triangular gray on black YWCA patch was sewn to the midsection of the right sleeve. It was a black semi-triangular patch with a grey thread triangle border, with the initials "Y.W.C.A." embroidered to the elongated center section.

YWCA women wore a black velvet tricorn hat with a light blue silk band, which terminated in the back of the hat in a flat bow. A triangular "Y.W.C.A." patch, similar to the previously described patch, was worn in the center of the hat.

The uniform illustrated was worn by Colonial Dame Mrs. William Adams Brown on the occasion of being officially presented to General Pershing at his headquarters in Chaumont. On this occasion, Pershing paid public tribute to American women who served in the war.[1193]

[1192] Report of the Committee on Relics, p. 11.
[1193] Ibid.

Silver bullion District of Paris patch on black backing, sewn onto the upper left sleeve. (Courtesy: NSCDA Coll.–NMAH/Smithsonian)

The black tricorn hat worn by members of the YWCA. The band is light blue. (Courtesy: NSCDS Coll.–NMAH/Smithsonian)

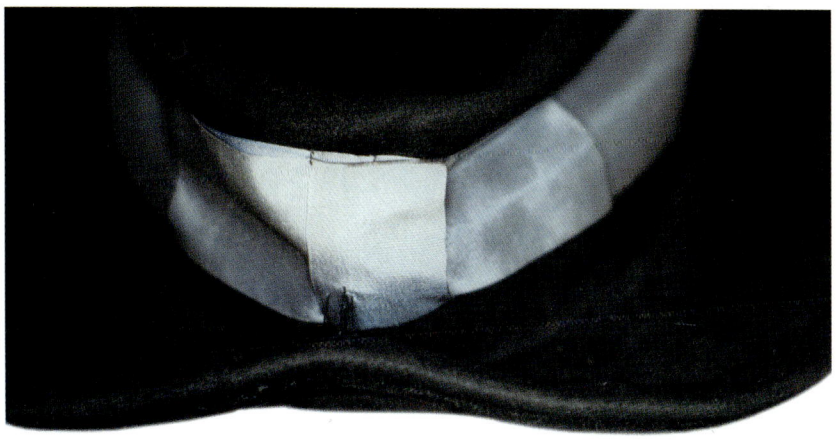

Bow on the back of the hat. (Courtesy: NSCDA Coll.–NMAH/Smithsonian)

Other Organizations

Air Force Aid Society contributor's card.

The Queen Mother greets girl drivers of the American Ambulance Service, Great Britain in late 1945. Note the circular unit patch which appears to be a crossed American and British flag, and the three 5-pointed stars on the shoulder strap.

450

"Children's Escort Corps, American Committee" brassard worn in England by American volunteers during WWII.

American Committee Relief in Near East pin back.

A member of the American Friends Service Committee in France, WWI. Note the sleeve patch. The design of the patch on the beret is unknown. (Refer to American Friends Service Committee chapter in Vol. 1, p 31.) (Courtesy: AFSC Archives)

This woman wears a variation of the American Friends Service Committee patch, France, WWI. (Courtesy: AFSC Archives)

This volunteer in Germany during WWII wears a garrison cap with the "Quaker Relief" arc and a smaller version of the AFSC patch. (Courtesy: AFSC Archives)

Terry Foss

452

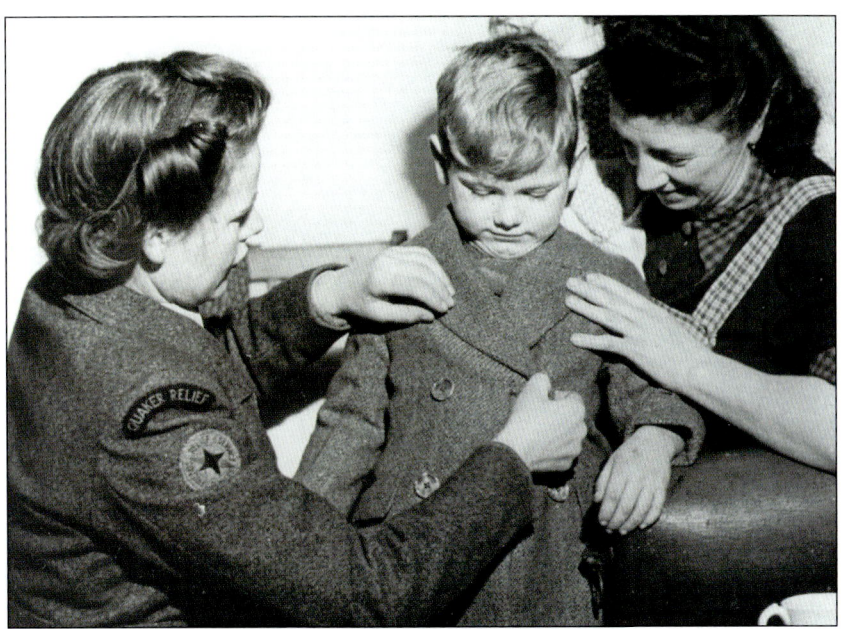

An AFSC volunteer fits a coat to a German boy, WWII. Note the "Quaker Relief" arc on the upper sleeve and the different design of the AFSC patch. It appears from photos that these patches may have been worn on both sleeves of the uniform. (Courtesy: AFSC Archives)

American Friends Service Committee volunteers in Hungary, WWII. (Courtesy: AFSC Archives) At left: An example of a hand-made AFSC patch. (Courtesy: Terry Foss)

Summer uniform of the American Library Association, Library War Service. (See Vol. 1, p. 35 for organization details.)

American Maritime Cadet's patch. (Courtesy: Phil & Linda Darling)

454

A bullion American Overseas Theater League patch. (Courtesy: The Johnson Bros.)

WWI American Women's Hospital driver's hat/cap badge. (Refer to AWH chapter in Vol. 1, p. 124.) (Credit: Thomas Schultz)

Winged wheel patch worn for a time by American Women's Voluntary Service (AWVS) Motor Corps drivers. The patch was positioned above the left breast pocket. (Refer to AWVS chapter in Vol. 1, p. 135.)

This WWI Army nurse wears an unidentified patch on her left upper sleeve, and her collar insignia is incorrectly positioned.

A WWI Army nurse wearing a 1st Army patch with a lighter, presumably white, backing with an embroidered caduceus.

Aviation Cadet Recruiting Aid garrison cap and related insignia. (See Vol. 1, p. 274, also "Air Cadet Recruiting Aides," p. 23, and "Army Air Force Aides," p. 158.) (Courtesy: John Cook)

"Bomberettes" pin back.

Minute Man patch. Yellow thread embroidery on slate blue material, Bronx War Service.

This women wears a uniform that varies from those worn by the other Bronx War Service women illustrated on the next page. Note her four pocket blouse, leather belt, and piped garrison cap. The Minute Man patch is clearly visible on the left forward curtain of the cap. A larger version of the patch is visible on her upper left sleeve. The patch appears to have an arc just below it. She also wears the Bronx War Service patch. This type of uniform suggests that this woman might have been a member of some sort of motor corps.

Bronx War Service hat.

These women wear the slate blue and yellow Minute Man patch on their hats and left sleeves. The woman on the right wears an additional patch on her left sleeve that reads, "Bronx War Service." Their uniforms were slate blue with yellow shoulder strap piping. A yellow knotted cord was worn on the hat.

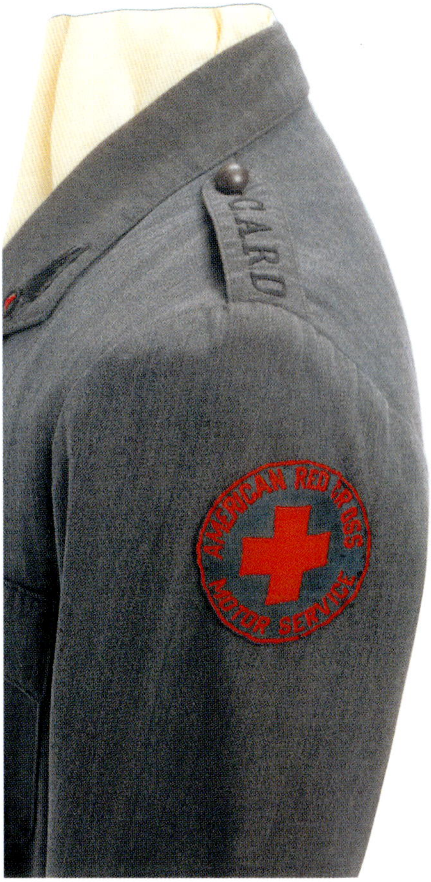

Unidentified World War I period woman's blue uniform. It has the French-style dark blue embroidered flaming bomb insignia with red embroidered "A's" in the center on each collar, a Red Cross Motor Service patch on the left sleeve, and "C.A.R.D." embroidered on the shoulder straps. (Photos by Ronda Sheel)

Detail of the embroidery on the left shoulder strap.

Detail of a collar insignia

Skirt with front pockets. (Photos by Ronda Sheel)

The Cavalry Corps of the American Woman's League for Self Defense holds a public drill on Broadway, New York City, WWI.

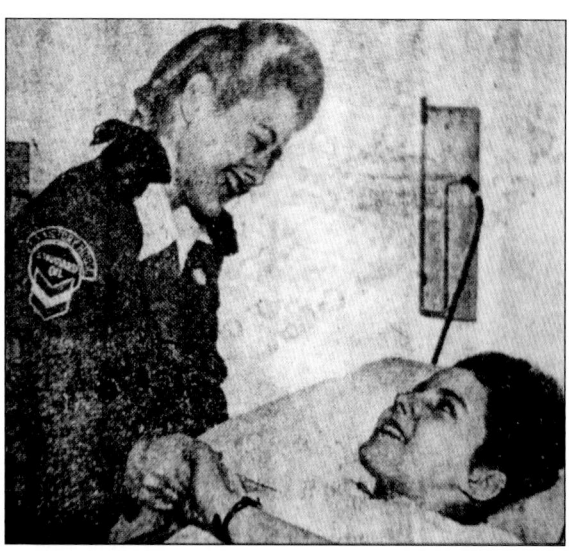

"Chevronette" Mary Bovard in her uniform. The tab above her "Standard Oil" patch reads "U.S. Victory House." (Courtesy: George Petersen)

Dorothy Lamour (center) and stamp girls Mary Gleason and Jean Kindley lick defense stamps to put in a savings book., These Chevronettes were based at the Defense House in Los Angeles which was sponsored by Standard Oil. This one segment of industry was instrumental in promoting sales of defense stamps, which were in denominations from 10¢ to $5 and available over store counters, at street corners, and at schools.

"ESSO" girls served in the same way "Chevronettes" did...to help sell Defense Savings Stamps.

Unknown women's tab. (Courtesy: The Johnson Bros.)

Junior Army-Navy Guild Organization (JANGO)

Created in 1943, this organization consisted of the daughters of military officers. They were in fact junior nurses aides, who assisted with basic patient care. The first thirty-five Jangos were capped at a ceremony on April 2 at the Washington, D.C. Medical Science Building. The JANGO co-chairman was Helen Almay. Though this organization started in Washington, it soon spread throughout the nation.

The girls were to be between the ages of fourteen and eighteen. By 1974, the daughters and sons of military personnel were admitted to the program. The age limit was changed to between fourteen and twenty-one. (Information, *"Life Magazine,"* April 26, 1943, pp. 37-38, and newspaper articles, provided by Shirley Kramer.)

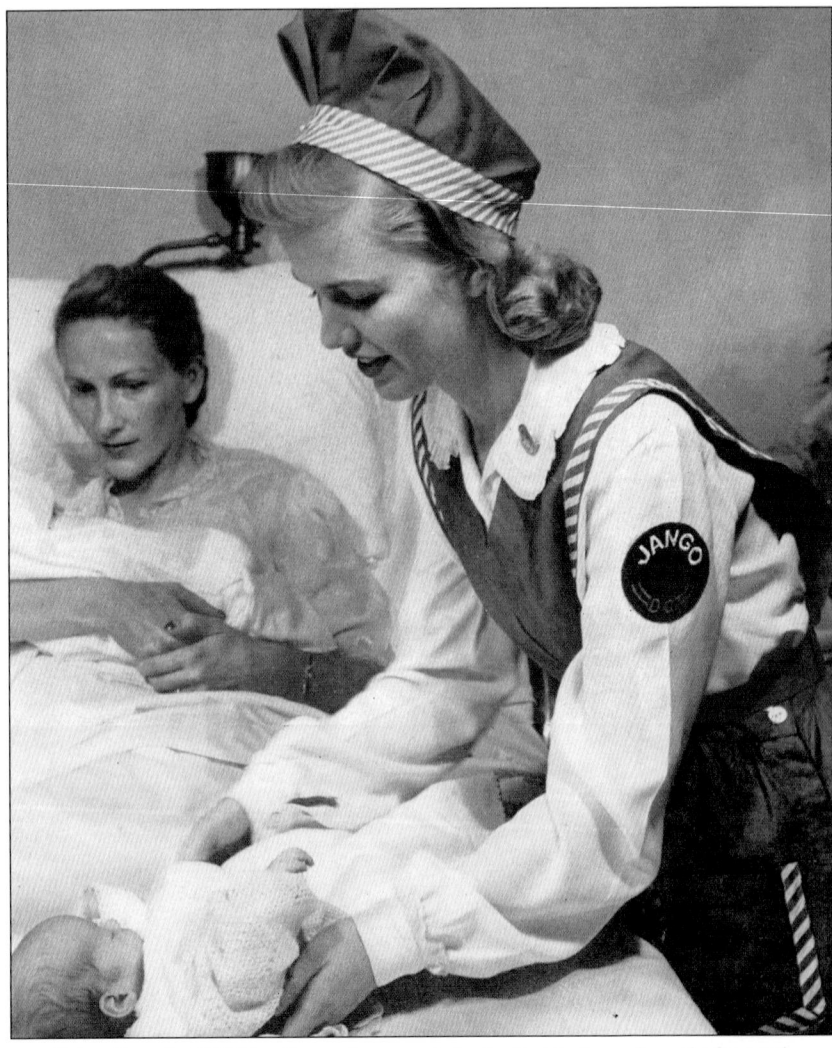

Helen Almy, in JANGO uniform, dresses a baby for its trip home from the hospital.

Miscellaneous JANGO insignia. (Courtesy: Shirley (Robl) Kramer)

Shirley (Robl) Kramer

JANGO Nurses Aide Pledge

Before God and this assembly I pledge a conscientious and a loyal service to the hospital which I serve. I will hold in confidence all personal and official matters which may come to my attention. I promise to be worthy of the JANGO tradition, to do my utmost in giving unselfish service and to conform to the regulations of JANGO with cheerful obedience and to respect my uniform. I further pledge to give every assistance and set an example for those to follow in my footsteps.

Shirley Robl

"Kansas City Canteen" dress and detail of the embroidery on the bodice pocket. (Courtesy: John Coy; photo by Ronda Sheel)

Brown leather shoulder bag worn by WWII era female Marines. For details on the organization, see Vol. 1, pp. 332-367. (Courtesy: John Mull)

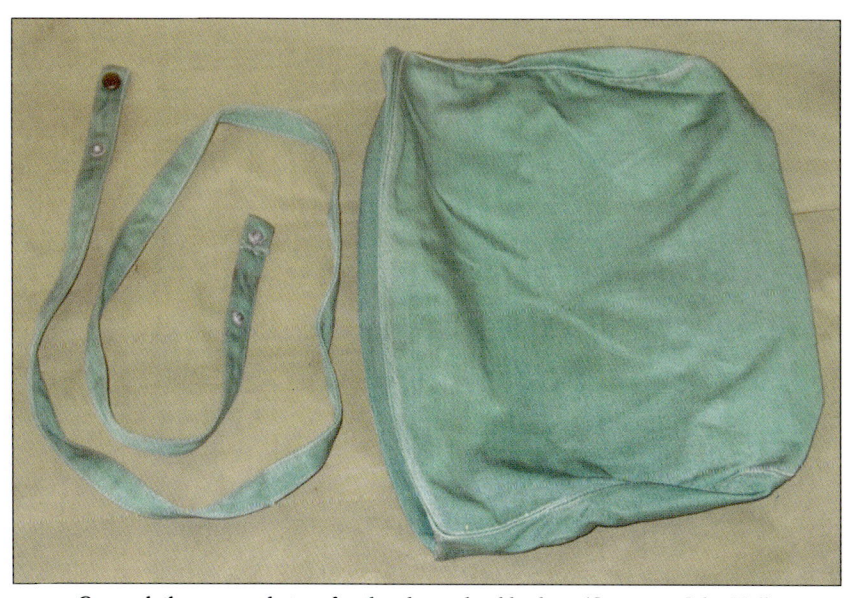

Green cloth cover and strap for the above shoulder bag. (Courtesy: John Mull)

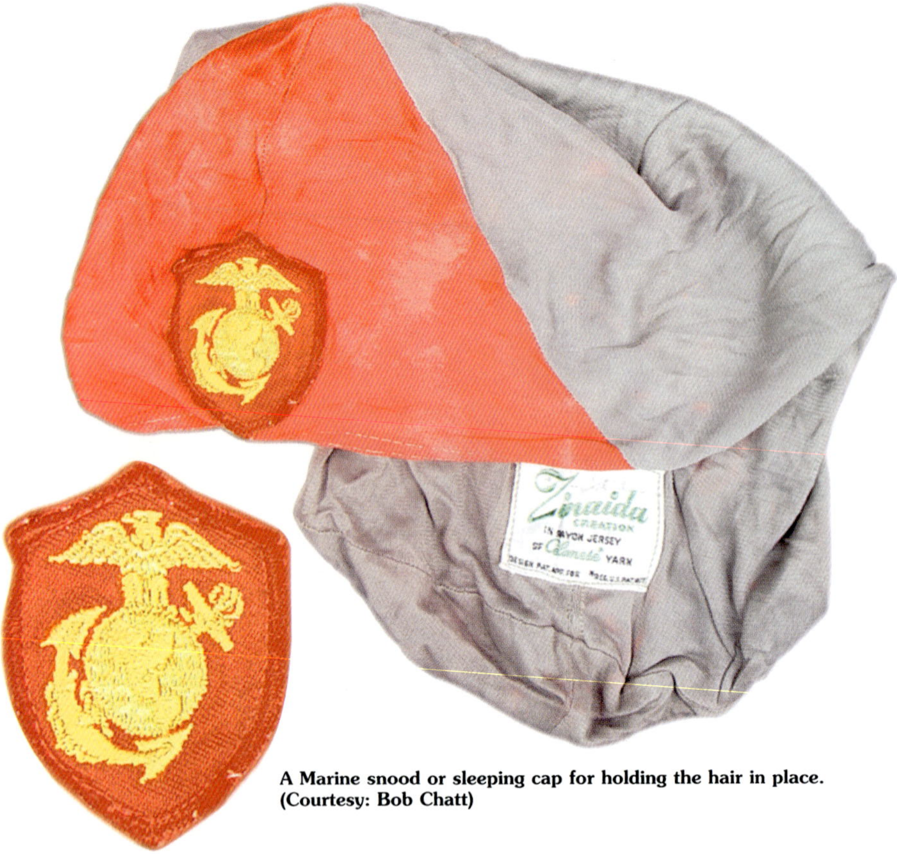

A Marine snood or sleeping cap for holding the hair in place. (Courtesy: Bob Chatt)

WWII era Marine compact. (Courtesy: John Mull)

This lady in the Massachusettes Women's Defense Corps wears that organization's brown unform. (Courtesy: Tom Schultz)

Massachusetts Women's Defense Corps collar flashes. (Courtesy: The Johnson Bros.)

Excellent photograph showing an officer of the Massachusetts Women's Defense Corps (MWDC). (Courtesy: Phil & Linda Darling)

MWDC decal.
(Courtesy: Phil & Linda Darling)

Massachusetts Women's Defense Corps officer's tunic. Right: A closer view of the collar insigne, shoulder strap stripes and medical patch. (Courtesy: Phil & Linda Darling; photo by Ronda Sheel)

Metal rank bars.

MWDC officer's blouse with metal rank insignia on the shoulder straps instead of the cloth stripes. (Courtesy: The Johnson Bros.)

MWDC enlisted woman's uniform. Note the lapel pin and sleeve patch. (Courtesy: Phil & Linda Darling)

Massachusetts Women's Defense Corps visored hat. (Courtesy: George Petersen)

Detail of the gold hat insigne and the maroon silk hat cords. (Courtesy: George Petersen)

MWDC service bars sewn horizontally on the lower left sleeve on an "enlisted" woman's blouse.

Massachusetts Women's Defense Corps (MWDC) enlisted woman. (Courtesy: Phil & Linda Darling)

Eugenia Jean Sahagian's identification card and "W" (warden) patch. (Courtesy: The Johnson Bros.)

MWDC canteen service patch.

MWDC flocked motor corps patch.

MWDC "enlisted" woman's yellow on black rank chevron. (Courtesy: The Johnson Bros.)

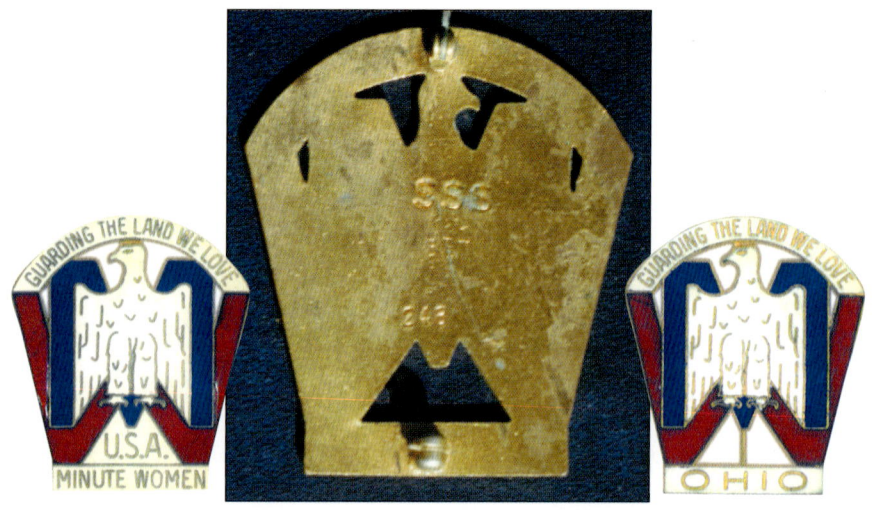

(Left) Typical "Minute Women" pin. (Right) Variant "Minute Women" pin with the "U.S.A." missing and the designation "Minute Women" replaced by "Ohio." (Courtesy: Phil & Linda Darling)

The Minute Women of Los Angeles served without pay, and were between the ages of 18 and 45. They were trained in advanced Red Cross and emergency work, and drilled as a soldier for benefit of discipline and co-ordination. The insignia of this Minute Women organization was a centaurette with first aid equipment superimposed on a bolt of lighting to indicate speed.

Another Disney-designed insigne for the vehicle repair section of the Minute Women of Los Angeles.

Paul Oostmeyer

A WWI poster depicting "The Motor-Corps of America" by the famed artist Howard Chandler Christy. (For details on the organization refer to Vol. 1, page 372.)

George A. Petersen

A uniformed member of the Navy League Service/Transportation Corps.

Members of the Mollie Pitcher Brigade. (Courtesy: Library of Congress)

National Association of Air Force Women wings.

Pre-WWI Navy Nurse Corps device.
(Courtesy: Dr. D.B. Patterson)

Navy Relief Society pin back, #1092.

Gold and black "National League for Woman's Service" variant hat band. For details on the organization refer to Vol. 1, page 381.

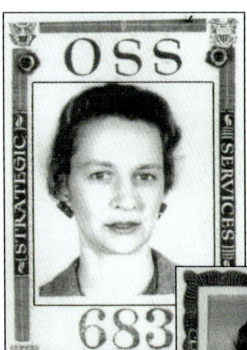

Left: Office of Strategic Services (OSS) headquarters identity badge, and below: an identity card. During World War II hundreds of OSS women served at posts worldwide. Most were not uniformed and worked in support of overseas operations as office workers, cartographers, cryptographers, etc. Those who were transferred from a uniformed service retained the uniform of their service. (Courtesy: Otto Spronk photo coll.)

1st Lt. Rolande Amundsen. She was a trained operative during World War II and was infiltrated into German occupied Europe to participate in the resistance movement in France. On her third parachute insertion, just before the invasion of Normandy in 1944, she was captured near the drop zone by Evron. She was interrogated at Gestapo headquarters in Paris and then transferred to Mauthausen Concentration Camp where she was to be executed. She was fortunately liberated by Allied forces before the sentence could be carried out.

Pennsylvania Reserve Defense Corps Auxiliary Brassard. (Courtesy: The Johnson Bros.)

Photo of the uniform worn by Physical Therapists during WWII. Fort George G. Meade, 29th General Hospital. (See Army Nurse Corps chapter in Vol. 1.) (Courtesy: Janet Sims)

WWII postal locator's badge. Worn by women who made sure that GIs received their mail overseas.

Seventh-Day Adventist Medical Cadet Corps patch and Women's Medical Corps garrison cap. (Courtesy: Phil & Linda Darling)

Part of a WWI poster for the "Stage Women's War Relief," showing an actress wearing a volunteer's uniform under her costume.

Staten Island Defense Motor Corps patch, WWII. (Courtesy: The Johnson Bros.)

Collar Insigne.

Rank chevron worn on the right sleeve only of the Staten Island Defense Motor Corps uniform. (Courtesy: The Johnson Bros.)

Texas Wing of Women Flyers patch.
(Courtesy: Mike Stacey)

Texas Wing of Women Flyers patch in wear. (Courtesy: Mike Stacey)

U.S. Navy Transportation Pool patch, worn by men and women employees at the 12th Naval District. (Courtesy: Ed Anderson, Jr.)

Supervisor.

Woman driver.

Photo identification tag for a female employee at the U.S. Navy shipyard at Philadelphia, PA. (Courtesy: Otto Spronk photo coll.)

Uniform worn by Uncle Sam's Girl Munitions Workers, WWI.

World War I period photo showing actress Bessie Love wearing a shield-shaped patch with an eagle and the words, "U.S. War Bonds Service."

Civilian woman employed by the U.S. Army Quartermaster Corps, WWI. (Courtesy: Joe Stone)

Victory Volunteers patch.

Uniform worn by women driving passenger vehicles for the Depot Quartermaster's Department.

A WAAM (Women's Auxiliary Aircraft Mechanic) in uniform.

Unidentified "W.A.M.S." half wing. (Courtesy: Jim Hester)

Women's Army National Defense (WAND) patch. (Courtesy: John Coy)

A driver of one of the War Camp Community Service lunch trucks. (See p. 95 of this volume for organization details.)

Unidentified "WARD" wing.

Unidentified khaki uniform. The blouse has black painted U.S. Army buttons, patch with spoked wheel and cross machine-embroidered in brown thread, "W.A.T.C.C." collar insignia and three rank diamonds on each shoulder strap. The garrison cap has gold and black flecked piping and a smaller version of the sleeve patch sewn to the left forward curtain.

W.A.T.C.C. patch and "enlisted" woman's chevrons. (Courtesy: Phil & Linda Darling)

Detail of the right collar insigne. Dull gold metal bar, pin-back, embossed with the letters, "W.A.T.C.C." The three diamond rank insignia on the shoulder straps are made of one piece of metal and are pin-back.

Woman's Committee Council of
National Defense pin back.
(Courtesy: Sylvia Leasure)

Patch and crest worn by women of the California-based "We Owe America," WWII. Crest has
"150 Hours Service" legend. (Courtesy: The Johnson Bros.)

Women's Defense Cadet Corps of America (Queens division). These women could drive trucks and shoot.

Women's Legion of Defense.

Women's Motor Corps sleeve patch. Note maroon medical color.
(Courtesy: Jim Hammack)

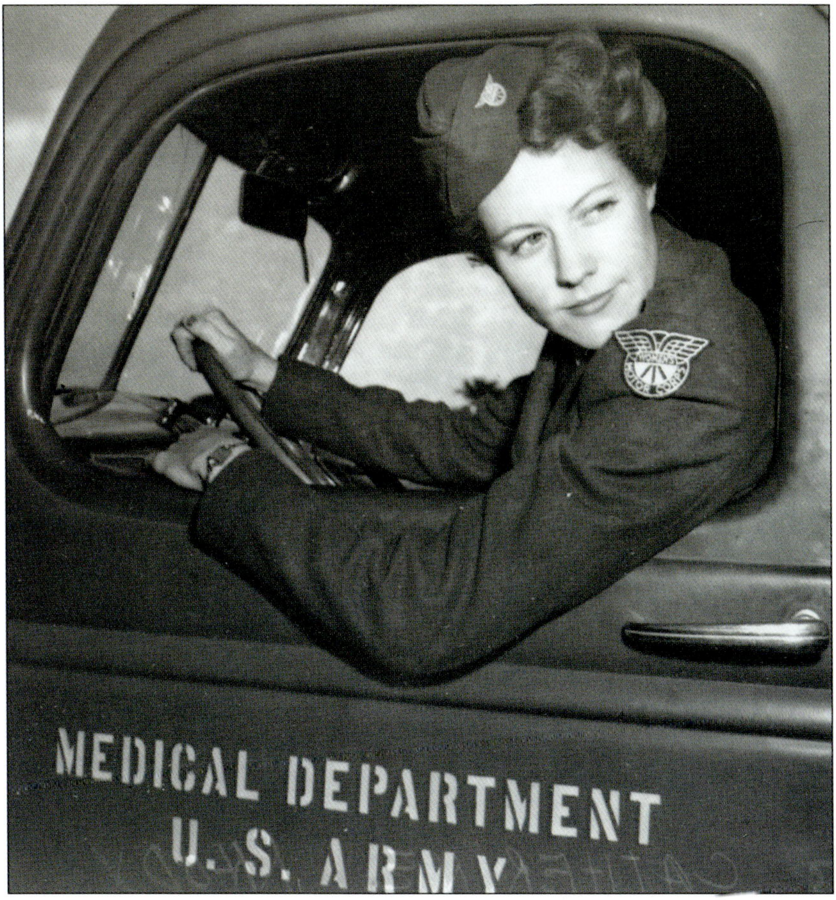

View of the Women's Motor Corps patch and garrison cap insigne. Virtually nothing is known about this organization, but it is thought that it was based in San Antonio, Texas. Note the similarities in the designs of the patch and cap insigne to that worn on the garrison cap of the National League for Woman's Service Motor Corps. (Refer to National League for Woman's Service chapter in Vol. 1, p. 381.) (Courtesy: Institute of Texan Cultures, San Antonio Light Coll.)

Small World War II Women's Motor Corps cap insigne for wear on the garrison cap or lapel.

(L to R) Mrs. Gene Reddick, Eva Wells, and Mrs. Esther Weeber wearing the Women's Motor Corps uniform. Note that two of the women are wearing piped garrison caps. Esther Weeber wears the ARC Emergency First Aid patch below the Women's Motor Corps patch, October, 1943. (Courtesy: Institute of Texan Cultures, San Antonio Light Coll.)

Mrs. Bessie Grayson wears the khaki version of the Women's Motor Corps uniform. San Antonio, Texas, 1941. (Courtesy: Institute of Texan Cultures, San Antonio Light Coll.)

The uniform worn by the women of the Radio Corps.

Unidentified WWI-period woman. (Courtesy: Barry Hooper)

Honorary Colonel Ruth Richy. Period and organization unknown (possible R.O.T.C. program). (Courtesy: Joe Stone)

492　　These unidentified women wear Civil War style kepis. (Courtesy: Joe Stone)

Blue garrison cap to the uniform. Note the silver "rank" insigne, red piping, and the red swastika patch on the curtain of the cap. (Courtesy: Sylvia Leasure, photo by Mark Riese)

Unidentified uniform. (Courtesy: Sylvia Leasure, photo by Mark Riese)

Note: It is believed the ornate uniform is for a high school cadet program in Oklahoma, circa World War I period. Different schools may have used different colored swastikas and piping.

Jane Driscoll served as policewoman in Washington, DC, during the war. She is shown here preparing for target practice, though DC policewomen did not carry guns. (Courtesy: Olio's)

It seems that just about everyone was in uniform during World War II. Sara Garcia, Plaza Hotel telegraph clerk in San Antonio, Texas is shown wearing her new uniform. (Courtesy: Institute of Texan Cultures, San Antonio Light Coll.)

Appendix 1: Honor Roll

(Note: This list is incomplete)

CIVIL WAR

Medal of Honor
Walker, Dr. Mary Edwards, Union Army.

Kearney Cross
Etheridge, Anna, awarded the Kearney Cross by Brigadier General David Birney (for more information, see p. 7, Volume 1).

WORLD WAR I[1]

AMERICAN AMBULANCE

Chevalier of the Legion of Honor
Gassette, Miss Grace, Superintendent of the hospital surgical dressing room at Neuilly, invented new orthopedic appliances when she saw that some of the old ones were not sufficient to bind certain types of fractures. Her inventions were so successful that the Government of France made her a Chevalier of the Legion of Honor.

AMERICAN RED CROSS

Florence Nightingale Medal
Hay, Helen Scott, contract nurse and general supervisor of the 1914 Red Cross Mercy Ship and senior supervisor of nursing units in Kiev, Russia;
Meirs, Linda E.;
Patterson, Florence M., member of the Red Cross Commission to Romania;
Stimson, Julia C., director of nursing in the AEF.

Distinguished Service Medal
Andress, Mary Vail, nurse, for her work at Toul, France
Cleveland, Maude, for her work at Brest, France
Delano, Jane A., director, Department of Nursing
Stimson, Julia C., chief nurse AEF, American Red Cross in France

US Certificate for Exceptionally Meritorious and Conspicuous Services
Austin, Mrs. C.K.
Cleveland, Maude

---

[1] Unless otherwise noted, all information about women who were decorated during World War I is reprinted with permission from the book, *American Women in World War I. They Also Served*, by Lettie Gavin. Niwot, Colorado: The University Press of Colorado, 1997, pp. 246-280, and from Colonel Stephen Durant.

Hunt, Georgia P.
Spaulding, Gertrude
Vanderbilt, Mrs. W.K. (Anne), chief, Red Cross Canteen Department, Paris
Walker, Hazel

Belgium:
Médaille de la Reine Élisabeth
Seamans, Mary F., chief, Red Cross GHQ

France:
Croix de Guerre
Andress, Mary, nurse
Daly, Mrs., canteen worker
Farwell, Mildred

Belgium:
Medal of Elisabeth
Anderson, Mrs. Isabel, awarded the medal by Her Majesty, Queen of the Belgians

Britain:
Military Medal
Parmlee, Eva Jean, Reserve Nurse, Base Hospital No. 5.

ARMY NURSE CORPS
Distinguished Service Cross
Jeffery, Jane, English Red Cross nurse serving with American Red Cross Hospital No 107. She was severely wounded during an air raid but refused to leave her post and continued to care for patients.

MacDonald, Beatrice M. (New York City, NY). Base Hospital No. 2. Wounded during an air raid while serving at a casualty clearing station in Belgium on August 17, 1917. She lost sight in her right eye.

McClelland, Helen Grace (Fredericktown, Ohio) Base Hospital No. 10, organized at Philadelphia, Pennsylvania. McClelland was serving with a surgical team at a British casualty clearing station and attended nurse Beatrice M. McDonald (see above) when she was wounded.

Parmelee, Eva Jean. Wounded while on duty during an air raid at Base Hospital No. 5 on September 4, 1917, but continued to serve during the attack.

Sloan, Emma S., Reconstruction Aide.[2]

Stambaugh, Isabelle (Philadelphia, Pennsylvania). Base Hospital No. 10. Stambaugh was seriously wounded on March 21, 1918 dur-

---

[2] Women Medal Recipents, http://userpages.aug.som/captbarb/medals.html.

ing an air raid while working in an operating room with a British surgical team at a British casualty clearing station at Amiens.

Distinguished Service Medal

Aubert, Lillian, assistant superintendent of the Army Nurse Corps.
Brennan, Cecelia, chief nurse, Toul Hospital Center
Brown Katherine, chief nurse.
Burns, Sophy Mary, Chief nurse of Base Hospital No. 16.
Cameron, Reba G., chief nurse at Plattsburg Barracks and Hampton, Virginia.
Coughlin, Edna M., Base Hospital No. 22,. Coughlin was a member of an emergency medical team caring for nontransportable wounded of six divisions in an advanced area under fire of shells and aerial bombs.
Delano, Jane A., Director of Nursing, ARC.
Flash, Alice, H., chief nurse at the Nesves-Blucy Hospital Center.
Goodrich, Annie W., first dean of the Army School of Nursing.
Howard, Carrie L., chief nurse of the Hoboken, New Jersey port of embarkation.
Leonard, Grace E., assistant director of the Allied Expeditionary Forces nursing service.
MacDonald, Beatrice Mary, chief nurse of the Presbyterian Hospital Unit,
McClelland, Helen Grace, Base Hospital No. 10,
Milliken, Sayers Louise, chief nurse, Camp Sevier, South Carolina, and assistant superintendent of the Army Nurse Corps;
Molloy, Jane G., chief nurse, Camp Devens, Massachusetts;
Mury, Edith A., assistant superintendent, Army Nurse Corps;
Poston, Adele S., chief nurse of the psychiatric unit of Base Hospital No. 117;
Rhodes, Marie B, chief of the Nurses' Equipment Bureau, Military Department, American Red Cross, Paris, France;
Rulon, Blance S., chief nurse of Base Hospital No. 27 and assistant to the director of nursing Services, American Expeditionary Forces (AEF);
Ryan, Lillian J., chief nurse of the base hospital at Camp Merritt, New Jersey;
Sheehan, Mary E., chief nurse of the Vichy Hospital Center, France;
Shelton, Neena, assistant to the director of nursing service of the AEF;
Sinnott, Catherine Glynn, chief nurse of the nurses' concentration camp at Savenay, France;
Stimson, Julia C, director of nursing service in the AEF;
Sweet, Ethel E., chief nurse, nurses' mobilization stations in New York, New York;
Thompson, Dora E., superintendent of the Army Nurse Corps;
Vandervort, Lynnette L., chief nurse of Mars Hospital Center, France and chief nurse of the nurses' embarkation center, Vannes, France.

Allied Expeditionary Forces Citation (Silver Star Citation)
Bridge, Ruth H., Field Hospital No. 103
Bunting, I. Gertrude, Camp Hospital No. 4
Frankhauser, Louise, Evacuation Hospital No. 6
Invernizio, Clementina, Evacuation Hospital No. 6
Leckrone, Linnie E., Château-Thierry
Low, Margaret, Field Hospital No. 103

US Army Citation
(Awarded for bravery and devotion to duty during a September 1918 air raid on the city where Field Hospital No. 103 was located)
Harlan, Elizabeth H.
Haviland, Sybella T.
McNamara, Della A.
Randall, Ethel
Roulston, Elizabeth Elliot
Zang, Mary Clara L.

General John J. Pershing Citation
Alexander, Catherine, Base Hospital No. 55
Allison, Agnes Winifred, Evacuation Hospital No. 4
Andersen, Emmeline, Evacuation Hospital No. 4
Bear, Laura Folsom, Evacuation Hospital No. 4
Bell, Bessie S.
Booth, May M., Evacuation Hospital No. 4
Bunting, I. Gertrude, Camp Hospital No. 4
Christman, Caroline H.
Clark, Margaret
Coyne, Adelaide, Irene
Deane, Pluma M., Evacuation Hospital No. 4
Fitzpatrick, Margaret M.
Grant, Jessie E., Base Hospital No. 55
Hall, Rosa H., Evacuation Hospital No. 4
Hatch, Inez Pearl
Hollindale, Edith Amy, Evacuation Hospital No. 6
Hosken, Beatrice
Hutton, Katherine A., Evacuation Hospital No. 4
Jones, Blanche
Jorgensen, Sigrid M., Evacuation Hospital No. 4
Kelly, Bree S., chief nurse of Base Hospital No. 65
Kingston, Edna E., Evacuation Hospital No. 4
Lawrence, Henrietta Gordon, Base Hospital No. 55
Leach, Goldie Alberta, Evacuation Hospital No. 4
Lee, Elizabeth C., Evacuation Hospital No. 4
Malloch, Grace L., Base Hospital No. 55
Marshall, Susan, Evacuation Hospital No. 4
McLean, Emily L., Evacuation Hospital No. 4
McQuillan, Rose C., Evacuation Hospital No. 4

Meyer, Minna Theckla, Evacuation Hospital No. 4
Moylan, Mary B., Evacuation Hospital No. 4
Newsom, Mary Palmer, Base Hospital No. 55
Pancoast, Mary E., Evacuation Hospital No. 4
Perkins, Margaret E., Evacuation Hosptial No. 4
Perrine, Mae, Evacuation Hospital No. 4
Rathbun, Katherine, Evacuation Hospital No. 4
Robinson, H. Victoria, Evacuation Hospital No. 4
Rottman, Marian E., Evacuation Hospital No. 1
Rutherford, Delia, Evacuation Hospital No. 4
Sands, Tyldesley L., Base Hospital No. 5
Shaw, Maybelle M., Evacuation Hospital No. 4
Thomasson, Ivy L., St. Mihiel Offensive
Tierney, Mary Jane, Evacuation Hospital No. 4
Tuthill, Carrie E., Evacuation Hospital No. 4
Ulmer, Florence H., Evacuation Hospital No. 4
Wells, Grace E. Evacuation Hospital No. 4
White, Cassie A., Evacuation Hospital No. 4

General Charles H. Muir Citation

Arnott, Ruth
Beardsley, Ethel Jean
Beckman, Ruth J.
Bowling, Gertrude H.
Brouilliard, Jennie
Conn, Jennie Elizabeth
Conyard, Mary E.
Fiester, Blanche I.
Heuter, Lucy M.
Jones, Annie E.
Kegrice, Mary O.
Macauley, Margaret M.
MacMillan, Grace E.
Sandelius, Elixabeth Dorothy
Swain, Mary L.

Foreign Awards

France:
Croix de Guerre
No information available.

Gilt Star to the Croix de Guerre
Jorgensen, Sigrid M., Evacuation Hospital No. 4;
Nye, Sylvene A.;
Radcliffe, Lillian E.;
Turner, Lila B., Evacuation Hospital No. 4;

Bronze Star to the Croix de Guerre
Connelly, Beth Clara;
Cornwall, Bertha;
Ferguson, Ida;
Gibson, Matilda M.;
Horn, Mathilda H.;
Hovey, Ruth;
Johnson, Lillian;
Lister, Hannah;
MacDonald, Beatrice Mary;
McManigill, Ella J.;
McNulty, Carolyn H.;
Meirs, Linda K.;
Perry, Jennie E.;
Richardson, Agnes Hope;

Rignel, Blanche S.;
Sahol, Elina P.;
Sharpe, Annie M.;
Smith, Alice O.;
Taylor, Phoebe F.;
Thompson, Sara R.;
Todd, Louise M.;
Vaugniaux, Emily.

Recommended for the Croix de Guerre
Durr, Mildred E.;
Engvall, Sarah C.;
Griffen, Cora;
McClure, Jean;
Purdy, Louise;
Wentland, May.

Médaille d'Honneur
Baker, Aurel;
Beers, Amy;
Broaddus, Emma;
Carother, Dora C.;
Cormier, Bernadette;
Diamond, Mary A.;
Drive, A. Madeg;
Francis, Mary L.;
Gardner, Agnes, J.;
Jeffrey, Lucy W.;
Kehoe, Frances M.;
Krans, Ella Mary;
Lombard, Arabella A.

Médaille d'Honneur des Épidémies
Aaron, Marjorie;
Arnold, Elizabeth;
Baker, Bessie;
Bedell, Ruth E.;
Borg, Ida A.;
Bowen, Mary M.;
Brendel, Myrtle L.;
Camblos, Jacqueline;
Cassidy, Rose, A.;
Clarke, Susanne;
Cloherty, Marie E.;
Corning, Alice;
DeLozier, Mary M.;
Dingley, Nellie M.;
Fisher, Madgalen C.;
Gavin, Mary;
Gough, Gussie;
Graves, Abigail B.;
Hadsell, Edith L.;
Hagadorn, Alice;
Hanchette, Lou;
Hartwell, Jennie V.;
Henry, Ethel;
Hill, Ada;
Hopkins, Anna B.;
Horner, Blanche;
Izen, Clara J.;
James, Agnes F.;
Johnson, Jane Hl.;
Knapp, Grace;
Laurisen, Karen M.;
Loughran, Nellie;
MacGregor, Flora;
Martin, Florence J.;
Mauffray, Helena;
McAuliffe, Julia;
McCauley, Alice;
McGee, Mary G.;
McGrandel, Robena M.;
McKernan, Inea G.;
Monroe, Edith;
Morrison, Edna M.;
Olsen, Lydia J.;
Patmore, Amy F.;
Perry, Edith V.;
Phillips, Laurie L.;
Radcliff, Lillian E.;
Reid, Agnes W.;
Reid, Elizabeth D.;
Ricker, Frances E.,
Robertson, RuthI.;
Roche, Katherine P.;
Rothwell, Martha D.;
Ryan, Lulu;
Strub, Ann;
Taft, Nora;
Tomlinson, Alva;
Warwick, Bessie Mae;
Watkins, Jeanette J.;
Watson, Isabel;
Wilkins, Maud M.;
Worley, Pearl M.

Médaille de la Reconnaisance Française
Cornwall, Bertha;
de Cairos, May, for reconstruction work in France, 1924;
Ferguson, Ida, for bravery under fire;
Hall, Carrie M.;
Jarves, Elsie Deming;

Stimson, Julia C.;
Van Horn, Mabel E.

Belgium:
Médaille de la Reine Élisabeth
Cromwell, R. Lee, chief nurse of Base Hospital No. 90.

Great Britain:
Commander of the British Empire
Hagar, Katherine Macfayden, Matron, 22nd General Hospital, Philadelphia Unit.

British Military Medal
MacDonald, Beatrice Mary, chief nurse of the Presbyterian Hospital Unit, Base Hospital No. 2.
Parmlee, Eva Jean, Base Hospital No. 5.

British Royal Red Cross Medal, First Class
Allen, Grace E., Chief Nurse, ANC, 9th General Hospital, Lakeside Unit;
Allison, Grace E., Lakeside Unit;
Butler, Rose Kate, Harvard Unit;
Christie, Janet B., Presbyterian Unit;
Claiborne, Estell Deane, St. Louis Unit;
Dunlop, Margaret Alice, Philadelphia Unit;
Folckener, Elizabeth M., Lakeside Unit;
Fraser, Katherine Margaret, Harvard Unit;
Hacey, Malinde I., assistant chief nurse, ANC;
Hall Carrie Mary, Harvard Unit;
Jardine, Georgina Mary, Harvard Unit;
McClelland, Helen Grace, Philadelphia Unit;
McLaughlin, Emily A., chief nurse, ANC;
Parsons, Marion G.;
Phillips, Lawrie L., chief nurse, ANC;
Scott, Eleanor, matron, US Women's War Hospital, Paignton, England;
Smith, Robina, Sister, 22nd General Hospital, Harvard Unit;
Spencer, Ruth Helen, Chicago Unit, 18th General Hospital;
Stimson, Julia C., director of nursing service in the AEF, 12th General Hospital;
Taylor, Mance, St. Louis Unit, 12th General Hospital;
Urch, Daisy D., Chicago Unit, 18th General Hospital.

British Royal Red Cross Medal, Second Class
Arvin, Mary W., ANC
Ascah, Nora Marjorie, Harvard Unit
Balen, Anna M., Presbyterian Unit
Berry, Nettie Josephine, No. 10 General Hospital
Briggs, Helen May, Lakeside Unit
Burcham, Daisy, ANC
Burky, Florence M., Philadelphia Unit

Carruthers, Isabelle E., Chicago Unit
Carson, Anne Loufheed, St. Louis Unit
Connelly, Betty Clara, ANC
Cuppaidge, Constance A., assistant chief nurse
Ebbs, Helen Jane, Harvard Unit
Elwood, Bessie Lydia, No. 3 Stationary Hospital
Engel, Austa White, Lakeside Unit
Evans, Isabel Wakeman, No. 8 General Hospital
Ferguson, Edna Allison, No. 5. General Hospital
Frederick, LaRue, ANC
Gerhard, Eve, assistant chief nurse
Gerrard, Gertrude Mary, assistant chief nurse
Gould, Elspeth Anna, assistant chief nurse
Harold, Mary R. Presbyterian Unit
Hayes, Myrtle Elizabeth, No. 5 General Hospital
Hill, Ada, assistant chief nurse
Kennedy, Mary E., No. 6 General Hospital
Lesper, Minnie A., assistant chief nurse
Lewis, Lydia, No. 11 Stationary Hospital
Lewis, Mary Elizabeth, No. 11 Stationary Hospital
Lyon, Elizabeth C., Chicago Unit
MacDonald, Beatrice Mary, ANC
MacNeal, Jane Crawford, Philadelphia Unit
McCloskey, Louise Helenne, Harvard Unit
McGillivray, Edith, No. 6 General Hospital
McKee, Inez, ANC
McKnight, Lillian Sarah, No. 3 Stationary Hospital
McLannan, Vera, No. 8 General Hospital
Miller, Elsie B., ANC
Miller, Lena Branson, Chicago Unit
Morton, Ruth, St. Louis Unit
Nicholson, Ann Estelle, No. 6 General Hospital
O'Brien, Agnes Veronica, No. 6 General Hospital
Parmelee, Eva Jean, ANC
Peterson, Hanna Sophia, Harvard Unit
Peterson, Hanna F., ANC
Powers, Margaret Alberta, Chicago Unit
Rignel, Jennie L., ANC
Roche, Mary Jane, ANC
Sands, Tyldesley L., ANC
Sarafini, Olive E., St. Louis Unit
Schmitt, Dolly Belle, ANC
Schorfield, Minnie, No 3 Stationary Hospital
Shepherd, Ada Louise Bascom, Harvard Unit
Stambaugh, Isabelle, Philadelphia Unit
Stephenson, Mary E., ANC
Stouffer, Barbara Ellen, ANC

Walkinshaw, Arvilla, Lakeside Unit
Wallace, Olive L., ANC
Wiseman, Katherine Julia, Harvard Unit

British Certificate of Merit
Krost, Carrie Gullickson

Sir Douglas Haig Mention for Gallant Service on the Western Front
Alexander, Bertha M.
Hall, Carrie M.
Marsh, Louise M.
Stimson, Julia C, director of nursing service in the AEF

Greece:
Silver Cross of the Order of King George I

Carr, Alice G. (1923)
Edison, Anna (1923)
Mathews, Stella S. (1923)
Nuno Christine M. (1923)
Smith, Lily Lyle (1923)
Thompson, Sara R. (1923)

Romania:
Order of the Croix Reine Marie

Donald, Jennie B., as a member of the Red Cross Commission in Romania, 1918
Meirs, Linda K, as a member of the Red Cross Commission in Romania, 1918
Patterson, Florence M.
Rowland, Adeline H.

Japan:
Order of the Crown
McGee, Anita Newcomb

Russia:
Silver Cross of St. Anne

(Awarded for service as a member of the Red Cross Commission in Kiev, Russia in 1915)

Bartlett, Kathryn
Cromwell, R. Lee
Echternach, Marion H.
Hansen, Anne
Hard, Gertrude
Hill, Mary E.
Horner, Blanche
Johnson, Cora
Pepper, Margaret
Reinhardt, Hettie
Smith, Anna R.

Army Dietitians
Hulsizer, Marjorie (Copher). One of the first dietitians to go overseas, she was assigned to the British Army and decorated by King George V and the French government.

ARMY SIGNAL CORPS TELEPHONE OPERATORS ("HELLO GIRLS")

Distinguished Service Medal

Banker, Grace D., chief operator, for her work at First Army Headquarters in September 1918. Presented in Coblenz, Germany in July 1919

General John J. Pershing Citation

(Awarded for exceptionally meritorious and conspicuous service in the AEF)

Keyser, Florence
Le Blanc, Marie A.
Le Breton, Louise

(Awarded for service at First Army Headquarters at Ligny-en-Barrois during the St. Mihiel drive, August 1918, and at Souilly during the Meuse-Argonne campaign, September-November 1918)

Arland, Berthe	Hill, Helen E.
Banker, Grace D.	Hoppock, Adele,
Belanger, Marie	Hunt, Berthe M.
Beraud, Louise	Lange, Marie
Flood, Maria	Peyron, Oeonie
Fresnel, Esther V.	Prevot, Suzanne

(Awarded for service as chief operator to the American Commission to Negotiate Peace, Paris, France, 1919)

Egan, Merle

Citation from General Edgar Russel, chief signal officer, AEF

(Awarded for especially meritorious and excellent services rendered in the AEF)

Arland, Berthe	Hoppock, Adele
Banker, Grace D.	Hunt, Berthe M.
Belanger, Marie	Johnson, Maud E.
Beraud, Louise	Lange, Marie
Dupuis, Cordelia	Peyron, Leonie
Flood, Maria	Prevot, Suzanne
Fresnel, Esther V.	Young, Jennie
Hill, Helen E.	

NAVY NURSE CORPS

Navy Cross

Higbee, Lenah Sutcliffe, superintendent of the Navy Nurse Corps

(The following three nurses gave long and devoted service during the war emergency period and died in a naval hospital during the influenza epidemic of 1918. Each was awarded the Navy Cross posthumously.)

Hidell, Marie Louise, Naval Hospital, Philadelphia, Pennsylvania

Murphy, Lillian M., Naval Hospital, Hampton Roads, Virginia
Pierce, Edna S., Naval Hospital, Philadelphia, Pennsylvania

Secretary of the Navy, Letter of Commendation
Brooke, Elsie, chief nurse
Elderkin, Mary
Leonhardt, Elizabeth, chief nurse
McClellan, Jeannette
Pringle, Marth E., chief nurse, Naval Hospital, Philadelphia, Pennsylvania
Van Ingen, Frances, chief nurse Navy Base Hospital No. 1

General John J. Pershing Citation
Van Ingen, Frances, chief nurse, Navy Base Hospital No. 1

Army Letter of Commendation
Elderkin, Mary
McClellan, Jeannette

Foreign Awards

France:
Médaille d'Honneur des Épidémmies
Hasson, Esther V., first superintendent, Navy Nurse Corps

YOUNG MEN'S CHRISTIAN ASSOCIATION
Distinguished Service Cross
Sloan, Emma S.–cited

Distinguished Service Medal
Cushman, Mrs. James S., chairman, War Work Council, YWCA of the United States

US Certificate for Exceptionally Meritorious and Conspicuous Service
Janis, Elsie, entertainment worker, AEF
Leonard, Katherine, Camp Stephenson
Miller, Bernetta A., worker with the US Army 326th Infantry
Roosevelt, Mrs. Theodore, Jr., worker with the AEF
Sweeney, Mary, canteen operator near the front lines
Sweeney, Sunshine, canteen operator near the front lines.

General John J. Pershing Citation
Francis, Dorothy

General Edwards Citation
Fleming, Louis Wellford

Divisional Commander Citation
Dennis, Dorothy
Gulick, Frances J.
Skelding, Marjorie
Warren, Maude Radford

Belgium:
Médaille de la Reine Élisabeth
Hall, Mrs. Gardiner, chief, YMCA women, GHQ
MacGruder, Emma, chief, YMCA women, GHQ
Tenner, Ethel, chief, YMCA women, GHQ

France:
Croix de Guerre
Arrowsmith, Mary Noel
Colby, Leslie Osgood
Davis, Cornelia Colt
Dwight, Jane R.
Ely, Gertrude
Fleming, Louise Wellford
Henthorne, Oril Elsie
Herron, Maria Clinton
King, Helen Maxwell
Lesley, Olive Mary
Miller, Bernetta A.
Nicoll, Ruby Bacon
Smalley, Evelyn
Sweeney, Mary E.--cited
Sweeney, Sunshine--cited

Fourragére
Boyd, Miss
Butler, Hope
Dunlap, Elizabeth
Ely, Gertrude
Landon, Cornelia
Morgan, Edith

Médaille de la Reconnaisance Française
Francis, Dorothy

Great Britain:
Order of the British Empire
Chisholm, Jessie Noyes
Davis, May Agnes
Dwight, Jane R.
Lynch, Gertrude

WOMEN PHYSICIANS
France:
Croix de Guerre
Tallant, Dr. Alice Weld, director of Smith College Relief Unit and a member of the American Committee for Devastated France.

Médaille del la Reconnaissance Française
(Awarded to the the staff of American Women's Hosptial No. 1 for service at Luzancy on the Marne; honorary French citizenship bestowed upon these recipients)

Bently, Dr. Inez
Bonness, Dr. Hazel D.
Cohen, Dr. Frances
Doherty, Dr. Kate A.
Douglas, Helen
Evens, Dr. Mary
Fairbanks, Dr. Charlotte
Fraser, Dr. M Ethel V.
Hunt, Dr. Barbara
Hurrell, Dr. M. Louise
Kinney, Dr. DeLan
Lehman, Emilie
MacLachlan, Dr. Mary
Manwaring, Dr. I. Jay
Prunell, Dr. Caroline M.
Ward, Dr. Edna

AMERICAN COMMITTEE FOR DEVASTATED FRANCE

Ann Morgan and Mrs. A.M. Dike, founders of the ACDF, were made honorary French citizens.

Dr. Nellie N. Barsness, an opthalmologist at the gas hospital at Cempuis, France, was decorated (decoration unknown) by the French Minister of War for her work "under hazardous conditions."

SALVATION ARMY OF AMERICA
Distinguished Service Medal
Booth, Evangeline Cory, commander of the Salvation Army in the United States

General John J. Pershing Citation
Burdick, Minnie Saunders

US Certificate for Exceptionally Meritorious and Conspicuous Services
Morton, Mae Isabella, for service in battle area in France
Rapson, Triselda (Della), for service in battle area in France
Van Norden, Cora, for service with the 77th Division

France:
Croix de Guerre
Burdick, Minnie Saunders

CIVILIAN WOMEN IN WAR SERVICE--WORLD WAR I
Distinguished Service Medal
Patterson, Hannah J., Women's Committee, Council of National Defense
Shaw, Dr. Anna Howard, chairman, Women's Committee, Council of National Defense

US Certificate for Exceptionally Meritorious and Conspicuous Service
Bousquet, Isabelle, for hospital work in France
Despecher, Clara, secretary to the chief of staff, AEF
Gunther, Elsie L, Quartermaster Corps, Tours, France
Herve, Eugenie, Gase Section No. 1., St. Nazaire, France
McCormick, Ruby, Air Service, Paris
Richards, Ruth (Law?), Air Service, Paris
Richardson, Florence, Quartermaster Corps with Salvage Service
Schunck M.A., Office of the Chief Quartermaster
Singleton, Ann Celestine, confidential secretary to the commander-in-chief
Spencer, Mildred, Quartermaster Corps
Steed, Leonara M., Office of the Chief Quartermaster, Salvage Service
Tracy, Mary Austin, personnel division, AGO, GHQ

France:
Légion d'Honneur

Cofer, Luisita L., founder, Fatherless Children of France society

Cushman, Emma, for her work with French prisoners of war in Turkey

De Roaldes, Annie Miller, president of *Le Secours Louisianais à la France*

Dike, Mrs. A. Murray, co-founder of the American Fund for French Wounded and the American Committee for Devastated France

Duryea, Nina L.

Gassette, Grace

Griggs, Emily R., director, Union Franco-American

Harjes, Mrs. H. Hermann, worked in hospitals and canteens, 1914-1919

Holt, Winifred, president, *Comité Franco-American Pour les Aveugles de la Guerre*

Lathrop, Mrs. Benjamin Girault (London, England), President in France of the American Fund for French Wounded

McIntyre, Anna, served with the American Red Cross, worked with French prisoners of war in Turkey

Morgan, Anne, organized the American Fund for French Wounded and its offshoot, the American Committee for Devastated France

Morgenthau, Mrs. Henry

Morhard, Jeanne Emma, for long and faithful services in the cause of France

Norton, Mrs. Henry

Sage, Cornelia Bentley, for services to French art, especially during the war

Skinner, Belle, for the reconstruction of the village of Hattonchatel, Meuse, France

Smith, Mrs. Joseph L.

Spencer, Carita, chairman, Food for France Fund

Tuck, Julia S., for benevolent work in France before and during the war

Tyler, Elisina, vice president fo the French Tubercular Children's Fund, and of American Hostels for Refugees, and of the Children of Flanders Relief Committee

Tyson, Mrs. Russel, for her work with the American Fund for French Wounded

Vanderbilt, Mrs. W.K. (Anne), for her work with the Red Cross in France

Wharton, Edith, for extensive relief work in France during the war

Whitney, Belle A.

Médaille de la Reconnaissance Française

Chew, Ada Knowlton, worked with the French nursing service in Paris and with the American Ambulance Hospital at Neuilly, 1916-1919

Morgan, Anne, and Dike, Mrs. A. Murray, founders of the American Fund for French Wounded and the American Committee for Devastated France
De Roaldes, Annie Miller
Morhard, Jeanne Emma
Spencer, Carita
Tyler, Elisina
Tyson, Mrs. Russell

Médaille d'Honneur des Épidémies
Tyson, Mrs. Russell

Croix de Guerre, with Palm
Harjes, Mrs. H. Herman

Belgium:
Médaille de la Reine Élisabeth
MacGruder, Emma, chief, YMCA women, GHQ
Seamans, Mary F., chief, Red Cross, GHQ
Spencer, Charita
Tenner, Ethel, chief, YMCA women, GHQ
Tuck, Mrs. Edward
Tyler, Elisina

WORLD WAR II

ARMY NURSE CORPS
Distinguished Service Medal
Florence A. Blanchfield, Colonel, Chief of the Army Nurse Corps, for her leadership of the ANC during World War II. DSM awarded on June 14, 1945. She was also awarded the West Virginia Distinguished Service Medal on July 19, 1963.
Anna Mae Hays, Brigadier General
Elizabeth Hoisington, Brigadier General

Legion of Merit
Davison, Maude C., Major, served in World War I and was a prisoner of war of the Japanese during World War II. Davison was awarded twelve medals.
Phillips, Mary G., Colonel (ret. 1951), Awarded the Legion of Merit on October 23, 1945 for outstanding service as First Assistant to the Superintendent, ANC.
Sullivan, Mary Ann, Lieutenant, awarded the Legion of Merit for her actions at the Kasserine Pass.

Distinguished Flying Cross
Lutz, Aleda E., Lieutenant, awarded the Distinguished Flying Cross posthumously after she was killed in a plane crash while on a mission to evacuate wounded servicemen.

Silver Star

Ainsworth, Ellen, Lieutenant--February 16, 1944, posthumous. Lieutenant Ainsworth was wounded while on duty at the hospital ward on the Anzio beachead on February 10th and died six days later.[3]

McCracken, Mary V., Lieutenant--December 12, 1944.

Nevin, Hilda, also awarded the Bronze Star for service in Casablanca, Algiers, Cairo, Russia, Tripoli and Teheran.

Roberts, Mary, for heroic service during the bombing of the 95th Evacuation Hospital at Anzio-Nettuno by the *Luftwaffe*, on February 10, 1944.

Roe, Elaine R., awarded for the same action.

Rourke, Virginia, awarded for the same action.

Schwing, Ruth, Captain--December 12, 1944.

Vitachnick, Pearl E., Lieutenant--December 12, 1944.

Bronze Star

Cook, Cordelia, Lieutenant
Davison, Maude C., Major
Gounder, Ann L., Lieutenant
Hodgson, Maralee R., Lieutenant
Kerlin, Ethel J., Lieutenant
Mitchell, Adelaide M., Lieutenant
Peterson, Mollie, Captain
Petting, Minnie M., Lieutenant
Smith, Evelyn E., Lieutenant
Wilson, Lucy Ina, Captain

Purple Heart

Ainsworth, Ellen, Lieutenant--February 16, 1944, posthumously.

Cook, Cordelia, Lieutenant.[4]

Fox, Annie G., First Lieutenant, though not wounded, was awarded the Purple Heart for "her fine example of calmness, courage, and leadership, which was of great benefit to the morale of all she came in contact with" during the Japanese attack on Pearl Harbor.

Whittle, Reba, Lieutenant. The air evac plane with Lieutenant Whittle on board was shot down by the Germans. All aboard were taken prisoner. During her confinement and though wounded, Lieutenant Whittle continued to perform her duties as a nurse, caring for camp prisoners.

Air Medal

Lutz, Aleda E., Lieutenant, flew over 190 evacuation missions and was awarded the Air Medal with four oak leaf clusters.

Ott, Elsie, Lieutenant, the first woman to receive the Air Medal. It was given "for meritorious achievement while participating in an aerial

---

[3] *The Women Who Gave Their Lives,* p. 3.

[4] *Women Medal Recipients,* p. 3.

flight.... [She] served as a nurse for five patients while being evacuated from India to Washington, DC. This was the pioneer movement of hospitalized personnel by air over such a great distance.... The successful transportation of these patients was made possible largely by the efficiency and professional skill of Lieutenant Ott and her unflagging devotion to duty. It further demonstrated the practicability of long-range evacuation by air of seriously ill and wounded military personnel from theaters of operations and reflected great credit upon Lieutenant Ott and the Army Nurse Corps."[5]

Richey, Margaret, Lieutenant.

Whittle, Reba, Lieutenant. The air evac plane on which Lieutenant Whittle was shot down by the Germans. All aboard were taken prisoner. During her confinement and though wounded, Lieutenant Whittle continued to perform her duties as a nurse, caring for camp prisoners.

Wilson, Lucy Ina, Captain, 13th Air Force.

Army Commendation Ribbon

No information available.

Florence Nightingale Medal

Blanchfield, Florence A., Colonel, Chief of the Army Nurse Corps during World War II. Medal presented on May 12, 1951.

Danielson, Ida W., Lieutenant Colonel, awarded the Florence Nightingale Medal by the International Red Cross for her work as the Director of Nurses in the ETO, 1944-1955. The medal was awarded to Lieutenant Colonel Danielson on June 11, 1947.

List of Superintendents of the Army Nurse Corps

Anita Newcomb McGee (unofficially)
Dita H. Kinney, 1901-1909;
Jane A. Delano, 1902-1912;
Mabel McIsaac, 1912-1914;
Dore E. Thompson, 1914-1919;
Major Julia C. Stimson, 1919-1937;
Colonel Julia O. Flikke, 1937-1943;
Colonel Florence A. Blanchfield, 1943-1947;
Colonel Mary G. Phillips, 1947-1951;
Colonel Ruby F. Bryant, 1951-1955;
Colonel Inez Haynes, 1955-1959;
Colonel Margaret Harper, 1959-1963;
Colonel Mildred Irene Clark, 1963-1967;
Brigadier General Anna Mae Hayes, 1967-1971;
Brigadier General Lillian Dunlap, 1971-1975.[6]

---

[5] Catherine Bell Palmer, "Flying Our Wounded Veterans Home," *The National Geographic* September 1945: p. 377.

[6] Women in Military Service Association, *The Register,* Washington, DC, "Special Drive to Honor Service Directors and Corps Chiefs," Summer 1996, p. 5.

Chiefs of the Army Medical Specialist Corps
Colonel Emma E. Vogel, 1947-1951;
Colonel Nell Wickliffe, 1951-1954;
Colonel Harriet S. Lee, 1954-1958;
Colonel Ruth Robinson, 1958-1962;
Colonel Lois Forsythe, 1962-1966;
Colonel Mary Lipscomb Hamrick, 1966-1969;
Colonel June E. Williams, 1970-1973.

NAVY NURSE CORPS
Legion of Merit
Bernatitus, Ann Agnes, Lieutenant (jg), the first person ever to receive the Legion of Merit. Bernatitus was the only member of the Navy Medical Staff who escaped after Bataan and Corregidor came under Japanese fire.[7]

Presidential Unit Citation
Bernatitus, Ann Agnes, Lieutenant (jg).

Bronze Star
Cobb, Laura May, Lieutenant Commander
Evans, Bertha Rae, Lieutenant
Gorzelanski, Helen Clara, Lieutenant
Hays, Mary Chapman, Lieutenant
Merrill, Goldia Aimee, Lieutenant
Nash, Margaret Alice, Lieutenant
Nelson, Mary Harrington, Lieutenant
Paige, Eldene Elinor, Lieutenant
Pitcher, Susie Josephine, Lieutenant
Still, Dorothy, Lieutenant
Todd, C. Edwina, Lieutenant
White, Faye Elmo, Lieutenant Commander

Gold Star in lieu of Second Bronze Star
Cobb, Laura May, Lieutenant Commander
Evans, Bertha Rae, Lieutenant
Gorzelanski, Helen Clara, Lieutenant
Hays, Mary Chapman, Lieutenant
Merrill, Goldia Aimee, Lieutenant
Nash, Margaret Alice, Lieutenant
Nelson, Mary Harrington, Lieutenant
Paige, Eldene Elinor, Lieutenant
Pitcher, Susie Josephine, Lieutenant
Still, Dorothy, Lieutenant
Todd, C. Edwina, Lieutenant

---

[7] Arthur E. DuBois, "The Heraldry of Herosim," *The National Geographic*, October 1943: p. 443.

Navy Commendation Ribbon
Pennington, Clyde, Lieutenant
Kreider, Anna M., Lieutenant
Lindner, Mary J., Lieutenant (jg)
Richardson, Catherine, Lieutenant
Kain, Catherine M., Lieutenant
Kozak, Stephany J., Lieutenant (jg)
Van Gorp, Dymphna M., Lieutenant (jg)

Distinguished Unit Badge (Army)
Bernatitus, Agnes Ann, Lieutenant
Cobb, Laura May, Lieutenant Commander
Evans, Bertha Rae, Lieutenant
Gorzelanski, Helen Clara, Lieutenant
Hays, Mary Chapman, Lieutenant
Merrill, Goldia Aimee, Lieutenant
Nash, Margaret Alice, Lieutenant
Nelson, Mary Harrington, Lieutenant
Paige, Eldene Elinor, Lieutenant
Pitcher, Susie Josephine, Lieutenant
Still, Dorothy, Lieutenant
Todd, C. Edwina, Lieutenant

Navy Unit Commendation Ribbon
Arnest, Gertrude B., Lieutenant Commander
Alkire, Lorene E., Lieutenant
Bogdon, D. Dorothy, Lieutenant
Ceaglske, Lorraine D., Lieutenant
Cohen, Ruth M., Lieutenant
Combes, Hilda W., Lieutenant
Conine, Freda, Lieutenant
Danya, Anna, Lieutenant
Davidson, Ann M., Lieutenant
Duggan, Teresa M., Lieutenant
Dolloff, Ellen M., Lieutenant
Erickson, Evelyn I., Lieutenant
Entriken, Helen, Lieutenant
Gibson, Winnie, Lieutenant
Haley, Margaret L., Lieutenant
Houge, Evelyn, Lieutenant
Lally, Margaret L., Lieutenant Commander
Nesgis, Rosella, Lieutenant
Richardson, Catherine, Lieutenant
Shaeffer, Clara, Lieutenant
Shurr, Agnes G., Lieutenant
Sonsalla, Frances L., Lieutenant
Terrell, Lenora, Lieutenant
Thompson, Ida K., Lieutenant

Vaubel, Valera C., Lieutenant
Von Stein, Majorie E., Lieutenant
Zalmon, Otilla J., Lieutenant

(Former NNC Members Awarded the Navy Unit Commendation Ribbon)

Antonelli, Eva
Banks, Lillian
Christensen, Elsie L.
Clohessy, Violet
Dana, Phyllis
Eno, Loretta M.
Gaililey, Irene D.
Hickey, Genevieve T.
Houck, Bertha
Jenkins, Beatrice
Semon, Nelly C.
Swann, Margaret M.
Tucker, Ann C.
Van de Drink, Geneva

Letter of Commendation
Blackman, Martha N., Lieutenant (jg)
Gregory, Mary E., Lieutenant
MacDonald, Constance G., Lieutenant
Seroka, Nell P., Lieutenant (jg)
Toenberg, Ruth, Lieutenant[8]

Purple Heart
No information available.

MARINE CORPS WOMEN'S RESERVE
Letter of Commendation with Ribbon
Towle, Colonel Katherine, "for meritorious service during the entire period of the growth and development of the United States Marine Corps Women's Reserve...."

WOMEN'S ARMY AUXILIARY CORPS/WOMEN'S ARMY CORPS
Distinguished Service Medal
Hobby, Colonel Oveta, Director of the Women's Army Auxiliary Corps and the Women's Army Corps, January 1945.[9]

Oak Leaf Cluster to the Legion of Merit
Boyce, Colonel Westray Battle (second director of the WAC), April 17, 1946, for "...exceptionally meritorious service from September 1944 to January 1946 as a staff officer in the Personnel Division of the War Department General Staff and later as Director of the Women's Army Corps. She conducted extensive studies that were extremely valuable in perfecting plans for the improved treatment of psychoneurotic personnel. As director of the Women's Army Corps, she demonstrated foresight and sound judgment that con-

---

[8] *White Task Force. The Story of the Nurse Corps, United States Navy* (Washington, DC: US Government Printing Office, 1945) pp.22-23.

[9] "Legion of Merit Awarded to Two WAC Officers," *WAC News Letter,* Vol. 3, No. 1 (December 1945): p. 2.

tributed greatly to an orderly demobilization of the Corps and a better understanding concerning the future role of women in the Army."

Hallaren, Colonel Mary A. (Named director of the WAC on May 7, 1947)

Legion of Merit

Bandel, Lieutenant Colonel Betty, 1946, WAC Staff Director for the Army Air Forces.

Bass, Lieutenant Colonel, Cora Webb, 1946, WAC Staff Director for the Second Service Command.

Belvin, Master Sergeant Adele B., 1946, for "...exceptionally meritorious service in the Economic Branch of the Military Intelligence Service where she was responsible for supplying intelligence material to field commands for operational use in the war against Japan."

Boyce, Colonel Westray Battle, September 1944 for services rendered as Staff Director in the North African Theater of Operations.[10]

Freeman, Lieutenant Colonel Mary C., former WAC Staff Director of the Army Air Forces Training Command, for her "...work in the Air Force utilization of WAC personnel, her direction of the recruiting program, and her outstanding achievements in the development of a training program aimed at preparing Wacs for their return to civilian life."

Hallaren, Colonel Mary A.

May, Lieutenant Colonel Geraldine P., WAC Staff Director, Air Transport Command, "...for her success in developing plans, policies, and a program for the use of WAC personnel in the Air Transport Command."

Newsome, Lieutenant Colonel Florence, Assistant Secretary to Army Chief of Staff General Marshall, for her handling of top secret documents.

Rice, Lieutenant Colonel Jesse Pearl, 1946, former Deputy Director of the WAC and Commandant of the WAC School for Personnel Administration.

Scheidenhelm, Captain Arlene, Commanding Officer of the WAC Detachments assigned to the Atomic Bomb Project.[11]

Stearns, Major Elizabeth, 1946, WAC Staff Director of the First Service Command.

Bronze Star

Carter, Nancy, 1st Sergeant, one of six Wacs awarded the Bronze Star by Brigadier General Allen R. Kimball, ETO Headquarters Com-

---

[10] "Colonel Boyce Addes Oak Leaf to Legion of Merit," *WAC News Letter*, Vol. 3, No. 6 (May 1946): p. 2.

[11] "Legion of Merit Awarded to Two WAC Officers," *WAC News Letter*, Vol. 3, No. 1 (December 1945): p. 2.

mandant, for moving into Paris on August 31, 1944 (six days after the Allies), as part of an advanced detachment and speedily arranging for thousands of Wacs to follow.[12]

Cornick, Frances S., Major, awarded for the move into Paris on August 31, 1944.

Fowler, Wilhelmina, Master Sergeant, awarded for the move into Paris on August 31, 1944.

Hallaren, Mary A., Colonel

Haluey, Mary, Staff Sergeant, awarded for the move into Paris on August 31, 1944.

Hoisington, Elizabeth P., Lieutenant, awarded for the move into Paris on August 31, 1944.

Lauwers, Barbara, Corporal--Assigned to the OSS (Office of Stategic Services) in Rome. Born in Czechoslovakia. Awarded April 6, 1945 at Rome for her participation in Operation "Sauerkraut," which resulted in the surrender to Allied Forces of more than six hundred Slovak and Czech soldiers who had joined the German Army on the Italian Front.

Magoon, Vivian G.

Petersen, Technical Sergeant Ruth, for meritorious service against the enemy while serving as a chief clerk at a supply base in New Guinea.

Russo, Staff Sergeant Elizabeth A., for the same action.

Wright, Margaret, Sergeant, awarded for the move into Paris on August 31, 1944.

Purple Heart

Gaylon, Leona J., Pvt., for injuries received from a German buzz bomb attack on London.

Gibbons, Effie M., Pfc., for injuries received from a German buzz bomb attack on London.

Johnson, Margaret, Pvt., for injuries received from a German buzz bomb attack on London.

Whitfield, Dorothy E. Pfc., for injuries received from a German buzz bomb attack on London.[13]

Air Medal

Williams, Sergeant Herietta A., 1946. Awarded Air Medal for flying more than twenty-five missions over China, Burma and India "...during a time when attack from enemy planes was expected and probable." She was the third WAC to receive the Air Medal.

---

[12] Lt.Col. Anna W. Wilson, *The WAC* (Paris: Orientation Branch, Information and Education Division, Hq., USFET, Immediate post-World War II publication), pp. 21-22.

[13] Ibid., pp. 16-17.

Soldier's Medal

Bilbo, Acting Staff Sergeant Virginia P., January 1946. "With four other companions, while on a rowboat in the middle of a lake, adverse weather conditions caused their boat to sink. Although not a competent swimmer Sergeant Bilbo noticed one of the other enlisted women in great danger of drowning and immediately went to her aid. Despite her exhaustion and the imminent danger of drowning, Sergeant Bilbo heroically remained with her companion and managed to keep her above water until help finally arrived."[14]

Army Commendation Ribbon

Winslow, Anne, Lieutenant--OSS--Award ribbon for her work in finding and interrogating German intelligence personnel. Fluent in Russian, German and French.

USA Typhus Commission Medal

Turner, Technician 4 Ida E., for service with the Commission in Southern Italy. Tech 4 Turner was the only enlisted person, male or female, to be awarded this medal.[15]

Unit Citation

WAC unit assigned to the OSS, London--Awarded citation October 1945 for its bravery during almost constant bombing of London and for their contribution to the OSS.

Certificate of Merit

House, Jane, Lieutenant--Awarded for Lieutenant House's work with the OSS as supply officer for the Air Operations Section.[16]

Lampton, Ida, Corporal--OSS, for her work as a Finnish language translator.

France:
Croix de Guerre with Gold Star

Hallaran, Colonel Mary A.

Croix de Guerre

Hallaran, Colonel Mary A.

WAVES
Naval Commendation Ribbon

Reynard, Elizabeth, Lieutenant, USNR--The first Wave to be decorated. She was given the Naval Commendation Ribbon for her ser-

---

[14] "Wac Awarded Soldier's Medal for Heroism," *WAC News Letter*, Vol. 3, No. 9 (September 1946), p. 3.

[15] "Officers, Enlisted Women Receive Many High Awards," *WAC News Letter*, Vol. 2, No. 3 (January 1946), p. 3.

[16] Elizabeth P. McIntosh, *Sisterhood of Spies. The Women of the OSS* (Annapolis, Maryland: Naval Institute Press, 1998), p. 92.

vice at the US Naval Training School (WR) in The Bronx, New York, where 50,000 enlisted Waves received their training during World War II.[17]

CIVILIAN WOMEN
Office of Special Services (OSS)
Distinguished Service Cross
Hall, Virginia--Awarded the DSC by order of President Harry S. Truman for her work in organizing, training and arming units of more than 300 agents who carried out sabotage against the Germans. Hall was also instrumental in the preservation of radio contact between OSS headquarters in London and resistance fighters in the district of Haute-Loire.

Distinguished Service Medal
Amelia Earhart Putnam was awarded the DSC.[18]

WOMEN AIRFORCE SERVICE PILOTS (WASP)
Distinguished Service Medal
Jacqueline Cochran, Director.

Distinguished Flying Cross
Earhart, Amelia, awarded for her successful flight across the Atlantic, 1932.

1946-1949
WOMEN IN THE UNITED STATES AIR FORCE
Soldier's Medal
O'Hara, Lieutenant Mary Patricia, Vancouver, BC, for saving Katherine Boening of Galveston, Texas from drowning. Presented by Major General Charles W. Lawrence, Commanding General at Lackland Air Force Base. "With complete disregard for her own safety, Lieutenant O'Hara dove into the treacherous Gulf Waters off Fort Crockett, Texas, and with considerable difficulty, succeeded in bringing the young woman safely to shore. The courage and quick action displayed by Lieutenant O'Hara reflected credit on herself and the United States Air Force."

THE KOREAN WAR–PRE-VIETNAM WAR

ARMY NURSE CORPS
Legion of Merit
Hayes, Inez, Colonel, Chief of the Army Nurse Corps, received the Legion of Merit on the occasion of her retirement on August 31, 1959.

---

[17] *Bureau of Naval Personnel Information Bulletin,* August 1944, p. 59.

[18] Charlotte Palmer Seeley, ed., *American Women and the US Armed Forces* (Washington, DC: The National Archives Trust Fund Board, 1992), p. 94, No. 107.32.

Second Oak Leaf Cluster to the Legion of Merit
Bradley, Ruby G., Colonel, ANC, awarded upon her retirement from the Army on March 31, 1963. Colonel Bradley was the most decorated woman in the history of the United States Army. In addition to the Second Oak Leaf Cluster to the Legion of Merit, Bradley was awarded the following:
Bronze Star with one Oak Leaf Cluster;
Army Commendation Medal with Oak Leaf Cluster;
American Defense Service Medal with Foreign Service bar;
American Campaign Medal
Asiatic-Pacific Campaign Medal with two bronze service stars for participation in the Philippine Island and Luzon campaigns;
World War II Victory Medal;
Army of Occupation Medal with Japan bar;
National Defense Service Medal;
Korean Service Medal with one silver star, in lieu of five bronze service stars, and two bronze service stars for participation in the UN Offensive, Chinese Communist Forces Intervention, UN Summer-Fall Offensive, Second Korean Winter, Korea Summer-Fall 1952, Third Korean Winter, and Korea Summer-Fall 1953;
United Nations Service Medal;
Philippine Liberation Ribbon with one bronze service star;
Philippine Independence Ribbon;
Distinguished Unit Citation;
Philippine Presidential Citation.
In addition, Col. Bradley had ten overseas service bars.[19]

Bronze Star
McConnell, Viola B., Captain. Awarded the Bronze Star for her "heroic performance of duty in assisting with the evacuation of Americans from Seoul...."[20]

Oak Leaf Cluster to the Bronze Star
McConnel, Viola, B., Captain. Awarded for outstanding service during the Korean War.

Florence Nightingale Medal
Bradley, Ruby G., Colonel, presented the decoration by the International Red Cross on June 15, 1955 for her service in Korea and for her services as a prisoner of war of the Japanese during World War II.

Associate Royal Red Cross--Great Britain
Dickson, Ruth, Captain-The medal, equivalent to the United States

---

[19] http://history.amedd.army.mil/ANCWebsite/bradleyres.htm., p. 23

[20] Feller, Carolyn M., Lieutenant Colonel, ANC, USAR and Major Constance J. Moore, ANC, eds, *Highlights in the History of the Army Nurse Corps* (Washington, DC: US Army Center for Military History, 1996), p. 23.

Distinguished Service Cross, was awarded to Captain Dickson on August 19, 1955 for her service to British Commonwealth Forces in Korea while Chief Nurse of the 8055th Mobile Army Surgical Hospital (MASH).

WOMEN'S ARMY CORPS
American Spirit Honor Medal
Sinatra, Private Theresa, Rochester, New York, received the award from Lieutenant Colonel Elizabeth C. Smith, commanding officer, WAC Training Center, Fort Lee, Virginia, June 1950.[21]

THE VIETNAM WAR

(All military personnel who served in Vietnam from July 3, 1965 to March 28, 1973 were awarded the Vietnam Service Medal and the Republic of Vietnam Campaign Medal.)

ARMY NURSE CORPS
Legion of Merit
Bryant, Ruby F., Colonel, awarded the Legion of Merit upon her retirement June 30, 1961.

Bronze Star
A number of Army nurses were awarded the Bronze Star for service in Vietnam, and Army Commendation Medals. At least one Army nurse was awarded the Purple Heart after having her jaw broken by a patient who was a prisoner of war. She was also awarded the Bronze Star.

Alexander, Eleanor Grace, 2nd Lieutenant, 85th Evac–posthumously.
Orlowski, Elizabeth Ann, 2nd Lieutenant, 67th Evac–posthumously.

Bronze Star with Valor Device
Lane, Sharon A., Lieutenant--posthumously.

Purple Heart
Lane, Sharon A., Lieutenant-posthumously.

Army Nurse Corps Medal
This medal was created in 1960 and was awarded to "the graduate of each Military Nursing Advanced Course at the US Army Medical Field Service School who best exemplified the ideal military nurse (male or female)." It is awarded twice a year. The first recipient of the medal was Captain Angeline Hennek, who received the award on June 9, 1961.

Basta, Particia J., Captain, December 1970
Boaz, Evelyn E., Captain, December 1972

---

[21] "Wac Wins American Spirit Honor Medal," *Woman Veteran*, Vol. IV, No. 7 (July 1950): 4.

Carson, Amelia, Lieutenant, December 1965
Condit, Mary, Major, June 1966
Groce, Joan R., Captain, March 1969
Hennek, Angeline, Captain, June 9, 1961
Hiers, Frances, Captain, June 1965
Johnson, Jean, Captain, December 1966
Johnson, Martha S., Captain, December 1968
Kingsley, Marthanne, Major, December 1963
Layman, Kay F., Captain, June 1972
Lee, Linda, Captain, December 1962
McQuail, Claire M., Major, June 1969
Munchbach, Rose, Major, June 1967
Nelson, Janice M., Captain, June 1970
Sater, Corinne, Captain, December 1961
Stallard, Sally, Captain, June 1962[22]

Republic of Vietnam Gallantry Cross with Palm
Lane, Sharon A., Lieutenant-posthumously.

National Defense Medal
Lane, Sharon A. Lieutenant

Navy Nurse Corps
No information available.

Silver Star
No information available.

Bronze Star
No information available.

Purple Heart
Four navy nurses were wounded in 1965 during a Viet Cong terrorist bombing. They were the first women serving in Vietnam to win the Purple Heart.

Air Medal
No information available.

Navy Commendation Medal
Several Navy nurses were awarded the Navy Commendation Medal and the Navy Achievement Medal for their service in Vietnam.

UNITED STATES AIR FORCE NURSE CORPS
Air Force nurses were awarded the Air Medal for numbers of hours in flight and for flying in combat zones. One nurse, who served from September 1971 to September 1971 with the 903rd Evacuation Squadron,

---

[22] Feller, Carolyn M., Lieutenant Colonel, ANC, USAR and Major Constance J. Moore, ANC, *Highlights in the History of the Army Nurse Corps* (Revised and Expanded) (Washington, DC: US Army Center of Military History, 1996), pp. 81-82.

was awarded three Air Medals. Another nurse who worked the repatriation flight of American prisoners of war, called "Project Homecoming," was awarded the Air Force Commendation Medal.[23]

---

[23] Elizabeth Norman, *Women at War*, p. 109 and 177.

Appendix 2: "Hello Girls"

The following is from a Signal Corps Telephone Operating Units commemorative booklet presented to Louise Le Breton on Christmas Day, 1918. See pages 56-64 in this volume for additional information. (Booklet courtesy: Mac West)

> The officers, men, and the young women of the Signal Corps have performed their duties with a large conception of the problem and with a devoted and patriotic spirit to which the perfection of our communications daily testify.
>
> John J. Pershing,
> Commander-in-Chief, A.E.F.

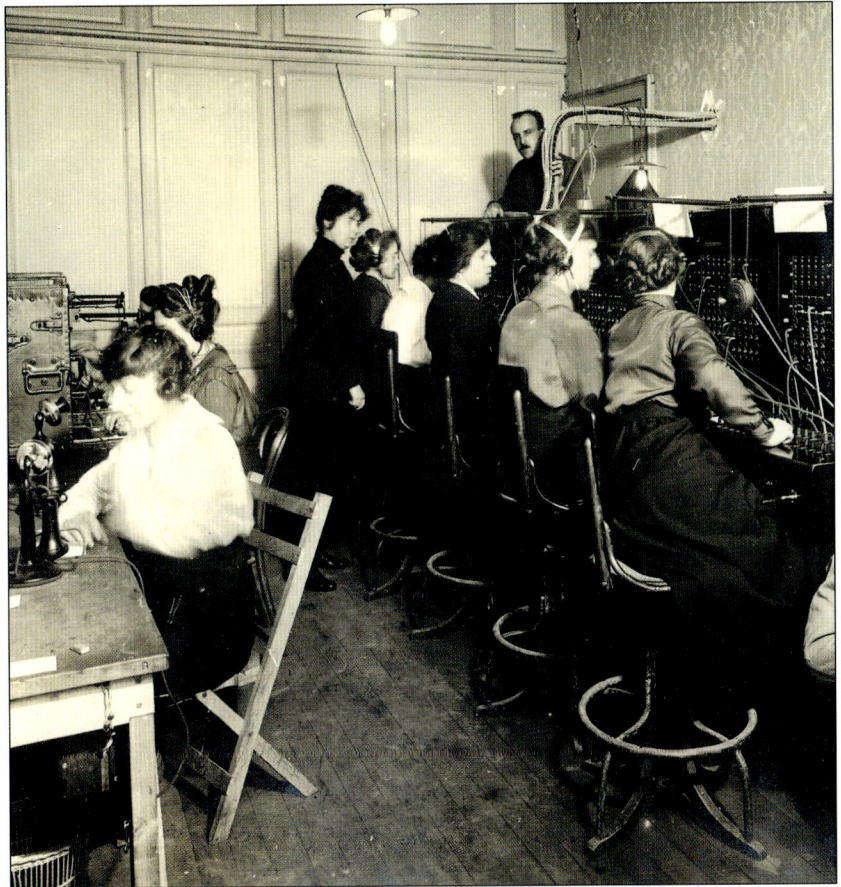

Third Party Headquaters at Toul, portable office.

Seated at desk:
Moussu, Eglantine
Gavard, Louisette

Standing:
Hunter, Elsie G.

At switchboard:
Hawkins, Alma
Anderson, Charlotte
White, Ethelyn
Macauley, Elizabeth
Van Gastel, Melanie

At left, Second Unit.
Seated:
  Perreten, Helene
  Heynen, Martina
  Libert, Marthe
  Mitchell, Kathleen

Standing:
  Ingram, Mrs. Denise
  Ponsolle, Marie
  Keyser, Ethel
  Keyser, Florence
  Taylor, Marion
  Gelinas, Lydia Warren

Below, Third Unit telephone operators. (List not in order and incomplete.)
Seated:
  Flood, Marie
  Bousquet, Marie (Johnson)
  Des Jardins, Frances
  Hoppock, Adele (Mills) 4th
  Robey, Elizabeth
  Snow, Nellie
  Beraud, Louise M.
  Belanger, Marie
  Gauthier, Yvonne
  Grand-Maitre, Blanche B.
  Sage, Dorothy
  Verkler, Lillian A.
  De Jersey, Lucile
  Verkler, Bertha J.

Standing:
  McMullen, Maude
  Blanc, Michele
  Jones, Janet
  Wuillemier, Berthe
  Milner, Marguerite (deceased)
  Kervin, Hope
  Hutchens, Margaret
  Hunt, Berthe
  Racicot, Eugenie
  Comeleach, Suzanne
  Beraud, Suzanne (deceased)
  Gavard, Louisette

Telephone Operators of the A.E.F.

NAME	HOME ADDRESS	UNIT NUMBER
Aarrents, Albertine	Lacken, Brussels	Second
Adam, Melina J.	Swansea, Mass.	First
Anderson, Charlotte	Berkeley, Calif.	Fourth
Anderson, Margaret	Creskhill, N.J.	Second
Arland, Berthe	Brooklyn, N.Y.	Fourth
Armand, Louise L.	New York, N. Y.	Fourth
Armanet, Irma	San Mateo, Calif.	Fourth
Audet, I. Eulalie	Jamaica Plain, Mass.	First
Banker, Grace D,	Passaic, N.J.	First
Barbour, Louise	Brooklyn, N. Y.	Fifth
Barrere, Julie St.	Mount Vernon, N. Y.	Second
Bartlett, Corah H.	Hillsdale, Mich.	Sixth
Batta, Madeline	New York, N.Y.	Fourth
Belanger, Marie B.	Rochester, N.Y.	Third
Belhumeur, Albertine M.	Providence, R. I.	Fourth
Beraud, Louise J.	Dallas, Texas	Fourth
Beraud, Suzanne M.	West Hoboken, N.J.	Third
Beraud, Louise Marie	West Hoboken, N.J.	Third
Bickford, Christine V.	Rockford, Maine.	Fifth
Bigou, Lucienne	New York, N, Y.	Fourth
Bixty, Helen	Indianapolis, Ind.	Sixth
Black, Sada Freelove	Yuma, Colo.	Fifth
Blanc, Michele F.	Thonon, Ht. Savoir, France	Third
Blazina, Agnes E.	Harrison, N. Y.	Fifth
Bleyeres, Marguerite S.	New York, N. Y.	Second
Boehrer, Georgette	Reading, Pa.	Fourth
Borresen, Alice J.	Pine Bluff, Ark.	Fourth
Boucher, Ruth	San Francisco, Calif.	Sixth
Bouchet, Jeanne	San Francisco, Calif.	First
Bourneuf, Beatrice P.	Haverhill, Mass.	Fourth
Bousquet, Marie Louise	San Francisco, Calif.	Third
Broderick, Marisu B.	Detroit, Mich.	Sixth
Brousseau, Emma Marie	Brockton, Mass.	Second
Brown, Eleanor, A.	Astoria, Oregon	Fourth
Brown, Jessie D.	Los Angeles, Calif.	Fifth
Browne, Elizabeth A.	San Antonio, Texas.	Sixth
Burke, Agnes G	Detroit, Mich.	Fourth
Campbell, Anna Marie	Emmett, Idaho	Sixth
Capistran, Aleria	North Yakima, Washington	First
Carey, Helen Hunt	Chicago, Ill.	Fifth
Caron, Estella I,	Brockton, Mass.	First
Carrel, Bertha A.	Ft. Wayne, Ind.	Second
Carrel, Martha L.	Ft. Wayne, Ind.	Second
Carroul, Marthe M.	San Francisco, Calif.	Fourth
Chaix, Louise	Gap, Haute Alps, France	Fourth
Chance, Anita Lenora	Denver, Colo.	Fifth
Chenot, Marguerite	Manhattan, N. Y.	Fourth
Coheleach, Suzanne	Astoria, L.I., N.Y.	Third
Conroy, Jane E.	Wilkes-Barre, Pa.	Sixth
Cook, Helen	Cleveland, Ohio	Fifth
Cooper, E. Tillears	San Diego, Calif.	Fourth
Courtial, Juliette	Los Angeles, Calif.	Fourth
Couture, Eugenia J.	Lynn, Mass.	Fourth
Couturier, Ruth	Westbrook, Maine	Fourth
Cunningham, Jean	Montreal, Canada	First
Davis, Anna Josephine	New Orleans, La.	First
de Jersey, Lucile	Covina, Calif.	Third
de Jersey, Miriam	Covina, Calif.	Third
de Montauzan, Rosemary	Lyon, France	Sixth
Des Jardins, Frances	Ontario, Canada	Third
Disbrowe, Ellen	Tacoma, Washington	Sixth
Dodson, Edith	Brussels	Fifth
Douchette, Bernadette G.	Alberta, Canada	Sixth
Dupuis, Cordelia	Rolla, N. D.	First
Egan, Merle	Helena, Mont.	Fifth
Erickson, Lydia	Chicago, Ill.	Sixth
Essirard, Louise M.J.	Paris, France	Second
Fairbrother, Sarah	Ellsworth, Maine	Fifth
Fecteau, Sara A.C.M.	Wilder, Vermont	First
Finch, Norma Gail	Hillsdale, Mich.	Fifth
Flood, Maria Dunne	Chicago, Ill.	Third

Name	Location	Class
Ford, Marie L.	Worcester, Mass.	First
Fox, Anne C.	Rochester, N. Y.	Second
Francfort, Beatrice	New York, N. Y.	Fourth
Fresnel, Esther V.	Yonkers, N. Y.	First
Gagnon, Marie A.	Grafton, N.D.	First
Ganley, Mae Alice	Brockton, Mass.	Sixth
Gauthier, Yvonne M.	Lowell, Mass.	Third
Gavard, Louisette	Newark, N.J.	Third
Gelinas, Lydia C.	Nashua, N.H.	Second
Gifford, Irene Alice	New Bedford, Mass,	Fifth
Goldman, Minnie H.	Chicago, Ill.	Sixth
Gordon, Louise	Lichfield, Mich.	Sixth
Grand-Maitre, Blanche B.	Minneapoliis, Minn.	Third
Greenlund, Helma	Riverside, Calif.	Sixth
Gridley, Laura	Los Angeles, Calif.	Fifth
Grimeke, Celia A.	Butte, Mont.	Sixth
Gyss, Charlotte	Yonkers, N.Y.	First
Hagan, Delta E.	Monticello, Minn.	Sixth
Hamel, Vivienne	Nashua, N.H.	Fourth
Hammond, Hazel, M.	Nampa, Idaho.	Sixth
Hardy, Winifred	Montreal, Canada	First
Hawkins, Alma H.	Bellingham, Wash.	Fourth
Hayes, Helen May	Lincoln, Mass.	Fifth
Henshaw, Martha May	Worcester, Mass.	Fifth
Henton, Darnaby	Versailles, Kentucky	Second
Heymen, Martina	Green Bay, Wis.	Second
Hill, Helen E.	New Haven, Conn.	Fourth
Honey, Faye Ruth	Detroit, Mich.	Fifth
Hoppock, Adele L.	North Seattle, Wash.	Third
Hoppock, Eleanor	North Seattle, Wash.	Fourth
Horsman, Elizabeth	Chicago, Ill.	Sixth
Houley, Agnes T.	Boston, Mass.	Sixth
Hunt, Berthe M.	Berkeley, Calif.	Third
Hunter, Elizabeth G.	Medford, Mass.	First
Hutchins, Margaret G.	New York, N.Y.	Third
Hyatt, Kathleen M.	Wenatchee, Wash.	Fourth
Ingram, Mrs. Denise	New York, N. Y.	Second
Jackson, Anallen	San Francisco, Calif.	Second
Johnson, Maude Edna	San Francisco, Calif.	Sixth
Jones, Janet R.	Newark, Ohio	Third
Joure, Oleda Ruth	Marine City, Mich.	Sixth
Keyser, Ethel	Seattle, Wash.	Second
Keyser, Florence F.	Seattle, Wash.	Second
Keeping, Ruth	Revere, Mass.	Fifth
Kervin, Margaret Hope	Reno, Nevada	Third
Kinney, Anna Adline	Muscatine, Iowa	Fifth
Knall, Grace Bernice	Los Angeles, Calif.	Fifth
Laborde, M. Anna	San Francisco, Calif.	Second
Lamontagne, Germaine	Montreal, Quebec	Fourth
Lamoureux, Leontine M.	Lowell, Mass.	First
Laney, Frances Willard	Lamona, Wash.	Sixth
Lang, Jane L.	Spokane, Wash.	Fourth
Lange, Marie	Colma, Calif .	Fourth
Langelier, Rose J.	Lynn, Mass.	First
Lanz, Ida B.	Brooklyn, N. Y.	Fourth
Lapp, Mabel C.	Evanston, Ill.	Sixth
La Riviere, Evelyn G.	Spencer, Mass.	Fourth
Lassalle, Marie A.	San Francisco, Calif.	Fourth
Le Blanc, Marie S. A.	Berlin, N.H.	First
Le Breton, Louise	Berkeley, Calif.	First
Le Breton, Ramonde	Berkeley, Calif.	First
Legallet, Jeanne	Oakland, Calif.	Fourth
Leguia, Celestine	Readville, Mass.	Fourth
Lemaire, Marie Jennie	San Mateo, Calif.	Second
Le Roux, Edmee	Washington, D.C.	Fourth
Levy, Hortense	Philadelphia, Pa.	Sixth
Lewis, Mildred	Bridgeport, Conn,	Fifth
Libert, Marthe M.	Brussels	Second
Lucier, Amelia C.	Nashua, N. H.	Fourth
Lumpert, Emelia C.	Salt Lake City, Utah	Fourth
Macauley, Elizabeth	New York, N. Y.	Fifth
Macdonald, Mary Isabel	Hartford, Conn.	Sixth
Maclin, Louise	New York, N. Y.	Fourth
Mahoney, Marguerite	San Francisco, Calif.	Fifth
Marsh, Geneva M.	Omaha, Neb.	Fourth
Marshall, Mary	Salt Lake City, Utah	Fourth

Name	Location	Session
Martin, Marguerite	San Mateo, Calif.	Fourth
Martin, Mellicent	Chicago, Ill.	Second
Messelin, Renee	San Francisco, Calif.	First
Milner, Marguerite H.	Berkeley, Calif.	Third
Mitchell, Abbie E.	Thomaston, Maine	Sixth
Mitchell, Kathleen	Denver, Colo.	Second
Moussu, Eglantine	Pendleton, Oregon	Fourth
Munoz, Lalla R.	Oakland, Calif.	Fourth
Munro, Eileen	Plattsburg, N. Y.	Fourth
McDermott, Mrs. Pauline	Brooklyn, N. Y.	Second
Mc Donnell, Pauline J.	San Francisco, Calif.	Fourth
Mc Intyre, Mrs. M.A.	New York, N. Y.	Second
Mc Killop, Marjorie L.	Silverdale, Wash.	Fourth
Mc Mullen, A. Maude	Fitchburg, Mass.	Third
Nadeau, Minerva G.	Boston, Mass.	First
Naismith, Helen A.	Los Angeles, Calif.	First
Noble, Lillie F.	Los Angeles, Calif.	Fourth
O'Brien, Florence	New York, N.Y.	Fifth
Olker, Margaret G.	Duluth, Minn.	Sixth
Orb, Helen, R.	Chicago, Ill.	Second
O'Rourke, Mary C.	New York, N.Y.	Fourth
Ostrander, Anna May	Los Angeles, Calif.	Sixth
Paine, Frances Bigelow	Bronxville, N.Y.	First
Palmer, Drucilla	Chicago, Ill.	Second
Pechin, Laurence H,	San Francisco, Calif.	Second
Perreten, F. Helene	New York, N.Y.	Second
Peyron, Leonie C.	Los Angeles, Calif.	Fourth
Plamondon, Bertha	San Francisco, Calif.	First
Ponsolle, Marie	Paris, France	Second
Prevot, Suzanne	New York, N.Y.	First
Racicot, Eugenie	Lowell, Mass.	Third
Raymond, Alice	Montreal, Canada	Fourth
Richards, Minnie R.	Van Buren, Maine	First
Rieder, Camille Fanny	New York, N.Y,	Fourth
Riendau, Emma	Providence, Mass.	Fourth
Robb, Ena	New York, N.Y.	Fifth
Robey, Elizabeth R.	Meriden, Conn.	Third
Robinson, Katherine H.	New York, N.Y.	Second
Ruffe, Louise	Sailiel Salat, Hte Garonne, France.	Fourth
Russel, Estella	Melrose, Minn.	Sixth
Sage, Dorothy Lewis	Evenston, Ill.	Third
Schaerr, Georgette	Omaha, Neb.	First
Sealey, Mary Ellen	Brookline, Mass.	Fifth
Shaw M. Olive	Boston, Mass.	Second
Sherin, Annie Frances	Somerville, Mass.	Fifth
Shovar, Elizabeth M.	Detroit, Mich.	Fifth
Sjostrom, Vera	Chicago, Ill.	Fifth
Snow, Nellie F.	Lowell, Mass.	Third
Steele, Mary A.	Portland, Maine	Sixth
Story, Mary Caroline	Halifax, N. S., Canada	Sixth
Summers, Doris E.	Seattle, Wash.	Fourth
Swan, Marion Campbell	Fall River, Mass.	Sixth
Swanson, Anna Maria	Douglas, Wyoming	Sixth
Taylor, Marion A.	Staten Island, N.Y.	Second
Theriault, Agnes Mary	Presque Isle, Maine	First
Thomas, Evelyn	Chicago, Ill.	Second
Thomas, Marjorie	Chicago, Ill.	Second
Thahan, Ida	Central Falls, R.I.	Fourth
Turner, Ellen M.	Seattle, Wash.	Fourth
Van Balkom, Fernande J.	Toronto. Ontario	First
Van Brunt, Hildegarde	Alameda, Calif.	Second
Van Gastel, Melanie, M.	Berkeley, Calif.	Fourth
Vannier, Mary S.	Deer Lodge, Mont.	Fourth
Verkler, Bertha J.	Chicago, Ill.	Third
Verkler, Lillian R.	Chicago, Ill.	Third
Viau, Stella M.	Fitchburg, Mass.	Fourth
Villiers, Isabelle	Reading, Mass.	Second
Ward, Alice Voronica	Montreal, Canada	First
White, Ethelyn	New York, N.Y.	Second
Wilcox, Louise Margaret	Detroit, Mich.	Fifth
Whitney, Clara	Butler, Pa.	First
Wilkins, Nell Suzan	Fremont, Neb.	Fifth
Wolloff, Elsie L.	Jamaica Plains, Mass.	Sixth
Wuilleumier, Berthe	St. Ymier, Switzerland	Third
Young, Jennie R.	Seattle, Wash.	Fourth

Index

A

Adams, Charity, Major, p. 347p
Adler, Larry, p. 44
Africa, p. 314
Air Force Aid Society, p. 450p
Air Medal, p. 314
Air Offensive over Europe, p. 309
Air Transport Auxiliary, (ATA), British, p. 155
Alaska, pp. 69, 76, 109, 121
Alert, The, p. 92
Algiers, p. 308
Alhambra Airport, p. 295
Allied Expeditionary Forces (AEF), pp. 56, 427
America, pp. 24, 39, 87
American Committee Relief in Near East, p. 451p
American Detachment, the, p. 23
American Forces Korea Network, p. 283p
American Forces Network Europe, p. 283p
American Friends Service Committee, pp. 451p-454p
American Friends of Yugoslavia, p. 37
American Red Cross, Army Rest Center, American Red Cross Club, Rome, p. 455p
American Telephone and Telegraph Company, p. 56
Ames, Winthrop, p. 426
Amico, p. 211
Anderson Air Activities, p. 149p
Andrews Sisters, the, p. 39
Anniston Ordnance Depot, p. 270p
Armistice, the, p. 57
Army Air Corps, Army Air Forces, Air Technical Service Command, p. 162
    Air Transport Command (ATC), pp. 149, p. 157, 159, 161-162, 167, 169p, 170, 171-172, 214p, 313 & p
    ATC Flight Traffic Technician's School, p. 313
    Eighth Air Force, p. 308
    Ferrying Command (ACFC), pp. 157, 169p, 295
    Ferrying Division (FERD), p. 157, 172
    First Air Force, p. 162
    Flying Training Detachment (AAFFTD), p. 205
    Fourth Air Force, p. 162
    Headquarters, pp. 161, 202
    Proving Ground Command, p. 162
    Second Air Force, p. 162
    Supply Division, p. 167
    Technical Training Command, pp. 144-145p, 161
    Third Air Force, p. 188
    Troop Carrier Command, p. 162
    Weather Wing, p. 162
Arnold, Henry Harley "Hap," General, Chief of the Army Air Forces, pp. 155-157, 160, 161-163p, 173, 202
Arrowsmith, Mary, pp. 428, 438p, 440p
Arthur, Mrs. Robert, p. 93
Associated Press, the, p. 275p
Astor, Mrs. Vincent, p. 424
Atherton, Gertrude, p. 283
Aumont, Jean-Pierre, p. 39
Australia, The, p 23
Austria, p. 427
Avenger Field, pp. 161, 190, 206, 217p
Aviation Enterprises, Ltd., pp. 206p, 219p

B

Bahamas, the, p. 139
Bailey, Mildred, General, pp. 405p, 409p, 412
Bang's disease, see Evans, Alice
Barnes, Florence "Pancho," aviatrix, p. 293
"Barretts of Wimpole Street," the (B.O.W.S.), pp. 49-50
Bastian Bros. Company, p. 41
Battle of Britain, the, p. 155
Bausch and Lomb Optical Company, p. 199
Beaverbrook, Lord, p. 155
Belgium, p. 446
Bendix Race, p. 155
Bengston, Ida, bacteriologist, p. 81
Benny, Jack, p. 44
Benny, Mrs. Jack, p. 93

529

Best & Company of New York, p. 439
Black, Winifred Sweet, p. 283
Blood and Fire New York No. 1, p. 23
Blue Bell Hat Co., Inc., p. 343p
Bocher, Main Rousseau, see "Mainbocher"
Bolling Air Force Base, pp. 225-226p
Bolling Field, DC, pp. 182, 211
"Bomberettes," p. 457p
Bond Center, p. 77p
Booth, Ballington, Commissioner, p. 26
Booth, Catherine, pp. 24,
Booth, Evangeline Cory, pp. 24, 26, 30, 32, 36
Booth, Maud, p. 26
Booth, William, pp. 23, 24,
Booth-Tucker, Emma, Consul, p. 26
"Boots," the airborne squirrel, p. 370
Boston Intercity Airlines, p. 156
Botulism bacillus, see Bengston, Ida
Bourke-White, Margaret, pp. 283, 285p
Boyer, Mrs. Charles, pp. 92- 93
Bronx War Service, pp. 457p-458p
Brook, Mrs. Clive, p. 92
Brooklyn No. 1, p. 23
Bronze Star, pp. 308, 321
Brown, Emma J., Captain, p. 26
Brown, Joe E., p. 39
Brucellosis, see Evans, Alice
Brunmark, Mrs. Walter J., p. 93
Buddy Poppy, p. 103p
Bulgaria, p. 427

C
C-9, p. 228
C-47, p. 370
C-123, p. 228
C-130, p. 228
Canada, p. 155
California, pp. 145p, 288, 310
   "Ft. Hollywood," p. 92
   Hollywood, pp 299, 301p
   Long Beach, pp. 160, 214, 295
   Los Angeles, pp. 144, 296, 462p, 474p
   Wasco, p. 314
   San Francisco, pp. 10, 46, 151, 297
Cam Ranh Bay Airbase, p. 228
Camel Cap and Cloth Belt Company, p. 100p
Camp Davis, North Carolina, p. 188p
Camp Pontanezen, France, p. 432p

Carlson's of Wilmington, pp. 165-167
Carnegie, Hattie, pp. 363, 366p, 372-373p, 380p, 384-385, 389, 401p-402p
Carroll, Madeline, p. 49p
Carter Memorial Laboratory, p. 82
Central Europe, p. 309
Chaffee, John H., Secretary of the Navy, p. 112
Champlin, Jane, first WAFS casualty, p. 162
Chapelle, Dickey, p. 273p
Chase, Edna Woolman, p. 371
"Chevronettes," pp. 461p-463p
Christy, Howard Chandler, p. 475p
Civil Aeronautics Authority (CAA), p. 160
Civil Air Patrol (CAP), pp. 160, 295
Clark, Deana, p. 173p
Clark, Mark, General, p. 49
Clarke, Mary E., Brigadier General, p. 412
Clemenceau, French Prime Minister, p. 57
Cleveland Air Races, p. 293p
Clyde, Mrs. William M., p. 93
Cochran, Jacqueline, pp. 151, 154-155, 157, 158-163p, 173-174, 176, 183, 187-189, 191, 197, 203p, 207, 210, 212
Cohen, George M., p. 426
Colbert, Claudette, pp. 93, 94
Colbert, L.C., Admiral, pp. 209-211p
Coleman, Bessie, pp. 151, 153
Collier Trophy, p. 155
Congress, p. 164, 366
   Public Law 554-77th Congress, p. 305
Consolidated Aircraft Corporation, p. 290p
Cooper, Mrs. Gary, p. 93
Cornell, Katherine, p. 48p
Coty, Inc., p. 19
Cowan, Ruth, pp. 273p-274p
Craddock Uniforms of Kansas City, p. 100p
Crandall, Marian, YMCA,
   Death of in France, p. 429
Crillon Exchange, p. 57
Croix de Guerre, pp. 428, 438p
Cuba, p. 139
Czechoslovakia, p. 446

D
Da Nang Airbase, p. 228
Danforth, Edward, Lieutenant General, p. 374p
Daniels, Mrs. Josephus, p. 447p

Davis, Bette, p. 48
Davis, Tobe Coller, p. 371
DDT (dichloro-diphenyl-tricholoroethane), p. 82
Debenhams, Ltd., p. 350, 353
Delano, Jane, p. 98
Delaware, p. 159
    Wilmington, pp. 77, 158, 165
Denver Ordnance Plant, p. 269
Deuell, Peggy Hull, pp. 272p, 283
Devers, Jacob L., Lieutenant General, p. 274
Dietrich, Marlene, pp. 39-41p, 43p, 48
Dietsch, Wersba & Cobbola, Inc., pp. 191
Disney, Walt, pp. 204, 206
Distinguished Service Medal, pp. 24, 36, 58, 107-108, 163, 391p
Dobbs Hats, pp. 335, 344,
"Doodle Bug," p. 57
Dorr, Rheta, p. 283
Dotty, Medallion, p. 283
Duncan Field, Texas, p. 144p
Dunhill Hat Corporation, p. 377

E
802 Pioneer Infantry, p. 427
814th Army Air Base Unit, p. 368p
"Eagle Hut," p. 429
Earhart, Amelia, pp. 151, 153
"Early Birds," p. 151
Egypt, p. 308
Eisenhower, Dwight David, General of the Army, pp. 306, 308, 314, 351, 381
    Forward Headquarters, p. 309
El Alamein Reunion, p. 40
Ellington Field, pp. 161, 172 &p, 206
Ely, Gertrude, pp. 428, 438, 440p
England, pp. 23-24, 156-157, 308, 310, 314, 327, 347p, 350, 353, 362p
    London, pp. 40, 274p, 309-310, 429
Esso, pp. 462p-463p
European Theater of Operations (ETO), pp. 274, 308, 314, 350
Evans, Alice, p. 81
Evening Standard, the (UK), p. 275p

F
1st Division, pp. 433p, 438p
14th Army Band, p. 366
41st Division, p. 29
42nd WAAC Post Headquarters Company, p. 315
44th Signal Battalion, p. 315
Fairbanks, Mrs. Douglas, Sr., p. 92
Fairfax Field, Kansas, p. 212
Fèdèration Aeronautique Internationale, p. 151
Fifenella, pp. 193 & p, 194p, 195p, 200, 204, 205 & p, 206
Fifth Army, pp. 49, 50
First Airborne Army, p. 366
First Army, pp. 57, 64, 372, 456p
Florida, p. 153
    Daytona Beach, p. 315, 455p
    Hollywood, p. 139
    Orlando, p. 112
    Palm Beach, p. 65
    West Palm Beach, p. 313
Forrestal, Mrs. James V., p. 112
Fort Benning, Georgia, p. 333p, 367, 371p
    Infantry School, p. 333p
    Parachute School, p. 367 & p, 370p
Fort Des Moines, Iowa, pp. 306-307p, 315, 316, 326p, 335p, 359p
Fort Dix, New Jersey, p. 315
Fort Jackson, South Carolina, p. 375p
Fort Lee, Virginia, p. 366
Ft. MacArthur, pp. 92, 95
Fort McClellan, Alabama, p. 366
Fort George G. Meade, p. 478p
Fourragere,
    Belgian, p. 238
    French, p. 238
    Netherlands, the, p. 238 & p
Le Foyers du Soldat, Union Franco-Américaines, pp. 428 & p. 429
France, pp. 34, 56, 61, 63-64, 151, 271, 314, 424-425, 427-428, 430p, 435p, 439, 444, 446, 477
    Aix-Les-Bains, p. 443p
    Ardennes, the, p. 309
    Argonne, p. 425
    Bordeaux, p. 27
    Brest, pp. 424, 426
    Chaumont, p. 448
    Evron, p. 477p
    Gièvres, p. 427
    Labouheyre, p. 271
    Le Belle Epegine, p. 56
    Normandy, p. 309
        Invasion of, p. 477p
    Paris, pp. 27, 56, 353, 426, 444p, 446, 477

Ste. Menehould, p. 429
St. Mihiel, p. 446
Tours, pp. 57, 60, 425
Fredericks, John, p. 180
Frothingham, Helen Losanitch, pp. 37-38
Frothingham, John Whipple, Major, ARC, p. 37

G

Galloway, Irene O., Colonel, p. 412
Garfield Custom Tailoring Company, p. 100p
Garfield, John, p. 48
"general's pants," p. 172
George, Harold, General, pp. 157, 160, 169
Georgia,
    Atlanta, p. 10
Germany, pp. 39, 87, 309, 427
    Berlin, p. 275p, 287p
    Coblenz, p. 59
    Frankfurt, p. 82p
    Rhineland, the, p. 309
Gestapo (Geheime Staatspolizei), p. 477p
Gillies, Betty Huyler, pp. 165-167
Gimbels, pp. 128
Girl Scouts of America, pp. 65, 167
"Glamour Buttons," p. 171
Goetz, Mrs. William, p. 93
Gopher Ordnance Works, p. 270p
Gorman, Emily C., Colonel, p. 412
Grand Army of the Republic, p. 104
Grand Central Station, p. 56
Great Depression, the, p. 153
Guardsman, the, p. 52
Gulf Coast Training Center, p. 206
Gulic, Miss Francis,
    Cited for service with the 1st Division, p. 433p
Gunter Air Force Base, Alabama, p. 253p

H

Hall, Mrs. Alexander, p. 93
Hallaren, Mary A., Colonel, p. 412
"Hallelujah Seven," p. 23
Hamilton Tailoring Company, the, p. 172
Hargrove, Rosette, p. 275p
Harper's Bazaar, p. 372
Harriman, Kathleen, p. 2
Haviland, Ruth, 151
Hawaii, pp. 47, 109
    Honolulu, p. 45

Hawthorne Club, the, p. 292p
Hays, Anna Mae, Brigadier General, pp. 382p, 389p-390p, 396p
Hepburn, Katherine, p. 288
Higgins, Marguerite, p. 285p
"Hobby Hat," pp. 335, 343p-344p, 363
Hobby, Oveta Culp, Colonel, pp. 81, 91, 157-158, 162, 305, 306p, 308, 314-316, 320p, 341 & p, 360, 364, 412
Hoefly, E. Ann, Brigadier General, pp. 227, 261
Hoisington, Elizabeth, Brigadier General, pp. 383p, 390p-391p, 412
Hollandia, p. 308
Hollywood Canteen, the, p. 48
Holm, Jeanne M., General, pp. 244p, 246p
Holston Ordnance Works, p. 268p
"Honey Bee Club," pp. 426-427
Hope, Bob, p. 39
"Hostess House," p. 446
Hotel Petrograd, p. 446
House Committee on the Civil Service, p. 162
Howard Hughes Airport, pp. 159-160
Hull, Peggy, see "Peggy Hull Deuell"
Hunt, Marsha, p. 296
Hunter College, pp. 65, 128
Huntsville Arsenal, p. 269p
"Hump," the, p. 314

I

Illinois, p. 304
    Alsip, p. 153
    Chicago, pp. 101p, 128, 264, 292p
    Des Moines, p. 324p
    Roseland, p. 101p
India, pp. 308, 314
Iowa Ordnance Plant, p. 269p
Iowa State Teacher's College, p. 65
Irwin, Virginia, p. 275p
Italy, pp. 314, 429-430p, 446
    Bologna, p. 429
    Fiume, p. 429
    Florence, p. 429
    Foggia, p. 429
    Genoa, p. 429
    Trenso, p. 429
    Milan, p. 429
    Rome, pp. 429, 440p
    Treviso, p. 429
    Trieste, p. 429
    Venice, p. 429

J
Japan,
    Hiroshima, p. 314
    Nagasaki, p. 314
Jayco (J.J. Sweeny Co.), p. 216p
Josten, pp. 211p, 212p

K
"Kansas City Canteen," p. 466p
Kantor, M.G., New York, pp. 401p-402p
Kaye, Danny, p. 39
Keystone Ordnance Works, p. 269p
King, Murial, p. 288
Kirkpatrick, Helen, pp. 274p, 283
Kirtland, Helen Johns, p. 283
Klumpke-Roberts, Mrs. D, p. 151
Knopf, Mrs. Edwin H., p. 93
Knox, Betty, p. 275p
Knox Hats, (Knox Division, Hat Corporation of America), pp. 43, 180, 182p, 200 & p, 335, 344
Koret, Richard, Inc., p. 360
Kovach, Ethel, Colonel, p. 261
Koverman, Ida R., p. 93
Korea, pp. 50, 285
Korean War, the, pp. 37, 65, 112, 227, 282p, 315, 366

L
Lackland Air Force Base, pp. 225-226, 232 & p
LaGuardia, Fiorello, pp. 19, 157
LaMarr, Hedy, p. 39
Lambert, Eleanor, p. 371
Lame, Ellen, p. 283
Lamour, Dorothy, p. 462p
Lane, Arthur Bliss, US Ambassador to Columbia, p. 335p
Langley Air Force Base, Virginia, p. 249p
Law, Ruth, p. 151
Lawrence, Mrs. Jock, p. 93
Lawson Field, p. 370
Lee, Anna, p. 44
Legion of Honor, France, p. 321p
Legion of Merit, pp. 309, 314
LeMay, Curtis, General, pp. 226-227
Lesco Limited, p. 361
Leslie's Weekly, p. 151
Ley, Frances, Colonel, p. 261
Leyte, p. 308
Liberty Field, Camp Stewart, Georgia, p. 208p
Life Magazine, pp. 51, 281p, 464
Life Saving Girl Guard, p. 27

Lineas Aereas Mexicanas, S.A., p. 176
Link trainer, pp. 77p, 137
Littlejohn, R.M., General, p. 353
Lloyd George, David, British Prime Minister, p. 57
London Sales Store, p. 353
Long, Westray Battle Boyce, Colonel, pp. 365, 412
Lord & Taylor of Manhattan, pp. 315, 372
Losanitch, Sima, p. 37
"Lost Class," the, p. 161
Louise, Anita, p. 93
Love, Bessie, p. 484p
Love, Nancy Harkness, pp. 151, 155-165, 166 & p-167
Love, Robert, p. 156
Lovette, Robert A., Assistant Secretary of War for Air, p. 155
Lowey, Raymond, p. 170
Lowry Field, Colorado, pp. 146-147p

M
Maine,
    Bath, p. 308p
McAfee, Mildred H. Commander, pp. 107, 112-114
McIntire, Ross T., Vice Admiral (MC), Surgeon General of the Navy, p. 132
Macy's, p. 128
Mainbocher, pp. 112-113, 119, 131, 141,
Mangone, Philip, p. 316
Manhattan Company, the, p. 166
Manhattan Project, p. 314
Manilla, p. 308
Marcus, Stanley, p. 174
Marine Hospital Service, p. 81
Marshall, George C., General, pp. 173-174
Marshall Fields, p. 128
Maryland,
    Bainbridge, p 112
    Baltimore, pp. 10, 91, 99, 158
Massachusetts,
    Boston, pp. 10, 151
    Dorchester Bay, p. 151
    Northampton, pp. 66, 109
Massachusetts Women's Defense Corps, pp. 469-473
Mauthausen Concentration Camp, p. 477p
May, Geraldine P., Colonel, pp. 225, 260

Mayberry, Lynn, pp. 41p, 43p
Mayer, Mrs. Louis B., p. 93
Menjou, Mrs. Adolphe, p. 93
Meritorious Unit "Service Award, p. 314
Mexican Army, the, p. 167
Michigan,
    Detroit, p. 455p
Military Air Transport Service (MATS), pp. 231p, 233p
Miller, Lee, pp. 274p, 284p
Mines Field, California, p. 295
Minute Women, p. 474
Missouri Ordnance Works, p. 270p
Mitchell Field, New York, p. 161
"Mollie Pitcher Brigade," p. 476p
Monsanto Chemical, p. 291p
Morrison Field, Florida, p. 313 & p
Mydans, Shelley Smith, p. 281p

N

9th Bombardment Division, p. 309
93rd Evacuation Hospital, p. 394
903rd Aeromedical Evacuation Squadron, p. 256p
Napoleon, p. 425
National Security Act, p. 225
Naval Air Navigation School (NANS), pp. 139-140p
Naval Air Transport Service (NATS), p. 130p,
Naval Reserve Midshipman School, p. 66
Naval Training Center, p. 112
Navy Recruit Training Command (Women), p. 112
Nebraska,
    Lincoln, p. 435p
    Omaha, p. 10
New Calidonia, p. 308
New Guinea, p. 308
Newcastle Army Air Base, pp. 158-159, 165, 190
Newsweek, p. 315
New York Evening Mail & Evening Post, p. 283
New York Herald Tribune, p. 275p, 285p
New York Infirmary for Women and Children, p. 271
New York No. 1, p. 23
New York Times, p. 23
New York, pp. 180, 200, 315, 372, 447
    Bronx, the, p. 108
    Elmira, p. 297p
    Governors Island, p. 372

Manhattan Beach, p. 65
New York City, pp. 10, 19, 23, 37, 56, 172, 189, 191, 287
Rochester, p. 41
Newspaper Enterprise Association, p. 275p
Nichols, Ruth, pp. 151-152p
Nieman-Marcus, p. 174
Nilssen, Anna Q., p. 93
Ninth Service Command, p. 264
North Africa, pp. 306, 308
Northern France, p. 309

O

149th WAAC Headquarters, p. 308
1453rd Aeromedical Evacuation Squadron, p. 254p
Odlum, Floyd, pp. 155
Ohio, p. 414, 474
    Cleveland, pp. 10, 99
    Logan, p. 309
Ohio National Guard, p. 272p
Oklahoma, p. 493p
Oklahoma A&M University, p. 65
Oklahoma City Air Depot, p. 148p
Olds, Robert, General, pp. 156-159
Omlie, Phoebie Fairgrave, p. 154
Order of Military Medical Merit, p. 407p
Order of St. Sava, p. 37
Order of the White Eagle, p. 37
Orlando, Prime Minister of Italy, p. 57
OSS (Office of Strategic Services), pp, 309, 477p

P

Pacific Theater of Operations, p. 308
Palm Beach Biltmore Hotel, p. 66
"Panama Hattie," p. 364
Paris Peace Conference, p. 57
Parker, Frank, Brigadier General, p. 433p
Pemberton, Brock, p. 46
Pennsylvania, 363
    Lock Haven, p. 161
Perry, Miriam E., Colonel, p. 261
Pershing, General John J., pp. 27, 56-57, 59p, 63, 426, 428, 448
Persian Gulf Service Command, p. 43
Philadelphia Ordnance District Headquarters, pp. 262, 263p
Picken, Mary Brooks, pp. 371-372
Pickford, Mary, p. 92
"Pioneer 440," p. 306
Piper Cub, p. 161
"play factories," p. 426
Plaza Hotel, p. 494p

Poland, p. 446
Pons, Lily, p. 43p
Portage Ordnance Depot, p. 270p
Porter, "Amazing Grace" Cleveland, p. 440p
Potsdam Conference, p. 309
"Powder Puff Derby," p. 152p
Pratt, Mrs. Harold Irving, p. 447
Prince Alexis of Serbia, p. 37
Pueblo Ordnance Plant, p. 269p
Purple Heart, p. 308

Q
Queen Mother, p. 450p
Quimby, Harriet, pp. 151-153

R
Railton, George Scott, pp. 23-24
Randolph Field, Texas, p. 211
Rasmuson, Mary L.M., Colonel, p. 412
Ray-Ban goggles, p. 199
Raye, Martha, p. 39
Redstone Ordnance Plant, p. 269p
"Ripples," pp. 128-129
Roaring `Twenties, the, p. 153
Rockwell, Norman, p. 264
Rogers, Edith Nourse, Congresswoman, p. 64
Rogers, Ginger, p. 288
Rogers, Will, p. 152
Romulus Air Base, Michigan, p 178
Rooney, Mickey, p. 39
Roosevelt, Eleanor, p. 155
Roosevelt, Franklin Delano, President, pp. 154-155
Roosevelt, Mrs. Theodore, Jr., pp. 429-430
"Rosie the Riveter," p. 264 & p
Royal Air Force, p. 156
  Pilots, pp. 155, 204
Royal Serbian Army, p. 38
Rubenstein, Mrs. Arthur, p. 93
Rumania, p. 446
Rundstedt, Gerd von, *Generalfeldmarschall*, 309
Russell, Rosalind, p. 18
Russia, pp. 429, 446

S
2nd Army, pp. 29, 60
6th Ferrying Command, p. 214p
6th Ferrying Squadron, p. 160
7th M.A.S.H., p. 375
7th Pennsylvania, p. 23
7th Service Command, p. 324p
6888th Central Postal Directory Battalion, p. 347p
7239th WAF Squadron, p. 225p
7708th WAC Detachment, p. 309
SAC (Strategic Air Command), p. 227
Saint Geneviev of Paris, p. 314ps
Saks Fifth Avenue, p. 172
Salyna by St. George (caps), p. 102p
San Francisco Bulletin, the, p. 283
Santa Ana Army Air Base, p. 310
Schneider,Hannes, Sports Company, pp. 172, 189, 191
Scotland,
  Edinburgh, p. 429
Scott, Blanche, p. 151
"Season Skipper," p. 188p
Second Ferrying Group, p. 158
Secretary of War, p. 202 & p
Serbia, p. 37
Serbia House, p. 37
Seventh Day Adventist Medical Cadet Corps, p. 479p
SHAEF (Supreme Headquarters Allied Expeditionary Forces) Psychological Warfare Division, French Intelligence Section, p. 321p
Shane, C.B., Corporation, the, pp. 172, 188
"Shank's mare," p. 198
Shaver, Dorothy, p. 372
Shaw, Wini, p. 44
Shore, Dinah, p. 39
Siberia Expedition, the, p. 272p
"Silkworms," p. 137
"Slum Sisters," p. 26
Smith College, pp. 82, 109
Snow, Carmel, p. 372
Societe des 40 Hommes et 8 Chevaux, La, p. 99
Sorbonne, the, p. 64
South Carolina,
  Dillon, p. 371p
South Pacific, the, pp. 315, 383
Spaatz, Carl, "Tooey," General, p. 309
St. Andrew's Hut, p. 429
St. Louis Ordnance Plant, p. 269p
Stage Door Canteen, p. 46
Standard Oil Company, pp. 461p-462
Stanwyck, Barbara, pp. 92, 93
Star-Maid Dresses, pp. 189-190
Stars and Stripes, the, pp. 278p, 427
  Pacific, p. 279p
Staten Island Ferry, p. 171
Stetson Hat Company (also, "Stetson

535

Hats, Inc."), p. 335, 342p, 344
Stinson, Henry, Secretary of War, pp. 156, 159
Stinson, Katherine, pp. 151-152p
Stinson, Majory, p. 151
Stout Field, Indiana, p. 368p
Stratton, Dorothy C., Commander, USCGWR, p. 65
"Submarine Air Corps," p. 83
Sullivan, Margaret, p. 288
Summersby, Kaye, Captain, p. 351

T
3rd Army, pp. 30, 57, 59, 61
3rd Division, p. 427
26th Infantry Division, p. 28
29th General Hospital, p. 478p
33rd Ferrying Group Exchange, p. 212
251st Station Hospital, p. 383
302nd Transport Wing, p. 309
318th AAFFTD, pp. 186, 213p
319th AAFFTD, pp. 194, 206
332nd Infantry Regiment, p. 429
3341st Signal Service Battalion, p. 309
3741st WAF Training Squadron, p. 225
3742nd WAF Training Squadron, p. 232
Tannenbaum, M. Hats, p. 377
Tan Son Nhut Airbase, pp. 228, 256
Tet Offensive, the, p. 315
Texas, p. 291
    Atlanta, p. 151
    Austin, p. 52
    Corpus Christi, pp. 52, 53
    Dallas, pp. 10, 51, 174, 197
    Houston, pp. 160, 161, 172, 207
    San Antonio, pp. 10, 489p, 491p, 494p
    Sweetwater, pp. 161, 186
    Westbrook, p. 162
"Texas Escadrille," p. 151
Thadden, Louise, p. 151
Thailand, p. 228
Tighe, Dixie, p. 274p
Toll Emergency Exchange, p. 56
Tomara, Sonia, pp. 275p-276p
Treadwell, Sophie, p. 283
Trevor, Clare, p. 92
Trout, Bobbi, Captain, pp. 293p-294p
Truck Company D, 103d Ammunition Train, p. 428
Turkey, p. 427

U
"Urban's Turbans," p. 164
USAF Officer Candidate School, p. 226
USAF "Thunderbirds," p. 261p
US Coast Guard Academy, p. 66
US Naval Training School (WR), p. 108
United Airlines, p. 175
United Nations, p. 282p
United States Food Administration, p. 413
University of Wisconsin, p. 128
US Army,
    Advance Section, p. 425
    District of Paris, p. 425
    Services of Supply, p. 425
    Vietnam, p. 396
Utah Ordnance Plant, p. 267p

V
Valley Forge Military Academy, p. 363
Vandenberg, Hoyt, General, p. 228
"Vicky Victory," p. 16
Victory Belles, USO, p. 51
Victory Medal, p. 58
Vietnam, pp. 37, 228, 255, 393p, 397p
    DaNang, p. 273p
    Long Binh, p. 315
    Saigon, pp. 112, 228
Vietnam War, the, pp. 37, 112, 250p, 261p, 315
Villa, Pancho, p. 272p
Virginia,
    Hampton Roads, p. 91
    Newport News, p. 91
Vogue, pp. 283-284p, 371
Volk Brothers Company, p. 197
Volk, Harold, p. 197

W
WAF Officer Candidate School, p. 225
Wainright, John, General, p. 36
Waische, Russel R., Vice Admiral, Coast Guard Commandant, p. 65
Walker, Nancy, p. 39
War brides, p. 446
War Cry, The, pp. 24
War Work Council, pp. 425-426p
Warner, Dr. Estella Ford, p. 82
Washington, DC, pp. 71, 78, 81, 114p, 115, 131p, 155, 158, 174, 187, 226p, 333p, 423, 464, 493p

Washington Women's Air Meet, p. 152
Welsh, Mary, p. 274p
Western Electric, p. 292
Westmoreland, General, p. 390p
Whalen, Grover A., p. 19
War Crimes Group, p. 309
Ward-Stilton Company, p. 379
White, M.G., General, p. 187
Whitehead and Hoag, p. 34
Whiteman Air Force Base, p 252p
Wilbur, Dr. Kay Lyman, p. 78
Wilson, Woodrow, President, pp. 57, 413
Women of the Royal Air Force (WRAF), p. 226
Women's Armed Services Integration Act of 1948, pp. 141, 226
Women's Army Auxiliary Corps Bill, p. 305
Women's Army Corps Training Center and Officer Candidate School, p. 366
Women's Transcontinental Air Derby, p. 152
"Woofteddies," p. 159
Works Progress Administration (WPA), p. 154
Wright Field, Ohio, p. 198

Y

Yank Magazine, p. 279p
"Yankee Division," p. 28

Z

Zeller, Dorothy, Colonel, p. 261
Zeller, Marina, Colonel, p. 260
Zeller, Verna, Colonel, p. 227
"Yeomanette Battalion," p. 423p
"Zoot Suits," p. 191

Bibliography

Ageton, Arthur A., Commander, US Army. *The Naval Officer's Guide.* New York: Whittlesey House, McGraw-Hill Book Company, Inc. No date.

Aldebol, Lieutenant Colonel Anthony, USAF (Ret.). *Army Air Force and United States Air Force Medals, Ribbons, Badges and Insignia.* South Carolina: Fountain Inn: Medals of America Press, 1997.

Anderson, Isabel. *Zigzagging.* Cambridge, Massachusetts: Houghton Mifflin Company, 1918.

Anderson, Colonel Robert S., MC, USA, editor in chief and Colonel Harriet S. Lee, USA (ret.) and Lieutenant Colonel Myra L. McDaniel, USA (ret.), editors. *Army Medical Specialist Corps.* Washington, DC: Office of the Surgeon General, Department of the Army, 1968.

Andrews, Maxine and Bill Gilbert. *Over Here, Over There. USO Stars in World War II.* New York: Zebra Books, Kensington Publishing Corporation, 1993.

Angel, Joan, USNR. *Angel of the Navy: The Story of A WAVE.* New York: Hastings House, 1943.

Balty, Bernard C., con. ed., and Russ A. Pritchard, tech. ed. *D-Day: Operation Overlord. From the Landing at Normandy to the Liberation of Paris.* New York: Smithmark Publishers, Inc., 1993.

Booth, Evangeline and Grace Livingston Hill. *The War Romance of the Salvation Army.* Philadelphia, Pennsylvania: J.B. Lippincott Company, 1919.

Boyne, Walter J. *The Smithsonian Book of Flight.* New York: Orion Books, 1992.

Britton, Jack and George Washington, Jr. *Military Shoulder Patches of the United States Armed Forces.* Tulsa, Oklahoma: MCN Press, 1985.

Bureau of Medicine and Surgery, Navy Department. *Navy Nurse Corps Relative Rank and Uniform Regulations.* Washington, DC: United States Government Printing Office, 1943

Dr. Charlotte Calasibetta, Ph.D. *Fairchild's Dictionary of Fashion.* New York: Fairchild Publications, Inc., 1975.

Carson, Julia M.H. *Home Away from Home.* New York: Harper & Brothers, 1946.

Chesham, Sallie. *Born to Battle. The Salvation Army in America.* New York: Rand McNally & Company, 1965.

Christie, Jeanne Marie, *Perspectives: Doughnut Dollies.* Vietnam, October 1999.

Claghorn, Charles E. *Women Patriots of the American Revolution.* New York: Continuum Publishing Co., 1989.

Cochran, Jacqueline, with Floyd Odum as Wingman. *The Stars at Noon.* Boston & Toronto: Little, Brown and Company, 1954.

Coffey, Frank. *Fifty Years of the USO. Always Home.* Washington, DC: Brassey's (US), Inc., 1991.

Coffman, Edward M. *The War to End All Wars. The American Military Experience in World War I.* Madison, Wisconsin: The University of Wisconsin Press, 1986.

Cohen, Stan. *V for Victory. America's Home Front during World War II.* Missoula, Montana: Pictorial Histories Publishing Company, Inc., 1991.

Cooper, Page. *Navy Nurse.* New York: McGraw-Hill Book Company, Inc., 1946.

Cosner, Shaaron, *War Nurses.* New York: Walker and Company, 1988.

Craven, W. F. and J. L. Cate. *The Army Air Forces in World War II. Services Around*

the World, Volume VII. Chicago, Illinois: The University of Chicago Press, 1958.
Denney, Robert E. *Civil War Medicine. Care and Comfort of the Wounded.* New York: Sterling Publishing Company, Inc., 1994.
Department of the Navy, *The Story of You in Navy Blue,* 1943.
Department of the Navy. *White Task Force. The Story of the Nurse Corps of the United States Navy.* Washington, DC: US Navy, 1945.
DeWitt, Gill, Lieutenant, USN. *The First Navy Flight Nurse on a Pacific Battlefield.* Fredericksburg, Texas: The Admiral Nimitz Foundation, 1983.
Division of Public Affairs (CODE PAM). *Women Marines in the 1980's.* Headquarters, US Marine Corps, Revised October 1986.
Dupy, Ernest R. *Five Days to War, April 2-6, 1917.* Harrisburg, Pennsylvania: A Giniger Book published in association with Stackpole Books, 1967.
Edwards, William S. *A History of the United States Uniforms for the Sea Services.* Washington, DC: Non-published, 1980.
Emerson, William K. *Encyclopedia of US Army Insignia and Uniforms.* Norman, Oklahoma: The University of Oklahoma Press, 1996.
Feller, Carolyn M., Lieutenant Colonel, ANC, USAR and Constance J. Moore, Major, ANC, eds. *Highlights in the History of the Army Nurse Corps.* Washington, DC: US Army Center of Military History, 1996.
"Flying Our Wounded Veterans Home." *The National Geographic,* September 1945.
Fosdick, Raymond B., Chairman of the Commission on Training Camp Activities, War Department. *Report to the Secretary of War on the Activities of Welfare Organizations serving with the A.E.F.* Washington, DC: The War Department, 1919.
Frothingham, Helen Losanitch, and Matilda Spence Rowland, ed. *Mission for Serbia. Letters from America and Canada, 1915-1920.* New York: Walker and Company, 1970.
Gavin, Lettie. *American Women in World War I. They also Served.* Niwot, Colorado: The University Press of Colorado, 1997.
Gillmore, Margalo and Patricia Collinge. *The B.O.W.S.* New York: Harcourt, Brace and Company, 1945.
Granger, Byrd Howell. *On Final Approach. The Women Airforce Service Pilots of World War II.* Scottsdale, Arizona: Falconer Publishing, 1991.
Hall, Richard. *Patriots in Disguise. Women Warriors of the Civil War.* New York: Paragon House, 1993.
Harris, Frederick, Managing Editor. *Service with Fighting Men. An Account of the Work of the American Young Men's Christian Associations in the World War, Vols. I & II.* New York: Association Press, 1922.
Hart, Philip S. *Up in the Air. The Story of Bessie Coleman.* Minneapolis, Minnesota: Carolrhoda Books, Inc., 1996.
Hartwick, Ann M. Ritchie. *The Army Medical Specialist Corps, the 45th Anniversary.* Washington, DC: Center of Military History, United States Army, 1995.
Harries, Meirion & Susie. *The Last Days of Innocence. America at War, 1917-1918.* New York: Random House, 1997.
Harris, Mary Virginia, Lieutenant, USNR. *Guide Right. A Handbook for WAVES and SPARS.* New York: The Macmillan Company, 1944.
Harrison, Carter H., Captain, ARC. *With the American Red Cross in France, 1918-1919.* Published by Ralph Fletcher Seymour, 1947.
Headquarters, US Marine Corps. *Women Marines in the 1980s.* Division of Public Affairs (Code PAM), revised October 1986.
Hess, Fjeril. *WACS at Work. The Story of the "Three B's" of the AAF.* New York: The

Macmillan Company, 1945.

Hewitt, Linda L., Captain, USMCR. *Women Marines in World War I.* Washington, DC: History and Museums Division, Headquarters, US Marine Corps, 1974.

Hill, LTC Nellie M., ANC. *Chronology of Uniforms, US Army Nurse Corps.* Washington, DC: August, 1971, non-published.

The Historical Section, Pubic Information Division, US Coast Guard Headquarters. *The Coast Guard at War, Women's Reserve, XXII* A. Washington, DC: April 15, 1946.

Holm, Major Jeanne, USAF (ret.). *Women in the Military. An Unfinished Revolution.* Revised Edition. Novato, CA: The Presidio Press, 1992.

Huff, Russell J. *Wings of World War II.* Bradenton, FL: Sunshine Press, 1981.

Huff, Russel J. *A Salute to America Wings. A Complete Study of the Military Wings of America.* 1993.

Hunt, Marsha. *The Way We Wore. Styles of the 1930's and '40's and Our World Since Then.* Fallbrook, CA: Fallbrook Publishing, 1993.

Hunter, Ann Arnold. *A Century of Service. The Story of the DAR.* Washington, DC: National Society Daughter of the American Revolution, 1991.

Jones, Rufus M. *A Service of Love in Wartime. American Friends Relief Work in Europe, 1917-1919.* New York: The Macmillan Company, 1920.

Jopling, Lucy Wilson. *Warrior in White.* San Antonio, Texas: The Watercress Press, 1990.

Keil, Sally Van Wagenen. *Those Wonderful Women in the Their Flying Machines.* New York: Rawson, Wade Publishers, Inc., 1979.

Lewis, Kenneth, *Doughboy to GI. U.S. Army Clothing and Equipment 1900-1945.* England: Norman D. Landing Co., 1993.

Link, Mae Mills and Hubert A. Coleman. *Medical Support of the Army Air Force in World War II.* Washington, DC: Office of the Surgeon General, USAF, 1955.

Litoff, Judy Barrett and David C. Smith. *We're in this War, Too.* New York: Oxford University Press, 1994.

Littlejohn, Helen W., Public Affairs Officer, Managing Editor/Research. *Fitzsimons Army Medical Center. The Life and History, 1918-1996.* Aurora, CO: The Public Affairs Office, Fitzsimmons Army Medical Center, 1997.

Manning, Thomas, Command Historian. *History of the Air Training Command, 1943-1993.* Office of History and Research, Headquarters, Air Education and Training Command, Randolph Air Force Base, Texas, 1993.

Maurizi, Dennis. *Breaking Barriers—The Bessie Coleman Story.* Flight Journal, August 1998.

McIntosh, Elizabeth P. *Sisterhood of Spies. The Women of the OSS.* Annapolis, Maryland: Naval Institute Press, 1998.

McKinley, Edward H. *Marching to Glory. The History of the Salvation Army in the United States of America, 1880-1980.* New York: Harper & Row, Publishers, 1980.

Millard, Shirley. *I Saw Them Die.* New York: Harcourt, Brace and Company, 1936.

Minnich, Mike. "WAVES Air Navigators: Charting a New Course." *Aviation History,* January 1999.

Morden, Betty J. *The Women's Army Corps, 1945-1978.* Washington, DC: Center of Military History, United States Army, 1990.

National Society of The Colonial Dames of America. *Report of the Committee on Relics. Uniforms of Women worn During the War.* Washington, DC: NSCDA, 1922.

Navy, United States. *Naval and Maritime Chronology, 1961-1971.* Annapolis, Maryland: Naval Institute Press, 1961-1971.

Neal, Harry Edward. *The Hallelujah Army.* New York: Chilton Company, 1961.
Neprud, Robert E. *Flying Minute Men. The Story of the Civil Air Patrol.* New York: Duell, Sloan and Pearce, 1948.
Noggle, Anne. *For God, Country and the Thrill of It. Women Airforce Service Pilots in World War II.* College Station, Texas: Texas A & M University Press, 1990.
Norman, Elizabeth. *Women at War. The Story of Fifty Military Nurses Who Served in Vietnam.* Philadelphia, PA: University of Pennsylvania Press, 1990.
O'Connor, Patrick. *Dietrich: Style and Substance.* New York: The Penguin Group, 1991.
Office of the Surgeon General, Department of the Army. *Highlights in the History of the Army Nurse Corps.* Washington, DC, 1965.
Officer's Guide, The, Washington, DC: The National Service Publishing Company, 1961.
Olsen, Kirsten. *Remember the Ladies: A Woman's Book of Days.* New Jersey: Pittstown: The Main Street Press, 1988.
Petersen, George, ed. *American Women at War in World War II, Vol. 1. Clothing, Insignia and Equipment of the US Army, WACs and Nurses, American Red Cross, USO, AWVS, Civil Defense and Related Wartime Women's Organizations, 1943.*
Peterson, George, ed. *World War II US Army Regulations for the Service and Field Uniforms: Clothing, Headgear, Insignia, Medals, and Equipment, Enlisted and Officer, Male and Female Personnel.* Reprint of the November 10, 1941 War Department Regulations.
Phillips, H.I. *All-Out Arlene.* Garden City, New York: Doubleday, Doran and Company, Inc., 1943.
Planck, Charles E. *Women with Wings.* New York: Harper & Brothers Publishers, 1942.
Pollack, Elizabeth R., Ruth Duhme, ed. *Yes, Ma'am! The Personal Papers of a WAAC Private.* New York: J.B. Lippincott Company, 1943.
Putney, Diane T., ed. *ULTRA and the Army Air forces in World War II: An Interview with Associate Justice of the US Supreme Court Lewis F. Powell, Jr.* Washington, DC: Office of Air Force History, United States Air Force, 1987.
Rankin, Colonel Robert H. *Uniforms of the Army.* New York: G.P. Putnam's Sons, 1967.
Rankin, Colonel Robert H. *Uniforms of the Sea Services from 1908 to the Present.*
Rattray, David, ed. *Reader's Digest Illustrated Encyclopedic Dictionary.* Pleasantville, NY: The Reader's Digest Association, Inc., 1987.
Rawls, Walton. *Disney dons Dogtags. The Best of Disney Military Insignia from World War II.* New York: The Abbeville Publishing Group, 1992.
Read, Phyllis J. and Bernard L. Witlieb. *The Women's Book of Firsts.* New York: Random House, 1992.
Rexford, Oscar Whitelaw. *Battlestars & Doughnuts. World War II Clubmobile Experiences of Mary Metcalf Rexford.* St. Louis, MO: The Patrice Press, 1989.
Richardson, Walter F., Department Historian. *History, Department of Maryland. The American Legion, 1919-1934.* Baltimore, MD: The American Legion, Department of Maryland, 1934.
Risch, Erna. *A Wardrobe for Women of the Army.*
Rosignoli, Guido. *Badges and Insignia of World War II: Air Force, Naval, Marines.* New York: Exeter Books, 1983.
Ross, Mary Steele. *American Women in Uniform.* Garden City, NY: Garden City Publishing, Inc., 1943.
Rottman, Gordon and Francis Chin. *Elite Series. US Army Air Force: 2.* London, Eng-

land: Osprey, 1994.

Scharr, Adela Riek. *Sisters in the Sky, Vol. 1: The WAFS.* St. Louis, Missouri: The Patrice Press, 1986.

Ibid, *Vol. 2: The WASPs,* 1988.

Schneider, Dorothy & Carl J. *Into the Breach: American Women Overseas in World War I.* New York: Viking Penguin, 1991.

Seeley, Charlotte Palmer, ed. *American Women and the US Armed Forces.* Washington, DC: National Archives Trust Fund Board, 1992.

"Service Uniforms of Red Cross Workers." *The Red Cross Magazine,* August 1918.

Simmons, Edwin H. *The United States Marines, 1775-1975.* New York: The Viking Press, Inc., 1976.

Stallings, Laurence. *The Doughboys. The Story of the AEF, 1917-1918.* New York: Harper and Row, 1963.

Stanton, Shelby. *US Army Uniforms of the Korean War.* Harrisburg, Pennsylvania: 1992.

Stein, Barry Jason. *US Army Patches. An Illustrated Encyclopedia of Cloth Unit Insignia.* Columbia, SC: University of South Carolina Press, 1997.

Stegemeyer, Anne. *Who's Who in Fashion.* New York: Fairchild Publications: 1980.

Strandeberg, John E. and Roger James Bender. *The Call of Duty. Military Awards and Decorations of the United States of America.* San Jose, CA: R. James Bender Publishing, 1994.

Stremlow, Colonel Mary V., US Marine Corps Reserve. *A History of the Women Marines, 1946-1977.* Washington, DC: History and Museums Division Headquarters, US Marine Corps, 1986

Stremlow, Colonel Mary V., US Marine Corps Reserve (Ret.). *Free a Marine to Fight: Women Marines in World War II.* Washington, DC: Marine Corps Historical Center, 1994.

Stimson, Julia C., MA, RN. *Finding Themselves. The Letters of an American Army Chief Nurse in a British Hospital in France.* New York: The Macmillan Company, 1918.

Tily, James C. *The Uniforms of the United States Navy.* New York: Thomas Yoseloff, 1964.

Treadwell, Mattie E. *United States Army in World War II. Special Studies: The Women's Army Corps.* Washington, DC: Office of the Chief of Military History, Department of the Army, 1954.

Verges, Marianne. *On Silver Wings. The Women Airforce Service Pilots of World War II, 1942-1944.* New York: Ballantine Books, 1991.

Voss, Frederick K. *Reporting the War. The Journalistic Coverage of World War II.* Washington, DC: The Smithsonian Institution Press, 1994.

Weatherford, Doris. *American Women and World War II.* New York: Facts on File, 1990.

Weiner, Willard. *Two Hundred Thousand Fliers. The Story of the Civilian—AAF Pilot Training Program.* Washington, DC: The Infantry Journal, 1945.

Wells, Helen. *Cherry Ames, Flight Nurse.* New York: Grosset & Dunlap, 1945.

Willenz, June A. *Women Veterans: America's Forgotten Heroines.* New York: Continuum Publishing Company, 1983.

Williams, Ralph Chester, MD, Assistant Surgeon General, United States Public Health Service. *The United States Public Health Service, 1798-1950.* Washington, DC: Commissioned Officers' Association of the United States Public Health Service, 1951.

Williams, Vera S. *WASPs: Women Airforce Service Pilots of World War II.* Osceola, Wisconsin: Motorbooks International, 1994.

Wingo, Josette Dermody. *Mother was a Gunner's Mate*. Annapolis, Maryland: Naval Institute Press, 1994.
Wisbey, Herbert A., Jr. *Soldiers Without Swords*. New York: The Macmillan Company, 1955.
Woodhead, Henry, ed. Echoes of Glory. *Arms and Equipment of the Union*. New York: Time-Life Books, 1991.

Contents of Volume 1

Aerial Nurse Corps of America
Air Cadet Recruiting Aides
Aircraft Warning Service—Aircraft Warning Corps (AWS—AWC)
American Ambulance
American Citizen's Relief Committee
American Committee for Devastated France
American Friends Service Committee
American Fund for French Wounded, Motor Corps
American Library Association (ALA)
American Red Cross (ARC)
American Red Star Animal Relief
American Woman's Hospitals and *Chauffeuses* (AWH)
American Women's Hospital Reserve Corps (AWHRC)
American Women's League for Self Defense
American Women's Voluntary Services, Inc. (AWVS)
America's Over-There Theatre League
Army Air Force Aides
Army Emergency Relief
Army Hostess and Librarian Service, Army and Air Force Hostess and Librarian Service,
Army Nurse Corps (ANC)
   Reconstruction Aides
Army Special Services Women Personnel
Aviation Cadet Recruiting Aides
British War Relief Society
Bundles for America, Bundles for Britain, Bundles for Bluejackets & Naval Aid Auxiliary
Cadet Nurse Corps
Caterpillar Club
Civil Aeronautics Authority Flight Instructors
Civil Air Patrol (CAP)
Citizens' Defense Corps, Civilian Defense Auxiliary Group, US Citizens' Service Corps
Colorado Hospitality Corps No. 1
Contract Surgeons
Daughters of the Defenders of the Republic
Daughters of the American Revolution Hospital Corps
Early Birds
Emergency Aid of Pennsylvania
High School Victory Corps
Jewish Welfare Board Women's Unit (JWB)
Junior American Nurse, Inc. (JAN)
Knights of Columbus Auxiliary (KC or K of C)
Marine Corps Woman's Reserve, United States Marine Corps Women's Reserve
Mother's and Widow's Organizations
Motor Corps of America
National Catholic War Council (NCWS), League of Catholic Women Canteen Services
National League for Woman's Service (NLWS), Junior Corps, Motor Corps
National Security Women's Corps, Inc.
National Service Schools
National Women's Council of the Navy League
Navy Nurse Corps (NNC)

Female uniforms, headgear, insignia, and accessories available—excellent reproductions and some originals. WWI, WWII, (WAC, ANC, WAVES, NNC, SPARS, Marine Corps, WASP, Red Cross, etc.), Korean War and Vietnam War. Contact: NCHS Inc., George Petersen, P.O. Box 605, Springfield, VA 22150-0605, USA. Ph: (703) 971-8535, email: GPETE@aol.com, web: www.NCHSINC.com